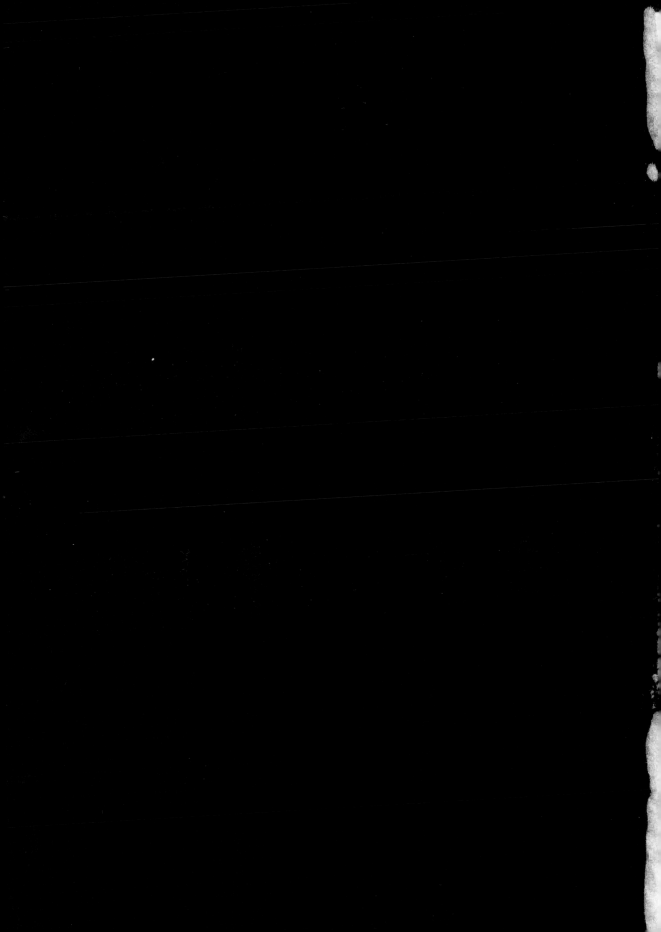

HISTORY UNDER THE SEA

HISTORY UNDER THE SEA

ALEXANDER McKEE

NEW YORK: E. P. DUTTON & CO., INC.

First published in the U.S.A. 1969
by E. P. Dutton & Co., Inc.
Copyright © 1968 by Alexander McKee
All rights reserved
Printed in Great Britain

Library of Congress Catalog Card Number: 69–20307

A15060

Designed by Georgina Bannister

To Miss Joan du Plat Taylor, Dr. George F. Bass,
Peter Throckmorton and Anders Franzén
whose work helped to found underwater archaeology
as a modern science

CONTENTS

For permission to reproduce photographs and diagrams on the pages listed, the author wishes to thank the following: John Brown and Son Ltd, Lifeboat Collection, Shoreham (p. 190), Niels Elswing, National Museum of Denmark (p. 137), Roger Hale (pp. 114–115, 116, 125), R. Kingsford Curram (p. 320), A. J. Greenland (pp. 130, 131), Leeds-London Universities Expedition (p. 277), National Maritime Museum (pp. 31, 33, 42–43, 63, 73), Robert Marx (Institute of Jamaica) (pp. 327, 329, 331), Borough of Newport (p. 45), Ora Pataharju (p. 165), Patent Office (pp. 7, 11, 12, 13), University Museum, University of Pennsylvania (pp. 271, 272, 273, 274, 275), Pepys Library, Magdalene College, Cambridge (p. 40), Portsmouth City Museums (pp. 9, 36–37, 44, 46, 48), the Controller of H.M. Stationery Office for facsimiles and transcripts of Crown-copyright records in the Public Record Office (pp. 14, 71), Royal Engineers Historical Society (pp. 51, 66), Jack W. Schott, California Dept. of Fish and Game (p. 235), Science Museum, South Kensington (pp. 4–5, 74, 75), Trustees of the Tate Gallery (p. 17), Peter Throckmorton (pp. 102–103, 105, 106), Sjörhistoriska Museet, Wasavarvet, Stockholm) (pp. 147, 148, 150, 153, 154, 155, 156, 158, 161, 163, 166).

Thanks are also due to Miss M. Pettman Pout for allowing the contents of the Deane portfolio of watercolour drawings to be photographed: these photographs, and all others not specifically listed above, are the copyright of Alexander McKee.

Part One
Spithead
A D 1500-1800

ENGLAND 1828-1844

1

'A safe and effectual method of descending into great depths of water...'

J. and C. A. Deane
The pioneer invention of 1828

The beginning of underwater archaeology is usually and conveniently assigned to the turn of the century, with the discovery by Greek sponge divers in 1900 of the wreck of a ship of the first century BC at Antikythera in the Aegean. The discovery was notable for three reasons. The cargo consisted of more-or-less imperishable works of art—bronze and marble statues—which were extremely valuable. Among the ship's gear also recovered was a bronze navigational instrument, now thought to be an astronomical clock—that is, a kind of computer. This was evidence of the technical level attained by the Mediterranean civilisation of the time, just as a radar set on a present-day ship would be valuable indication of twentieth century technology to historians of the very distant future who might be probing back 2,000 years into the past in order to understand our present, with little to help them in the documentary line except, perhaps, some fragments of narrative written by a sailor called Sir Francis Chichester. If indeed he ever existed, and was not merely an epic hero whose legendary exploits were perhaps based on the experience of many ocean voyagers, from which some unknown poet had woven a romantic but unsubstantial tale.

The third important facet of the discovery was that the Greek divers reported their find to the authorities in Athens, showing them artifacts to prove their story, and that the authorities acted responsibly by sending a salvage vessel to collect the rest of the sunken cargo, with a professional archaeologist on board to direct the work from the surface. Under his orders, they brought up much of the cargo and also scraps of ship's gear. But no attempt was made to map the wreckage as it lay underwater or to examine and excavate the hull. The operation was confined to the easier, but still difficult and dangerous, task of recovering cargo and collecting artifacts. Strictly speaking, it was not archaeology at all; for by then, land archaeology was half-a-century past the stage of casual collection of unrelated bits and pieces, and was able to reconstruct not merely single buildings, but a series of occupation layers where many buildings had been raised on the one site and then fallen into ruin or been largely demolished. Nor, apart from noting the deterioration of those parts of the marble statuary which had been exposed to the sea, did the experts of the time study the corrosion of materials or consider the problems of conserving them from further deterioration.

But the discovery at Antikythera, and the archaeological emergency measures taken there in the years 1900–1901, do not in fact mark the start of underwater archaeology. Discoveries as important, and archaeological measures of a comparable if not superior order, are recorded some seventy years earlier. In one important respect, these operations were markedly superior to those carried out much later in the Aegean. Whereas the Antikythera project resulted from an accidental discovery, the work of 1828–1844 was deliberately planned; whereas the work at Antikythera was carried out by primitive divers ignorant of history, directed by land archaeologists ignorant of diving (a situation which still obtains for much of the Mediterranean area), the earlier work was undertaken by divers who fully realised its importance, took pains to record what they found,

4

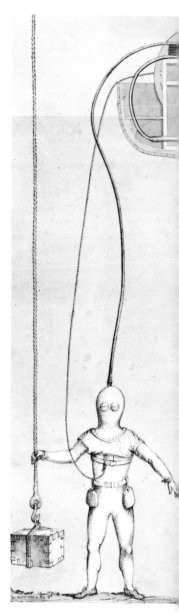

Sketch of diving apparatus dated 1811, from the Goodrich Papers. It may be connected with a plan put forward by James Hicks for raising the *Royal George*, which was officially approved in 1813, but never carried into effect.

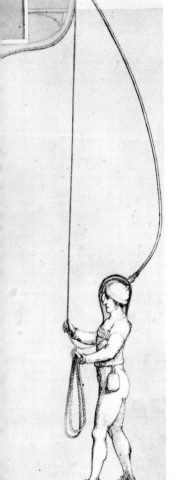

and who, far from being sea-going peasants using diving gear which they did not wholly understand, had themselves invented the apparatus which they used—and with which, some seventy years later, the Greek sponge divers were to make their Mediterranean discoveries. A totally different type of man was involved, and it may be said therefore that underwater archaeology began in a burning farmhouse in Kent in about the year 1828.

In his book, *Whitstable, Seasalter and Swalecliff: The History of Three Kent Parishes*, Robert H. Goodsall quotes from the recollections of the late Mr. W. Humphrey, whose grandfather was the Water Bailiff of the Whitstable Oyster Fishery Company at the beginning of the nineteenth century:

Whitstable was the birthplace of the diver. The first man to go underwater in a diving dress was named John Deane, who married Matthew Browning's daughter. Very curious and interesting is the story of how he became a diver. About 1830* a fire occurred at a large farm. First haystacks caught fire and then one of the stables, where the best team of horses was put away for the night. Great efforts were made to extinguish the flames, but there was no fire engine in those days. Pails of water were used, and then an old pump, with a long pipe attached, which was placed in a large pond. This threw a small jet of water on the fire, but without much effect. Several attempts were made to get the horses out, but without success.

A large crowd assembled, among whom was John Deane, a powerfully built man, who quickly thought out a plan to save the horses. In the hall of the farmhouse stood an old suit of armour. Being a friend of the farmer, he asked if he might use the helmet and try to save the horses. Consent was readily given, and placing it over his head, he secured the pipe from the old pump to the inside and asked the farmer to pump air slowly. Then he walked into the stable through the dense smoke, and brought out one horse after another, until all were saved. Everybody cheered and congratulated Deane on his bravery and success, but he had not finished with the old pump. He borrowed it and rigged up the helmet with a water-tight dress. The helmet had two large round pieces of glass to look through. On a calm day he tried it at high water along the seashore, but found when the water covered his head, the air pumped into the dress caused him to turn upside down. To alter this he made fast to his shoes some pieces of lead, which kept his feet down, and enabled him to walk under water quite easily. Later Deane went off with the sweepers (men who go sweeping for anchors and chains which are lost by ships). When they came fast to an anchor, he would go down in his diving dress, the men on deck pumping air to him. He would then make fast a chain, and they would heave up the anchor. He then went out to a wreck, and sent up several things that had lain there for years. This success encouraged him to try a bigger job. A suitable wreck he considered was the Royal George, *which sank at Spithead on 28th August, 1782. He took with him the ingenious apparatus which he had invented and improved. He now had a rubber dress, made perfectly water-tight, and a helmet large enough for him to turn his head round at pleasure,*

* More probably about 1820, as Deane's brother, Charles Anthony, patented a smoke apparatus in 1823.

having three glasses to admit light, and a flexible rubber tube on the top to supply air from above by means of an air pump, worked by a man in attendance. In this simple dress, Mr. Deane, although he had attached to his shoes about 90 lb. of lead to make him sink, could readily walk about at the bottom of the sea. He could use a hatchet freely, and stay under water for more than an hour at a time.

John Deane himself wrote a brief account of his invention:

A safe and effectual method of descending into great depths of water appears to have been unknown, or but very imperfectly developed, until the introduction of that now well known diving apparatus invented by myself and my brother (Charles Anthony Deane). The Invention, after a long series of experiments, vast study and labour, was brought to full perfection in 1828.

The naval correspondent of the *Hampshire Telegraph*, Captain Basil Hall, R.N., wrote in September, 1840:

The merit of having first introduced the diving helmet, etc. into general use, and applied it to practical purposes of a most important nature, is due to Messrs. Charles and John Deane, and their apparatus is the simplest that has yet been suggested, and is very serviceable for general purposes, as it never fails, excepting when the diver's head by any accident becomes lower than his body, in which case the water must necessarily enter, and drives out the air, upon which his safety depends. In the same year, a similar verdict appeared in Colburns' *United Service Journal*.

But whatever improvements have been or may hereafter be made in it (the diving dress), there can be no doubt that Mr. Charles Deane deserves the credit of having first brought it to an efficient state, indeed, we may say, to considerable perfection, and of having proved to the world by his own example and exertions, how very useful it may be. For it will be allowed, that whatever was suggested or done, in respect to the diving-helmet, before he undertook to improve it, was either a matter of mere speculation, or of occasional experiments, which were never applied to any useful practical purpose.

A detailed technical description of Deane's apparatus also appeared in 1840, under the signature of Colonel C. W. Pasley, Royal Engineers, in an unpublished, confidential report on diving gear addressed to the Inspector General of Fortifications, for onward transmission to the Master General and Board of Ordnance.

Deane's Diving Dress consists of a waterproof-dress, which comes up as high as the Diver's Ears, and is tied round his neck by a handkerchief, which keeps it in its proper place. The wrists are confined by tight bandages, so that water cannot enter there. The Helmet is then put on which rests on the Diver's Shoulders, and is fitted with an Air pipe, by which fresh air is continually forced into the Helmet, from the Air pump above, whilst the foul or waste air escapes by the opening between the bottom of the Helmet, and the Waterproof dress. Whilst the Diver's head is upright or nearly so, the helmet acts as a portable Diving Bell, and the water cannot possibly get in by the bottom of it, though open, on account of the compressed air above. A couple

Deane's specification for a smoke apparatus, 1823, which is the basis of the diving helmet and dress.

6

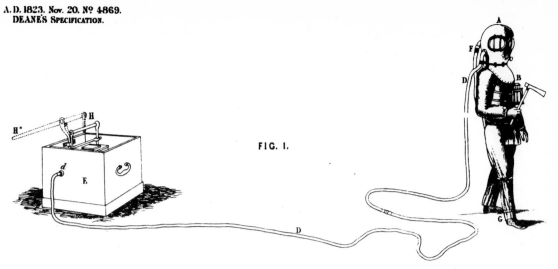

FIG. 1.

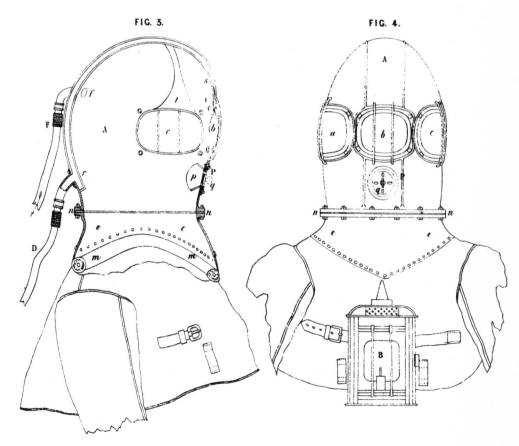

FIG. 3.

FIG. 4.

of leaden weights, connected with the helmet, are fixed in front and rear, and Shoes weighted with lead at the Soles, are worn, to enable the Diver to descend to the bottom, and remain there conveniently. These weights together with the helmet usually amount to about 100 lb., but are not oppressive or even felt in the water. This diving apparatus was first proposed by Mr. Charles Deane, who brought to perfection and introduced into general use, the Diving Helmet, which had been suggested some Centuries before, but which had never been applied to any useful practical purpose. But Deane's Apparatus, which is the simplest of all, though very efficient for common purposes, and highly approved by many of the best Divers, does not admit of a man lying down or Stooping with his head lower than his body, without a risk of his helmet filling with water, and if he should by accident, or by neglect of his assistants fall over into a hole, or down from the Side of a Wreck head foremost, he will be drowned, if not hauled up immediately.

These authentic descriptions, compiled morever by witnesses who were not merely contemporary but expert, contradict all existing stories of the development of the diving helmet, as those familiar with the subject will realise. They came to light in 1965–1967 during my own research into the work previously carried out underwater on some of the historic Spithead wrecks which I was now personally investigating on the seabed. I began by believing, and even quoting, the existing histories, then doubting them, and, finally, disbelieving them almost entirely. By 1966, I was close to the truth.

Evidence now began to fall into place as neatly as the pieces of a prepared jigsaw puzzle, although not in chronological order. My own research began in the local, Portsmouth archives, then following a clue from the Royal Engineers Historical Society at Chatham, moved to the Public Record Office for a search among the red-taped files of Ordnance in-letters, Pasley's technical report, from which the above is taken, being found in WO44/613. This report described also two other types of diving apparatus tested by Pasley in 1840—those of Bethell and Siebe—but as Siebe's alone was illustrated by a diagram I was left to guess at what Deane's and Bethell's looked like; and this was true also of Fraser's apparatus, of which I had come across brief descriptions elsewhere. But at the same time, Mr. A. Corney, of Portsmouth City Museums, then busily engaged in turning Henry VIII's Southsea Castle into a modern museum, was instrumental in rescuing from oblivion a lithograph of Deane working on the *Royal George* in 1832, which clearly showed the apparatus and, more-over, named all the various parts. Also at the same time, Mr. B. W. Bathe of the Department of Sailing Ships at the Science Museum, South Kensing-ton, was building up an exhibition to show the history of diving. In pursuit of a missing portfolio of watercolour drawings of artifacts recovered by John Deane, I contacted Mr. Bathe, who did not have this portfolio but did possess three books of watercolours drawn for Colonel Pasley in about 1840 and, although most were of artifacts, one was of an unidentified helmet stated to have been used by his divers in 1840. As it was neither Deane's nor Siebe's, it could only be Bethell's.

A representation of HMS
'Royal George' of 108 guns,
now lying sunk at a depth
of 60 ft. at Spithead,
having been underwater
fifty-one years. Mr. Deane
equipped in his newly
invented Diving Apparatus,
engaged in taking off one of
the hoops of the bowsprit
in August, 1832. This is a
detail from a large
lithograph designed to
show how Deane's 'open'
dress actually worked.
B—Two leaden weights
suspended from the neck of
the helmet [with a quick-
release for emergency];
C—Air tube passing from
the Pump under the arm
and entering at the back of
the helmet; D—Air Pump;
E—Signal Line; F—
Ladder for ascending and
descending with weights at
its feet. The ladder was a
rope ladder with wooden
slats intended to be held
vertical by the weights
about two feet above the
top of the wreck. The
diving boat is the sloop
Mary.

More was to come from this source for, shortly afterwards, a great-
great-granddaughter of John Deane, Miss M. Pettman Pout, heard of
Mr. Bathe's project and sent him a number of documents among which
was a printed diving manual of 1836 entitled *Method of Using Deane's
Patent Diving Apparatus*. Mr. Bathe passed this information on to me and
also put me in touch with Miss Pettman Pout, who was able to offer much-
needed information on a number of points. Finally, I began to make
enquiries at the Patent Office in London and this produced the original
patent for the smoke apparatus, 1823, plus the patents for Bethell's

9

apparatus and Frazer's apparatus, both dated 1835.

This meant that I had now both technical descriptions and detailed diagrams of the four main types of diving apparatus which evolved during the most important phase of development which turned diving from an inventor's dream into a practical, workaday proposition; and, for once, the information was entirely authentic.

The primary invention was Patent No. 4869 of 20 November 1823, granted to Charles Anthony Deane, Ship Caulker, of Deptford, Kent, in respect of an *Apparatus to be worn by persons entering a room filled with smoke or other vapour for the purpose of extinguishing fire or extricating persons or property therein*. John Deane was born in 1800 and Charles Anthony was an elder brother, and this smoke apparatus was the start of a career in underwater engineering which lasted all their lives; at the age of fifty-six John Deane was diving under the ice of the Crimea to salvage sunken Russian warships. The smoke apparatus they invented was very compact; it consisted of a wooden box containing the bellows to supply air, plus a space for the hose, helmet, jacket, trousers, and tools. The copper helmet was attached to a jacket made smokeproof at the sleeves and at the bottom; and had a metal turning plate fitted to the helmet in connection with a mouthpiece, which enabled the man inside to breathe the air outside when this was fresh. Just before going into the smoke, another man began to operate the bellows, and then the 'fireman' moved the turning plate to the 'closed' position, thus shutting off outside air, in much the same manner as with an air regulator for stoves.

With a few small modifications, this invention became Deane's Patent Diving Apparatus, the value of which lay in its neatness and simplicity. The turning plate was eliminated, presumably because it would have been almost impossible to make it pressure proof, as distinct from air proof. The jacket also was eliminated and replaced by a waterproof suit, as protection against the chill of the sea; the suit came up to the chin and was loosely tied in place around the neck. The helmet then merely rested on the diver's shoulders; it was not bolted or screwed onto a neckring at the top of the dress as it is in modern 'standard' helmet diving gear. The weak bellows were replaced by a more powerful force pump to supply air at the much greater pressures required under water, and the escape route for this air was under the bottom of the helmet; in effect, it was a scaled down diving bell. The main weights were in basically the same position as in a modern helmet dress, that is, back and front, but they were attached to the helmet and not to the body. The reason for this was partly comfort and partly safety. The rope securing them had a quick-release loop very similar to that of some modern weightbelts, so that the weights, and the helmet also if necessary, could be removed very quickly in the boat while the diver rested, or could be ditched altogether in an emergency underwater. One of the main hazards facing these early divers, owing to unreliable materials, was the possibility of a burst air-pipe, and Deane's design gave perhaps a fifty-fifty chance of an emergency ascent in that eventuality, whereas, even today, a diver wearing the totally enclosed dress would almost certainly be killed, unless he was very quick

Deane carrying out repairs to the hull of a two-decker line-of-battle ship.

The salvage of cargo from a wreck: above, a telescope is used to survey the seabed; below, lifting bags filled with compressed air are used for bringing up heavy objects. Bethell's Patent.

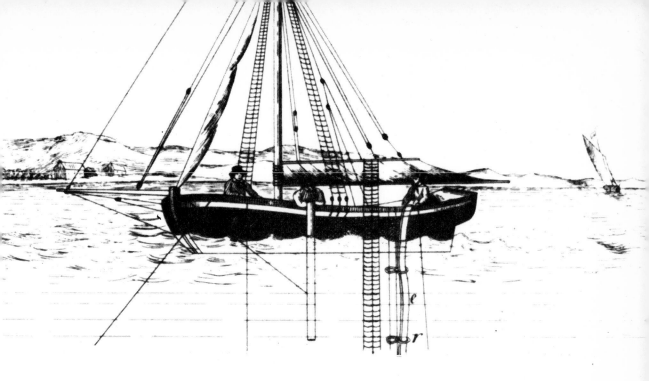

indeed to close his outlet valve. The latter would also be killed by the 'squeeze' if he fell any distance. But Deane's design was not safe against the hazard of falling either, except that the manner of death would be different; the diver was liable to be drowned instead of pulverised.

In both cases the hazards can be met only by thinking out and then applying a practical safety procedure, and Deane's booklet is the earliest diving manual I know. It covers not merely the technical details of the apparatus and the pump, but also meets a range of customer's queries, from how to anchor the diving boat to the safety precautions and signalling procedures. The manual details specific instructions for the attendant on the safety line to keep this line taut at all times, as a guard against the possibility of the diver falling or stumbling, and adds, that if the line should tend to run out through his fingers, he should immediately haul up. The code of signals, both on the line and on the air hose, is too detailed to recount here,

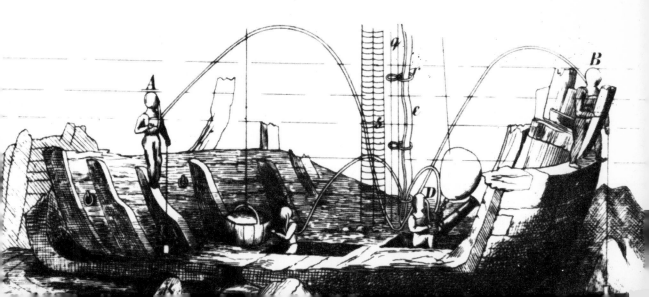

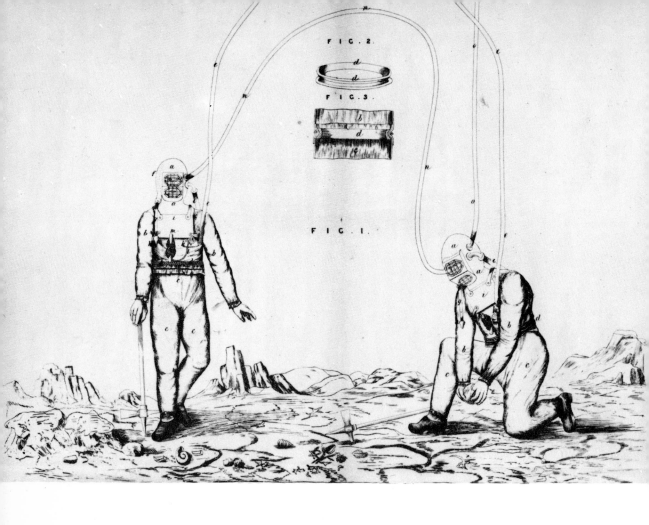

F I G . 2 .

F I G . 3 .

F I G . 1 .

but includes the note: *No person should, on any account whatever, be suffered to descend in the Diving Apparatus, or to attend to the signals, unless they are perfectly sober, calm, and collected; and not then, unless they thoroughly understand all the signals, and can repeat them without hesitation.* The manual also makes the point that *A knife should always accompany the Diver, to cut away any ropes, etc. etc. with which he might become entangled.* A weighted rope ladder, instead of the modern shot rope, is recommended, but apart from this Deane's instructions of 1836 are not out of date in 1968. Also, it is now clear, the Deane apparatus itself is not out of date. The men who feed the dolphins in some American Marinelands wear diving gear identical in principle, and differing only in minor detail from Deane's original invention.

In 1835, two 'tight', or completely enclosed diving dresses were invented. The first was Patent No. 6757 of 31 January 1835, granted to John Bethell, Gentleman, of Mecklenburgh Square, Middlesex. The drawbacks of this apparatus, when it was tested by Pasley in 1840, will be described in the appropriate place, but basically it was a two-piece suit, the waterproof seal between jacket and trousers being at the waist. The

Bethell's specification for a 'tight' diving dress, 1835.

12

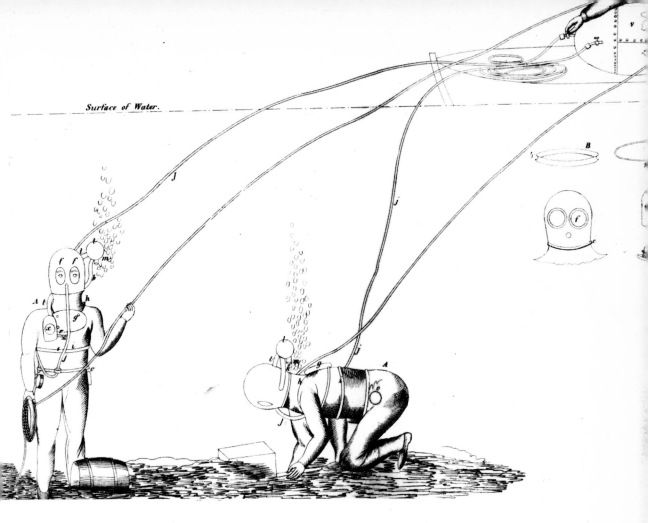

Surface of Water.

Fraser's specification for a 'tight' diving dress with compressed air cylinder and crude demand valve, 1835.

patent was not merely for this apparatus, however, but for a range of accessories some of which sound very modern. For instance, there was an outlet pipe from the helmet specially designed for filling buoyancy, or lifting bags, with compressed air, it being specifically stated that the principle of the air bag was not new. There was provision for diver-to-diver and diver-to-surface speech (in theory at least); an underwater lamp; an anti-shark cage for pearl divers; a light-weight diving bell made of indian rubber or of cloth, and also a diving helmet made of the same materials. Many of these innovations were by no means unsound, they merely required many years of practical underwater experiment, which Mr. Bethell was not in a position to carry out.

The second invention was Patent No. 6929 of 14 November 1835, granted to John William Fraser, Artist, of Ludgate Hill, London, in respect of a diving apparatus very similar to Bethell's, being a completely closed two-piece suit. The difference was that, while other diving dresses were pump-fed with air, Fraser's dress was supplied by a large cylinder of compressed air placed in the boat, the air being compressed to thirty times surface pressure, i.e., 30 atmospheres compared to modern capaci-

13

ties of about 120–200 atmospheres. No man can breathe air at this pressure when in shallow water and therefore the apparatus included a device which balanced the internal air pressure in the suit with the external water pressure, automatically compensating for alterations in depth. This arrangement very closely foreshadowed the demand valve invented by Cousteau and Gagnan in the 1940s, and Fraser used much the same language, stating that:

The object of my escape pipe is, that by allowing the air to escape at nearly the same depth in the water as the diver, it causes the air to be compressed according to his depth, and by being of a larger area than those used heretofore, and always floating as high or as higher than the upper part of his dress, the air escapes from the helmet without inflating the dress.

It has been necessary to describe all these developments fully because, firstly, Deane's original apparatus was used by him during a long career of diving to the sunken ships of history, many of them famous names; and secondly, because the story as outlined above is not merely unknown, but actually contradictory of the currently accepted version, which is based very largely on information given in Part Two of the late Sir Robert Davis's monumental manual, *Deep Diving and Submarine Operations*. A passage in Part Two is responsible for the widespread belief that Augustus Siebe, the founder of Sir Robert's firm, invented an 'open' diving dress in 1819, in which the helmet was fixed to the jacket, and which was used by Deane on the *Royal George* in 1834. An illustration in the book, described as depicting Augustus Siebe's 'open' diving dress, appears to be identical except in minor detail to Charles Anthony Deane's patent for a smoke apparatus of 1823. Slight discrepancies might be explained if it had been muddled with John Deane's Patent No. 63 of 10 January 1853, which details a reversion to the jacket design for diving purposes, to enable the diver to bend down, but lacks a diagram. Equally unfortunate is the fact that neither the Patent Office nor the Science Museum can trace a patent in Siebe's name for diving apparatus. It is true that he took out a patent in 1819—but it was for a weighing machine; also that he took out a patent in 1828—for hydraulic machinery; and again in 1852—for machinery for manufacturing paper. The only contemporary diagrams of a Siebe 'closed' dress are those drawn for Colonel Pasley in 1840, and they do not entirely agree with the representation in Sir Robert Davis's book.

To confuse matters further, in an appendix to his book, Sir Robert contradicts the story told earlier in Part Two, that Siebe invented the 'open' dress, and states instead that Siebe 'made the acquaintance of a working diver named Deane, who was using a very crude dress of the "open" type. Siebe produced an improved version of this type consisting of a metal helmet attached by rivets to a jacket extending below the waist.' The explanation may be that Siebe manufactured diving gear to designs invented by the Deanes and perhaps made some modifications of his own.

By the time I was beginning to question the accuracy of some of these

Detail from a large working diagram of Siebe's 'tight' diving dress as used on the *Royal George* and *Edgar* in 1840, with modifications made at Pasley's suggestion that year. The original diagram was a watercolour drawn by Corporal Samuel March for Colonel Pasley to submit to the authorities with his recommendation that the dress be universally adopted in the Services. It was.

14

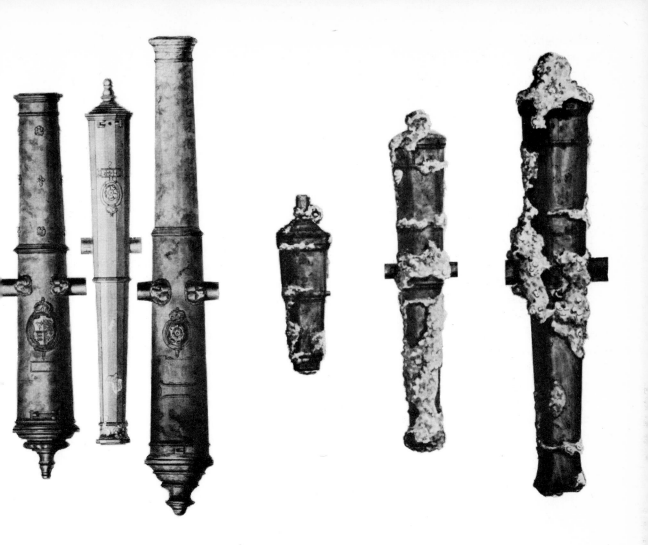

Above (*left*) the three brass guns raised by Deane and Edwards from the *Mary Rose* in 1836; from left to right, 68-pdr Cannon Royal, 9-pdr Culverin Bastard, and 32-pdr Demi-Cannon: and (*right*) two cannon and a carronade recovered by Deane from the wreck of H M S *Collossus*, one of Nelson's 74 s wrecked in the Scillies.

statements Sir Robert Davis had unfortunately died and it was impossible to obtain clarification direct. However, Captain W. O. Shelford, R N, the manager of Siebe Gorman's underwater division, was kind enough to explain that: '*Deep Diving and Submarine Operations* is primarily a technical work on Diving. The second part of the book is added for the interest and amusement of people connected with diving and was never intended as a serious historical document to be used as a reference for research without consultation of collateral documentation.'

It is again unfortunate that Siebe appears to have left no memoirs or other documents which might explain the connection between what we now know is Deane's 'open' dress and what is still known as Siebe's 'closed' dress. That there was a connection is clear. The 'tight' or 'closed' dress is simply Deane's full-length, one-piece suit made watertight by inserting a neck-ring at the top, to which the helmet is attached, making a pressure-proof seal. With a valve to control the escape of air, this is basically today's standard helmet diving dress. The late Mrs. Grace Pettman Pout,

15

granddaughter of John Deane, left written notes on his career, including the statement:

Together with a brother, Charles Anthony, John Deane invented the helmet diving apparatus, very much as it is used at the present day. Before he could register the patent, his brother sold the 'rights' to Siebe. John continued his diving career. It was he who laid the underwater piles for the present Houses of Parliament (my mother, née Agnes Deane, was a visitor to him at this work).

This is going back very close to the source, and there are also contemporary hints of a collaboration between Siebe on the one hand and the Deanes with their associate, William Edwards, on the other.

It would seem that Siebe has been over-sold as an inventor, and undersold as an engineer, for Pasley pays tribute later to his vital work in improving the pumps essential to deep diving. In 1836, John Deane stated in his manual that he had on one occasion remained underwater for five hours and forty minutes (presumably in the shallows), and that a considerable depth could be achieved, of 20 fathoms (120 feet), with the possibility of reaching 30 fathoms (180 feet). This depth capacity was largely a matter of the efficiency of the air pump and hose, and not of the helmet and dress, and the value of Siebe's later work in this connection should not be underestimated. The balanced verdict is probably that of Captain Basil Hall, who gave the credit for original invention and the long years of practical experiment to John and Charles Deane, but stated that Siebe's closed dress in its 1840 form *combines so many improvements, though not all of his own invention, and are so complete in all their details, that they seem to approach as near to perfection as can be expected of any apparatus of this nature.*

Naturally, there had been previous inventors of diving apparatus. The earliest British patent, No. 56, is dated 1632. Even when actually built and tested, however, these designs achieved little. Whereas the Deane's apparatus was such a practical proposition that they were able to go into the salvage business as 'submarine engineers'. In the *Mary*, a smack owned by their associate, William Edwards, and with a total team of not more than seven men, seamen as well as divers, they operated all round the coasts of Britain for an all-in charge of five guineas a day.

The separate case of the diving bell is easily disposed of. John Deane in a public lecture on the history of diving apparatus referred to it as 'old-fashioned'. It may be objected that some deep salvage work had been done with diving bells, including the raising of many cannon from the Swedish galleon *Vasa* in the seventeenth century. This is true, and indeed when Colonel Pasley entered the underwater salvage field in direct competition with the Deanes, he considered that a diving bell would be a vital part of his equipment. When he actually came to use it, however, it was discovered that to operate the bell the labour of no less than forty-nine men was required, together with much heavy equipment which necessitated the use of a large lighter as a floating workbase.

In comparison, Deane's gear was light, portable, and cheap. For

Possibly the earliest, and certainly one of the best, representations of a 'concretion'. Deane's artist has carefully recorded the exact appearance, fresh from the sea, of a mass of copper coins, rope, and other artifacts recovered from the *Indostan*, an East Indiaman wrecked off Margate in 1803. This watercolour cannot have been painted later than 1839 and therefore antedates Mediterranean and American discoveries by well over a century. The growth shown has been identified as a hydroid, possibly *Certularia*.

16

transport, a small fishing vessel would suffice. The diver required a team of four men only to support him—two men working at the pump, one man holding taut the signal and safety line, another man carefully paying out the air hose and attending to the signals on that for more or less air. Additionally, the helmet diver was comparatively unencumbered when compared a bell diver, although the principle employed was the same. A pump, a hose, a helmet, and 90 lb. of lead—those were the basic requirements.

It was an innovation as far-reaching as the invention of the aqualung, and in the same direction; for the real point of Commandant Cousteau's device was that the support team was reduced to nil. The basic operating unit could be scaled down to one man in a one-man dinghy, backed by compressor facilities for re-filling the cylinders. Both commercial salvage and also archaeological work can be done, and has been done, with resources no greater than this. Both inventions, for their times, represented also a great increase in manœuvrability. While the aqualung has finally enabled the excavation of wrecks to be carried out to the same standards of precision and thoroughness as that of the best of land excavations, Deane's apparatus enabled divers for the first time to pay attention to small historical finds in and around wrecks, when previously only bulky obvious items such as cannon could normally be hoped for. There were exceptions, of course, on sites where the water was very clear and shallow;

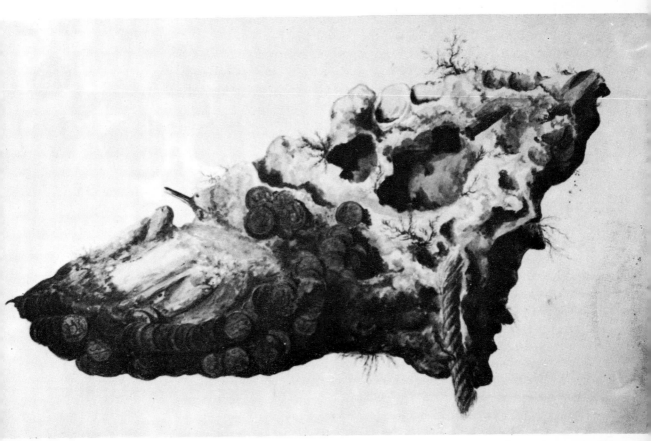

and where the artifacts were also of sufficient value to justify the immense trouble and expense involved. An early example was the recovery of treasure worth £200,000 in the year 1687 from a Spanish ship sunk off 'Hispaniola'. The salvage director, William Phipps, used 'a square iron box, open at the bottom, with windows and an inside seat for the divers,' according to the author of a history of diving published in the *Cornhill Magazine*, 1868. Spanish gold is clearly treasure. What was exceptional about the Deanes, quite apart from the effectiveness of their apparatus, was that they realised that historical knowledge was also treasure, and went out of their way to obtain and record it. Furthermore, the significance of their discoveries was instantly recognised and the more important reports, and artifacts also, were submitted immediately to the highest authorities. Literally the highest—to the Crown—in the person of William IV, the 'Sailor King'. In England, there is nothing quite like Royal Patronage to get things moving at the right speed and at the right level.

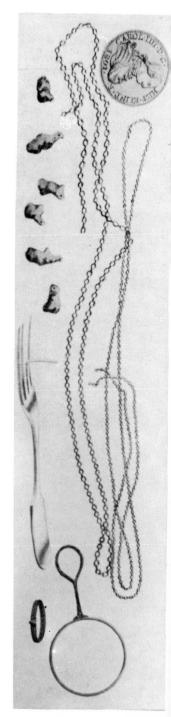

The Deanes had professional watercolour drawings made of the most important or more curious of the artifacts they recovered, usually to scale, and with details recorded, and by 1836 had amassed a sufficient number to be able to plan for publication. If recording is the first step in archaeology, publication is the second, and they were therefore setting a valuable precedent. By December 1839, the portfolio was before the Lords Commissioners of the Admiralty and due to be passed by them to the Board of Ordnance, with a long list of subscribers already attached. In his covering letter, Deane described the portfolio and attached manuscript as 'An entirely original work, and contains a selection of facsimile specimens of antique pieces of Cannon, and a variety of interesting relics curiously incrusted and covered with Marine animal and vegetable productions, which during the last 12 Years I have recovered by means of my Diving Apparatus from the bed of the Sea, and from the wrecks of H M Ships *Mary Rose, Royal George, Collossus, Venerable, etc. etc.* with an historical account of the losses and recoveries of the same with notes and experiences'.

Both the Admiralty and the Ordnance Board (then responsible for equipping both the Army and the Navy with guns) subscribed for ten copies, at two guineas each, plus single orders from individuals such as the Duke of Buccleugh, Admiral Sir Phillip Durham (a survivor from the sinking of the *Royal George* fifty-eight years before), the Earl of Egremont, Admiral Sir Edward Codrington, and organisations such as the Gosport and Alverstoke Literary and Philosophical Society (who had backed Deane's work for some years). I came across these clues in November 1966, and there appeared to be some connection with five items previously shown to me by Mr. Corney at Cumberland House Museum. One was a lithograph depicting guns raised by Deane and Edwards from the *Mary Rose* and *Royal George* in 1836, the others were large watercolour drawings of artifacts. One Mr. Corney was able to identify as representing relics from the Ordnance transport *Guernsey Lily*, on which I knew the Deanes had worked: another I was able to identify as representing relics known to have

18

Relics from some of the many wrecks visited by John Deane: a doubloon, a gold chain, a gold eyeglass, ring, gold nuggets, and a silver fork—exactly recorded with one bent tine.

been recovered by the Deanes from the *Mary Rose*. Mr. Corney believed that these drawings were probably prepared in connection with an auction of wood and duplicated artifacts held by Deane in Portsmouth on 12 November 1840, which he knew about because a copy of the advertising poster was also in the Museum. These drawings gave an indication of the high quality to be expected of the portfolio pictures, if I could lay my hands on them. Enquiry indicated that the portfolio and attached narrative manuscript had never actually reached the public in a published version, so that my search must be for the elusive originals, last heard of at the end of 1839.

Among the many letters I wrote was one to Mr. Bathe of the Science Museum. At the time this produced the three books of watercolour drawings of artifacts from the *Royal George* and *Edgar* sketched on Colonel Pasley's instructions in around 1840; valuable indeed, but not the main quarry. Then, on one and the same day, I received two letters. One from my publishers, to say that they were shortly going to press with this book, the other from Miss Pettman Pout, writing to me as a result of a letter from Mr. Bathe. She had possessed the portfolio I was looking for,

John Deane, at about seventy years of age.

but had lent it to a Councillor Willis of Monmouth, who had since died. What had happened to it was unknown, but she was trying to recover it by contacting his widow. It was now July 1967. But before she could act, a radio firm which had taken over the late Councillor Willis' antique shop went bankrupt—and the Official Receiver moved in! Then burglars broke in—and actually spent several nights in the lock-up flat above the shop in which the portfolio was thought to be. And therefore the Police moved in! In October, after an urgent letter from me, Miss Pout went to the Police and was granted permission to search the flat. It then became clear that the burglars had found the portfolio before me—their muddy footprints were clearly marked on some of the drawings, which presumably had become Police evidence, as well as evidence of the earliest known recordings in the whole of underwater archaeology!

On 30 October I met Miss Pettman Pout at Hutchinson's London office, where she loaned me the portfolio for study. The finished watercolours were of the same high quality as those at Cumberland House. A specific directive must have been given to the artist to reproduce exactly the state of the artifacts immediately they came out of the sea; and he must have had the originals in front of him very shortly afterwards. The state of the deterioration of the various materials can be clearly seen, and various types of encrusting shellfish, red weed and algae tentatively identified by me. Some appeared identical to those attached to a pottery bowl I had previously recovered from the remains of the *Royal George*, and it was clear that the Deanes took as great an interest in the biological fate of wrecks as they did of the archaeological aspects. This is a very modern approach, quite lacking from the early work in the Mediterranean. Indeed, it is superior to much modern work in the Mediterranean and elsewhere, in cases where the archaeologist can hardly wait to scrape off the encrustations and then let the artifact dry out, before recording. This effectively destroys half the information which could have been obtained. In many cases, the physical state of the materials, having altered once, from immersion in the sea and the achievement of semi-stability in that medium, promptly loses this stability on return to air. Recording should take place at once; or, alternatively, the artifact should go into a polythene bag with some seawater to retain both stability and the biological record until it can be photographed on land. The Deanes saw this 140 years ago, and today the watercolours they commissioned to be made are more eloquent than most of the photographs and draughtsmanship of many modern expeditions.

Even a casual glance at these watercolours showed that the artifacts had been raised from a number of different wrecks lying in quite distinctly different sea areas, although all were around the British Isles, as the pencilled notes indicated. Consequently, they are now to be examined by a marine biologist, as constituting first-rate evidence of the biological nature of those sites in the 1830s; quite valuable information, in fact. Even more valuable, in the archaeological field, was one painting showing two views of one of the old-fashioned 'built-up' guns recovered from the *Mary Rose* in 1836. This deteriorated almost at once from contact with

20

The modern aqualung diver
fully equipped: Alexander
McKee about to do some
underwater photography.

the air and is at present in a sorry state at Woolwich, while the Science
Museum drawings of it were made obviously after, and not before, the
deterioration had taken place. But from Deanes' drawings we now know
what this very early gun looked like and from various rings and bolts
attached, may profitably speculate as to how it was trained and elevated,
matters by no means clear before. Further, the inclusion of a number of
other artifacts, such as bows and bottles, also raised from the *Mary Rose*,

will probably aid the identification of that wreck in due course, possibly in 1968.

The Deanes were not alone in their intelligent approach to a new problem, for the first recorded scientific studies of the deterioration of differing types of materials after long periods of immersion in the sea, were made in the year 1839 by various interested parties salvaging wrecks off Portsmouth in Hampshire, an area the Deanes knew well.

This is not really so surprising after all, for the scientific age had been in full swing in England for more than fifty years by this time, although the founder of scientific archaeology was then only a boy of twelve. As a General, Pitt Rivers was to operate in Dorset, the county adjoining Hampshire to the west, and to enunciate principles which are valid to this day. He wrote:

A discovery dates only from the time of the record of it, and not from the time of its being found in the soil. . . . Excavators, as a rule, record only those things which appear to them important at the time, but fresh problems in Archaeology and Anthropology are constantly arising, and it can hardly have escaped the notice of anthropologists . . . that, on turning back to old accounts in search of evidence, the points which would have been most valuable have been passed over from being thought uninteresting at the time. Every detail should therefore be recorded . . . and it ought at all times to be the chief object of an excavator to reduce his own personal equation to a minimum.

The General's practical work stands up to modern examination, and the essence of it was military method and thoroughness.

The first era of undersea archaeology was to be conducted on the same lines, although in a much more difficult medium, and a number of generals were eventually to be involved. But first an adequate diving apparatus had to be invented, as we have seen, and then the inventors had to enter a quite unknown world, where the very principles of existence were different from those to which they were accustomed. There was no one to teach them, they had to train themselves; there was no one to signpost the hazards, these they had to anticipate, where no precedents existed. And there *were* hazards, some foreseeable. Other dangers, however, were invisible, as well as being unknown and even unsuspected, and these were the most deadly of all. It is hardly surprising that they began cautiously. Indeed, had they not done so, they would not have survived to succeed.

2

The Battle of the *Boyne*

Beginnings of underwater archaeology
Spithead 1832-1840

Like almost every other beginner, Deane did his first dives from the shore. Next came simple salvage, the recovery of lost anchors and items of that nature. This was followed by dives to modern wrecks in shallow water— that is, stranded wrecks of the 1800s. The degree of difficulty and danger is normally decided in such cases by the way in which the ship lies. If upright, and especially if the masts had been cut away before she struck, the hazards of entrapment and entanglement are reduced. A ship lying on her side, however, presents to the diver much the same picture as a barbed-wired minefield would to a descending parachutist. If anything, a twentieth-century ship is even more dangerous than a nineteenth-century wreck, as the rigging is of steel wire and the superstructure staunchions, railings and ladders present the effect of a series of superimposed gratings, topped by radar aerial, radio direction-finding loop, and so on, below which the diver must penetrate. All that can be said in favour of a fairly recent wreck is that it contains a certain logic, perfectly recognisable once the angle of the ship from the vertical has been established. An older wreck, on the other hand, which has been badly broken up and then covered with a deep layer of laminaria weed, algae, and miscellaneous growth, represents rather a series of well-concealed booby-traps. Into this tangle the early helmet divers had to descend feet first; and in British waters at any rate, in many cases with visibility so bad that they could not see their feet. Consequently, it was vital for the lifeline to be kept taut by the attendant in the boat above; for if the diver stumbled or fell, or—simply unable to see on what he was walking—just stepped off into space, the consequences were liable to be fatal.

These hazards could be greatly reduced by choosing in the first place a stranded rather than a sunken wreck. That is a ship which has been destroyed by running aground or, more usually, been blown ashore by a gale from the wrong direction. The great majority of wrecks during the era of sail came into this latter category. Their subsequent fate depends on the depth of water in the place at which they strike. A true stranding only occurs on a gently sloping seabed or barely submerged sandbank or reef. If the coast consists of a steeply sloping rock face, with considerable depths at its submerged foot, then the tendency is for the ship eventually to descend the rock face to the bottom, which may still be rock, although it can also be sand or mud. The exact circumstances determine both the amount and the nature of the preservation of the remains, and are therefore of paramount interest to underwater archaeologists. At one time it was believed, and frequently stated, that a ship wrecked in the shallows must inevitably break up rapidly and that, therefore, only deep water could contain historically interesting wrecks. As we shall see, this idea has recently been exploded and the sandy shallows are shown to contain their fair share of history. For the salvage diver, such a wreck, when it is recent, affords a life-saving opportunity to reconnoitre the layout at low water, when some part of the ship will probably be visible and the swirl of current and eddy round it will provide further preliminary information as to the safest approach.

It was on such wrecks as these that the Deanes first learned their trade, and the shallows of the Kentish coast on the shores of the Thames Estuary provided profitable work. Without Deane's manuscript to guide us, however, the first named wreck of which we know is the *Carnbrea Castle*, East Indiaman, which fell victim to the dreaded 'Back of the Wight' in July, 1829. This south-west stretch of rocky coast on the Isle of Wight is a lee shore in all normal conditions. It must have taken many Roman ships, and possibly Phoenecian traders also, although none has been found so far, and it still takes a fair quota of modern steamships. It is in fact a recognisable accident 'black spot' of Channel trade. The unfortunate Indiaman was embayed in Chilton Chine; that is, she was blown into a bay and was unable to work her way out as long as wind strength and direction remained unchanged. In brief, at certain angles from the wind, sailing ships travel sideways faster than they make way ahead, and on a lee shore there is usually only one end to that. Last-minute expedients consist of cutting away the masts, to help reduce weight and the wind-exposed area, and anchoring. Neither is infallible. Even a modern steamship, or motorboat for that matter, will tend to travel downwind, the sides, superstructure, and funnel, if fitted, all acting the part of unfurlable sails. If the sea is very bad, which in such a case it almost always is, another last-minute expedient is to get rid of weight from high up in the ship—deck cargo, or, in the case of an old-fashioned warship, dumping overboard the upperdeck guns and ready-use ammunition. In underwater archaeology, these facts become important, because a wrecked ship can leave a trail of clues a mile or more long; although, if these expedients get her out of trouble, the clues are false—or, at any rate, misleading. The *Carnbrea Castle* left just such a trail. She failed to get out of the bay, grounded on the rocks near Ludmore point, then drifted on to within half-a-mile of the mainland of Mottiston, where she took the ground finally, in 28 feet of water. A few days later, a gale began to break her up, and masses of wreckage drifted onshore at Chilton Chine. The *Cornhill Magazine* records that Charles and John Deane worked on her that same year, 1829, and this may have been their first visit to the area of their greatest exploits. In any event, within a few years John Deane took up residence at 72, North Street, Gosport, which is on the west side of Portsmouth Harbour and also housed a rival salvage operator, the shipmaster Henry Abbinett, who lived in Castle Row. Thus the scene was set for the 'Battle of the *Boyne*'.

What is usually called the 'Solent area', comprising roughly the civil port of Southampton, the Naval base of Portsmouth, the Isle of Wight, and various channels and anchorages, such as Spithead and St. Helens, at that time contained a very considerable and genuine underwater treasury. And this undoubtedly was why the divers congregated there. There were no 'treasure ships' as such, of course, because the Spaniards did not route the Plate Fleets through the English Channel, and very wisely so. True, it lay along the 'Black Diamond' route from the coal ports of the north-east coast, and still does, and therefore a high proportion of the local wrecks are colliers, both wood and steel. But it was then, and still is, the largest battleship graveyard possibly in the world. In one small area of it, less than a mile square, there lie today the remains of no less than five historic ships of size and force. Overall, it contained then, and contains today, more than a dozen examples of the development of the European wooden warship, from the floating barracks of the fourteenth century to the ultimate development of the 100-gun three-decker. Most are English, but not all. Three at least are French, sunk in action during battles long forgotten, the precise positions in which they went down equally obscure. But in 1832, three of the British wrecks were not merely known, but buoyed—because they represented dangerous obstructions either to the Spithead warship anchorage or to the navigational channel into Portsmouth Harbour. They were the first-rate three-decker *Royal George*, 108 guns, laid down in 1746, sunk in 1782 by a structural failure; the second-rate three-decker *Boyne*, 98 guns, sunk by fire and internal explosion after grounding off Southsea Castle in 1795; and the third-rate two-decker *Edgar*, 70 guns, reputed the oldest ship in the Navy when sunk by internal explosion in 1711. There was also the ordnance transport *Guernsey Lily*, sunk in Yarmouth Roads, Isle of Wight, in 1799. The treasure potential of all these ships was not gold but guns—brass guns. As the wrecks were prominently buoyed, there was no question of a tedious search. Their treasures had remained comparatively undisturbed for many years, because there was no really efficient diving apparatus available. Now the Deanes had invented one, and had gained sufficient experience to be confident of success in these generally deeper and more dangerous waters. At the same time, they had rivals, because their invention was so easily copied that it was now known generally as the Common Diving Dress.

The year in which preliminary operations began was 1832, the evidence being contained in Admiralty and Ordnance Board files and in the current issues of the *Hampshire Telegraph*. The Deanes had applied for permission to work three wrecks, *Guernsey Lily*, *Royal George*, and *Boyne*. Abbinett had applied for permission to work the *Boyne*. By an oversight, all these permissions were granted, but Deane went to work first. Up from the *Guernsey Lily* came the artillery, and because she was an ordnance transport, it was field artillery. That is, mainly light guns with large-diameter spoked wheels. Had a modern archaeologist made such a find, he might have been somewhat winded by discovering field guns on the seabed, and much bizarre argument might have ensured. The *Boyne* was eventually to produce an even more startling artifact. This was a single brass field gun four feet long and with a calibre of $3\frac{1}{4}$ inches, with an inscription in Swedish. Translated, this read: 'With God's help by King Charles XII, taken at the battle of Clitzow, 9th July, 1702.' What was a Polish trophy, taken by the Swedes in battle on the plains near Warsaw in 1702, doing in a British line-of-battle-ship sunk off Southsea Castle in 1795? This single example, and there are others, must amend somewhat the modern view of sunken ships as 'closed finds' or 'capsules in time', in which, it is some-times explicitly stated, everything must be contemporary. It is for this reason that the present author prefers to use the term 'closed community', because this form of words allows room for the human idiosyncrasy for the

26

The sinking of the *Royal George* at Spithead on the morning of 29 August 1792 in the heart of the fleet assembled to relieve Gibraltar. Lieutenant Bligh (later Captain of the *Bounty*) was then serving in the first-rate HMS *Cambridge* and probably assisted in the rescue work. The painting is by John Christian Schetky marine painter to George IV, William IV and Queen Victoria.

collection of the antique and the curious, as well as stating explicitly that the people who used the ship are of more interest to us than the ship itself. In short, that archaeology is a method of studying history, and that the details of artifacts are only a means to that end. This case is also a salutary reminder of the need for caution in identifying and dating wrecks. A Polish gun, with a Swedish inscription, in a British warship of a later era; and the gun a fieldpiece, not a naval weapon. To anticipate somewhat, the only artifact inscribed with a ship name and date which was to be recovered from the *Royal George* was a dog-collar with the inscription: 'Thomas Little, HMS *Victory*, 1781.' Midshipman Little did in fact go down with the *Royal George* in 1782, his previous ship having been the *Victory*. Of course, no one was for a moment misled, and indeed the *Victory*, far from being sunk, has survived time, collision, the devouring beetle, several Luftwaffe bomb hits, and reports in the patriotic French Press in 1967 (that she had been sunk by the *Redoubtable* at Trafalgar in 1805), and

27

still remains as a unit of the Royal Navy at Portsmouth, in which the Commander-in-Chief flies his flag.

But let us suppose that many centuries have passed and that historians and archaeologists of the long-distant future had only three pieces of evidence on which to base a judgement: the finding of a wreck at Spithead with one artifact marked H M S *Victory*, and two contradictory pieces of documentary evidence, that H M S *Victory* had been sunk at Trafalgar in 1805 and that she had been hit by German dive-bombers at Portsmouth in 1940. All too often, the investigator is in fact compelled to pick his way through such lethal evidence. Generally speaking, the best evidence is circumstantial, and often decidedly undramatic. If a mass of small, accumulated facts point entirely, or even mainly, in one direction then one can be fairly sure that one is on the right lines.

The early divers were at any rate spared this problem, together with the equally vexatious difficulties of location. The *Boyne* was not buoyed, but its position was repeatedly being discovered by vessels entering or leaving Portsmouth Harbour. Abbinett, in his petition of 2 May 1832, for salvage rights, mentioned that there were only three feet of water over the wreck at low tide and that he had, at one time or another, seen a troop transport, a naval storeship, and a revenue cutter hard aground on it, and had taken part himself in towing the latter off. After catching fire at Spithead, the battleship had drifted with the flood tide towards the harbour mouth, until she grounded on the Horse Sand at the side of the navigational channel, a sheet of flame from head to stern, her guns firing from the heat of the blaze, and three hours later blew up. A contemporary picture depicts a column of smoke ascending in atomic cloud proportions. All this resulting from target practice by the ship's marines. A musket cartridge had been blown by the wind into the Admiral's quarter galley, and started a fire which took only five minutes to consume the rigging, a reminder that all wooden ships, and especially sailing ships of the gunpowder era, were peculiarly liable to destruction by fire. Unlike the *Royal George*, however, which had gone down with some 900 men, women, and children aboard, the casualties in the *Boyne* amounted to the Captain's clerk, six seamen, four women, and, it is believed, three children. (Relatives, friends, and traders of all kinds were customarily allowed on board the warships anchored at Spithead.) A number of sheep were killed while grazing on Southsea Common, by the cannon shot, and the final explosion of the after magazine showered Southsea Castle and Common with red-hot debris.

The Deanes began work on her in July, 1832, and quickly recovered two guns, a quantity of copper sheathing, cutlasses, bottles of wine, and a human bone. Abbinett arrived, found them at work on his wreck, and complained to the Admiralty,

I found to my very great injury that C. A. Deane had a letter which he says he has received from your Lordships Board authorizing him to operate on the Rl George and Boyne and to Commence on the latter first. . . . I have lately been at very great trouble and almost ruinous expense, exposing my self my wife and very large family to all the horrors of want and famine,

Artifacts recovered by Deane and Edwards from a number of wrecks, including two copper cooking pots, two iron cauldrons, three glass bottles from the *Mary Rose* site, wardroom crockery, and what may be a chimney or ventilator. All of them, as well as the three human bones from the *Royal George*, are liberally encrusted with oysters.

should your Lordships withhold from me your protection in this my very great undertaking . . . I would humbly point out to your Lordships that it is impossible for two parties to work on the same wreck.

This letter was written on 9 August and annotated by the Admiralty the next day.

Explain to Mr. Deane that he must confine his operations to the Royal George—permission as to the Boyne having been given under a misapprehension. This and other correspondence shows, incidentally, that the postal service between Portsmouth and London was rather better in the 1830s than it is today in the 1960s.

Charles Deane went to London to sort out the matter, diplomatically taking some interesting artifacts with him—three bottles of wine from the *Boyne*. One was given as a present to Earl Grey and the other two to the King, William IV, thus helping to ensure a Royal interest in the historic side of the operations. The *Hampshire Telegraph* reported:

Mr. Charles Anthony Deane, who has volunteered to explore the wreck of the Royal George, *is descended from Sir Anthony Deane, who in 1663, improved the building of the 60 and 70 gun ships, and whose son (the great great grandfather of the present experimentalist) in 1699, was sent to Moscow, to assist Peter the Great in the construction of a Navy, and from whom some interesting communications will be found in* Pepy's Memoirs, *Vol. XI. Mr. Deane, on Monday last (20 August), descended in 11½ fathoms water, to inspect the* Royal George; *he alighted on her, and immediately slung a gun, but the purchase in his vessel (the* Albion) *was not sufficient to haul it up, he then cleared a fisherman's cable, the stone of which had been used for an anchor having got down what Mr. Deane conjectured to be the main hatchway.*

That stone anchor is archaeologically interesting in itself, because it tends to resolve much contemporary argument about the use of stone anchors in the Mediterranean by the ships of antiquity. The answer is simple rather than scholarly. Wrecks and rocks provide much better fishing ground than barren seabed, and so are popular with fishermen; but any anchor is liable to become fast and therefore be lost in such circumstances, and the astute fishermen use an expendable anchor— a stone, an old lump of iron or even a bag full of sand or shingle. These are less likely to get hung up, but if they do, the monetary loss is much reduced. The argument has tended to rage around the Mediterranean use of so-called 'sand anchors' and so-called 'rock anchors', but is best considered as being merely the difference between an efficient, expensive anchor and an expendable anchor for use on what the local English fishermen call 'fasty ground', a most eloquent and all-embracing definition.

The *Royal George* had now been on the bottom for fifty years. The cause of the disaster had been a war crisis, the siege of Gibraltar. A fleet had to be gathered to go to the relief of the Rock, at all costs. On 15 February 1781, the condition of the *Victory* had been marked as 'doubtful', and that of the *Royal George* as 'very bad' (Tomlinson Papers). On 7 November the same year, the *Royal George* headed a list of ships under the heading 'Must be Docked' (Sandwich Papers). She was docked and Vice-Admiral Milbank later testified at the Court Martial: *I found her so bad, that I do not Recollect there was a Sound Timber in the Open. The Officers of the Yard said they should be able to make her last a Summer.* That was the summer of 1782, when every ship was needed. On the morning of 29 August 1782, she was slowly foundering at her moorings among the assembled fleet at Spithead. The fact was partially camouflaged by the incident of a minor repair to a watercock just below the waterline which required the ship to be heeled over to port slightly, which was done by running out the port-side guns and running back the starboard-side guns to about the centre line of the decks. This produced surprisingly, even suspiciously, little effect. Some people began to get worried at the sluggishness of the ship and the nearness of the lower deck ports on the port side to the water, at about the time that the last of the stores—heavy rum casks—began to come aboard, on that side, from the store sloop *Lark*. This combination of circumstances brought a quick end. John Smart, gunner's yeoman,

the Illustrious and Aspiring Glory of the British
Most ANTIENT ORDER of the THISTLE, this
now in Execution, for the effectual raising His
massively subscribed by His Royal Highness's

Nation, PRINCE WILLIAM HENRY, &c.
Plate, being an Exact Representation of the approved
MAJESTY's Ship the Royal George, is most
most hble & obed Servt.
William Tracey

Publ. according to Act by W. Tracey Dec 19, 1782 London.

testified that the angle of heel was slight until he heard a 'Bodily Crack'
from below decks. *She gave a great Jerk or Crack first, and within a moment
after, another, and went down, and I jumped out of the starboard Stern port.*
Several survivors actually escaped from under water. Henry Bishop saw
the port-side gun-ports go dark, as they went below the sea, cutting off

31

the light; then the inrush of water pushed him up a hatchway, in which he met a starboard-side gun on its way down; with three fingers broken by the collision, he burst to the surface and was taken up by a boat. James Ingram, one of the crew of number three gun, lower deck, starboard battery, tried with others to run this gun back into its original position, but the ship heeled so quickly that the gun came back on them; and Ingram, thinking quickly, leapt for the gun-port and got through, by which time it was horizontal instead of vertical, and had his hat blown off by the rush of compressed air from the starboard side of the ship, which was now completely on her side. She hung there for long moments, then went down, righting herself as she did so, coming to rest with her masts and flags out of the water, heeled to port.

The detailed narratives of Ingram and others enabled me to time approximately the fatal heel. I simply repeated in detail their last described actions, with the aid of the *Victory*, an almost identical ship, and the results of a rough-and-ready time-and-motion study in the *Victory* gave a figure of between twelve and fifteen seconds. The effect of the heel could not be reproduced, but all the distances were accurate. The speed with which the ship went over, and then filled, bore out the Court Martial verdict that there had been a structural failure; that, literally, part of the bottom of the ship had broken and that she had filled mainly from below, and only afterwards partly through the open gun-ports on the port side. But this verdict was kept secret at the time, for obvious reasons of military security, and public happiness, and the story put about that the slight heel to careen her, together with a sudden 'land breeze', had been responsible. Just as, during the Second World War the R.A.F. ran newspaper stories of how they fed their night-fighter pilots on carrots in order to improve their eye-sight, as a cover for the development of airborne radar and the resulting decimation of enemy night-bombers. The early salvage operators did not know this, however, and were puzzled and angry at the apparently malicious sabotage of their well-meaning efforts. The last thing the Admiralty wanted to see again was the *Royal George*.

Shortly after the disaster, when the upper parts of the ship were only about twelve feet under at low water, sixteen guns were recovered by divers. The following year, 1783, William Tracey attempted to raise the *Royal George* complete, but only managed to move her about 40 or 50 feet to the westward. Contemporary lithographs produced for him depict the seabed in that area with great accuracy. As a result of his failure, partly connived at by the Admiralty, he was ruined financially. After this there were several stillborn schemes to raise the wreck, because she obstructed a considerable part of the best berth in the anchorage and was now an embarrassment to the Admiralty, and on 11 June 1817, she was officially inspected by a Dockyard diver, Mr. Ancell, from a diving bell. He reported:

The wreck appears to lay with her head about W.S.W. with a considerable list to port. The quarter-deck, forecastle, and round house with the larboard

top-side, as low down as the range of the upper deck, are entirely gone. The oak strakes, amidships of the flat of the upper deck, are very much eaten by worms in several places, so as to show the beams and framing beneath. The whole of the fir appears sound, and as perfect as when first laid, but the deck is much twisted by the ship's falling over so much forward and aft. The wreck has a beautiful appearance when about a fathom above the deck, being covered with small weeds, interspersed with shells, star-fish, and a species of the polypos, lying on a thin, greasy, grey sediment, about an eighth of an inch thick. Below the upper deck, is a perfect solid mass of fine black mud. When suspended over the larboard side of the ship, she appeared a rude mass of timber, lying in all directions, and I have every reason to believe the after part has fallen in, as I found it so much more perfect, and less inclined as I approached the midships. There can be no doubt, I think of the state of the ship being such, as to preclude the possibility of her removal either together or in detached parts.

This was the state of the wreck after thirty-five years under the sea. When the Deanes first dived on her, half a century had passed since the sinking and the great structure had deteriorated further. *We found her to be one huge, indescribable mass of old decayed timbers, and materials confusedly mixed and intermingled with mud, clay, sand, etc.* stated John Deane. Their descents to the wreck were made down a ladder (in one diagram stated to be a rope ladder) which was heavily weighted at the bottom end. Although not in use nowadays, this was clearly a safety measure to avoid some of the hazards of an unknown obstruction in bad visibility. The distance to the upper parts of the wreck was stated to be 60 feet, the seabed being perhaps another 15 to 20 feet down, so that when the divers left the ladder to search for guns and other valuable items, they would have to move slowly and cautiously to avoid a fall. Nothing of great value was recovered in 1832, but they went back to work on the *Royal George* for three continuous seasons during the years 1834–1836 when, stated John Deane,

'This gun, which formed part of the armament of the *Royal George*, was recovered from the wreck of that ship by Mr. Chas. Anty. Dean in the year 1834.' The weapon, a brass 24-pdr, was for many years on view outside the Garrison Church in Old Portsmouth, but has now been moved to the new museum at Southsea Castle.

We used our best exertions on the wreck, and our labours were crowned with success in the discovery of eighteen brass 24-pounders, beautifully wrought, three 18-pounders, and eight iron. 32-pounders, together with human bones and many other curious relics. The brass guns were in a high state of preservation. Our proceedings were carried out entirely at our own expense; government received half of all we recovered; this being the case, it was not surprising that we did not continue our operations after 1836.'

34

When the encrusting shellfish were scraped off the brass guns, it was found that the molluscs retained a perfect impression of the moulding, and some were preserved as curiosities. One of these 24-pounders, raised by Charles Anthony Deane in 1834, was placed on the green by Portsmouth Garrison Church, overlooking the harbour entrance, and was there, much frequented by child climbers, until moved in 1967 to Southsea Castle when this was brought back to its condition at an early period and opened as a museum. It is interesting for two reasons, that it was cast by Andrew Schalch, the first Master Founder of Woolwich Arsenal in 1743, and that the *Royal George* was the last British battleship to be fitted with brass cannon.

The correspondence between the Admiralty and the Ordnance Board regarding salvage rates acquit them of meanness. They made enquiries as to precedent, and had discovered that while a one-third award to the finder was the normal rate paid, exceptions had been made where salvage would remove an obstruction from a dangerous position. For this reason, Abbinett, who was busy trying to remove the *Boyne* with 'low' explosives, was granted a very favourable rate and the Deanes a better-than-average rate. The correspondence also reveals, however, that in considering precedents the authorities had not taken into account the comparative difficulties of different sites. Even the prospective salvors of the guns of the *Endymion*, sunk in that underwater paradise, Jamaica, had asked for one-half of the value instead of the normal one-third. The *Boyne*, only 3 feet under at low water, might have appeared easy, but from the fast currents and a marked wind-against-tide effect half the time, is difficult. The *Royal George*, lying in 75 feet of water at low tide, and 90 feet at high, and with equally poor visibilities, is not everyone's favourite choice of diving site. But it was not long before the Inspector of Artillery was recommending payment to the Deanes of further sums under a quite new category—historic, or museum, value.

On 20 June 1836, the Board of Ordnance received an astounding letter signed, *Your Most obedt Humble Servants, John Deane and Wm Edwards of the Smack Mary*, with an accompanying letter from the Gun Wharf at Portsmouth. Deane and Edwards reported finding at Spithead, on 16 June, and the Civil Officers reported receiving from them on 18 June, a brass demi-cannon, 32-pounder, calibre 6.4 inches, length 11 feet, with the Rose and Crown upon it and the inscription:

HENRICVS. VIII

ANGLIE. FRAN

CIE. ET.HIBERN

IE.REX.FIDEI.DE

FENSOR. INVICT

ISSIMVS. F.F.

MDXXXXII

HRVIII

ARCANVS.DEARCANIS

CESENEN. FECIT

The Civil Officers added, significantly, *There are some letters on the Breech Ring of this Gun which are not legible. The Metal appears to be corroded, and has several small holes in it.* The brass guns from the *Royal George* had been perfect, and all the inscriptions 'as sharp as when first from the foundry', even after more than fifty years under the sea. Mr. Richard Byham, Secretary of the Ordnance Board, endorsed his subordinates' report with the words, 'Let me have a copy of the Deane's letter to send to the King'.

The inscription, being translated, meant: that the gun had been made for Henry VIII, King of England, France and Ireland, Invincible Defender of the Faith, in 1542, by Arcanus de Arcanis of Cesenen, a famous gun-founder of the sixteenth century.

Further the shot, wad, and powder were still in the gun, loaded for action, and the gunpowder was pronounced as still possessing 'properties of ignition'. The cast-iron shot, however, although of regulation size for a 32-pounder, now weighed only 19 lb., owing to a change in its composition resulting from long contact with seawater.

But the full significance of the discovery was not known until Deane and Edwards wrote a further letter, revealing the exact circumstances of the find.

Honble. Gentlemen,
With reference to the Ancient Gun refered to in your letter dated 22nd June 1836 we most respectfully beg leave to state to your Honble. Board that it was recovered thro' the instigation of 5 poor Fishermen, who had frequently got their lines etc entangled in something, but could not find out what it was. That in consequence of getting again entangled on the 16th June they applied to us to descend to discover what was the cause of their frequent losses, and the obstruction to their daily occupation; That previous to descending to prevent any dispute, an arrangement was made, that if anything was found whether of great or trifling value, it should be equally divided between them-selves and us, and on going down about half a cables length from the bow of HM *Ship Pembroke their lines was found to have caught in a piece of old Timber, which was extricated, but on searching in the vicinity, some more old Timber was found, and the Gun in question recovered.*

We humbly hope your Honble. Board will be pleased to take into considera-tion that from its great Age, and length of time lost, although cast in the Reign of Henry 8th by a foreigner, and in a foreign part, the impossibility of ascertaining for certain, whether it ever belong'd to his Government, as it appears in those days, it was not unusual for the Cinque Ports etc to furnish the Government with ships fully equpd. for Naval purposes.

We therefore humbly trust that on the inspection of the said Gun, if Your Honble. Board should decide upon retaining it, that as there must be great doubt respecting it, Your Honble. Board will be pleased to favour us with the benefit of that doubt, and considering the importance of the removal of such obstruction to the safe anchorage of HM *Ships, and also that an equal portion, with our own, belongs to the Fisher-men, that it will meet the appro-bation of Your Honble. Board to allow us the value as old Metal.*

Lithograph reproduction of two of the guns taken up by John Deane and William Edwards at Spithead and landed in HM Gunwharf, Portsmouth, 15 August 1836 (*left*) the 68-pdr brass Cannon Royal, made by Robart and John Owen Brothers in 1535, from the *Mary Rose* (compare the watercolour reproduction of the same gun on p. 15) and (*right*) a 32-pdr iron gun, reign of George III, from the *Royal George*.

With this letter, written on 18 July, Deane and Edwards enclosed certificates from the Captain and Lieutenant of HMS *Pembroke*, as to their recovery of the gun and the importance of clearing the anchorage. They duly received the full price as old metal, which was £220 19s. 0d., instead of one-half or one-third. Authority did not haggle about the price on this occasion, because they saw the significance of those pieces of old timber. This was not a casual find, but must represent the wreck of a large Tudor warship. They thought they knew which one, but set up a committee to establish the facts definitely; the committee was headed by Major-General Sir William Millar, flanked by Colonel Sir Alex Dickson, K.C.B., and Major William Dundas. Simultaneously, the Portsmouth and Portsea Literary and Philosophical Society began to consider acquiring recovered artifacts for their museum.

Deane and Edwards, of course, had known from the beginning that it must be a wreck, hence their agreement to go shares with the fishermen. As for the apparent mercenary tinge to their letter, the clearing of fishermen's lines or nets from an unknown obstruction must always bring a mixture of hope and fear—hope that it will be a rich wreck, fear that, in visibility of only a few feet, reducing rapidly to nil as the work goes forward, one will be fatally entangled on the seabed, far from all help. No doubt they felt, when they had finished, that they had fully earned the money. We know, from an account which Deane gave to Horsey, the local historian, that this wreck was not at all like that of the *Royal George*. Nothing of the ship or armament showed higher than a foot out of the ground, whereas the *Royal George* still stood in places two gun-decks high. Whereas the *Royal George* was in an area which was basically clay mixed with black harbour mud, the ground around this new wreck included sand. And we know also that generally it was very soft, for it was possible to dig. *Mr. Deane, with spade, shovel, etc., then excavated a portion of the sand, etc., and fired a charge of gunpowder, and found on descending again that he had got into the hold of the unfortunate ship, having made a crater of large dimensions by this explosion. After this he made numerous descents at various times, and secured a variety of articles; a list of which Mr. Deane has kindly furnished. The greater portion of these singular articles were, by order of Mr. Deane, disposed of by public Auction, and realised a considerable amount.* The guns, of course, had to be delivered to the Ordnance Board, and three more complete guns were raised from the wreck in August of the same year, plus a broken gun which the local Society wanted for their museum. The contrasted nature of these guns produced a furore; indeed, some people simply would not believe that they all came from the same ship.

Two of the guns were brass. One was a culverin bastard, 9-pounder, calibre 4.56, length 8½ feet. It was not round, but twelve-sided, bore the Rose and Crown in relief, the letters 'H.R.' and the inscription: 'This colveryn bastard weys ZZ99.' The purpose of this piece was to throw a light iron cannonball a long way. The other brass gun was towards the opposite end of the scale. Technically, it was a cannon royal, 68-pounder, calibre 8.54, length 8½ feet (without counting the cascabel, which measured a further 15 inches). This gun fired a shot more than twice the weight of the heaviest guns carried by the 2,000-ton *Royal George*. It was an enormous piece, but it is necessary to see the actual cannon in order to realise fully that it could only have come from a major warship. This also had been made for Henry VIII, but in 1535, seven years earlier than the 32-pounder, and by a British foundry, Robert and John Owyn Brothers, instead of in Italy. It also was loaded for action and the shot had lost weight by submersion and now weighed only 45 lb. 6 oz. The original iron shot, fired from a gun like that at fairly close range, would have severely shaken an enemy ship.

It was the two iron guns, however, which fairly put the cat among the pigeons. They were of the same type, but one was broken. The intact piece was still mounted on its wooden carriage, which began to deteriorate as soon as it was exposed to the air and dried out. The barrel was 9 ft. 8 in. long and was literally a barrel; it was built up of wrought-iron hoops shrunk on to wrought-iron bars. It was a breech-loader, not a muzzle-loader like the others. And the wooden carriage was rather a bed than a carriage; had no wheels, and never had possessed them, but was pivoted behind the breech on a wooden beam and trained by means of a directing bar fitted into a groove under the bed. Its total length, including bed, must have been about 14 feet and its calibre approximately 8 inches— a 60-pounder at least. The recoil was taken by the wooden beam or 'bitt', instead of by backward movement checked by ropes, and therefore the charge could not have been very powerful. The powder was put into a detachable chamber, which was then dropped into place and fixed with a wooden wedge. By the use of a number of such chambers, a fairly high rate of fire could be kept up. The gun was apparently what Tudor gun-lists referred to as a 'Port Piece' and would have fired stone shot, the shrapnel of the time. Stone, being light, would require a lighter charge. In fact, in basic design—although not in size—it was one of the earliest types of gun, developed in the fourteenth century.

In some experts, its discovery among the brass guns, 'which in beauty of design and workmanship are equal to anything that could be produced in the present day', roused a holy fury of denial, and any hypothesis would serve to demolish it. It was even suggested that, 'if indeed they were ever on board' the same ship, then it must have been 'for ballast or some other illegitimate purpose'. This erratic and ill-tempered analysis (a theory had been badly dented by the Deane's discovery) will be found under the name of Mr. C. D. Archibald in *Archaeologia*, vol. xxviii, p. 386, a contemporary publication. This, indeed, is one of the primary functions of underwater archaeology; to prevent the scholars wasting their time and ours, by providing them with sufficient facts. Deane and Edwards were certainly alive to the historical importance of their discoveries, for in this year John Deane makes reference to his 'Cabinet of Submarine recoveries' as being in preparation, and requests the Board of Ordnance not to allow unauthorised persons to make sketches of the guns, as he wishes very accurate representations to be made by his own artist.

This letter was dated 14 September. For their part, Major-General

Millar's committee came to final conclusions about the same time and submitted their report on the guns and the identification of the wreck on 30 September. On 16 October the report was accepted, and, together with the scale drawings of the guns it contained, ordered to be recorded in the Minutes of the Board of Ordnance, and by 24 October had 'been submitted to his Majesty's Inspection by the Master General'. After describing in detail the five pieces of ordnance recovered from this unknown wreck, together with notes on state of preservation and subsequent deterioration of some of the materials, the historical enquiry was prefaced by the sentence: 'In reference to this discovery, and in support of the conjecture that the Guns in question formed part of the Armament of the *Mary Rose*, the following details have been extracted from various authorities, which all tend to confirm the correctness of the supposition.'

The *Mary Rose* was what Anders Franzén, the discoverer of the *Vasa*, defines as a 'fully identified ship'. She appears in the Roll of the King's Ships made by Anthony Anthony for Henry VIII. This was a kind of Jane's *Fighting Ships*, but in colour. Each ship is represented by a coloured picture of her afloat, with details of crew, armament, ammunition, and even small arms because fighting soldiers were then part of the armament of a warship. She was built at Portsmouth in 1509 and then rebuilt to 700 (Tudor) tons in 1536, and sunk in 1545. She was one of the very few really 'key' ships of history. Around 1500 experiments in armament were

Brass guns from the *Mary Rose* now at the Rotunda, Woolwich.

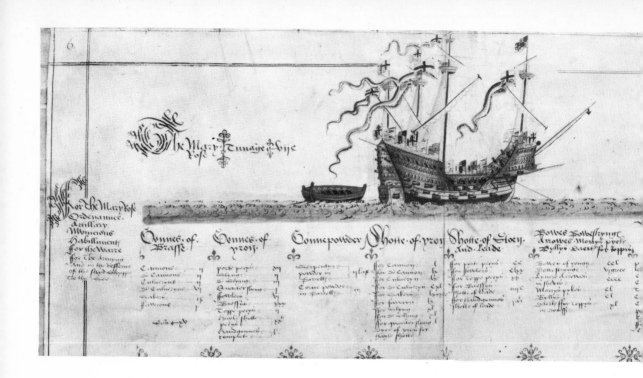

Gonnes of Brasse

Cannons	2
de Cannons	2
Culveryns	2
de Culveryns	6
Sakers	2
Fawcons	1

Gonnepowder

Serpentyn powder in barrells	2 last
Corne powder in barrells	3 last

Men

Souldiours	185
Marrynars	200
Gonnars	30

Gonnes of Yron

Porte pecys	12
Slyngs	2
de Slyngs	3
Quarter slyng	1
Fowlers	6
Baessys	30
Toppe pecys	2
Hayle shotte pecys	20
Handgonnes	1

Bowes of yough	250
Bowestryngs	6 × 144
Lynere arrowes in shevis	300
Morrys pykes	150
Byllys	150
Daerts for toppys in doussn	40 × 12

The *Mary Rose* as depicted
[by] Anthony Anthony for
[K]ing Henry VIII, with lists
[of] her armament,
[am]munition and stores, etc.

going on, and the warship was in process of changing from a floating castle fitted with many small-calibre anti-personnel guns and manned largely by soldiers, to a floating castle armed with many heavy guns firing through gun-ports, supported by small-calibre anti-personnel guns, and manned still by soldiers, but with a higher proportion of professional gunners. The end of this process was to be the floating battery, represented by the *Victory* at the end of the scale, and also, in an earlier stage of development, by the galleon *Vasa* of 1628. The *Mary Rose* was well over a hundred years older than the *Vasa*, and at the time she was built was a warship of revolutionary design—the first we know to be fitted with complete gun-decks rather than with nests of guns in various strategic places. Nevertheless the gun lists and, more spectacularly, the actual guns recovered from the wreck, show with certainty that, unlike later ships, she was not equipped with uniform batteries. The *Victory*, for instance, is fitted with 32-pounders on the lower gun-deck, 24-pounders on the middle gun-deck, and 12-pounders on the upper gun-deck. The *Mary Rose* must also have conformed to the principle of avoiding excess weight high up, although she would be better able to stand it because she was, comparatively, a much wider ship of the 'carrack' type, very broad and shallow for her length. But various points of evidence lead the present author to believe that her guns may have been sited in a more intricate manner and upon definite military principles. In brief, that each slow-firing, heavy gun of a battery was covered and supported by quick-firing light guns and possibly by infantry also, halberdiers and bowmen.

To test this idea, more than the recovery and recording of artillery would be required. Nothing short of either raising the ship completely, like the *Vasa*, or an underwater excavation of mammoth proportions to superlative standards, would produce the required evidence. As land excavation techniques did not become efficient until 1880, this was too much to expect for the divers of 1836.

Potentially, however, there was still more to be gained, because it was not merely the ship which was 'fully identified'; some of the individuals concerned were identified personalities also. The senior officer aboard was Sir George Carew, son of Sir William Carew of Ottery Mohun; his wife Mary, daughter of Henry Norreys, was a witness to the disaster and was standing with the King, Henry VIII, when the ship went down in front of their eyes. Two other relatives were in the fleet and also witnessed the sinking—Sir Peter Carew, 31, younger brother of Sir George, and Sir Gawen Carew, his uncle. Sir George was the Vice-Admiral, not the captain as is usually stated; the Captain of the *Mary Rose* was Roger Grenville. In many cases, underwater archaeology produces only technical drawings of a ship and some vague indications of how the crew lived and what sort of plates they ate from. But in this case, we know the very thoughts of the people concerned, because John Hooker, born 1524, wrote the biography of Sir Peter, who succeeded to the estates as a result of the loss of Sir George in the *Mary Rose*. These were not published until 1857, and therefore were probably unknown at the time of the discovery of the wreck in 1836. The ethos of the time was that of the age of chivalry, of armoured

knights and fair maidens, described in Malory's *Morte d'Arthur*, in which he cloaked the headquarters of a possible Romano-British general with the armour, equipment, clothing, and general sentiments of his own age. The wreck presented, therefore, and still presents, the possibility of bringing Tudor times most sharply into focus for the present age; and this is its importance. Complete, rather than fragmentary, understanding.

However, at the time of the discovery in 1836, there was a tale (still current in some places, particularly the U.S.A.) that the *Mary Rose* had sunk inside Portsmouth Harbour, as she was setting out; this was probably a misreading of Holinshed, a contemporary historian, but the committee had to go into the matter. That is, the first stage was preliminary identification by site location. This was particularly interesting to me, because I had employed the same principle in connection with the re-discovery of the *Royal George* and *Boyne* in 1965 and by 1966, knew to within an accuracy of a few hundred feet, where the remains of the *Mary Rose* lay buried. The committee knew where the remains were; what they had to prove was, were these definitely from the *Mary Rose*. Could she have sunk in that spot?

After recapitulating the known details of the fact of the Battle of

The 'Cowdray Picture' of the Battle of Portsmouth, 20 July 1545, engraved by James Basire in 1778 from the original painting at Cowdray House, Sussex: in the *right foreground* is 'Old' Portsmouth enclosed within fortifications which cover by short-range gun-fire the navigational channel into Portsmouth Harbour, and in the *left foreground* the main English Field Army is encamped round Southseas Castle, the gun emplacements here also covering the navigational channel, which is up to 70 ft. deep. In the centre Henry VIII himself rides into camp on a black horse

with his attendants. In the *right background* forts on the Gosport side of Portsmouth Harbour overlook the main assembly area of the smaller vessels of the English Fleet on the shallow Hamilton Bank and Monckton Patch, and in the *left background* the French Fleet is massed round the south-eastern tip of the Isle of Wight, with a galley group forward at No Man's Land to draw out the English from the shallows. The *Great Harry* engages them and the *Mary Rose* has just sunk, her masts and yards showing above the water.

Portsmouth, 1545, in which a French fleet of 235 ships came into attack an English fleet of about 60 ships, under the eyes of the English king, court, and privy council established in and around Southsea Castle, the committee went on to quote Holinshed:

The twentieth of Julie, the whole Navie of the Englishmen made out and purposed to set on the Frenchmen but in setting forward, through too much follie, one of the King's Ship's, the Mary Rose was drowned in the middest of the Haven, by reason that she was overladen with Ordinance, and had the ports left open, which were verie low, and the great Artillerie unbreached, so that when the Ship should turne, the Water entered and suddenlie she suncke. In her was Sir George Carew Knight and four hundred Soldiers under his guiding. There escaped not past fortie persons of the whole number.

The committee next took advantage of the fact that the affair had occurred under the noses of the English Government, and that it, and subsequent events, were very fully described in surviving State Papers. They were able to quote chapter and verse on the salvage attempts, beginning with the letter from Lord Russell to Sir William Paget on 23 July.

43

I am verie sory of the unhappy and the unfortunat chaunce of the Mary
Rose: *whiche throughe such rasheness and great negligence, soulde be in
suchewise cast awaye, with thos that werr within her whiche is a great loss of
the Men, and the Shipp also, notwithstanding ye give me good hope by your
letters that the Shipp shall be recovered againe, which I praye God may be so.
I understand also, that there ar besides Saint Ellens point, to the number of
8 score seale, and that the King hathe determyined that my Lorde Admirall
shall give them Battaile, if they abide. And that even then, att the wrytinge of
your Letters 17 of the gallies cam in the order of battaile to the fight, of the
whiche on was sunke, and the Shippes begane to retyre, which I believe
will not come againe.*

The Venetian salvage contractors, Petre de Andreas and Symone de
Maryne, worked on into August, trying to raise the wreck, which lay
heeled on her port side with her masts and yards well out of the water, by
the classic method of stationing two hulks on either side, running cables
under the hull of the wreck, and using the rise of the tide for a series of
'lifts', meanwhile lightening the sunken ship as much as possible. By 5
August, her sails and sail-yards had been removed and brought to land,
but the marked angle of heel was making it difficult to position the hulks
correctly; and in an endeavour to get her into the upright position before
beginning the series of lifts, cables were attached to her masts. But the
Mary Rose did not come upright; instead, the foremast broke, proof of
the lifting strain they were able to bring to bear. Subsequently, some of
the guns were salvaged from her by an Italian diver called Peter Paul.

Then the committee came upon the final proof that the hull was never
salvaged, in a few lines from Sir William Monson's *Naval Tracts*.

The Mary Rose, *next to the* Regent *in bigness and goodness after this was
cast away betwixt Portsmouth and the Isle of Wight, the very same day King
Henry boarded her, and dined in her. Part of the ribs of this Ship I have seen
with my own Eyes. There perished in her, four hundred persons.*

To the committee this was conclusive, and they commented:

*Sir William Monson was born in 1569 and he died in 1643: his Tracts
were published in 1623. The* Mary Rose *therefore was lost 24 years before he
was born, but such an unfortunate event would be well remembered for many
years beyond that period, and the exact situation where she sunk would be well
known to all persons residing at Portsmouth. Sir William's statement of
having seen her remains seems consequently to be beyond the possibility of any
mistake, and he further establishes certainty as to the situation where the
accident happened, which by the preceding details remained in doubt; whether
it occurred within the Harbour, or without. . . . On the whole subject, it appears
quite certain that the* Mary Rose, *was lost at Spithead, that the Ship never was
weighed up, and from the description of the Guns lately discovered there is
every reason to believe that they formed part of her Armament. It may fairly
be presumed therefore, if the wreck the Guns were laying on could be displaced
in some degree, that more Guns and other articles of an interesting character
might be discovered and weighed up, indeed the same observation holds good,*

44

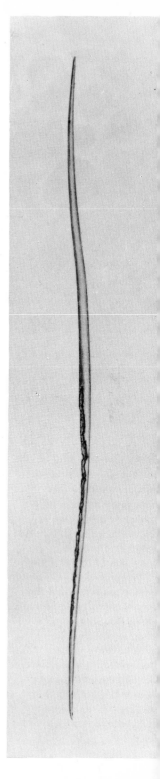

Yew bow among the artifact
recovered by Deane and
Edwards from the *Mary
Rose:* it is about 6 ft. long.

The 'Old Ligger' or Ledger Book of Newport, opened in 1567 contains this illustration which appears to depict the French landings on the Isle of Wight in 1545. Shore positions are being fired on by three galleys and a large 'roundship', the latter armed with four heavy guns on the lower deck, apparently brass cannon and built-up iron guns arranged alternately to cover each other, with a row of light guns on the deck above.

with regard to the Edgar, *and other Vessels that have perished in a sudden and violent manner in shallow Water, to which it would be advisable that the attentions of Mr. Deane be called and that every encouragement be given to him.* (SIGNED) *Wm. Millar, M.Genl., Woolwich, 30th Sept. 1836.*

That letter can fairly be said to mark the beginnings of official interest in underwater archaeology, some seventy-four years previous to its currently-accepted start at Antikythera in 1900. It would be fitting to record here also the names of the five Gosport fishermen who really found the *Mary Rose*. They were John Henry Richard, William Burnett,

45

Sir Peter Carewe, brother of the Vice-Admiral, who was also present at the action and subsequently described the sinking of the *Mary Rose* to his biographer.

Jas. Richard, Job. Redman, and William Burnett, Jr.

It was not until 1840, however, that the next major series of discoveries was made, and Deane and Edwards reported to the Ordnance Board:

In accordance with authority and privilege granted to us by the Lords Commissioners of the Admiralty, and approved by your Honble. Board, we have at various favourite intervals pursued our Diving operations in searching and surveying the place where the Mary Rose is supposed to have sunk at Spithead, and we have the honour and satisfaction of acquainting your Honble. Board that our exertions have at length been crowned with success. . . .

This was written on 5 September, and the most valuable piece was a brass culverin, 17-pounder, calibre 5.20, length 10 ft. 11 ins. (11 ft. 8 ins. with cascabel). It bore exactly the same inscription as the first gun recovered, on 16 June 1836, and had been made for Henry VIII by the Cesenen foundry in the same year, 1542. Deane and Edwards reported that they had recovered also:

46

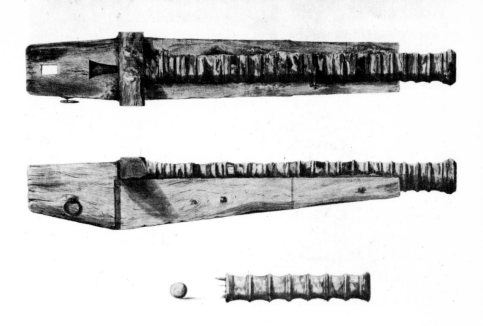

he large wrought-iron, reech-loading gun, and art of a smaller but milar gun, recovered by Deane and Edwards om the *Mary Rose* in ugust 1836. One of the atercolour illustrations intended to be reproduced a John Deane's *Cabinet*, it particularly important in hat it shows the wood and on fresh from the seabed efore deterioration had et in. Later drawings were artly guesswork and the resent state of the gun is ery sad. These pieces were aded with stone shot, uch as is illustrated here eside the broken barrel of he smaller gun.

Four iron 32 pdrs from 6 to 8 feet long, constructed of wrought iron bars and hoops, containing powder and stone shott, these are very antique and have a hole [the bore] completely through, although they have no appearance of being broken, but of a perfect muzzle at each end.* Also several smaller Guns, swivels and parts to the number of 7 or 8 of the same make, together with a perfect human skull, two of the Archers bows, and a small quantity of timber, etc.

The archers' bows, about 6 feet long and made of yew, went to the Tower of London, where they still are; at the time, they were the earliest known examples of a warrior's bow (as distinct from a practice bow), and were, of course, precisely dated. Remains of bows found on the site of a land battle cannot be dated with such certainty. Another interesting artifact found in this year was a jug. This was of a well-known type of Cologne-ware, but came as a surprise to the experts, who had hitherto assigned a much later date to the type. Again, a shipwreck had provided an almost unarguable dating.† In lending it to the Victoria and Albert Museum, London, in 1916, the owner, Mr. Everitt, had written that the jug had 'been in possession of the family, from whom I recently obtained it, since about the year 1840 when it was given to one of the members of that family by a diver who stated that he obtained it from the wreck. . . .' Until recently, the jug was on loan to Cumberland House Museum, Southsea, and will probably go into the *Mary Rose* Room in the new museum at Southsea Castle.

* i.e., they were breechloaders.
† As no drawings or descriptions of the objects as they lay *in situ* exist, there is the possibility of both jugs and bottles from the *Mary Rose* site being 'anchorage artifacts' put over with the garbage from ships of a somewhat later date. Only the most careful observation and recording of the stratification above and around the wreck would have revealed this, and even on land this technique had not then been developed.

In the same letter, Deane and Edwards referred to 'the delay and expence of repeated attempts and failures of discovery' and 'continued exertion and perseverance, entirely at our own expence and risk', and asked the Board 'to take the same liberal and favourable view' as they had before in estimating the value to be awarded. This was done. On the brass culverin, the Inspector of Artillery recommended a payment 25 per cent greater than that of the value of the metal, because 'as a specimen of Ancient Ordnance, it is, in my opinion, extremely valuable'. The iron guns had no intrinsic value, but the recommendation was that those guns selected for retention should be paid for. To anyone acquainted with bureaucracy, this recommendation is astounding, but the memo was signed by Lt.-Col. Dundas, a member of the *Mary Rose* Committee of 1836.

On 13 October Deane and Edwards, signing themselves for the first time 'Submarine Engineers', solicited from the Board 'the grant of a few old condemned bomb shell (13 in) for the purpose of exploding gun powder in continuation of our operations on the Wreck of the *Mary Rose*'. They were granted six unserviceable 13-inch shells, and on 30 October reported that they had 'recovered two more large iron guns, and several parts of others from the *Mary Rose*' and were now discontinuing operations for the season. What they had recovered, when compared with the list of guns in the Anthony Roll, appears to represent less than half the main armament of the *Mary Rose*. Did the Tudor divers recover the other half when the wreck was still visible from the surface, or are those guns still there, deep in the light clay? They may be, indeed the whole trend of the evidence leads this way, for at this point the *Mary Rose* again disappears from the record, apart from one unsubstantiated and unlikely statement that Colonel Pasley had the remains blown up in 1844. Not merely did she disappear from the record, but all trace of the position in which she lay was also lost until in 1965, I launched a project to re-locate and investigate the historic Spithead wrecks with modern archaeological policy in mind, and after visiting the *Royal George* and the *Boyne* at last came across lost evidence for the position of the *Mary Rose*. The project was extremely economical in diving time, because most of the work consisted of research on land, which unearthed in turn the authentic story of the development of diving apparatus; the record of what had been done to, and recovered from, various historic wrecks, including the *Mary Rose*, and in many cases the present whereabouts and condition of those artifacts; the authentic story of the battle in which the *Mary Rose* was sunk; and facts from various operations, including those of Colonel Pasley, which exploded many myths widely-held by Mediterranean underwater archaeologists; and underpinned the results with carefully-directed underwater survey during the two seasons 1965–66. These latter bore out the highly surprising, but hitherto neglected, findings of the extremely ambitious underwater operations carried out by Pasley during the period 1837–1844.

The Mary Rose jug, an early example of Cologne ware, recovered by the Deanes in 1840.

3

'A black earthenware teapot, much cracked…'

Operations of Colonel Pasley, 1837-1844
First scientific analysis of artifacts
Further development of diving apparatus

It may appear strange that I, hoping to uncover the *Mary Rose* again shortly, should apparently regard with equanimity the explosion by the Deanes of bomb shells filled with gunpowder among the remains. The answer is, that having regard to the nature of the seabed at that point and to the explosive force in question, their effect would be rather to uncover than to destroy; in the context of 1840, they would be the equivalent of either the 'airlift', a kind of underwater vacuum cleaner, or more directly the pressure pump. They would do little more than blow away the exceedingly light clay, overlaid with patches of harbour mud and beachsand, which is the basic ground there. The cushioning effect would be considerable, and the force of the explosive used negligible. The 13-inch bomb shell was just an explosive cannonball designed to be fired from a mortar, with a hole for the fuse which burned in flight. They were used for close-range bombardment of sea defences by small, oddly-rigged vessels known as Bomb Ketches; and indeed I have helped recover one from the seabed. They were conveniently water-tight, except for the fuse-hole, and under-water explosions were contrived with them by connecting the open fuse-hole, via a pipe, to the surface and then either popping a match down or igniting a long length of fuse inserted in the pipe. Necessarily, the salvage boat was more-or-less on top of the explosion, but as gunpowder is only a 'low explosive' the quantity contained in the bomb was insufficient to do any damage. As long as this form of ignition was used, in fact, the explosion of really heavy charges underwater was virtually out of the question. It was Colonel Pasley who changed all this.

Charles William Pasley (who was to retire as General Sir C. W. Pasley, K.C.B., F.R.S., D.C.L.) was a Napoleonic figure. That is, he had dined with Nelson on board his ship the year before Trafalgar (*His appearance, a thin middle-sized figure, would be by no means striking if the want of an arm, and a shade over one eye, did not suggest to you the memory of the high service he has rendered his country . . . I remarked the keenness of his look and gesture, which announced the decision of his soul . . . His Lordship's ardent mind is so much bent on the destruction of the enemy that he thinks and talks of nothing else.*) He was at the battle of Maida against Regnier's Division in 1806 (*I attached myself to the Light Infantry, who were the first corps engaged, and had the pleasure of witnessing the famous charge in which they ran down the heroes of Marengo like a flock of sheep. . . . The French waited the onset with the utmost firmness till the points of the bayonets almost crossed each other, then they turned their backs, to a man, as if by word of command, and in a moment the field of action was covered with their dead and wounded*).* He was with Sir John Moore at

---

* This description is more revealing of Pasley than of the battle, which is famous in military history as being the first proof of what was before only a theory, that British infantry drawn up in double-linear formation had a great fire-power advantage over the traditional Napoleonic blitzkrieg method of attack in double-column. Three volleys from the 1,000 men of the British Light Brigade virtually destroyed the 1,600 men of the French 1st Léger. Undoubtedly the British were much steadier and more disciplined than their attackers, but the shame of unexpected defeat made the French General Compére ride right in among the British although disabled by two musket balls in his left arm and shoulder, 'cursing and swearing with the most voluble bitterness'.

50

Corunna (*I was present when he died, but did not enter the room until he was nearly insensible and speechless . . . I assisted that night and next morning at his burial, which was private, only the Aides-de-Camp, and the clergymen being present*). He was at the landing on Walcheren in 1809 (*The French were making counterworks, and do them faster than ours . . . such circumstances would put life into a statue, by heavens it would have called a dead body from the grave, but what could we do with a parcel of old women at our head, with fellows without souls, to direct the operations of armies, with fellows old in years, poor in spirit, beardless in military experience, destitute of knowledge, not merely blockheads but blockbodies*). He was with Wellington at Waterloo—in 1814, one year before the battle, while that prudent general was reconnoitring the approaches to Brussels. In 1837, he was fifty-seven years of age and had been Director of the R.E. Establishment at Chatham, on the southern side of the Thames Estuary, for some time. Whitstable, where John Deane had developed his diving apparatus, and which had subsequently become a kind of centre for shallow water diving, on account of the steadily increasing number of available wrecks, was only a short distance away. It was one of these new wrecks, the 200-ton coal-

51

A 13-inch bomb shell (with fuse) in the stubby mortar normally used for firing it, preserved by the Garrison Church, Old Portsmouth. The Deanes used condemned shells for excavating wrecks and blowing holes in the seabed.

brig *William*, sunk near Tilbury Fort in the Thames in May, 1837, which brought Pasley into the underwater business. At this time, there were about 1,000 new wrecks each year round the coasts of Great Britain, and of these approximately half became total losses. The average number of lives lost was in excess of one thousand. There was no obvious reason why this should affect Pasley, who was not in any case an active man. He had received crippling injuries at the Siege of Walcheren, when aged twenty-eight, and the nature of them—multiple musket and bayonet wounds—show that he was 'up the sharp end' at the time. There was even less reason to suppose that he was to be responsible, quite incidentally for certain developments in underwater archaeology which were soon to be forgotten and not to be repeated for well over a century.

His involvement came about because a salvage attempt on the *William* failed, the vessel was a danger to navigation, and the London Water Bailiff asked the Board of Ordnance if they could help to blow up the wreck. As mining was an engineer responsibility, the papers landed on Pasley's desk. In point of fact, Submarine Mining was included in his training programme at Chatham, where small charges were exploded in shallow water, usually in the River Medway. But the *William* lay in seven fathoms at low water—just over forty feet—and in a fast tideway with virtually no visibility. Pasley asked for two or three weeks in which to make experiments, 'as the attempt to blow up a ship in such deep water has never been made since the invention of gunpowder'. Pasley was a business-efficiency expert, long before anyone had got around to describing proper planning by fancy names, and this factor shows in all his operations. He decided: deep water equals great difficulty in the placing of charges and a high failure rate, therefore employ a small number of large charges, carefully prepared, rather than many small ones. He

52

identical bomb shell
[un]derwater, with a
[gra]pnel-fluke inserted into
[the] fuse-hole, as raised from
[40] ft. of water near
[Hor]mansland Fort, Spithead,
[1]5 June 1965. Taken with
[nat]ural light only, the
[ph]otograph shows how
[art]ifacts are camouflaged
[by] algae and seaweed.

planned to use a diving bell to take down and prepare the charges, and
two helmet-divers to check (entirely by feel, for there was no visibility)
that the charges were correctly placed and in contact with the hull of the
wreck. He first asked Deane and Edwards if they would undertake this
task, but complained that although they 'urgently requested to be employed they would not name their terms'. This should have been a timely
warning, that diving operations are a chancy business, always liable to
delay by weather, and that to quote a fixed price or a stated time is
unwise. Deane and Edwards knew it well enough, and Pasley was to learn
it; but his immediate reaction was characteristically bold and decisive.
Deane and Edwards normally had a standard charge of five guineas per
day all in, which included hire of diving boat, crew, diving gear, and
divers. Pasley decided to save the government money by hiring a helmet
dress from Mr. Kemp, another salvage operator, and train two of his men,
from the Corps of Sappers and Miners, to use it. For the bell, he engaged
the famous George Dewar. Dewar had been the bell diver employed during
1825 and 1826 on the Spanish 'treasure galleons' of Vigo Bay, rumoured
to have been the only successful raiding of those famous remnants of a
'Plate Fleet'. He had certainly recovered during 1831 and 1832 the
treasure from the frigate *Thetis*, sunk off Cape Frio, Brazil.

There were many setbacks in the experiments to detonate charges at
depth by means of a lead tube with a fuse inside, and it was not until the
spring of the following year, 1838, that Pasley's preparations for his first
underwater operation began to take shape. What he was proposing looked
sensible on paper, but was positively horrifying from the practical point
of view. He had to train two absolute novices—Serjeant Young and Corporal Henry Mitchell—to use a primitive diving helmet in more than
forty feet of totally black, tidal water among the tangled masts, spars and

53

rigging of an unseen wreck, and, moreover, to do all this at a time of the year when the water is bitterly cold and severely affects the confidence and efficiency even of an experienced diver. When Pasley had been shot down and then bayoneted, he had been leading a storming party; he led this one, too. On 28 April he made the first practice dive in person, reporting that the diving-helmet was 'very comfortable'; and then gave it to Serjeant Young for that NCO to try. On 5 May, with the actual operation imminent, Corporal Mitchell made his first practice dive. Pasley reported:

This morning I sent a Corporal down to the bottom of the Medway, who fixed two eye-bolts to a piece of timber placed there, and went through the same process that I propose to adopt for fixing the charges under water as near to the bottom of the brig as possible. This man had never used a diving helmet before, and yet he remained under water for three-quarters of an hour, which has satisfied me that there is neither difficulty nor danger in the use of this apparatus, which I also know by my own experience, having gone down first myself, which I thought was the best way of forming an opinion of the practicability of the proposed operation. One of our Serjeants has also made the same experiment, so I have no doubt that we shall be able to manage the diving operations at probably one fiftieth part of the expence that would have been incurred by accepting the offer of Messrs. Deane and Edwards, who urgently requested to be employed but would not name their terms.

On the morning of 21 May the diving lighter was moored over the wreck, and Corporal Mitchell was making his second dive of the day, to fix the charges. He had been down a long time and was apparently forgetting to make signals via the lifeline. Captain Yule ordered the attendant to give the lifeline a pull—and it came taut, immovably fixed in some obstruction down in the black water. At this moment of crisis, Pasley arrived and took over. Although slack water was past, and the tide was now running, he went down in the diving bell with Captain Yule to search for his NCO. The attempt failed. Another search was carried out, this time by Serjeant Ross. And that failed. Only at low slack water, twelve hours after Mitchell had failed to answer signals, did they find him, hanging dead in his diving-helmet nine feet above the seabed and hopelessly entangled in some projection from the wreck. As some measure of his grief, Pasley paid for a headstone to be placed on the grave, recording the manner of the man's death, which had been brave indeed.

On 28 May, Pasley's divers destroyed all but the bows of the brig *William* with a single large charge containing 2,500 lb. of gunpowder. He had prepared two such charges, so used the other to blow the wreck of the *Glamorgan*, lying over by the Essex shore. As a result of these experiments he drew two conclusions—that the lighted fuse method was unreliable and that a new gadget in process of development, using what is now known as electricity, would be preferable; and that, for use in a current, a diving bell needed to be angled at both ends. This preoccupation with gadgets, some to prove vital, others a total loss, strikes a distinctly modern note, as does the optimism resulting from these small successes. And also the rivalry between different groups. Pasley learned via the grapevine—the 'old boy net' of 1839—that Deane had applied to the Ordnance Board for powder and bomb shells with which to blow the *Royal George*; and this news was speedily followed by information from another source which told him the far worse news, that Deane had approached the Polytechnicon Institute for the same 'voltaic batteries' which Pasley was trying to get hold of. So, on 19 March 1839, Pasley wrote a private letter to protect his interests—for he, also, was planning to deal with the *Royal George*, jumping from a 200-ton collier to a 2,000-ton warship, from 42 feet to a minimum of 72 feet. On 25 May, his proposed plan of operations against the *Royal George* was ready, all 14 pages of it. It was very thorough. He stated that, according to Dockyard soundings taken in February that year, 'certain parts of the hull must stand from 33 to 36 feet above the bottom of the Anchorage.' That 'Mr. Dean the ingenious improver of the Diving Helmet' had recovered guns worth more than £3000, for which he had been paid £1,512 6s. 2d., or half the value; and that guns to the value of £5,637 4s. 3d. must still remain in the wreck to repay salvage costs. That, 'as the Hull is imperfect', four large explosive charges, plus 44 small charges, should suffice to remove the entire wreck and free the anchorage altogether of this obstruction. Diving time in manhours was worked out in detail: as the weight of the *Royal George* and her stores was calculated to be 15½ times that of the brig *William*, which had required 30 descents by 2 helmet-divers in 18 days, then 'we may suppose that about 465 descents of divers of this description would be required, to clear from the anchorage the fragments of the *Royal George*'. But also, in order to keep the lighters fully employed, a diving bell, with three shifts of divers, would be necessary. A surface support party of 'about 20 Royal Sappers and Miners with Non Commissioned Officers in proportion would be required'; plus a party of seamen, with Petty Officers in proportion. Gunpowder, wages, and stores were costed—'the whole will not exceed £2,500; and if operations began in the current year, 1839, then 'there can scarcely be a doubt of the Anchorage at Spithead being put into a fit state for a British fleet, in the course of the Year 1840'. In fact, it was to take until 1843 because, as the Deanes had known, underwater operations are awkward to evaluate. Nevertheless, a salvage operation of this magnitude had never before been undertaken, and such careful planning was not to enter the archaeological field until American expeditions, under Mr. George Bass, had been successfully mounted, and the experience digested.

On 4 July, Pasley was given authority to proceed. Only now could he prepare the giant cylinders to contain the gunpowder and assemble stores and the men. On 20 August, the surface support force was anchored around the buoy of the *Royal George*. This consisted of the frigate hulk *Success* as accommodation ship, and three Dockyard lighters as diving platforms and working salvage platforms, for the wreck was to be removed, piece by piece, until only the smaller fragments remained. The two helmet-divers were George Hall, of Whitstable, and John Smith, who had worked with Abbinett on the *Boyne*. Both were civilians, as was George Dewar, the senior bell diver. Operations began next day, 21 August.

On 23 August, red flags were hoisted by the surface support force, to indicate that two of the giant cylinders, each containing 2,400 lb. of gunpowder, were to be fired. These cylinders, looking rather like aerial bombs of a later age, were to be lowered mechanically by ropes and chains into their approximate positions against the wreck, then finally checked by the helmet-divers. A vast concourse, including Royalty, had assembled at Spithead to witness the double explosion. But the down-haul ropes of the first cylinder would not move—they were tangled in the wreck—and that cylinder could not even be lowered to the seabed. The second cylinder only was placed in position, the trumpets announced the imminent explosion, the electrical contact was made, the apparatus sparked—and nothing else happened. The next few days were spent recovering the giant cylinders and in testing small oil casks for their resistance to pressure on the seabed. Abbinett had used these to contain explosives while blowing up the *Boyne* in 1833 and 1838, and they had worked in that shallow water. At Spithead, with more than twice the depth, they simply stove in. On 26 August, Pasley sacked the bell-diver Dewar, for being absent from his post, and went down in the bell himself. In spite of the compressed air being pumped down to it, the water rose $2\frac{1}{2}$ feet into the bell, because of the greater depth and the inability of the pumps and pipes to cope with it, and, before they had even reached the bottom and seen the *Royal George*, a curious gentleman in a pleasure yacht came too close and rammed the lighter from which the bell was suspended. A fortnight later, Pasley returned the bell to the Dockyard and it was not seen again at Spithead. On 1 September, he sacked John Smith, the helmet-diver, because he seemed unable to remain underwater so long as George Hall. About this time, it was discovered that the work-men at Chatham had failed to waterproof the priming apparatus of the giant cylinders, contrary to instructions, so this was remedied and on 5 September a properly treated cylinder was sent down, the red flags hoisted, the trumpets sounded, and, with their Lordships of the Admiralty watching closely from a nearby steamer, this cylinder again failed to fire. When raised, it was found that the powder was wet from a leak which could not be traced. Pasley decided that the large cylinders must be re-tested and in the meantime only small charges fired. On 21 September, a new but experienced helmet-diver, Hiram London, was hired by Pasley to take the place of Smith. Soon, he had them both diving two or three times a day, not merely at the low water slack depth of some 72 feet, but at high water of spring tides also, nearer 90 feet.

On 23 September, one of the giant cylinders fired at last, causing a beehive-shaped column of water to shoot up 30 or 40 feet into the air, and now the archaeological aspect of the affair began, in spite of the fact that when the fragments of the wooden cylinder floated to the surface, they were carried off by some of the spectators as souvenirs of the *Royal George*. Three people were directly involved, encouraged by Pasley, and they began to record not merely artifacts but facts. Lieutenant William Reid, R N, was a draughtsman who had studied ship-building at the Naval College and was therefore able not merely to draw the fragments

A lithograph published by Augustus Siebe showing Army and East India Company divers at work on the *Royal George* using his 'improved diving dress'. Two of the lighters and the frigate-hulk *Success*, used as a base ship, can be seen— with Ryde Pier, Isle of Wight—in the background.

recovered, but usually able also to say what they were. Again, a very
modern touch, because it has been discovered that an archaeologist on an
underwater site is not enough, unless the remains are those of buildings;
a naval architect, or someone with very similar qualifications, is required
for identification and the eventual theoretic reconstruction of ship
remains. Also employed as a draughtsman was Serjeant Samuel March,
who recorded several hundred artifacts and fragments. According to the
official *History of the Royal Sappers and Miners* by T. W. J. Connolly,
'Many of the sketches of the wreck were executed by him with the assistance of the camera lucida, kindly lent for the purpose by the late Captain
Basil Hall, R N, from whom he received much useful instruction'.
Captain Hall, the naval correspondent employed by the *Hampshire
Telegraph* specially to cover the operations, made copious notes; and was
especially interested in the deterioration of various types of materials
after, now, 57 years under the sea. Again, a very modern touch. Reporting
the 'beehive' explosion and its results for his paper, he wrote:

> One brass gun, a 24-pounder, of great beauty, 9 ft. 6 in. in length, and quite
> uninjured by time, has been recovered; as well as four iron 32-pounders, of

one of which the carriage is quite perfect. Those parts of the iron which have been exposed are reduced to a soft substance like plumbage; but those which have been under the mud are as hard and quite entire as ever. This remark applies also to every description of timber. For example, to the capstan, the upper drumhead of which, with its welps, is almost worn away, while the lower drumhead and all its other parts, are as fresh and firm as when they were first made! Two tillers have been got up, quite entire, and much ironwork, including the shank painter, but the whole worn to a thread.*

The interest in these relics, particularly the local interest, was intense; and whereas nowadays such detailed reports would appear only some years afterwards and in some hard-to-obtain specialist publication, small local printers took upon themselves the task of immediate publication and with commendable enterprise produced a series of small pamphlets, well researched and documented, and in very hard covers—to wit, wood from the *Royal George*. Horsey of Portsea was one, Charpentier of the High Street another (in collaboration with Ackermann of London). The latter asked Captain Hall if he would kindly submit a full report on the recovered artifacts for publication, and on 29 July 1840, Hall replied:

In compliance with your request, I proceed to give you a short account of some of the most interesting relics saved from the wreck of the Royal George, *which Col. Pasley has kindly permitted me to examine, and if the description appears likely to prove useful to your little publication, you are welcome to print it accordingly.* Charpentier did so in his second edition, the same year.

In the first place, there were brought up two inkstands—one of ebony, and the other of lead: the ebony one is 14 inches long by 8 inches broad, and not quite an inch in height; it has one large and one small ink-glass remaining of three, which it originally held; it has a brass handle and a brass candlestick fitted to it. Near this lay an ivory paper cutter, the flat end of which is much decayed; also a huge red lump of sealing wax, nearly as thick as my wrist, about three inches long. It seems doubtful whether the mass was originally formed of this magnitude, or whether it be composed of a dozen sticks run together. I have heard it said, that formerly sealing-wax was used in sticks of this large size. It is remarkable, that while the ebony ink-stand is quite perfect, the leaden one is much corroded. A fragment of a penknife, also, was found near the same spot; and as the position was not far from the stern, there seems every reason to suppose that these things may have belonged to Admiral Kempenfelt himself.

In the same neighbourhood were found several beautiful specimens of real dragon china ware, blue and white, some of it in perfect preservation; also sundry wine glasses, of rather a dumpy shape; and several small punch

---

* The earliest study on the corrosion of cast iron appears to date from 1831, when Berzelius commented on the state of cannon balls recovered from a wreck sunk off Karlskrona half a century earlier (*Traité de Chimie*, vol. iii, p. 274). Mallet described the state of an old anchor and analysed contemporary reports of the raising of guns from the 'Tobermory Galleon' in 1740 (*British Association Reports*, 1838, pp. 259–260). Wilkinson refers to this and additionally studied the state of iron recovered from the *Mary Rose* by the Deanes (*On the Extraordinary Effect produced on Cast Iron by the Action of Sea-Water*, London, 1841, pp. 238–239).

glasses, all of them tinged of a faint brown, manifestly produced by the action of the water, and the mud. Along with, or near these, were two salt-cellars, with two horn egg spoons, and three cruet bottles. None of the glass, except the salt-cellars, is cut, and most of it is of a rude construction. The two helmet-divers did not work together, but from separate lighters moored over different parts of the wreck, so that they got to know their own areas and took an interest in them. These artifacts came from the stern, where the Admiral's and Captain's cabins were, and also the Wardroom where the officers dined. From this part also, several dozen of wine have been brought up. The wine, both in taste and smell, is more abominable than anything which these submarine operations have brought to light, wrote Captain Hall, anticipating similar observations by Cousteau's divers on Roman wine by rather more than a century. He then went on to make a penetrating observation on the deterioration of glass, anticipating modern scientific work on this subject by 120 years. The surface of the glass of which the bottles is composed, has, in most instances, undergone a slight degree of decay; in some the corrosive process has formed a series of very thin plates, some of them highly coloured. Where possible, the highest scientific advice was sought, and the artifacts sent away for analysis.

One of the great explosions invaded the purser's store-room and covered Spithead with tallow candles, well known to professional men under the name of Purser's Dips. These have been analysed by Mr. Faraday, who says that the matter is very little changed, chemically speaking. Time has, indeed, crystallised them a little, but when they are melted and allowed to cool, they resume their old character; the only perceptible change being analogous to that of fat which has been saponified.

Mr. Faraday was, of course, the most eminent physicist of his day and was at this time also scientific adviser to Trinity House, where he was responsible later for replacing tallow lamps in lighthouses with the first electrically-powered beams.

In great social contrast to the contents of the flag officer's cabins and the Wardroom area were other revealing discoveries. In another part of the wreck was found a black earthenware teapot, much cracked, which must have belonged to some thrifty personage, as it is tied round and across with wire-string, not only at the top, but at the bottom, to prevent its falling to pieces; the handle also is tied on. The lid of this elegant affair is gone, but in its stead, another has been found, bearing on its top a very solemn lion for a handle.

There was no great interest in the ship itself, because—in absolute contrast to the Mary Rose, of which little was then or is now known—scale models of the Royal George were in existence and very similar ships were still afloat. To study this aspect of nautical archaeology would have been superfluous in the case of the Royal George.

I do not trouble you with an account of the innumerable beams, timbers, knees, planks, and other portions of the poor old ship; nor with an enumeration of old casks, powder barrels, coals, firewood, ballast, shot, guns, spars, a box of tools, another of locks, panes of glass, and such other commonplace

UNIFORM 1843

fragments which Colonel Pasley's ably-conducted operations having dis-
lodged, the divers were enabled to sling from time to time; I rather take
notice of one or two apparently minor items, possessing, as it seems to me, a
more enduring interest, from the associations with which they are connected,
being of so popular a description as to be intelligible to every one. Of these,
the most striking, perhaps, are the well-preserved remains of a woman's
gipsey hat. It is composed of chip, covered with silk, and trimmed with gauze:
the crown is entirely gone, but the head-lining, also of gauze, is complete; it is
slightly drawn together with silk thread, where a neat handed person would
have hemmed it. Some weeks after this hat was brought up, the hood and collar
of two silk cloaks were found—one of a woman's size, trimmed with lace; the
other, which is evidently that of a child, is without trimming. It is probable,
from these cloaks being intertwined, that their wearers—perhaps mother and
daughter—perished, at the same moment, in one another's arms.

Of seamen's dresses, there have been many torn fragments brought up, such
as arms and breasts of jackets and of frieze coats, several silk handkerchiefs,

60

many shoes, and some shoe buckles—of which last I saw several fished up one day. Many skulls, too, and other human bones have been recovered, mixed with broken crockery, mess kids, and a confused heap of heterogeneous articles. One of these is a checker board for playing draughts, very rudely carved with a knife, out of a bit of plank. The imagination can readily fancy a merry party at their game, unconscious of their impending fate, as the ship went down.

In a similar spirit, we may conceive the spy-glass which was recently brought up, to have been in the hands of the officer of the watch—who by the way is now alive, the gallant Adml. Sir P. C. H. Durham. The glass bears Dollond's celebrated name, and is of 40-inch focus, of the kind called a deck glass: it is greatly to be regretted that the object glass—which would have been a real treasure—did not come up with the tube: the remaining glasses are entire, and all the screws work perfectly. The only other philosophical instrument, if so it may be called, which has been recovered from the wreck, is an old-fashioned wooden quadrant, made by Cole, of London; it is of 16 inches radius, graduated to 95 degrees, each degree being divided into three parts of 20 minutes each, and furnished with a vernier reading to single minutes, but without any tangent screw. A portion of the quicksilver remains on both the index and the horizon glasses. In place of the usual eyehole in the 'sight vane' there is fitted a small disk of ground glass: the width of this disk is nearly half-an-inch. Between the index and the horizon glasses are placed two coloured glasses, both of a deep red, one being considerably darker than the other. It is curious that no plate has yet been discovered, and no money, except I believe, two guineas—nor, so far as I have heard, any watches, nor any silver coins.

Silver objects, including a dish and spoon from the area of the Admiral's cabins, were to be recovered later. Some of the artifacts, including the anchor cable, although thought unremarkable in 1840, were to be of great use later, when HMS *Victory* was being restored to her Trafalgar state, and the authentic details of much of the gear of the period had been forgotten. Items from the *Royal George* enabled them to be copied accurately. But by far the most important lesson learned is implicit in Captain Hall's attitude: he is interested primarily in people; in the shipboard community of the late eighteenth century, as revealed by the objects they used, the clothes they wore, and even by their bodies, or what was left of them. This is truly archaeology. It is a dramatic illustration of what I mean by emphasising that an underwater investigation is primarily that of a 'closed community', and only secondarily a technical or technological investigation. One has only to imagine what equally detailed information, obtained by far more thorough, modern techniques, would produce for a Tudor community from the *Mary Rose*, in which at least 400 men went down, or of an earlier French society, which in 1419 had two great carracks sunk in a raid on Southampton, one of them lost in deep water, 'in which there perished eight hundred men in light Harneys', and never discovered to this day. How many still remain? Very few were found aboard the foundered *Vasa* when she was raised recently, but this is explained partly by the fact that her full complement had not joined when the disaster

took place; virtually nothing of this sort has been found in the Mediterranean, which may be partly explained by circumstances special to that
limited area, but also no doubt because Mediterranean archaeologists
tend not to think in these terms. A great many bodies floated off and
out of the *Royal George*, and were buried in mass graves at Portsea and
in the Isle of Wight. Perhaps half of the drowned 900 in all. But very
many still remained to be uncovered by the somewhat violent methods
of Colonel Pasley. We may suppose that large ships which sank very
quickly still retain among their timbers a substantial, and not too unrepresentative, selection of the community which manned the ship, and,
if applicable, the visitors aboard at the time.

During 1840, three different types of helmet-diving dress were in use,
and under test, on the *Royal George*, both by the experienced civilian
divers and by novice divers who had volunteered from the ranks of the
Sappers. Because, as he said, *every Inventor recommends his own peculiar
Apparatus with confident assertions of its superiority over all others, and
as the most skilful Divers, who have used one apparatus only, have strong
prejudices in its favour and against all those that they have not used,* Pasley
submitted his own report on them to the Inspector General of Fortifications on 30 December that year. *Our Diving Dresses were two of Deane's
pattern, made by Mr. Sadler, of Tooley-Street, which were used during the
whole of our operations for two Successive Seasons, and two of Siebe's pattern,
during the latter part of the present Season only. Mr. Bethell's was tried
repeatedly, but objected to by the Divers, as will be explained.* Pasley's
report, with covering letter, runs to eighteen pages and is extremely
explicit. Bethell's dress was one attempted solution to the problem of
what happened to a diver wearing the Deane pattern dress if his helmet
was to flood. It was a 'tight' dress—that is, it was watertight—and the
basic problems here are how the diver is to get into it and, having got into
it, how is it then made watertight; or rather, pressure-proof, because this
is not a matter of merely keeping off the rain. Bethell's answer was a
two-piece suit consisting of jacket and trousers, the bottom of the former
folding over the top of the latter and held tightly together by a ligature.
As the air was continually being renewed by the pump, there had to be
an aperture for the foul air to escape by, and this was provided by
a small pipe, three inches long, projecting at the side of the helmet.
When first tried by diver Smith for Pasley in 1839, the waistbelt join
proved to be anything but watertight and the dress was sent back to
Mr. Bethell. He returned it with a new type of join, consisting of two
metal hoops which engaged, with leather in between, and pressure
applied to the joint by 12 screws. This method has been used in
modern times for frogmen's 'dry' suits, and there is nothing wrong
with it, in principle. But Bethell's screws proved cumbersome, and *finding that it took about 20 minutes to screw them up, and that it required
nearly the same time to unscrew them, the Divers objected to this arrangement,
as causing them a great deal of unnecessary fatigue, for they seldom descend
fewer than 3 times in the Course of each Slack tide, and often 6 or 7 times, or
more, and they always wish to have their helmets taken off, as a relief to them*

62

during the intervals. The objections to Mr. Bethell's Apparatus, chiefly on this account, were so Strong, that I could not with propriety insist upon their using it, in a Service not absolutely free from personal danger . . .

So Pasley rejected the jacket and trousers, soldered up the hole in the helmet, had the small-aperture airpipe replaced by wider ones, and, as he said, *it had then ceased to be Mr. Bethell's plan; for the Helmet had been converted into Deane's, and the Airpipes were those of Mr. Sadler, so that no part remained unaltered, but the pump alone, in which there was nothing unusual.*

Pasley mentions that he had seen, but not tried, a similar two-piece 'tight' dress designed by Mr. Fraser of the Salvage Company; the difference being that the trousers came up to shoulder-height under the jacket, and that the waste air escaped by an 8-inch long India rubber tube or 'Snout' instead of a 3-inch metal pipe. The diver could grasp this 'Snout', close it to shut off the escape of air from the dress, and so blow himself up to the surface. Pasley did not appreciate that this was foolproof, because if the diver overdid it and the suit blew up to rigidity, his hand would automatically be forced away from the 'Snout' and so the air would rush out again and deflate the dress.

An oddity of Bethell's helmet was that it had a small lamp screwed on to the escape pipe outside, to give the diver light to see by; but Pasley never actually tried this out. Bethell also experimented with speaking tubes. The verdict must be, that Bethell's apparatus was too complicated, too ingenious.

The third apparatus to be tried was Siebe's. This also was a 'tight' dress, but it differed from the other two in being a one-piece design, the diver stepping into it at the neck. The actual dress was virtually the same as Deane's, and the single major difference was, that instead of the helmet resting on the shoulders, with the air escaping from underneath it, the helmet screwed down on to a fitting at the top of the dress and made a more-or-less watertight joint. The waste air escaped by a spring-loaded valve, which shut automatically if the pressure of air inside the suit should drop dangerously for any reason. *Mr. George Hall, of Whitstable, the excellent Diver, who has distinguished himself so much in the removal of the wreck of the* Royal George, *first recommended Mr. Siebe to me, as having supplied better workmanship to those who employed him, than any other maker of Diving Apparatuses,* explained Pasley. This dress is similar to those still in use today, but Pasley shows that a development process took place during the early Spithead operations which, as it is not mentioned in Sir Robert Davis' history of diving, is probably worth telling.

The watertight connection on Siebe's dress was made by thumb screws, instead of screws requiring a key or a screwdriver, and it took only two minutes for a team of men to fix the helmet on or take it off again after the diver had come up for a breather between jobs. The process of taking the *Royal George* apart bit by bit, slinging each part separately, meant that the diver's work was all up-down, up-down, up-down while slack water lasted. They complained that two minutes was too long to get the helmet off, contrasting it unfavourably with the even simpler Deane dress,

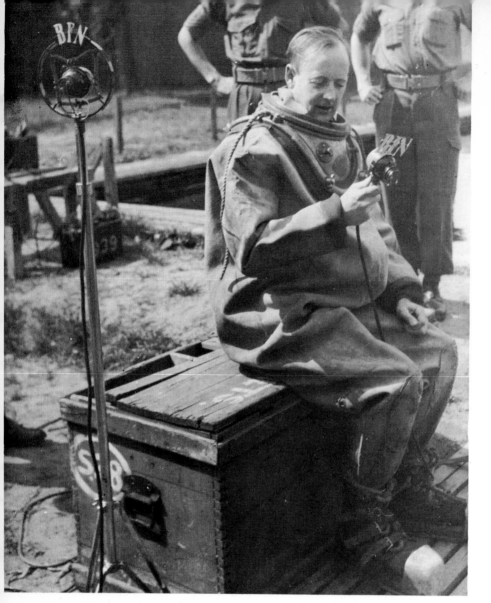

Recording a radio commentary at the Royal Engineers Diving School, Hamburg, in 1952. I am wearing a modern Siebe-type dress, the apparatus being in principle the same as the 1840 model.

from which the helmet and weights combined could be removed in 15 seconds. With this in mind, Siebe had already made it possible to unscrew the front glass of the helmet, but nevertheless the divers were not satisfied, and so Siebe introduced a refinement which did not stand the test of time, although it was used at Spithead. This was an ingenious arrangement by which the helmet was made in two parts, the top being capable of being removed in a few seconds. The other alteration to Siebe's original helmet was proposed by Pasley himself. According to Pasley a modification had in the first place been proposed to Siebe by Edwards, and consisted of a complicated siphon-shaped pipe for the escape of the foul air to the outlet valve. *I therefore took the liberty of Soldering up the Airpipe in Mr. Siebe's Apparatus, cutting a hole through his helmet directly opposite*

64

Detail (*above right*) from the diagram of Siebe's dress, which includes Pasley's signature. The front-weights differ from today's model and the diver wore shoes instead of boots, with stockings to protect the suit from abrasion. The helmet (*below*) is from Bethell's 'tight' dress, as used on the *Royal George* in 1840 in competition with Deane's 'open' dress and Siebe's 'tight' dress: it had provision for a lamp. Drawn for Colonel Pasley.

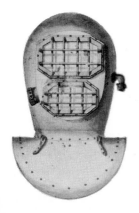

to the valve. This Simplication of Mr. Siebe's Apparatus saves workmanship and expense, and at the same time gets rid of an erroneous principle, and he will adopt it in his future constructions, as he came down to Chatham himself, and saw it tried.

Pasley attached a large working drawing of the entire apparatus to his report, and the diver resembles rather an Irish navvy or a Mummerset agricultural labourer than the present-day idea of a diver, because, in addition to the Guernsey dresses and worsted stockings worn under the dress, for warmth, he wore outside the dress, with the idea of protecting it from abrasion, a canvas jacket and trousers and another pair of even larger worsted stockings.

Pasley concluded that of the three designs, 'Mr. Siebe's is best adapted to the Public Service'; and he was undoubtedly right, especially for deep diving, although as we have seen the Deane pattern is still convenient for some forms of shallow water diving. His enthusiastic claims, however, that Siebe's dress could be used for head-first diving should be taken with a pinch of salt, as he had not then discovered that the waste air cannot escape when the diver is in this position, and he is in danger of having his suit blown up to complete rigidity, leaving him helpless. In fact, there was still a great deal to be learned about diving, and Pasley's Spithead operations involved one death, that of Skelton off Southsea Castle, many injuries, partly from defective air pipes, and odd twinges and indistinct ailments of that nature. 'Of the seasoned divers, not a man escaped repeated attacks of acute rheumatism and cold,' wrote Connolly. When he adds that 'the divers were six or seven hours a day, and sometimes more, under water, at depths of sixty or seventy feet', one no longer has to wonder why this was, although the six or seven hours mentioned probably included the waiting time on the surface as well as the descents and ascents. Even so, around forty minutes would be an accepted seabed working time for those depths, not to be exceeded without serious risk of a 'bend'. This is known today, but was not known then, although it is curious how the experienced civilian divers would not work the long underwater hours at depths that Pasley demanded, and were eventually all replaced by military personnel.

The underwater visibility was exactly as it is today—there has been no change resulting from the growth of industry—and Pasley gives an eye-witness description of it:

The Glasses in the Helmet are to enable Divers to See in clear water, but this is quite impossible in the Thames & Medway; and even at Spithead the water is generally far too thick, to allow them to distinguish objects, except as opaque masses, when very near. When I went down I could just discern the Rope-ladder by which I was descending. Occasionally the water has been clear, so that George Hall said he saw a number of small fishes playing about him, and Corporal Harris when at the bottom saw John Fullager descending from the same lighter, and went to Shake hands with him. But this Extraordinary clearness of the water at Spithead, was only observed during two or three days of the whole Season. That is a very fair statement.

Nevertheless, despite these difficult conditions in 1840, that year saw no less than three salvage organisations working four separate, historic wrecks—Pasley on the *Royal George* (1782) and his Lieutenant Symonds on the *Edgar* (1711), Abbinett on the *Boyne* (1795) and the Deanes on the *Mary Rose* (1545). Many important principles were established in that year. One occurred as a result of a comedy over the wreck of the *Boyne*. Abbinett had borrowed the voltaic battery from Pasley, in order to blow in the sides of the wreck by two charges, and was having trouble. Pasley came over in a huff, to defend the battery, and blamed the failure on Abbinett's diver. The third salvage operator, John Deane, was also present, purely as a spectator, and he volunteered to dive and place the two charges—which this time exploded. These charges contained only 300 lb. of gunpowder each, but nevertheless their shock effort gave a sharp rap on the helmet to George Hall, working underwater at the time on the *Royal George*, more than one sea mile distant. The speed of sound in water is very much greater than in air. Additional information on the deterioration of metals was noted, in the *United Services Magazine:*

All the brass guns recovered were as perfect as the day they sunk, and only required cleaning, the iron guns were very little injured, but not yet serviceable, as the surface of the metal was softened to the depth of about one-eighth, or not exceeding a quarter of an inch, being partially changed into plumbage, or carburet of iron, to that depth. Several of the iron guns and their carriages came up together, they having been held fast by the iron capsquares of the carriages embracing the trunnions of the guns. Indeed the first iron 32-pounder, when landed, was moved about on its carriage from one part of the Dockyard and Gun-Wharf to another, the carriage being in a very serviceable state, with its trucks complete. But none of the brass guns were brought up with carriages, because their trunnions, being in contact with the iron capsquares had caused the decay of the latter, and thus separated the guns and carriages. This affords a useful hint not to employ two metals in the fastenings of the gates of docks, etc., exposed to the action of salt water.

This referred to guns from the *Royal George*, which had now been fifty-eight years under the sea, the hull of which, until recently, had stood to a height of over 30 feet above the seabed. The sides of *Boyne*, likewise, had stood up some 8 or 10 feet off the bottom, despite previous fire and explosion, until Deane had blown them flat with two charges.

The *Edgar* was even more remarkable, for she had been built at Bristol in 1668 and sunk by internal explosion in 1711. In 1840, only a part of this wreck was found, and some guns and pottery recovered. Apparently, she had been blown in three by the explosion of both fore and after magazines, the bow and stern being scattered. But, in Pasley's last year at Spithead, 1844, the untouched centre-section of the hull was found by sweeping. Connolly wrote,

The sweeps from the boat having been caught by an obstruction below, Corporal Jones descended by them till he found himself astride a 32-pounder iron gun, which was peeping through a port-hole in the lower deck. It happened

66

The *Resolution* (70 guns) painted by Van de Velde, an almost identical ship to the 70-gun *Edgar* blown up at Spithead on 16 October 1711, with the loss of more than four hundred lives.

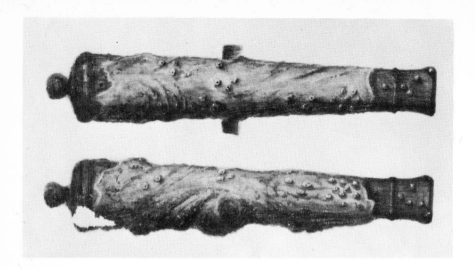

Iron gun recovered from the *Edgar* by Pasley's divers after 133 years' submergence.

at the time to be unusually clear at the bottom, and to his amazement there stood upright before him the midship portion of the vessel, with an altitude above the general level of the ground, of thirteen feet and a half. From the open ports, in two tiers, yawned the mouths of about twelve pieces of ordnance, grim and deformed with the incrustations of 133 years . . . The midships, sharing but little in the convulsion, went down like a colossal millstone, scarcely heeling on the bottom; and the armament of the decks remained as if ready for battle, without a carriage unjerked from its platform, or a gun from its carriage. All the woodwork, however, was so completely decayed by the ravages of worms, and the insidious action of the sea, that when the guns were slung, they were hauled through the decks, as if no obstruction interposed.

We therefore get the following extraordinary figures for the four historic Spithead wrecks investigated by the pioneer divers:

SHIP	Mary Rose	Edgar	Royal George	Boyne
Observation Year	1836	1844	1839	1840
Sunk	1545	1711	1782	1795
Submerged	291 years	133 years	57 years	45 years
Height	1 ft.	13½ ft.	33–36 ft.	8–10 ft.

It needs to be remembered that the two earliest ships were two-deckers, the two later ships three-deckers; that the *Mary Rose* sank on much softer ground than the others, and that the *Boyne* was burned to the waterline. It is also possible that the remains of the *Mary Rose*, of which only part of a gun and some fragments of timber were visible when first found, may at times have been completely covered up and so protected by temporary alterations of the seabed. But, for the sake of certainty, and ignoring the *Mary Rose*, we are still left with three wooden ships, two still fairly well

68

Along the artifacts recovered from the *Royal George* by Pasley's divers and recorded in watercolour (probably by Corporal Samuel March) were a 'carved hand' (*above*) brought up on 19 October 1840 and a block brought up in June of the same years (*below*)—in the latter case the watercolour was based on a sketch made by Captain Basil Hall, R N.

preserved above the seabed for around half a century, and one rather fragile but still standing well above the seabed for 133 years, until deliberately destroyed.

By the standards of all other seas, except the Baltic, these figures are not merely astounding—they are impossible. Cousteau, who pioneered the study of wrecks in the Mediterranean, has given it as his judgement that iron lasts no longer than sixty years, and wood less than twenty Throckmorton has more recently confirmed the figure for wood. In the Mediterranean, all surface trace of wood disappears inside twenty years. In Southern California, an experiment with artificial reefs as homes for fish produced exact and repeated figures—wooden tramcars were destroyed inside five years, and some barely lasted three; metal motor car bodies also disintegrated within a three to five year period.

When I set out to plan a wreck investigation project in the Solent area, I bore these figures very much in mind. They needed, first, to be confirmed; and if confirmed, to be explained. Positive results were obtained within two years. But in the interim, between the Spithead investigations of the 1830s and 1840s, and those of the mid-1960s, important developments had taken place elsewhere. In particular, divers had discovered in the Mediterranean many ships far older than the wooden warships of North-West Europe; they had first found, then plundered, and finally learned to excavate, the trading ships of antiquity—of Rome, of Greece of Byzantium, of Phoenicia. They had gone back 3,000 years in time.

Part Two
The ancient world
1200 BC-AD 700

4

Art and amphorae

Sponge-divers and the aqualung pioneers
1900-1958

By accident, and not by design, the progression *Mary Rose, Edgar, Royal George,* and *Boyne* illustrated the development of the heavily-gunned wooden warships of North-West Europe with a nice precision: for the *Mary Rose* was a 'key' ship—the start of a process which was to result in the great three-deckers of the Napoleonic period. After that, in rapid succession, came steam auxiliary engines, iron ships, composite ships built of wooden planks on an iron frame, steel ships, efficient steam engines, turbines and so on, until the Spithead scene of the mid-1960s has produced an array of 'key' vessels—the first British nuclear-powered submarine, ships with atomic weapons, the first hovercraft and the first commercial hovercraft service in the world, and in small vessels only as yet, the use of plastics formed from moulds as a constructional material. In size, development has been even more fantastic, even nightmarish. Where once 2,000 tons had represented an enormous ship, oil tankers of 100,000 tons and upwards were in use, with plans for the future which specified ships of quarter-of-a-million and even half-a-million tons. Where once the length of a ship could be calculated conveniently in feet, the lengths of these ships are best expressed as quarter-of-a-mile, half-a-mile long, and so on.

Clearly, the technology of European civilisation is moving fast, and visibly accelerating. But where, precisely, is it going? And is it wise to go there? And if we get there, will it be worth the journey?

The principal function of underwater archaeology in the Mediterranean, in fact if not in theory, is to escape. The value of the many sunken ships of antiquity does not lie in the knowledge they give us of methods of ship construction or patterns of trade, but of the contact with an older and to us, apparently a calmer, more settled, nobler civilisation, centred around a smiling, eternal sea. Practically, much of this is probably a dream. Into the civilisations of both Greece and Rome there erupted from time to time events as barbarous and horrible as anything the twentieth century has yet experienced; nevertheless, there also comes across the feeling of solidity, of settled values, of a timeless calm. True or untrue, and regardless of the fact that if true such a life might well become tedious, this vision of his past is a soothing one to modern man, particularly if he does not himself live by the shores of the Mediterranean, but is only three and a half hours away by jet aircraft. This, oddly, does not seem at all incongruous to him, because there is a link between the functional piece of metal machinery which annihilates distance for him and the functional shapes of the antique liquid-containers which he finds in the sea on arrival—both are beautiful. Because they are perfectly designed, or nearly so. Between, on the one hand, the Winged Victory of Samothrace —which is the simplified representation in stone of a figurehead on the bow of a war-galley—and on the other, say, the undecorated, bronze scale-model of the early mark of Vickers-Supermarine Spitfire, an eight-gun fighter of the Battle of Britain, there is this link. They are lovely in their lines, and in their proportions. They represent human aspirations and purpose. They are beautiful. They satisfy. That is their justification, and they need no other.

But this beauty from the shores of the Mediterranean, and from its silent depths also, has subtly coloured, not merely the archaeology of the area but the development of underwater archaeology as a whole.

As we have seen, the British approach was strictly scientific and firmly historical, from the first; an attitude which has been maintained. Spithead was sordidly unromantic. The attraction of the *Royal George* was not beauty but tragedy—the loss of Kempenfeldt and his 'brave eight hundred' (nearer 900, actually, counting whores and traders), one of the greatest naval disasters of all time, and certainly of the locality. The attraction of the *Mary Rose*, apart from the quaintness of her armament, was schoolbook history—the almost direct contact with Henry the Eighth, much-married, middle-aged now, standing at Southsea Castle with the wife of the doomed Admiral, as he died in front of their eyes. And, to be remembered also, Henry the Eighth was and is England's idea of a real ruler; strong, ruthless when necessary but not gratuitously so, astute as a bagful of monkeys, and far from being harmed by his reputation with the women, the wine, and the food. A most interesting character who, if he could enter politics today, would win a runaway victory at the polls, with no particular objection to be made if he employed the public headsman to clear up public life a bit afterwards. In brief, the attraction, the importance, the value of the Spithead wrecks was, that they were known, named ships, identified with important historical personages and events, which they brought closer and made more personal. Three were buoyed and therefore the 'discovery' was more a matter of improved diving apparatus than of search; one was an accidental discovery, made by fishermen. There were no deliberate discoveries as a result of search.

As we shall see, the pattern in the Americas was, from first almost to last, that of treasure-hunting. Appropriately so, because real treasure fleets really did pass that way. The treasures, although valuable, were not particularly beautiful; interesting, as showing the trade pattern; but hardly compelling in their attraction except to a minority who could be thrilled by tales of Spanish gold and the pirates of Hispaniola. In the Americas, where these were local wrecks and there was a chance of finding them, or of reading about some other more fortunate person finding them, that minority was and is fairly substantial. Many of the wrecks were found by deliberate search and then identified from historical records, and there was some gain as a result to historical knowledge of shipbuilding. By far the most interesting aspect, as far as North America is concerned, however, is that a high proportion of the most talented individuals never gave a thought to Spanish treasure, but gave up all possibility of it by seeking to explore methodically in the Mediterranean for ships 2,000 years older, carrying in many cases nearly valueless cargoes. They found many hundreds of them, mostly from fishermen's information, some by chance, a few by deliberate search of likely areas for wrecks, none so far as a result of deliberate search for a known, identified ship. These wrecks have no provenance, apart from such evidence as may be gleaned from their remains. But it was these North Americans—a mere handful of them—who made the vital technical advance: from the salvaging of treasures to that full excavation of all the remains which ensures that not one scrap of knowledge is lost. The locals did not do this, mainly because of the enormous, overwhelming impact upon them of coming at face-mask range across the lost ships of Greece and Rome. They were led away by the fascination and beauty of that lost world into careless, enraptured recovery of some traces of it. Even the Northerners fell under that spell, and dubbed it 'amphorae fever'. There is a definite psychological reaction to a shipwreck of antiquity which is not matched by the effect of any other type of wreck. Henry Morgan and Spanish gold have not half the pull of great Caesar and the fairytale isles of Greece. Solemnity and joy are fairly mixed in a unique proportion, for this latter is like coming across the hearths of one's household gods.

But it was here where the distortion in the development of archaeology occurred. The Mediterranean finds were highly personal archaeology: for, it must be admitted, there are a great many traces of the ancient civilisations still visible on land. The tremendous lure of the ancient wrecks was, incongruously, that they were new: no one had ever seen them before. They had not been fingered, handled, examined, inspected by generation after dusty generation. They were, on the contrary, the raw material of Rome and Greece. Actual physical contact with an authentic uncontaminated mystery: what would they reveal? Who were the long-dead men who had sailed the 'wine-dark' seas in these lost ships of long, long ago? It is terribly true that the full experience value of such a wreck is known only to the first diver to see her; and then the value decreases with each succeeding diver, until finally, after excavation, it has reached its lowest point. If the ship herself, or the contents of it, are beautiful then that value may still be high; but if not, then they are as near nil as makes no matter. Of interest only to students of shipbuilding and trade patterns, serving to solve some scholarly problems, and to pose many additional ones. Most of them, after all, are seen then to be merely freighters engaged in the coasting trade, like today's steel collier, oil-tanker, or general-cargo ship. No mystery remains, and Rome and Greece are gone.

But it is the mystery which matters, and therefore one has some sympathy with the early underwater explorers in the Mediterranean. However, the archaeologists, rightly, were not at all pleased to see take place a process which was in effect the unrecorded dismantling and pillage of valuable archaeological sites, even when the object was to obtain, by means of a personal souvenir, some direct contact with the past; and not, as in so many cases later, the commercial plundering of such sites, sometimes with explosives, for personal profit. At this time, neither side was really in a position to throw insults at the other. The divers, like happy retriever dogs, came splashing out of the water to lay at the feet of the archaeologists some unrecorded treasure, expecting to be praised, and got kicked in the teeth for their pains instead. But the archaeologists, full of lofty advice as to the necessity for leaving sites undisturbed until they could be recorded accurately in the various stages of efficient excavation, themselves made the most monumentally stupid and disastrous mistakes. Either they would not dive, and sent down power-operated grabs from a dredger to dig destructive craters in wreck and cargo; or they organised divers to uncover the wreck, and then foolishly left it uncovered for a whole winter, so that storms, gales, and the effect of oxygen and minute organisms could in the interim demolish it completely—and then looked surprised, the following spring, when they found it gone; or they had so little method in their excavations that though worldwide publicity was given to such sites as Grand Congloué, which became household names for a period of years, spoken of in awed whispers, these are now, only a few years later, merely four-letter words, archaeologically speaking.

The entire development process was held up for ten to fifteen years by this artificial conflict between paper tigers: between, on the one hand, the ignorant and the incompetent, and on the other, by the incompetent and the ignorant. Divers knowing nothing of archaeology, and precious little of ships; archaeologists knowing little of diving, and nothing whatever about ships, even when intact and afloat, let alone wrecked and submerged for a few thousand years; and few on either side aware of the problems of deterioration and conservation. Compared to the work done at Spithead well over a century before, long before archaeology itself had become a semi-science, this appeared as crude, knock-about farce; it was high time for the North Americans to move in. Probably the most absurd aspect of the whole affair was that some British divers went off to the Mediterranean to learn underwater archaeology from the locals, and that some people began to lecture those who stayed at home, for all the world as if they had committed, or were even likely to commit, such atrocities themselves in British waters. Fortunately, neither the British divers, nor for that matter the Scandinavians, took the slightest notice of the work done in the Mediterranean, let alone considered that it contained any examples to be followed, prior to the excavations of Bass and Throckmorton. Even here, however, they had their own different reservations, as we shall see, because the problems were rather different and therefore pointed to original solutions.

By far the worst effect of the Mediterranean influence was the danger, at one time, that the conflict of diver v. archaeologist might be repeated quite pointlessly in other areas, and that the basic purposes might be obscured by the smoke of battle and the dust of verbal shot-and-shell. In fact, this very nearly did happen. In self-protection, the divers began to mouth archaeological catch-phrases, to please the grown-ups, but without understanding a word of it; and in self-protection also, the archaeologists began to give little deprecatory coughs, explaining how old and infirm and unbrave they were, compared to those romantic, daring, dashing, bold heroes of the deep, superbly exhibiting their exceptional skills, upside down at 300 feet firmly clenched in the grasp of an octopus. Indeed, for some fifteen to twenty years, this *was* underwater archaeology in the Mediterranean, as recorded in numerous books; and for a time it seemed as if this attitude might gain a foothold elsewhere. However, there was a revolt against it, and in North America, Great Britain, and some of the Scandinavian countries also, it was eventually by-passed. Where British divers in British waters were concerned, there was in the beginning no real problem. The archaeologists had no practical suggestions as to what the divers should do, and the divers mostly did not want to do anything anyway. Therefore there was no conflict. There was merely well-meant advice on what to do if by chance anything was found and, understandably, considering what had happened in the Mediterranean, great play was made of base-lines and simple triangulation. But, apart from casual references to 'trade routes', there was virtually nothing to explain what underwater archaeology in the Mediterranean was actually about. And this really needed objective consideration.

The record of better known wrecks in the Mediterranean reads very strangely, and is best appreciated in tabular form:

Wreck site	Dating	Discovery and diving
ANTIKYTHERA S. Greece	1st century BC	1900–1, 1953
MAHDIA Tunisia	1st century BC	1907–13, 1948, 1954–
ANTHEOR S. France	1st century BC	1948 onwards
ALBENGA N.W. Italy	1st century BC	1950, 1957
GRAND CONGLOUE S. France	2nd century BC	1952 onwards
TITAN (Ile du Levant) S. France	1st century BC	1956, 1958
DRAMONT S. France	1st century BC	1956–9
SPARGI Sardinia	2nd century BC	1958
GELIDONYA Turkey	12th century BC	19586–0
YASSI ADA Turkey	7th century AD	1958 onwards

Marine Archaeology, edited by Joan du Plat Taylor for C.M.A.S. (World Underwater Federation), first published in 1965, covers most of them in detail and authoritatively; for Antheor, Philippe Diolé is a useful guide, and George Bass has written a book about his work in Turkey, *Archaeology Under Water*, 1966, which should be read in conjunction with Peter Throckmorton's *The Lost Ships*, 1964. There is therefore no point whatever in recounting the stories of these discoveries in any detail, whereas an analysis of the apparent pattern which they present is long overdue.

The list contains both a valid pattern and an apparent pattern. The former first. The dates of discovery show two ships in the first group around 1900, then a gap of some forty years. These two wrecks were accidentally discovered by sponge divers using a copy of the Siebe dress developed at Spithead some seventy years previously. In spite of the two world wars which followed, one might have expected their work to be followed up; but it was not. The rush of discoveries which came shortly after the Second World War arose from the invention and popularisation of the aqualung by Commandant Cousteau and his associates, which, together with the earlier invention of swimfins, made it practical for the common man to explore the sea, the bold adventurer being swiftly followed by the timid tourist. These people had good visibility, mobility, leisure, curiosity, and above all, numbers on their side.

The apparent pattern is quite hopelessly absurd, and must be wrong. The dating of the wrecks, all first and second century BC, with the startling exception of the two Turkish finds, themselves wildly different, cannot be taken at face value. The Turkish group is in fact explained by the purposeful operations of the North Americans: Throckmorton spent two years with the Turkish sponge divers and got them to show him some thirty wrecks which they (but no one else) knew about, or had not bothered about; and reported this to the University of Pennsylvania Museum, who sent out George Bass to explore and excavate those which appeared to be the most promising. This specialised later group is therefore the result of active human intervention, and marks the first real archaeological work to be done underwater. The surprising concentration of all the other dates at a point just before the birth of Christ, is partly coincidence, partly failure to report finds, partly failure to circulate reports more widely. In short, the list is quite wildly unrepresentative; all it represents are the names of famous sites on which some archaeological work was carried out.

All these wrecks were of cargo ships; and all the cargoes, with three exceptions only, consisted of amphorae. That is, wine or slimy-goods containers (fish and fruit were other possibilities). The three exceptions were by far the most important. The Gelidonya wreck was a Phoenician boat carrying scrap metal, mostly copper. This could never have been guessed at by consulting documents, and indeed its discovery and careful excavation fractured many scholarly theories and reputations irreparably. But by coincidence, the first two discoveries, those of Antikythera and Mahdia, both carried cargoes of M. & B. (marbles and bronzes), which were really beautiful and valuable works of art. In both cases, the operations of the sponge divers in helmet dresses were directed from the surface by land archaeologists or antiquarians, and no attempt was made at the time to excavate the hulls. Even so, there were casualties, the depths being very great and the divers ignorant. These were the operations which, until recently, were taken to mark the very earliest beginnings of underwater archaeology.

There were no warships in this list; nor in any other list. No warship of antiquity has been found, at the time of writing, and these are known only from some not-very-explicit descriptions and illustrations. The word 'galley' appears not infrequently in some works on underwater archaeology in the Mediterranean; but this means merely that the author either does not know what was actually found or, alternatively, does not know what a galley was. Basically, the warship of antiquity was a long, thin rowing boat very lightly built and with little freeboard, attached to a fairly strong bow sporting a metal ram just below the waterline. An extremely unseaworthy type of vessel, many of which must have come to grief. The probable explanations for their absence so far from the lists of discoveries are two-fold. Firstly, the wind-driven cargo ship tends to fall victim to the various aspects of the lee shore: it can be blown straight on-shore if the wind rises to gale force, or if the wind-direction changes, may be unable to weather a headland and end up on the point, or, in fog or at night, mistake the course, come too close to a headland and be unable to manœuvre off in time. Headlands habitually collect ships, even modern ones. The galley, however, was unlikely to be destroyed by any such circumstances, as the oars gave not merely the necessary power to get the vessel out of wind-trouble but also the split-second manœuvrability to avoid sudden danger of collision; by backing one bank of oars and going ahead with the other, the craft could be spun on a sixpence. So can modern steamships, of course, but their speed and impetus, aided by radar, is usually so great that nothing can be done. I well remember when I witnessed the awe-inspiring sight of 45,000 tons of modern battleship get slightly out of control of its tugs and decide to charge a public house in Old Portsmouth; in spite of all the tugs could do, the monster went its own way remorselessly, riding up the beach and being stopped by the shingle only just short of the astonished topers. A modern ship has no brakes, whereas a galley had; she could be stopped dead in the water, if necessary, in a very short space indeed. The galley lasted, in various forms of development, right into the sixteenth century, precisely because a galley fleet could be manœuvred and drilled exactly like a regiment of soldiers, unlike the clumsy wind-driven ships which, in some circumstances, could require five or more miles in which to reverse their course. A galley wreck is therefore unlikely to be found in the type of known accident black spot which tends to collect sailing ships. On the other hand, it was very susceptible to swamping and could tend to be sunk in those places where heavy or very steep, breaking seas are to be found. The second reason why no galley wrecks have been discovered is the very simple one implicit in the study of the cargoes which have been found. It was the cargoes which were found, in the first place, not the ship; the hull was never seen until the excavation had been nearly completed. And all the cargoes concerned were both bulky and imperishable. By the same token, a cargo ship carrying a load of, say, silk or cloth would be an unlikely discovery; the cargo would have rotted away and there would be no sign on the seabed to indicate the presence of a wreck, although in sand, mud or clay the lower part of the hull at least would certainly remain. This principle applies to galleys also, of course, but is additionally a warning not to place too close a reliance on the trade pattern analysis of lists of cargo-ship wrecks. Until search systems have been much improved, no list can be representative.

So far, we have been considering death by natural causes, but of course by far the best place to look for the wreck of a galley would be in the area of a famous sea-battle, and Throckmorton has suggested Actium and Lepanto as a start, aided by the latest instruments designed to detect anomalies below the seabed. Another possibility, less romantic, is that ships also die of old age and are sometimes left on a mudflat to rot; although here, naturally, the hull would have to be of over-riding importance as nothing could be expected in the way of human remains or intelligible artifacts.

A point normally much neglected in the Mediterranean until recently has been just this possibility of deliberate search. Most Mediterranean discoveries have been accidental, and as all have been those of cargo ships, the sites are usually very close to shore, often within a hundred yards of the cliffs or of a reef. Position-finding skills, which are the essential start-point to underwater archaeology elsewhere, are in consequence not much exercised. One of the few exceptions was the re-discovery of the Mahdia wreck by Cousteau's team in 1948. It lay three miles from shore and its re-location took an uncomfortably long time: six days. Whose fault it was is not clear, but the archaeological investigations of 1908–1913, following on the discovery in 1907, had produced a reconstruction which placed the heavy part of the cargo—massive stone columns—on the deck of the hypothetical ship, with the valuable works of art, mostly fragile, below decks. Scholars have since postulated this remarkable form of cargo-stowage whenever they wanted to get rid of awkward pieces of submerged stonework which spoilt their theories; but then, they were not required to set sail in a ship so loaded. What is really amazing is that the Cousteau team did not question this unlikely story, and it was left to the sceptics of the local Club for Underwater Studies of Tunisia to explode in 1954–1955. This was a much better piece of work than the average for the Mediterranean and produced intelligent results from a wreck which had already been worked over and confused by helmet divers and aqualungers alike.

Possibly the difference in dates, between 1948 and 1954, is the difference between the accepting approach in archaeology and the enquiring one. Cousteau and his associates were not the pioneers of what they called 'free diving' (to distinguish the underwater swimmer from the helmet-and-line man), as this was a wartime development of the warring powers. They were, however, what was probably much more important, the pioneers of undersea exploration; although, in justice, one should include also Hans Hass and his associates, with the proviso that his interests were concentrated on various aspects of marine biology and zoology. The Cousteau team were interested in everything they saw, and this included wrecked ships of antiquity as well as a great deal which, necessarily, they did not understand. The best example of a failure, not to see, but to understand what was seen, is represented by what still tend to be called the Marbles of Saint Tropez. These consisted of fourteen rocks 250 yards from shore in 3½ fathoms of water (21 feet) off one of the more popular resorts of the French Riviera. Anyone can dive 21 feet in warm, clear Mediterranean water just by holding his breath; and in champagne visibility, of course, such objects can be clearly seen from the surface. Nowadays, they would be instantly recognised as the remains of a small, stone-carrying freighter of around 250 tons, and someone would send for Peter Throckmorton to make a survey. The local divers knew them well, because the fish liked them and the divers liked fish. To the men who actually touched them, they were just 'those old rocks'. Marble, it must be admitted, is a rock; much building material is. And all rocks are old. The first simple question, which was not at first asked, was: Is this material, in shape and composition, natural to the geology of Saint Tropez? The second question: What is the local tradition concerning them? would have received a false answer, but not wholly misleading.

The fishermen believed they were old millstones which had been 'thrown into the sea' long ago. This at any rate would be an indication that the site was not that of a submerged building. However, the number of unlikely objects which continue to be 'thrown into the sea' or merely 'fell overboard', according to scholars and other theorists, is legion. Very odd indeed, because stonework, for instance, is valuable; it can be sold for money. In this case, when the divers from the Club Alpin Sous-Marin came from Cannes to carry out an intelligent investigation, they discovered that the Saint Tropez rocks were marbles from Carrara in Italy, quite some distance away, and that the largest weighed some 38 metric tons. They could, of course, have taken the scholarly view that in ancient times there existed a race of men so indifferent to riches and so extremely well muscled that they were in the habit of throwing 38-ton blocks of marble into the sea in a fit of worldly disdain. Being examined, this basic field of explanation may be diagnosed as an attitude: 'I am far too lazy/insufficiently interested to go into this matter, but at the same time I do not care to admit that I simply do not know/am afraid I may be hoaxed'.

The Cannes divers did call in a scholar, but a good one, Monsieur F. Benoit. And he was wise enough to resist their diagnosis, that the 'mill stones' were capitals; he thought they were bases. The base is the foundation for a column, necessary large and heavy; the capital is a stone similar in shape and purpose which 'caps' it, and forms the foundation or base for the next storey or the roof. Necessarily, it must be lighter; in accordance with the simple principles of construction for buildings. There is no getting round these. If the walls of a high, heavy building were of the same thickness from top to bottom, instead of growing lighter as they went up, the stonework at the bottom would dissolve into powder under the weight. This gives a simple table of proportions for different types of stonework and of construction and M. Benoit could see at a glance that if the 'millstones' were capitals, then the building was impossibly large for the historic context of the area, whereas if they were bases, then they could have been intended for a known type of Roman construction. Later, when most of the 'rocks' had been raised by a crane, it was seen that a number of different types of rough-cut blocks were involved and that the 'capitals' were indeed bases. The divers had been at fault, in that they had made a judgement in a technical matter instead of encouraging the right sort of expert to dive with them. They found no trace of the ship which had carried this cargo of building material, but M. Benoit suspects that it was intended for the construction of the Temple of Narbonne in the second century A D. This was the first of the stone-carrying freighters to be found and surveyed, but at the time no great importance was attached to it; it was not recognised as pointing to a definite and obvious trend in the trade pattern, which should be further investigated.

Nevertheless, it should be added to the list given earlier in this chapter, together with another art-cargo wreck which was so inefficiently handled that it was not even hypothetically dated. In 1926 fishermen caught a bronze arm in their nets at a point off Cape Artemision in Greece, antiquarians in Athens launched an expedition using helmet divers with the

object of recovering statues, were stopped by the Greek police, and succeeded by a Government-sponsored project. The sum total of all this was one bronze statue of Zeus and one broken bronze of a galloping horse and rider. It is not hard to see why archaeologists prefer to forget this confused operation, but when added to the list it makes the third art-cargo wreck in a row: that is, all three of the first discoveries were carrying statues and all were dealt with by helmet divers directed by surface archaeologists. This may appear as casual coincidence, but most probably is not. There are uncounted wrecks of antiquity in the Mediterranean and many of them are known, either directly to sponge divers using helmet dress or by trawlfishermen who get 'hung up' at certain points, or on certain courses, and occasionally find a part of the obstruction in their nets. If what comes up is a statue of great beauty and value, and provided that the sponge divers or fishermen can be prevented from melting the

bronze down and selling it for scrap, and provided also that an archaeologist or antiquarian learns of the discovery, then an expedition is much
more likely to be launched than if the wreck were to be carrying amphorae
or roof tiles. In fact, aqualung divers have found several small wrecks off
southern France which were carrying cargoes of tiles, thus adding yet
another item to the pattern. Around Frioul, near Marseilles, there were
three; two only a few hundred yards apart and carrying an identical
cargo dated to the second century A D.

It was, however, the report of a single art-find brought up in a trawl
which led eventually to the discovery of the world's oldest known wreck
and, with it, the establishment of underwater archaeology proper.

Undersea mountaineering in
the Mediterranean, where
cliffs may plunge steeply
down for over a hundred
feet, and exploration was
impossible until the invention
of the aqualung. A horde of
hungry demoselles follows
the diver. Round the
British coast rocky scenery
is even more spectacular
because of the immense
variety of waving weed,
but—because of the bitter
cold—less well known.

5

The Demeter of Bodrum

The North Americans in Turkey
Gelidonya and Yassi Ada
1958-1967

'We were all instantly convinced it was a masterpiece, the more we looked at it the more beautiful it seemed,' said Margaret Bean in a talk on the B.B.C. The masterpiece was the head and shoulders of what had once been a full length bronze statue of Demeter, the corn goddess, mourning for her lost daughter, Persephone. The bust and back of the head were covered in a grey concretion—the marine sediment of more than two thousand years—and a tube worm had left its shell around the neck of the statue, like a coiled sea serpent. The crown of the head was broken in, but the emotional force created in metal by the sculptor was un-affected: the mother sorrowing for the death of her child, so that winter seemed about to engulf the world. Or so it seemed to Margaret Bean. Then she noticed something odd—the lips and cheeks of the bronze appeared to be a strange, rusty red. The statue, having only just been taken out of the sea by a fisherman, was now stored temporarily in a shed guarded by gendarmes, and it turned out that it was these soldiers in the remote Turkish village of Bodrum who were responsible for the colours: they had been applying make-up. She was their pin-up girl. The message had certainly got across. It had leapt the space of 2,300 years and the unknown depths of the Aegean, to produce a profound impression upon such diverse people as English archaeologists and Turkish peasants. A statue which can do that is most certainly a masterpiece, even if it had not subse-quently been identified as an original work of the fourth century BC, the age of Praxiteles. But where was the ship that carried it and what was the rest of the cargo like, and could that ship be found?

In 1958, some five years later, Peter Throckmorton arrived in Bodrum on the track of the Demeter. He was a New York photo-journalist with both diving and archaeological experience, but of no fixed abode; he was restless and rootless, with a longing to travel far and talk to people in their own tongue; in fact, exactly the man for the long, tedious task ahead. Bodrum had once been Halikarnassos, but now it was just a Turkish village at the back-of-beyond. It had one claim to fame only: it was the centre of the sponge-fishing industry. The divers and trawlermen had a wide knowledge of the seabed and what it contained; and were sometimes willing to talk about it—if the interrogator could speak Turkish. For two years, Throckmorton lived with those fishermen, sailed with them, dived with them, drank with them, talked to them. What he did was not, of course, archaeological excavation but the vital preliminary to it—archaeological reconnaissance. Sounding out the possibilities of the area. He collected samples from each wreck and sat up late, making copious notes. The result was partly to confirm an apparent trend in the list given in the last chapter. Out of every ten wrecks, one only was earlier than the time of Alexander the Great. A high percentage were from the period first century BC to second century AD. This was the time when the Romans were known to have stamped out piracy, resulting clearly in a great increase of seaborne commerce. Few wrecks dated from the period of the collapse of the Roman Empire between the third and fifth centuries AD. Many, however, dated from the period immediately after when the Roman Empire in the East—Byzantium—having survived the barbaric invasions which had wrecked the Western half, was rising to independent power. As these were Byzantine waters, it was natural that they should be rich in wrecks of that period and place. On the reef of Yassi Ada, outside Bodrum Throckmorton marked down two wrecks in particular which, being on sand, should be well preserved and therefore offer fresh evidence of this unknown aspect of Byzantium. There was still no hint as to the location of the Demeter wreck—the captain of the ship which had trawled up the statue seemed always to be at sea, and when at last Throckmorton did manage to meet him, the position of the find had turned out to be imprecise. He did say, however, that they had nearly thrown it back, had then decided to try to sell it for scrap, but that it had been confiscated by the Government, which had compensated them by giving a reward equivalent to rather less than ten dollars.

Then, in conversation with another captain, Kemal Aras, with whom he usually sailed, Throckmorton heard of a hoard of bronze ingots on the seabed at a place about 185 miles away, off Cap Gelidonya, which Kemal intended to dynamite soon and then sell for scrap; not that it would fetch much, for the bronze was 'rotten'. The penny did not drop until several hours later. Bronze was hardly at all affected by long immersion in the sea; for this metal to become corroded, it must have been submerged an inconceivably long time ago. And the bronze ingots of the type described did suggest a date prior to 1000 BC. Throckmorton still had to get there, still had to re-locate the wreck, prise loose a sample and have it properly identified and dated, then urge people and institutions to raise money for a proper expedition, and in the meantime prevent his friends from blowing the wreck to pieces. He succeeded.

The University of Pennsylvania Museum decided to send an expedition to Bodrum, with the object of excavating to the highest standards current on land, both the Bronze Age wreck off Gelidonya and one of the two well-preserved Byzantine wrecks on the reef at Yassi Ada. As director of the excavation they appointed George Bass, a specialist in Mycenean studies—that is, the period of the Bronze Age in that particular place. In order to carry out this excavation, Bass had first to learn to dive. Out of some dozen divers he used, only a few had already learned to dive; the others had to learn while actually on the site at Bodrum. Their justification was, not that they were divers, but that they were specialists— archaeologists, draughtsmen, photographers, and so on. This was to treat an underwater site exactly like a land site. Aqualung diving gear was regarded merely as transportation, much as a jeep would be. This was in fact exactly how the old helmet divers had regarded their equipment, although possibly with a greater sense of wonder, because the underwater world was then so new. But with the director himself an underwater novice, it was necessary to hire at least one really experienced aqualung diver to handle training and technical direction. The expedition employed the very best—Frédéric Dumas, one of the original Cousteau 'big three', who had great comparative experience of ancient shipwrecks and was aware, moreover, of the more obvious shortcomings of Cousteau's experiments in underwater archaeology. In fact, it was not archaeology at all;

they just dug a big hole in the seabed over some part of the wreck, they did not know which part, and proceeded to enlarge the crater, with everything sliding into it, and as they never recorded any stage of their progress anyway, they never did find out what part of the wreck they had been digging on, or even which was the bow or which the stern. An intelligent bomb could have done as much.

But if the French efforts, and for that matter the Italian also, had been archaeological blasphemy, the University's casual approach to diving skills was heresy in the Mediterranean. A significant proportion of archaeological reports from that area contain over-blown and romantic references to the heroism and wonderful diving skills of the personnel involved which, even if true, would be irrelevant. The whole attitude of the American expedition was to puncture this balloon of vanity, which may have had its birth in the traumatic verdicts of 1940, and perhaps to overstate a case, slightly. George Bass, for instance, was later to claim that an archaeologist can be taught to dive in a week, whereas most Mediterranean diving schools regard ten days, or even two weeks in some cases, as the minimum training time to enable a novice, under supervision, to reach 120 feet and enjoy himself when there. More difficult waters, naturally, require a slightly extended and more versatile training, but nevertheless it is true, and the Pennsylvania expedition underlined it, that simply to go down and come up is not very difficult. The control and management of an expedition, however, does require much more skill and experience; but even so, hardly to full-time professional standards. The professions which count are those concerned with excavating, recording, conserving, and interpreting the finds.

The Pennsylvania expedition, apart from having a distinguished French expert on hand for the initial phases, also joined forces with the Institute of Archaeology at London University, a liaison which was to endure. The Institute lent an expert in Bronze Age studies, who was able to undertake conservation, to the Bodrum expedition. This was Miss Joan du Plat Taylor. Less permanently associated was Miss Honor Frost, who had briefly visited Throckmorton at Bodrum, with a small bottle (of compressed air) under her arm, during the reconnaissance phase and had used her skill as a draughtswoman to record some of the artifacts for identification. Miss Frost was English, lived in the Lebanon, toured many of the underwater excavations going on, and because she was an archaeologist was able to make the most penetrating observations; her analysis of Grand Congloué in her book *Under the Mediterranean* is a masterpiece. Miss Taylor was not a diver, however, and after even a few lessons from Dumas himself had failed to accustom her to go underwater, resigned herself to the fact. Since then, she has performed the most valuable work, particularly in the fields of organising, liaison, and forward-planning.

The Gelidonya wreck lay in 90 feet on a rocky bottom and in good visibility, but with a fast current at times. It had been there so long that the sediment had formed rock-hard concretions which bound the cargo to the rock and because the bottom was rock, little remained of

88

the vessel. In short, quite a new type of wreck formation. To meet this unexpected problem, a new method was devised on the spur of the moment. After the chaotic shapes of the concreted cargo had been photographed, mapped, and tagged with identification numbers as they lay on the seabed, they were chipped into lumps weighing some 200 to 300 lbs. and raised to the surface, where the plans and tags enabled them to be reassembled. Then, and only then, was the concretion chipped away to reveal the cargo, fragments of the ship, and some of the tools and other artifacts used by the crew. Because of the previous care taken in recording, they could then be shown on a plan in their original relative positions on the bottom; although not, of course, necessarily all in the position they had occupied before the sinking. A wreck is like a car accident in some ways: it tends to alter the original pattern of the vehicle and its contents. Nevertheless, with some idea of the principles involved, and provided that the scene of the accident is carefully recorded before it is disturbed, it is usually possible to reconstruct with fair accuracy the nature of the vehicle, the contents, and the cause of disaster. Archaeology has, in fact, many affinities both with accident investigation and the murder enquiry by detectives. The basic principles are mostly common sense, although some of the techniques—such as finger-printing or metallurgical analysis—may require the services of an expert, a filing system, and a specialist laboratory. But because most archaeological sites are buried, the process has to be repeated most carefully many times, as the dig proceeds down through the different levels. A really complicated excavation site could represent the equivalent of a six-storey house in which one or more murders had occurred on every floor, and with petty theft rife everywhere; or, alternatively, an accident black-spot which had never previously been properly cleared of the first crash before the next vehicle ran into the wreckage and disintegrated, intermingling with it, and so on over a substantial period of time during which grass and weed spouted on some of the wreckage and considerable corrosion and deterioration took place, but differing sharply with the material and the climate involved.

This is why archaeology is 'fun'; it is something less than a science and gives an opportunity for the exercise of intellectual debate, even if only with one's self. And with the result, if properly carried out, providing in its turn one more piece of evidence for a much greater and more important debate. And so, in the end, perhaps providing a very much clearer picture of a certain part of history.

This excavation proved to be a simple one. There was only one wreck, the remains of which were preserved in one thin layer between the concretion on top and the rock underneath. The vessel was only a boat, about 24 feet long. The cargo had been scrap metal, quite unromantic copper and tin ingots, from which new bronze can be made. There were also the simple tools one would associate with this. Where wood, brushwood, and a wicker basket had been trapped under the cargo and so insulated from the oxygen in seawater, the state of preservation varied from fair to almost as good as new. It was in fact just such a vessel as Homer describes in *The Odyssey*, and, moreover, of the same date. The crew of this one, however, were clearly not Greeks; they were Phoenicians. That fairly put the cat among the pigeons.

The scholars believed that Homer was not even a near-contemporary of the gods, people and events about which he writes; and their reason was, that they had found him out by his continual references to Phoenician sea traders. These, they well knew, did not enter upon the scene until very much later, and therefore Homer was writing of a distant world which he could have but imperfectly understood. What the wreck said to the scholars was: Homer was right and you were wrong. What Mr. George Bass said to the scholars was: You complain about the cost of underwater archaeology, but you have been taking good money all these years under false pretences to knowledge, which would have been much better spent in obtaining real knowledge, such as this. He phrased it a little more politely and a little less explicitly, but that was what he meant.

Nor did the translators escape unscathed. They were specialists, of course, but they lacked technical knowledge of seafaring; and this was hardly their fault. The wreck did show, however, how unreliable and various different translations could be, if the simple background was not understood. Homer had said something about brushwood being used in the vessel, and when fed to the translators this came out in different ways. All started with the raising of the height of the gunwales, to keep out high seas, by making a wickerwork or wattle fence all round. Then came the brushwood. One version had it, that the brushwood was used to reinforce the wickerwork; another, that the brushwood formed a bed; and in yet another, that it was ballast, not brushwood, which was added next! What Homer really said was, 'he spread out or heaped up a lot of brushwood.' The position of the brushwood in the wreck, directly on top of the bottom planks and cushioning the heavy, jagged metal cargo placed on top of it, made it perfectly clear what Homer meant, and also that he knew what he was writing about.

In the following year, 1961, the expedition moved to Yassi Ada to excavate the Byzantine wreck, otherwise known as the 'Globe Wreck' from the large, globular amphorae on top, lying at 120 feet. This was a sand excavation, of the type which had produced so many collapsible craters in the past. The normal reaction of a Mediterranean-type diver, on being confronted with such a wreck, was to grab the first unbroken amphora in sight and rise to the surface in triumph, brandishing the trophy as evidence of his courage and skill. In northern waters, too, this attitude is not entirely unknown. Part of the blame must be shared by the gallery, which ranges all the way from the urchin with his plaintive cry of 'Wotchergetmister?' to the glossy colour-magazine which demands artifacts, large, colourful, and in numbers, before it will print a story. On reflection, the two appear to have something in common.

Yassi Ada was therefore unusual in that, in the first place, Throckmorton had carefully selected the artifacts for recovery and the object of that exercise was dating and identification; part of the reconnaissance process. In the second place, the excavation which followed was unusual, because, before beginning, the archaeologist sat down to have a good look at it, metaphorically speaking, just as on a land site the director does not begin his dig haphazardly. And there, too, of course, there is the same problem, in many cases, that there is little or no surface trace of the buried building, he does not know either its plan or extent, and if he did there would be precious little point in excavating. A land archaeologist normally achieves renown among his colleagues according to the accuracy of his early guesses; the man or woman who hits a key point of the building with his first or second trench has pulled off a 'grand slam'. Many land sites are just as difficult to make out as seabed sites, sometimes more so; the level of a grass-covered field not quite even in places, with anomalies of no more than an inch or two, thickly camouflaged by vegetation, this frequently is all the archaeologist has to go on. There is little to tell him, apart from the keenness of his eyesight and his reading of the ground and of local histories, whether he is confronted by a palace or a pottery.

The Yassi Ada wreck was a good deal more obvious than the Gelidonya cargo, which had been hardly visible at all to a first glance. There was a roughly rectangular mound of big, pot-bellied amphorae, with a mass of what looked like entangled, concreted anchors at one end, and at the other small amphorae, tiles and so on. Bass guessed that this might be read as bow, cargo hold, and crew's quarters. In fact, the anchors represented amidships; these were the spares, and the bow, having been held up out of the sand, had largely disintegrated; the ship proved to have been some 70 feet long instead of 60 feet. Eight years after the Grand Congloué excavation had begun, people were still arguing as to the alignment of the vessel, and which end was which, and were there one or were there two wrecks there; and so the Pennsylvania party's preliminary assessment seems more startling than it really was. Knowing that the surface appearance might be deceptive, and that this was the first experiment in a controlled, recorded underwater 'dig', Bass went cautiously. Everything was recorded in exact detail; all the amphorae in the mound even, were drawn in with painstaking accuracy, although, since this represented the cargo hold, there was probably nothing of significance there. Nor was there, but the methodical principle paid off with some unrecognisable concretions at the stern. Georges Barnier, the Frenchman, had been the first to discover and publicise the importance of concretions. Anything submerged in the sea for any length of time (sometimes only a matter of months) begins to grow a 'fur' of algae and sediment, which eventually hardens into an enclosing shell. Metals such as iron tend to dissolve, forming a chemical combination with the shell as they change their physical structure, until eventually nothing is left but the shell—which is now, in effect, a perfect mould. Cut open carefully, it can then be used to 'cast' the shape of the original object. Therefore the position of all concretions on and around and in this wreck was noted, they were labelled and recovered, and eventually used to mould representations of the artifacts they had enclosed.

So carefully was all this work done, that the cabin space of the Byzantine ship could eventually be drawn with fair accuracy. The position of the forward bulkhead could be deduced and it was seen that the cabin had

had a tiled roof, and that about a quarter of the deck had been tiled. These tiles had been laid on a bed of clay supported by long iron bars, of which only the covering shell of concretion now remained, and this space obviously represented the remains of the galley. The mass of artifacts which came from this area could therefore be regarded as ship's gear and crew's possessions; as distinct from cargo. The Greek name, George Senior, was inscribed on one artifact, a bronze balancer for weighing cargo; presumably, he was the master of the ship. A number of coins dated between AD 610 and 641 dated the wreck and all that was in it; and, applied to many of the pottery bowls and lamps, showed that land archaeological datings were in some cases several centuries out—an important matter, because the study of chronology is vital; such objects are the basic evidence, almost the only clues available, in many cases.

If the recording here was careful, the care taken with the wooden hull can only be described as finicky; and necessarily so. Not only was each piece of wood noted, but it was drawn with every 'nail hole, bolt hole, score-line, mortise, or any other significant feature' recorded, and from plans based on such evidence Frederick van Doorninck was later able to reconstruct with fair accuracy those wooden portions of the ship which had been preserved under the sand. The reason for this was, that the methods of construction in the first place could not be taken for granted. Below the waterline, the vessel was of conventional build for her time and indeed similar to many earlier ships of Roman construction. It has been said that this method was nearer to cabinet-making, with its careful joinery, than to the ship building of our time. In principle, it is well known in aviation and used to be called monocoque, or shell construction, in the days when aircraft also were made of wood. Briefly, the planks of the hull go into place first, joined end to end by wooden tongues, and only then are the weak points stiffened with the normal ribs, frames and keel. The strength of such a ship lay primarily in the shell, like a lobster, whereas the ships of the north are built around a strong framework, like a fish, which is put into position first. The interesting point about this vessel was, that the upperworks had been built quite differently, with the skeleton first and the planks added afterwards, in the modern manner; possibly she was a transitional vessel.

George Bass had proved that a seabed excavation could be carried out to land standards, and without great cost; but he had not forgotten the Demeter which had brought Throckmorton to Bodrum in the first place. In April 1967, he stopped off in London on his way to open the new season in Turkey and talked informally to a small group at the Institute of Archaeology. Not merely the Demeter, but the equally famous 'Negro Boy', had been trawled up in an area which could now be defined as a known four-mile square, with a flat bottom and a depth of about 275 feet. Beyond the effective range of divers breathing compressed air, but well within the range of the more elaborate and more expensive oxy-helium mixtures which were about to become generally available. The previous year, they had attempted to survey the area by various modern means, all of which had proved inadequate to the task. Their research submarine could not cope, because there was no known method of accurately navigating such a submarine. In order to obtain the advantage of surface navigation, they had tried towing a special diving-bell; this worked, but it found nothing. Underwater television was used also and proved very versatile. It showed up at one point a big Roman wreck at 180 feet—a huge vessel—but it was not the statue-carrying wreck. This year, they hoped to be able to try side-scanning sonar (which shows the bottom at a oblique angle for some distance, instead of in effect drawing one thin, wavy line profile directly under the keel). At this, a member of the audience pointed out that the Royal Navy had just developed an ahead-sonar device which gave one a TV-quality picture, not just a series of wavy lines, and, moreover, showed you where you were going, not just where you had been; at the moment, it had been passed to Lowestoft for fisheries research.

These failures were due, of course, to the fact that the rarest feat in underwater archaeology is the deliberate discovery of a known wreck, when the area of error is miles across. Strictly speaking, this has been performed once only; by Anders Franzén on the *Vasa*. He used documents, not gadgets.

When Bass turned to his plans for Yassi Ada, however, the immediate future of underwater excavation became plain. He planned to deal with the second Byzantine wreck, believed fifth or sixth century, in one year, as compared to the four years required to excavate the first one. This was a matter of logistics in the first place, of proper staff planning, based on analysis of previous cost-performance figures. The plan for the operation really divided into two parts—archaeological and technical. They would use the familiar technique of an undersea 'dig'; the air-lift, to suck off the sand on vacuum-cleaner lines, would be used to trench around the wreck, not on it; and the bulk of the amphorae would be removed to a nearby part of the seabed, clear of the excavation area, and left there. This contrasted strongly with other people's excavations, because they would insist on raising the amphorae to the surface, where they had to be catalogued and given to museums, which then stored them in the basement. Samples only would be lifted, of the cargo. Technically, the picture was of a modified land 'dig'. The airlift, an unwieldy big tube reaching to the surface, could run on a monorail track laid on the seabed, making it much easier to operate. The workers would do their stint with surface-demand apparatus; that is, connected to a pump above; then switch to aqualung cylinders for the swim up the slope to a seabed decompression chamber in the shallows. The tanks would also be used to effect conversation, as the only effective inter-com method had been found to be a kind of telephone booth full of compressed air, inside which both divers could take out their mouthpieces and converse normally. When they dug down to the timbers of the wreck, these would not be raised to the surface; they would probably be too fragile. Instead, they would be walked along the bottom, up the undersea hill, and so on to the island beside the reef.

One very puzzling point was that the distance between this wreck and the previous excavation site was a mere 40 feet laterally, and it was only ten feet deeper—around 135 feet at the most. No undue inefficiency from narcotic effects had been felt by anyone at around the 120 feet level during previous years, but these had most definitely been noticed on the new wreck, only slightly deeper. Nobody understood this.

As yet, the results of this 1967 season off Turkey have still to be published, but the most important item of news to come from Mr. Bass so far is that of the success of the side-scan sonar for deliberate wreck location. During his 1965 season the Pennsylvania expedition carried out a month-long search for a statue-carrying wreck lying at around 300 feet somewhere within an area four square miles in extent, this being calculated from the evidence of sponge-draggers who had caught bronzes in their nets. The methods used then included both underwater television and the Towvane, a one-man towed observation chamber. These combined failed to locate so much as a single amphora! But in 1967, the use of a side-scanner on two mornings only picked up the target. The two-man submarine was sent down to investigate the contact, which proved to be a huge Roman shipwreck. This discovery came late in the season and it was impossible to investigate by submarine other promising contacts made by side-scanner, which may also include statue-carrying ships among their number.

A little more than a month later, as will be told, our own Spithead effort had the use for fifteen minutes only of a more intricate set-up-side-scan sonar and pinger probe combined—and scored yet another historical success by the use of really helpful scientific instruments. Peter Throckmorton and Elisha Linder are also using side-scan in a search for an eighth century BC Phoenician wreck off Israel. These searches are equivalent to the work done by Anders Franzén, being deliberate efforts to locate certain very important known wrecks for excavation, and should not be confused either with accidental discoveries or treasure hunting, although it is true that the bronze statues lying on the seabed off Turkey are likely to be priceless because few contemporary examples exist on land. They should also make clear the severe limitations, even in seas of good visibility, of underwater television considered solely as a search instrument; although, purely for surface inspection purposes by qualified experts who do not care to dive, this device is not without value. It is a method of examining sites which have already been found by other methods, rather than a search instrument in its own right.

6
The stone ships

Marzamemi, Methone,
Gulf of Taranto, Pantano Longarini
1959 - 1966

Meanwhile, Throckmorton had gone to live in Greece and from this base, with the aid of the Hellenic Federation for Underwater Activities and the University of Pennsylvania, among others, had been able to carry out a number of reconnaissance surveys. Up to this time, there had been two waves of underwater discovery. The first three finds had consisted of art-cargoes, but this trend had been lost in the succeeding discovery of, and fashion for, amphorae wrecks. The wine-trade loomed large at this time, so much so that it seemed that the Roman Empire fell because its inhabitants were all drunk. What Throckmorton did was to help put the building trade back on the map.

The first wreck of this kind was carrying the enormous 'Marbles of St. Tropez'. The next discoveries to be reported had been in Sicily, not far from Syracuse. A local nobleman, Piero Gargallo, and an experienced German underwater archaeologist, Gerhard Kapitän, had surveyed two 'off-beat' wrecks. The first had been carrying general cargo, which included statuettes of great beauty and liveliness, and could be dated to the second or third century A D. The second had been carrying a pre-fabricated Christian Church of a very early period. The material included columns, bases, capitals, various decorated pillars, and an altar.

In 1962, Throckmorton and John M. Bullitt surveyed two wrecks in shallow water off Cap Spitha, near Methone, in southern Greece. The first consisted of heaped columns scattered over a large area of seabed in 30 feet of water, almost on the point of the cape; clearly a shipwreck and not a submerged building. The columns were of pink granite, which could have been quarried in distant parts of Greece or, alternatively, at Aswan in Egypt. A very careful survey of the columns produced a plan which showed that this was not in fact a quarry shipment; the columns were old stonework, much chipped, worn and broken but which, unlike a jig-saw puzzle, did not fit together. The deduction was, that they were from a ruined or demolished building. No trace of the ship remained, except a little broken pottery wedged under rocks and giving a date to the late Roman period. They assumed that the ship had gone completely to pieces as a result of the pounding it must have endured in the shallow water.

The second wreck was discovered by accident, again in shallow water on a sandy bottom, and all that remained was the cargo and some ballast stones. The cargo consisted of unfinished sarcophagi, granite coffins with lids, and this was the first wreck of the kind to be discovered. Again, no excavation was considered necessary, but the cargo was carefully surveyed and drawn.

In 1964 Throckmorton advised by John B. Ward-Perkins, worked in the Gulf of Taranto and again there were two wrecks to be studied. The most important lay off a bathing beach at San Pietro, south-east of Taranto, 110 metres from the shore at a depth varying from 9 to 18 feet only. Twenty sarcophagi were visible on the bottom, which was sand, and there had been rumours of sarcophagi under the sea since at least 1935; although they had not been investigated until 1960 when a local diver, Dr. Congedo, had located and photographed them. He also located a wreck carrying columns. Throckmorton surveyed the twenty sarco-

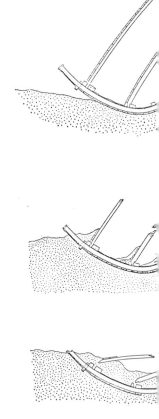

Stages of disintegration of a Mediterranean mud wreck, as reconstructed by Throckmorton in the case of the 'Austrian brig' of about 1860. This shows the process on a fairly firm seabed combined with a saltwater environment containing many organisms highly destructive of wood, plus chemical qualities inimical to metals.

10·70 metres to surface

Level before

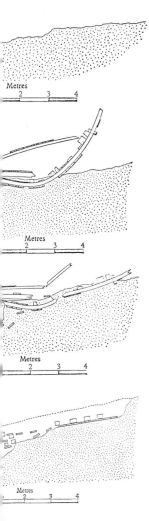

phagi first, using buoys to mark the points to be fixed. Two more sarcophagi were discovered, then an October gale, the notorious sirocco which
blows from the south, buried most of these in the sand, but uncovered
a new one. Again, the sarcophagi were rough-cut and some were doubled;
that is, two coffins joined together. In one case, a small coffin had been
placed inside a larger one. These features were obviously for ease of shipment, the final work to be carried out by masons in the country of dis-
charge. A few ship fragments pinned under a coffin, together with pottery
fragments and the evidence of the stonework itself, gave a dating of the
third century A D. The coffin nearest to the beach was only 30 feet away
from the water's edge. When the column-carrying wreck was found, some
of the columns proved to be of green marble. What these finds represented
in general was the second stage of the grandiose Roman building plan.
The famous Carrara quarries were opened in about 40 B C, but later proved
inadequate to meet the demand for both white and coloured marbles
produced by the programme of public works initiated by Augustus. What
happened then might be considered as the equivalent to the replacement
of the local 'shop round the corner' by a giant supermarket. In short,
bulk handling; and, in this case, the materials imported rough-cut in
quantity and stored at various convenient ports and central points to
feed the building programme at the required rate. What effect this had
on cargo-handling techniques has not been studied.

In the intervening year, 1963, Throckmorton had carried on at Methone,
but had turned decisively away from a detailed study of antiquity in
favour of a general study of wrecks of all ages, to determine what happened
to them under various conditions, but especially on soft seabeds in the
shallows. The results were staggering; they were also encouraging. Of
the building-trade wrecks virtually nothing was left except the substantial,
indestructible cargo, and this seemed to bear out the dictum of the old
hands of the Mediterranean, such as Dumas, who had declared that 'well-
preserved wrecks are found *only in deep water*'. The italics are those of
Dumas.

Throckmorton, on the evidence of the Yassi Ada wreck, suspected that
this pessimistic diagnosis (because deep water means difficult diving, or
none at all) was of limited application only. Certainly, it was true in many
cases. But in each and every case? Regardless of the configuration and
nature of the seabed? Of the currents and gale patterns? Even so, the
results of a season's work in and around Methone came as a shock. The
first objective had been H.M.S. *Columbine*, sloop, sunk in Porto Longo
harbour in 1824. A wreck was duly found in the approximate position of
the sinking and the air-lift turned on to it. After the top two feet of mud
had been cleared off, what showed on the harbour bottom was the bulwarks of a large ship, some of the timbers retaining their oiled finish, and
with an intact deck below that. Eventually some thirty feet of the bulwarks was uncovered, complete with upper-deck gunports, and the taff-
rail and counter of the stern intact ten feet down in the mud. Instead of
just a keel and floor timbers, with all else rotted away, they had here a
ship preserved in parts from keel to bulwarks complete! The reason was,

97

of course, the soft nature of the seabed, coupled with the fact that the ship had sunk heeled right over to port; what they had found nearly intact was the port side of the vessel, somewhat flattened out, whereas the starboard side, which had been uppermost, had almost entirely gone or was in a collapsed and flattened state. By this time, they knew that it was not the *Columbine*, but an Austrian brig sunk later on, in 1860. But did the length of time matter, so long as the remains lay below the mud?

Throckmorton went on to study this point and got an answer when he found the wreck of the schooner *Heraclea*, sunk by dive-bombers in 1940. The general picture was much the same, the hull being flattened out and with one side far better preserved than the other; but there was less left of the *Heraclea* than there was of the Austrian brig which had gone down eighty years earlier! Of the *Columbine*, on the other hand, when eventually found, there was hardly anything left at all. A careful study of the seabed and the circumstances convinced Throckmorton that in Mediterranean conditions—and he stressed Mediterranean—all the exposed parts of a vessel were rotted or eaten away by marine organisms within a short time, perhaps twenty years, but that relative stability was achieved after some fifty years. The buried parts of the wreck, in their collapsed or partially-collapsed state, would be preserved virtually for all time. To establish these points, Throckmorton cut trenches through the wrecks and drew sections of what actually was preserved. On the seabed, little or nothing showed; in the case of the Austrian brig, the only evidence that a large ship lay there was a single tiny piece of heavily concreted wood protruding slightly from the mud. All previous work in the Mediterranean had stressed the concept of the 'shipmound'—the tumulus or grave, often with amphorae protruding, which had drawn the divers to inspect more closely. But what Throckmorton's trial trenches showed, was no mound at all in these cases, but if anything a depression or scour-mark, not really visible to the eye until a trench had been cut right across the wreck, carefully recorded, and then drawn in on a master plan. This was bad news for the diver looking for wrecks; but good news for the diver who found a valuable wreck in such conditions, for it meant that the state of preservation would be high. Throckmorton did not, of course, excavate these wrecks, as they were of little or no historical value; their real worth was as test cases in an enquiry into the physical, chemical and biological processes which determined the eventual state of preservation.

Only a year or two later, Throckmorton was to take part in the excavation of a shipwreck not unlike this, which was, however, preserved on land! At the south-eastern tip of Sicily there is a flat, marshy coastline known as the Pantano Longarini which was at one time an anchorage and the site of the ancient harbour of Edissa. Both harbour and anchorage had silted up and become a marsh, so that the modern town is several miles away from the original site. And this marsh, in which the salt water lay only a few feet down, held an ancient wreck sunk when the area was a shallow seabed. The discovery was made when the marshes were being reclaimed by the owner, Sig. Francesco Spatola. In the winter of 1963–

The Greek merchant ship of AD 500 on the Pantano Longarini, showing the starboard bulwarks near the stern, seen from the inside. In the foreground (*right*) is a Weda pump used for keeping the excavation area dry; the basket in which it is placed serves as a filter. In the foreground (*left*) Helena Wylde examines a small artifact before placing it in the polythene bag as an immediate conservation measure.

1964 the mechanical excavators being used to dig drainage channels struck a mass of wood at a point about 600 metres inland from the present shoreline. So good was its condition that the workmen thought they might be able to sell it to the nearest shipyard, at Marzamemi, and took there samples of their wares. This was the area where Gerhard Kapitän had been working with Piero Gargallo on a number of wrecks, and

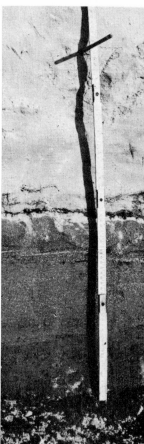

the wood samples were brought to his notice. The local Director of Antiquities asked him to make a preliminary examination, which he did the same year. The timbers of a large ship came to light and its alignment was discovered more or less by feel; Kapitän swam along the bed of the channel in virtually non-existent visibility, groping with his hands for the remains of the shattered timber. Samples were removed for a test by the carbon 14 method, which gave a dating of A D 500, plus or minus 150 years.

100

The Pantano Longarini wreck: (*above left*) the waterline wales and smashed bottom planking after removal of floors, frames, and transom pieces; (*lower left*) the transom and the starboard after frames; and (*right*) the sand layers— the streak in the centre, between the light and dark layers, is *Poseidonia* grass, as are the streaks at 10 and 15 cms. from the bottom.

As the drainage project could not be held up indefinitely, a rapid excavation was planned, with Kapitän and Throckmorton as joint directors, the draftsmen being Joan Throckmorton and Helena Wylde, the latter an American student at the London Institute of Archaeology. It was vital to record every detail of each piece of wood, but there was no urgency regarding the conservation process, which is expensive and time-consuming, as the timbers could be temporarily stored in wet tanks. A bulldozer was used to erect temporary dams around the excavation area, and the water level was lowered by the use of marine salvage pumps, so that the work could be done in air. They then dug down through the alluvial sand and soon came on a layer of darker sand containing the stern of a large ship. Each timber was tagged, sketched to scale in relation to its neighbours, and then drawn in detail; the details being as fine as those of nail holes, adze marks, scores and, occasionally, their own footprints—for some of the wood was very soft. The oak used for the ribs and frames was in this condition, whereas the cypress wood used for the planking and the reinforcing wales had retained much of its strength. The softness of the oak raised serious handling problems when, after being drawn, beams weighing perhaps half a ton, but having 'no more strength than hard cheese', had to be moved to the water tanks.

The very careful draughtsmanship was fully justified only at the end of the excavation, when the vicissitudes to which the ship had been subjected in the past had become clear. The shattered condition of some of the bottom planking indicated that the vessel had struck in shallow water, probably on a sand bar, and no doubt as a result of a sirocco, and there been pounded with terrific force. As a result of this hammering, the vessel had partly broken up and the upper part of the starboard side had been washed ashore. The remainder of the wreck had then been attacked by the local inhabitants, who had chopped up, probably for firewood, such timbers as they could get at; the proofs of this were the marks of axe and adze on some of the timbers, dating clearly from the time of the shipwreck. Shortly afterwards, what remained of the vessel had been covered over with sand and so preserved at that stage of disintegration. The next stage in the process of destruction did not occur until 1963, when the bulldozer struck the wreck. The extent of this damage was difficult to reconstruct, however, because the local villagers as well as the site workers, had removed some of the wood for present-day use. Careful questioning of the men who had found the ship in 1963 led to the conclusion that some 15 metres of planking and wales on the upper starboard side of the wreck had then been removed. This woodwork had included a hardwood plaque affixed to the stem post, inscribed with a horse's head and a Greek inscription some five or six letters long—clearly, the name of the ship.

It was decided that the best way to reconstruct the vessel would be to build a scale model, by first making 1:10 scale copies of each piece of timber and then assembling them. This work has not yet been completed, but it appears that the stern section can be reconstructed with accuracy, from keel to upper bulwarks, and the remainder of the hull estimated with fair accuracy. This is a remarkable achievement, because the upper parts of the hulls of Roman ships are known only through survivals of pictorial art, such as the Porto bas relief. Previous underwater excavations had failed to produce an actual example, in some cases possibly because only the keel and floor timbers had been preserved, but in most cases probably because the excavation had been incompetently conducted and the evidence destroyed without even being recognised. The details of construction show a vessel about 30 metres long between perpendiculars (i.e., from stem to stern post) and about 40 metres long overall, of about 300 tons gross burden, built probably in southern Italy or Greece for a Greek shipowner, and bearing a much closer resemblance to the Byzantine ship of Yassi Ada than to the earlier Roman wrecks.

Throckmorton's work also included a welcome change from the casual, even childish, assumptions of many earlier investigators, who tend to assign the reason for all shipwrecks of antiquity to careless overloading by the owners. Lacking, as we do, all details of marine insurance in the Ancient World, it is impossible to say how great or small a part this played; but most certainly both trade and wreck patterns, for wind-driven ships, are determined by the wind, and in the area he had studied, from Sicily in the west to Turkey in the east, the prevailing wind of summer was from the north-west and the period of greatest danger was in the autumn, with the coming of the strong southerly gale, the sirocco. The reason was, that ships sailing from Africa and Egypt for Rome rarely could, or would, go direct. Those from Alexandria traced a semi-circular course via Rhodes, Crete, Greece, and the Gulf of Taranto at the heel of Italy, for Syracuse and the Straits of Messina. A northerly gale would merely blow them out to sea, out of sight of land, whereas a southerly gale would tend to put them ashore. Hence their vulnerability to the sirocco, rather than the north-easterly gale, the gregale. Of course, there are many other reasons for shipwreck, including collision, fog, darkness, piracy, and war; plus the tendency of all wooden ships to leak all the time, and especially in bad weather when the hull tends to open at the seams.

Underwater archaeology is still so new, with most of its historic sites still awaiting discovery, that the apparent pattern shifts drastically with each investigation. From statue wrecks to amphorae wrecks to stone-cargo wrecks, and with the sum totals so small that nothing really substantial can be based on them. Further, the impression left by the foregoing must be of undisturbed excavations, whereas generally this is not true. The necessary corrective to all this is provided by two small islands in the Tyrrhenian Sea about a dozen miles off the Italian coast just north of Rome: the Isola del Giglio and the Isola di Giannutri. It will be recalled that there were only some four or five 'old faithfuls' for all the underwater archaeology books of a decade—Antikythera, Mahdia, Antheor, Albenga, and later Grand Congloué, they were trotted out time after time, potted and rehashed in versions which became increasingly remote from the original, and very interesting, eye-witness reports. Yet when these two islands were investigated in the early 1960s, they were found to contain

102

evidence of no less than seven wrecks of antiquity, the oldest dating to 700 BC, plus a probable 'Spanish Galleon'. More wrecks, in fact, than the entire record for the whole of the Mediterranean, as popularly presented, at any rate. Furthermore, the real question here was not of good or bad excavation techniques, but instead: what, if anything, could be saved from swift and wholesale destruction? And it must be admitted that this, rather than the careful surveys or excavations described earlier, is the more typical picture: an almost embarrassing surplus of archaeological riches being rapidly reduced to vanishing point within a few years of discovery. Worse, although most of these vessels had been carrying amphorae, two new trends were apparent. One small ship of the third century BC had been carrying a cargo of dinnerware and a mysterious wreck of the seventh century BC had been carrying a general cargo of mixed Etruscan, Phoenician and Greek goods. And the datings covered a far wider range than anything previously suspected. From the Etruscan to the late Roman of the fourth century AD in the space of four wrecks, for the others have not been dated.

One of the four is now dated merely because I was there and took the trouble to collect the bases of three different types of broken amphorae in it, and sent drawings of them to Miss Joan du Plat Taylor. This was during a brief visit in 1962. But the bulk of the dating and 'rescue' work generally was carried out by Reg Vallintine and Roger Hale, instructors at the diving school on Giglio, in co-operation with the Italian authorities. It was they who put the new names on the map—Le Scole, Campese, Punta del Morto, Capel Rosso, Castellare, Giannutri—and saved what they could, while they could.

Giglio was in the western half of the Mediterranean and formed part of the same complex of trade routes as those represented by the early French and Italian discoveries between Marseilles and Genoa; it was much nearer Rome and Naples, but in no other respect did it differ from them. Trade routes today are divided into Deep Sea, Short Sea, and Coasting. As far as we know, the Romans did not cross the Atlantic—although Pytheas of Marseilles explored the British Isles and further north in a 7,000 mile voyage undertaken before 300 BC—but there was a Mediterranean equivalent of the modern short sea voyage. This was the route taken by the grain fleet which supplied Rome from Alexandria. These ships were very large and they ran direct to Egypt with the north-west winds behind them, although on the return trip they were forced to circle back. Their exact size is much disputed and will only be established when a wreck is found—just possibly the ship caught by George Bass's television camera may be one of them. However, we know from the ceremonial ships uncovered in Lake Nemi by Mussolini that a 250-feet long vessel was within their capabilities, and indeed it would be surprising if it was not. But most wrecks found so far have proved to be nearer 200 tons than 2,000, and this is not surprising either, because they were engaged in the coasting trade. Even today, although the largest oil tankers are over 100,000 tons, these vessels are all deep sea, running direct from oil fields to refinery, at both of which deep water facilities exist. The average-

103

size oil tanker engaged in the coasting trade, however, is nearer 1,000 tons than 100,000, and the reason is that the greater number of potential ports of call are small and poky. A large vessel could not approach much nearer than five miles, which is an impractical distance for handling purposes. Tankers are not allowed to take the ground, but the 'mud berth' is traditional in Europe for other classes of small ship; even so, some have first to be partially discharged into lighters in a deep water berth before being able to come alongside the quay. Small size therefore offers advantages today, just as it did in the ancient world.

Coastal navigation probably did not differ much in principle, either. The basic rule is to take the short-cut 'from headland to headland', and the most prominent ones were marked by lighthouses in Roman times just as they are today; indeed, a Roman lighthouse is still visible on the cliffs above Dover. In the case of Giglio and Giannutri, which are both islands lying a dozen or more miles out to sea from the Argenterio peninsula in Tuscany, we would expect ship traffic to pass through the channel between, whether southbound for Rome or Naples from Gaul or Northern Italy, or outward bound from Rome for the north and west; and that most of the wrecks would occur on the side of the islands facing the mainland, which is in fact the case. Quite a number, however, are suspiciously near harbour entrances, which may imply an attempt to enter in bad weather. Without exception, they are all deep water wrecks, as deep as 165 feet, because both islands are really submerged mountains. Giglio, for instance, rises steeply to a height of 405 metres, where it is crowned by a fortified Moorish town. These mountain gradients are continued below water, and many of the wrecks lie on a sand slope below the underwater cliffs, mostly deeper than 100 feet, and with depths of 400 or more feet only a short distance away. These slopes are immensely deceptive, because the diver feels that he is simply swimming over the bottom when in fact he is going very deep, very fast. Indeed, even by 1962, Giglio had taken four lives already: two German aqualungers whose skeletons and equipment had been recovered by Vallintine and Hale from the base of a cliff 220 feet down, and two Italians who have never been found.

7

Giglio and Giannutri

Le Scole, Campese, Punta del Morto, Capel Rosso,
the 'Plate' Wreck, etc. 1961-1965

The wrecks of Giglio and Giannutri were not discovered until amateur aqualung diving in the Mediterranean had become, not merely a sport of the locals, but a branch of tourism. The virgin scenes described in Cousteau's first book, *The Silent World*, and equally vividly in the works of Diolé, had by 1960 become items of interest on the itineraries of conducted underwater tours, with the professional guide knowing every octopus by its first name. For those whose total experience beneath the sea had been enjoyed only from an armchair sited in front of a television set, this introduction to reality proved truly wonderful. Unfortunately, however, the astonishment of being underwater and alive palls after a few years. Also, the easy availability of the waters around the south of France drew hordes of sportsmen eager to shoot fish or obtain a souvenir from a wreck of antiquity. Very soon, there were few ancient wrecks or large fish left within diving range. Consequently, a demand arose for diving holidays in areas more remote from civilisation than Cannes or St. Tropez, but which could offer spectacular underwater scenery well populated by large natural fauna, and properly provided with warm, exceptionally clear water. Giglio was just such a place. The little fishing harbour of Giglio Porto and the Moorish fortress on the mountaintop above were beginning to draw ordinary surface-breathing tourists, too.

The instructor of the diving club set up there in 1961 was Reginald Vallintine, a Londoner. The clientele was international—French, Italian, Swedish, German, British. In the first season, six wrecks were found, beginning with the most famous, that of Le Scole. On 16 June, Vallintine led two members of the Munich Underwater Club to where a group of rocky peaks projected above the surface to seaward of a cape just south of the harbour of Giglio Porto. 'Visibility was close on a hundred feet,' he wrote for his Club magazine, *London Diver*. 'Clouds of black sea bream parted, and Sargi slid down into the rock clefts. The bottom swallow-dived down in great rock reefs. We followed a rock ledge to 140 feet and here the sand began. We swam down the slowly shelving slope and the vegetation began to disappear. Suddenly in the distance we became conscious of something unnatural. A huge mound with what looked like a mass of tiny tubes sticking out of it—we swam close . . . suddenly realisation dawned. We were looking at the wreck of a great Roman Galley and the "tubes" were the necks of hundreds of amphorae sticking out of the sand. I shall never forget the sight. Squeaking wildly into our tubes and pointing like half-wits, we thrashed around the wreck. Every amphora was complete and encrusted with red, white and brown growths. In and out of them swam tiny pink and blue fish—out of one of them a Moray poked its head. Euphoria possessed us, we felt as though we had found Atlantis. During later months I took many divers to this wreck. In September some of the Italians who had been diving with us announced it as a new discovery in *Mondo Sommerso*. It was also featured in *L'aventure sous-marin* later in the year. The authors of these articles, so anxious to claim the wreck as their own, did not check on the historical facts. They wrote of it as "Etruscan". In actual fact these amphorae are late Roman from AD 400.'

An amphora from the wreck of the Roman cargo ship of *c.* AD 400 at Le Scole, Giglio Porto: all were of the same type with pointed bases designed to fit into holes in racks, the so-called 'shipping amphorae'.

It was true—the discovery of a Roman ship had exactly the same effect upon Englishmen and Germans as it had on the French, the only difference being the grandeur of the French language, which in translation promptly invites derision. The journalist's mention of 'Etruscan' was a confusion with yet another discovery made by Vallintine.

'Perhaps the most interesting of the other five wrecks that we found during last summer (1961) off Giglio was some miles further north of the one I have just described. Here is an underwater island or "sec", with its summit only a few dozen feet below the surface. This was a wonderful place for fish. Ombrine, sar, corvina and huge shoals of salpe were always flitting through the rock grottoes. There was a great, wily and incredibly ancient grouper who gazed at us lugubriously as we paddled towards him and then slid lazily into a great rock cleft when we got to within six feet or so. In August, we started diving deeper at this spot. Once again we followed the rocks down. This time they opened into broad sand valleys. Over a dividing ridge we went and suddenly on the "valley" below us were mysterious scattered objects and amphorae. Every pot, amphora and bowl that we found here was a different shape. This then had not been one of the cargo galleys (sic), but some other type of vessel. The pots that we found here were Greek and Etruscan and dated back to 700 BC—nearly 3,000 years. Bogie Kane found what we all thought was a Roman oil lamp but it turned out to be a kind of plate with a curved lip running round the edge. There were also many large unidentified objects in this wreck, some of which we hope to have the chance to bring up this year. One thing *was* clear—the cause of the tragedy. In the rock clefts surrounding the wreck were pieces of charred wood. She had burnt, but whether at the hands of pirates or accidentally it was impossible to say.' Vallintine then went on to add: 'Never forget to make a preliminary survey and sketch before moving anything. The location of each object is a clue to the archaeologist . . . and irreparable damage can be done by one careless action. Some of the Roman anchors and amphorae that we found are now in store on the island awaiting the opening of a new museum which will be furnished entirely with objects brought from the sea.'

Vallintine's assistant for the height of the season was Roger Hale, a member of Southsea Branch of the British Sub-Aqua Club. His reports of the delights of Giglio led to visits the following year, 1962, by nearly a dozen members of that branch, including me. In the eleven full days I personally was there, I was able to make twenty-one aqualung dives and visit five wrecks of antiquity, plus the 'Galleon'. The situation then was, that Vallintine was working with the authorities of the nearest Italian museum and managing to damp down looting of the more important wrecks, by stipulating that if anyone wanted an amphorae from the Le Scole wreck, he must raise three for the museum (few took advantage of that offer, because the labour was considerable) and by allowing small souvenirs to be taken only from the totally smashed cargo of another wreck which was beyond all archaeological aid. This was, in effect, a holding action, because it was understood that, very shortly, proper excavations would be carried out by a fully equipped Italian expedition. But no one could control the independent Italian divers who came pouring off the boat from Orbitello, laden with twin-cylinder aqua-lungs and the knowledge that amphorae were fetching the equivalent of £150 each in New York.

No one had prepared us for this situation. Such articles as were published on underwater archaeology invariably smacked of the schoolroom; they did not tell us that the place was about to catch fire, less still what wonderful treasures it contained. There was obviously little time to lose, because the waters of Giglio were such a paradise that they had become famous. While we were there, an Italian film party arrived to carry out scientific tests on different types of colour film and apparatus, including the then brand-new Calypso camera, the first to be designed from the start for underwater use. This party was led by the diving inventor, Victor de Sanctis, and included the leading cameraman, Maurizio Sarra (who was killed by a shark about a week later); and, as it happened, it was with de Sanctis that I visited the two wrecks previously described by Vallintine.

We came straight down on the Le Scole wreck, as hard as we could go, so as not to waste precious air; it was visible long before we arrived, and was, quite clearly, a large, intact ship, still shipshape. It was on a sand slope, with one end, presumably the bows, at 150 feet and the other end lower down at around 165 feet. In the top 50–70 feet there was plenty of light, but at this depth all colour and shadow had been filtered out to a uniform shade of grey. The amphorae were still stacked in apparently orderly rows and indicated a fairly large vessel more than 100 feet long by surface indications. Clearly, the larger part of the hull must still be preserved underneath the sand. But there were several ominous 'bomb craters' in the rows of amphorae, to show where 'pirates' had been digging out quantities of the wine jars. All were of the same type, long, narrow and with pointed ends for fitting into wooden racks. At about 150 feet I went into slow motion, so as to keep to a minimum the narcotic effect of breathing air compressed to this high pressure; but even so, noted that I was now tending to think in slow motion also, and with the sharp edge taken off the sense of self-preservation. The effect, which is believed to be due to nitrogen, is to induce lightheartedness at precisely that point where critical survival calculations have to be made. In this case, I had to time my stay on the bottom to twelve minutes, and then decompress for ten minutes at ten feet on the ascent. I ignored the amphorae and began to search methodically for more significant artifacts, in the area where I thought the stern might have been. I came across what looked like an iron box, open at both ends, and about a foot long, clearly a 'mould' formed by concretions. Even in slow mental motion, it was possible to memorise its shape and proportions; but how accurately I do not know, because I left it exactly where it was, in the belief that this vessel was to be excavated. The total time for the dive was 25 minutes, including descent and decompression stop, but less than half of that was bottom time. The only other dive that day had to be on a shallower site, about 75 feet, because the level of nitrogen in my system was high. On a

108

Artifacts from the wreck of 700 B C in Campese Bay, Giglio: from top to bottom (*left*) 18-in. diameter dish, 4-in. diameter jug, 10-in. diameter oil lamp, and 6-ft. long lead anchor stock, one of three seen; and (*right*) 3-in. diameter goblet, 24-in. diameter Phoenician amphora and 30-in. high Phoenician amphora, both these last matching finds at Motya.

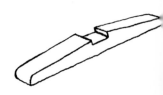

site such as Le Scole, breathing conventional compressed air, one could hardly get more than 30 minutes work a day out of a diver, and not very efficient work at that. Possibly this was the reason why the site was not in fact excavated. This was the scene in 1962, but by 1964 there was nothing left at all of this briefly famous Roman vessel, according to Roger Hale, who had then replaced Vallintine as chief instructor. The wreck had been totally destroyed by 'amphorae pirates', in spite of the depth at which it lay and the many hundreds of tons weight which its cargo represented. Of its construction, ownership, destination, we know nothing.

It was Hale, however, who was mainly responsible for saving some scraps of knowledge from the most interesting wreck of them all, that on the underwater island in Campese Bay, also described by Vallintine. He made scale drawings of the more important objects, whole or broken, recovered from this site. There were many broken amphorae, all of different shapes and sizes, from very small to very large, and items such as goblets, jugs, dishes, etc. This enabled the Italian authorities to identify some as Etruscan and Greek of about 700 BC; and later Miss Joan du Plat Taylor was able to say that two of the amphorae were Phoenician and matched with similar items from a current land and underwater excavation being undertaken at Motya, a Phoenician trading settlement in Sicily. The Etruscans are a shadowy people who were nevertheless an important power in Italy before Rome became an imperial city, and full details of this cargo would have been invaluable. It was an older shipment than any so far discovered, apart from that of Gelidonya (unless there have been others which have been destroyed but not reported, which is perfectly possible). My own impressions of the site are something less than precise, except that the wreck started at about 140 feet and went on down the slope, appearing to have been very badly smashed among the rocks which jutted out of the sand here and there. This dive occurred on my third day at Giglio, and owing to a series of minor mishaps, starting with the snapping of one strap of my mask, which left me behind and so forced a burst of speed to catch up with the others, I over-exerted myself and so brought on a severe narcotic effect, the result of which was that I went on down the slope from 140 feet feeling very giggly and extremely pleased with myself, fanned away some sand to find a lovely amphorae handle which I was sure no-one would miss, and then swam down the slope to greater depths after what looked like another handle, and then looked like a curled sea-cucumber, and in spite of my swimming hard, didn't seem to come any nearer—and that rang the warning bell in what was left of my mental faculties. As my depth-gauge had flooded from the pressure, I have no idea how deep I went; but as I started to rise, my air started coming 'hard', and I had just sufficient wits left to grope around behind me among the bottle-straps for the thin wire which, when tugged released the reserve air supply. I had recognised the onset of the 'narcs' because I had read about it often enough, but a sudden giddiness when about 70 feet from the surface, was not then in the books. This is caused in fact by the transfer from the cold water layer below the thermocline to the warm water layer above affecting the organs of balance, but it felt

109

just as though a blackout was coming on, and I stood by both to drop the amphora handle and release my weightbelt in a panic 'bail-out'. Somewhat shaken, but still with weightbelt on and amphora handle in hand, I hit the surface of Campese Bay and looked around for the boat, which had temporarily disappeared (actually it was I who had moved away from the boat, not the other way round).

I give these embarrassing and, indeed, humiliating details because they are instructive. They go far towards explaining the 'magpie instincts' of Mediterranean divers and the meaningless meanderings in ancient wrecks which used to pass for archaeological excavations. There is this extreme lightheartedness (and lightheadedness) which first becomes really noticeable at around 140 feet, which can be dangerously increased by over-exertion and also by cold, coupled with a sapping of will power and of the critical faculties. It occurs when breathing compressed air, but can be avoided by the use of expensive 'mixtures', in which the nitrogen, for instance, is replaced by helium. The danger is perhaps more acute in the Mediterranean than in, say, British waters, because the Mediterranean looks so safe and easy. At this time, the deepest I had ever been in British waters was a mere 75 feet, and for a very amateur diver it had been no joke; for the site was five miles from the nearest land, in the middle of a

Rows of amphorae, like multiple-mortar barrels, projecting from the sand at 165 ft. below the rock of Le Scole. This photograph was taken just after the discovery of the wreck, some 1,600 years after the ship sank, and the lower part of the hull at least must have been intact. Within two or three years 'amphorae pirates' had totally destroyed the site without any recording of ship or cargo having been made.

racing current, in an area which had never been dived before, and, for the most part carried out in total darkness until when, less than 18 inches from the seabed, it became just visible from reflected light. My companion and I had pulled ourselves down the anchor-rope, our bodies blown out like flags by the current, and if we misjudged the ascent and surfaced astern of the boat in the choppy sea which was running, we would be swept helplessly astern and out of sight. We were not in the mood for fun, we were trying to find a lost anchor for some friends; and I at any rate spent most of the totally blind descent into blackness wondering if I dared invent a technical excuse for abandoning the dive (which, incidentally, would be perfectly routine for a professional diver in British waters: however, he would have logged more than the bare dozen dives which was all I had done at that time). The point of the contrast is that there is currently an effort by some theorists to explain the troubles experienced by George Bass's party, for instance, at around the 140 feet level in the Mediterranean by obscure references to psychological disturbances rather than the straight physiological effect of having the body saturated by gases under high pressure. It is therefore necessary to stress the fact that I indeed suffered a severe pyschological disturbance during the 75 feet dive in British waters—i.e., I was scared stiff!—but the effect of twice that depth in the Mediterranean was purely one of over-confidence and lightheartedness; precisely the opposite effect, and rather more dangerous, in fact.

All this has a direct bearing on the problems of what is sometimes called 'deep water archaeology'; but the solution is doubtless technical rather than psychological. The only truly psychological effect experienced during the Campese Bay dive was an overwhelming desire to obtain some physical souvenir of a ship (and therefore of a civilisation) some 2,700 years old, qualified by the proviso that the item should be both beautiful and broken (a fragment only, so as to reduce the plundering to a tiny archaeological sin); and that the curve of the handle was indeed beautiful, particularly as it broke the surface, when it could be seen with all the rich pink and white hues of the fresh sea-growth on it. This, indeed, was the very oddest thing, psychologically, in that perfectly mundane cargo containers, such as amphorae, appeared to take on the status of works of art, truly satisfying to the eye of every beholder, regardless of his rank, race, trade or occupation. A member of this branch of the pseudo-sciences might well find useful employment in studying the various facets of this field, which occur on land as well as underwater. As a helpful hint, it is a fact that visitors to the current excavation of the great Roman 'palace' at Fishbourne in Sussex sometimes wish to know exactly where the Romans walked, so that they can walk there, too. The requests are made somewhat shamefacedly, but the really significant thing is that this reaction occurs far more frequently in connection with Roman remains than with those of any other period. The number of people who would apparently have preferred to live in a prehistoric community is much smaller, although a case can be made out for this kind of life. Almost certainly, a value judgement is involved, as well as instinctive preference, and it does not follow that a Chinese would react in the same way, in a European as opposed to an Asiatic context. But it means also this: that for the questioner, the Romans were real people and their occupation of Britain a real event. Without this feeling, there would of course be no history and no archaeology either. But it must also be admitted that the opposite reaction is also not uncommon, particularly in connection with comparatively recent events. In our own time, for instance, a generation has grown up for whom, in most cases, the Battle of Britain and the Normandy landings are 'history' in the schoolroom sense: dry, non-events which never really happened, not to people at any rate, but rather to mythical gods and heroes, engaged in a conflict which has no importance because we now know how it ended.

Most of the wrecks around Giglio did not in fact give much sense of contact with real sailors and a real shipwreck, but only with their civilisation in general; the reason being that the remains had little or no height, and they were being regarded through blinkers from above. So little did they resemble ships that most of these piles of amphorae were believed by many of the divers to be merely dumping grounds for rubbish, and not wrecks at all. One opposite view was represented by Reg Vallintine, who pointed out shrewdly that one ought not to ignore even single, broken amphorae lying on the rocks without a context because, although these might well have been dumped overboard from a ship, because broken, others might represent the deliberate ditching of cargo by the crew of a ship in trouble, or the displacement of some of the upper cargo as the ship sank, or the activities of 'amphorae pirates' at work on a wreck nearby. In any of these three latter cases, anyone taking the casual, pessimistic view was simply passing up three chances of finding a wreck. That was not very clever.

As to the 'doubtful' wreck sites, I arrived at conclusions firmly and early. Without exception, they were all wrecks. Indeed there might be more wrecks there than at first appeared. This optimistic estimate sprang from the fact that, apart from writing history—which means the careful weighing of evidence to at least legal standards—I had also been part-time editor since 1954 of the house magazine of a large group of companies prominently associated with the shipping, handling and distribution of coal, oil and general cargoes of all kinds to the south-east coast of England. Their origins went back to the old days of the small sailing coaster which was sometimes discharged by the simple expedient of running the vessel up on a beach just short of the top of the tide, where it was met by horse-drawn carts, the coal being transferred in baskets; the power was sometimes provided by a process known as 'jumping the basket'. While as much moved as anyone else by the sight of an ancient amphora neck, glowing with purple and reddish hues, as it rose into daylight for the first time in 2,000 years, at the same time, I was able also to consider it coldly, as a practical cargo container—to be filled, marked, stowed, shipped, discharged, examined by Customs, checked, handled, transported, distributed, and the contents sold. The size was determined by ease of handling, but it was unlikely that the Romans at any rate made unproductive use of

112

The three different types of amphora base represented among the smashed cargo of the freighter from Marseilles wrecked in the third century BC off Punta del Morto, Giglio: with the aid of these the vessel was eventually dated and identified.

manpower by getting people to run up and down gangways with them; at least, not at major ports with crane facilities. More probably they discharged in bulk by use of nets, or by stringing a number of amphorae together by lines through the handles and round the bases, common Mediterranean practice today. The watertight pottery container was succeeded by the watertight wooden cask, which had a shorter run. In various sizes, it was still in use; but basically the sizes were determined by the necessity to man-handle it. Measurement of liquid contents was still carried out by a cooper, on behalf of various interested parties, including HM Customs, and he also inscribed on each cask a code number for the ship which brought it and another code number denoting the customer to whom it was to be delivered. Code numbers or lettering on the stoppers and handles of amphorae clearly served the same purposes in ancient times; indeed, this was necessary information, because neither the amphorae nor the casks could speak, and they had to pass through many hands on their journey. They also had to be, not merely man-handled, but taken through constricted spaces into ships' holds and narrow cellar entrances.

In 1962, I was already aware that this procedure was about to come to an end, because the first shipment of wine—'Cinzano' Vermouth—had already arrived at Shoreham in 500-gallon metal containers. No smuggler would ever stagger ashore with one of those on his back; indeed they had to be discharged by powered crane to the loading platforms of special vehicles, four to a vehicle. Even this was only an interim measure, because

113

forward planning envisaged the logical treatment of liquid cargoes on the same lines as those for crude oil; that is, a 'wine tanker' which pumped the wine ashore through pipes into 'farms' of large wine tanks ashore. This raised some interesting speculations as to how the Romans handled their bulk cargoes, such as grain. But the basic economics of the business destroyed the concept of the pile of broken amphorae on the seabed as merely a dumping ground for rubbish.

The most controversial was that lying at 125 feet under the northern headland of Giglio, which goes by the surely significant name of Punta del Morto, or Headland of Death. This was an obvious point of accidental arrival for any cargo ship a little off course in bad weather or fog at night, when bound from Spain, France, or northern Italy for Rome or points south, such as Naples. What was left of the heap of completely shattered amphorae lay among a stream of sand in a rock gulley which began at about 90 feet below the surface and sloped steeply to the remains at 125 feet. I made several dives to this one and judged that the ship had descended with some force into the rock gulley and either broken up badly there and then, or had burst her sides under the weight of the cargo shortly after; at any rate, the amphorae had poured down the slope in a typical 'cascade', with devastating effects. Apart from that, the site was being used as a jumble-sale bazaar to provide free souvenirs for visitors, in the hope of preventing them from looting more important and more intact wrecks. As the cargo was in fragments, the amphorae had never been identified, let alone dated. I therefore carefully selected one neck and handle and bases of three different types; of the latter, one had a sharp-pointed end, while two were broad-based and not dissimilar. Later, I included drawings of these in a Branch report on Giglio, from which Miss Joan du Plat Taylor was able to identify their port of origin as Marseilles and give their date as between 400 and 300 BC. Clearly, therefore, they were the cargo of a single vessel sailing from France and southbound towards Rome when she struck 'Dead Man's Point' on Giglio 2,200 years ago.

This disposed of the 'dumping ground' theory, which in any case I had intemperately dismissed at the time in an article for *Diver* magazine, as follows:

'Let us assume that a merchant has accumulated a large number of broken, cracked, or otherwise unserviceable amphorae, and that they are taking up valuable storage space. If he is a bad business man, he begins to scratch his head and wonder just who will be likely to buy them from him. If he is a good business man, he can think at once of at least three possible customers, and will immediately send a slave round to ask for quotations. Building contractors, roadmakers, wharf constructors, anyone engaged on levelling and preparing sites—those are the obvious customers, then and now. There's lolly in rubble. But let's suppose that the Great Roman Depression has arrived and the tycoon can't find a customer. Well, he hires a labourer with a cart to dump the stuff on the nearest tip, or, failing that, into the sea off the harbour wall. Instead of making a profit, it sets him back a bit; but not very much. The only thing that never

that remained of the
nta del Morto wreck was
s 'cascade' of broken
phorae filling a steeply
ping rock gulley at
5 feet.

occurs to him is to hire a ship (plus the crew and dock labour involved) and take the lot miles away from the harbour and dump it overboard. If you have the slightest doubt about this, ring the nearest shipping company and get a quotation for the hire of a 1,000 tonner for twenty-four hours. You won't have much change out of a year's salary. And as there were no old Roman steam engines, our ancient tycoon is faced

115

with the very real possibility, if the wind is foul, of having to hire the ship for several days, possibly even a week (if a mistral hits him half-way through). If the Romans really did carry on like this, then the reason for the decline and fall of their empire is evident. It went bankrupt.'

Theoretically, the southern headland of Giglio, known as Punta del Capel Rosso, should have collected slightly off-course ships headed north for France and Spain. In fact, there was a local legend of a sunken 'Spanish Galleon' at this place. Since Schliemann, such legends have been taken much more seriously than was once the case. The wreck area here is a steep sand slope at the base of an even steeper rock cliff, at a depth of 140 feet. One wreck is immediately obvious, even from 70 feet above, because the stump of a mast sticks out of the sand. At the time I first saw the mast, a man in an aqualung was sitting on top of it, master of all he euphorically surveyed. Unlike British waters, where a wreck has sometimes to be explored foot by foot, because a foot at a time is all you can see of it, the lie of this one was obvious. A trail of debris littered the sand slope parallel to the nearest undersea cliff, and high up and towards the cliff, there was an anchor in a rock crevice; I know this because, my mask having misted up, this was where I chose to stop, flood, and then clear it. I then lay down on the water about six inches above the sand and 'blew' the sand gently away by fanning one hand at it; a few inches under, there was a wooden deck in a state of excellent preservation. Further down the slope, there were a number of tightly-packed metal plates, rims upper-most, showing at one point, and then, moving back up the slope past the stump of the mast, there were a number of long, thin concreted 'moulds', which had formerly enclosed octagonal ironwork bars. And a little further on, a cache of musket balls. Proceeding to what I presumed to be the bows of the ship, I saw off to my left a litter of broken pottery fragments, which proved to be from amphorae. And having on this occasion only a large, single high-pressure cylinder on my back, my time was up. The scene was so fascinating, that I felt I could have stayed there for ever. The site had been discovered by Reg Vallintine on 28 June, 1961, and in his judgement there were three wrecks at that place, intermingled. Taken with the local story of a 'Spanish Galleon' wreck at that point, the musket balls seemed good evidence for the nature of one of them.

This site appeared to offer a most interesting excavation, whereas another site near the harbour did not. Around a large rock formation called Castellari, Roger Hale later reported masses of broken amphorae, concreted together in rock crevices, presumably the remains of one or more cargo ships; as the extreme depth was only 50 feet both ships and cargo had presumably been smashed by wave action long ago. At a very remote site, the location of which it is probably advisable not to mention, there were similar broken fragments at about 60 feet, from which how-ever he recovered a small, intact vase. Around the shores of Giglio, the main island, there appear to be therefore a minimum of seven wrecks of antiquity, plus the galleon, with heaven knows how many completely buried under the sand or in deeper water. Although Hale went as deep as 260 feet on several occasions, and other members of Southsea Branch went

A sar comes down to nose among the disturbed fragments of the Punta del Morto wreck for newly-exposed tubeworms and other food.

to 225 feet while I was there, prolonged search at these depths is impossible. However, in addition to the seven ancient wrecks around Giglio, there are two more off the neighbouring island of Giannutri, giving a total of nine in all so far discovered in comparatively shallow water within a very small area.

On the day we went to Giannutri, visibility was about 140 feet and water temperature 77° F. We went first to the still unidentified wreck lying at 110 feet on mud just to seaward of one of the most savage rock cliffs I have ever seen. Vallintine had originally been shown it by Maurizio Sarra and Claudio Ripa on 9 July, 1962, six weeks previously. This site consisted of a high-piled heap of amphorae, many broken, so that you could actually lie down among them, have them tower above you, and get some sense of really being in the ship which had carried them. The impression given was that the ship had burst its sides on impact, although it is possible that the damage was done mainly by battering against the rock face before sinking, and the sides had simply unfolded like flowers later on, once the wood had become soggy. For the first time, there was some sense of the human drama involved, in place of coldfish appraisal

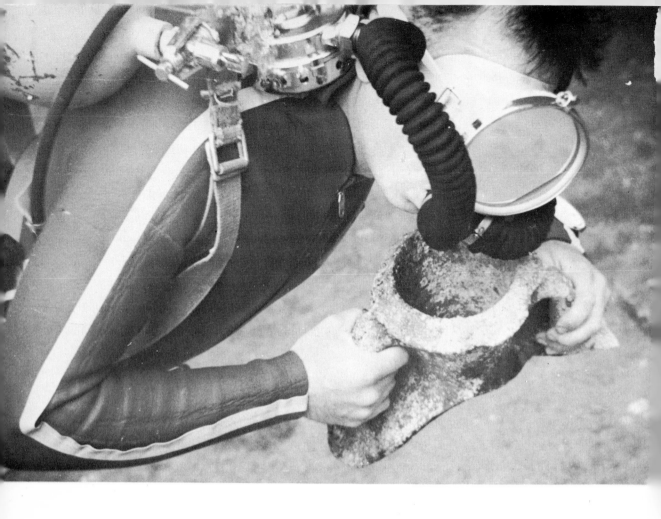

Bringing a sample amphora
neck to the surface from the
Punta del Morto wreck.

and one's own survival considerations. No quick, single-handed identification was possible, so I took nothing from the wreck until, having pulled
the reserve air lever and on my way up over the shoreward end of the
jumble, I caught a brief glimpse of a diver's knife in a yellow sheath
among the amphorae about 20 feet below and went down again to get it,
thinking a member of the team had lost it. However, it belonged to none
of them and, though waterlogged, proved to be of the 'floating' type. I still
have this artifact as a reminder that 'closed finds' are sometimes not as
closed as all that.

We then went round to the tiny harbour below the ruined Roman
palace on the cliffs above, and turned land tourist. Giannutri is uninhabited today, but the palace was apparently built for a relative of
Nero's, or so I was informed, and commanded a wonderful view out over
the sea towards the coast of Tuscany about a dozen miles away. It was
utterly peaceful in the dozing warmth of summer, but the underfloor
central-heating system installed there was a clear necessity for winter.
Almost directly below the cliff on which this palace stands there was yet
another wreck, lying in 140 feet, which we did not have time to visit.

118

e 'Plate Wreck' at
nnutri, Italy. The
ire cargo consisted of
mpanian ware dating
m about 300 B C, which
l obviously been tightly
ked into crates. The
sel, a small ship lying
140 ft. just off an
pressive 'villa' or seaside
nsion, was excavated by
eam from the
haeological frigate
ino.

Vallintine believes that he and Sigfried Koster of the Munich Underwater
Club were the first divers to see this site, on 15 June, 1961, although its
discovery was claimed by divers whom he took there later on. It appeared
to be a small ship and the cargo consisted of crates of dinner ware. The
crates had disappeared, of course, but the dishes were still perfectly in
place, fitted inside one another, and with some of the packing material
still visible. The plates and bowls were subsequently dated by the British
Museum to around 300 B C and were identified as Campanian ware.
This, therefore, represented yet another type of cargo to emerge from
undersea exploration. Koster took photographs of the wreck in its original,
untouched state.

Later, in 1963, the Italian frigate *Daino* arrived to carry out a three-
month excavation. Fully fitted up for diving and underwater archaeology,
this vessel had been on loan to the International Institute of Ligurian
Studies for some years. This was the organisation which had investigated
the Roman wreck at Albenga by using the crane-grab of a salvage vessel
to dig a crater among the amphorae. The *Daino* had been put to some use
in surveying the remains of submerged buildings and harbours, in carry-

119

ing out the not-very-notable excavation of the wreck at Spargi on the north coast of Sardinia, and for a perfectly useless and wasteful general underwater survey which, predictably, found nothing whatever. Meanwhile, the accurately known, important wrecks of Giglio were being destroyed. What could be done there by British divers, based a thousand miles away, was of course minute; but at least there was an attempt at the equivalent of the 'rescue dig' which takes place on land when a site is immediately threatened by bulldozers. The great tragedy lay in the faulty strategical direction of the Italian archaeological authorities who, with a large, splendidly-equipped vessel at their disposal, chose to throw it away on a number of projects which were either hopeless of accomplishment, unnecessary, or with no urgency about them. The submerged towns and harbours which they attempted to survey were in no danger whatever from pillage, these structures being the very reverse of fragile. Indeed, they were not even portable.

Whenever the conflict between divers and archaeologists in the Mediterranean is mentioned, it is as well to remember that it was not only divers who miscalculated.

Part Three
The North:
AD 200-1800

8

The gaps in the chain

Roman wrecks in Britain: Viking Ships:
Medieval Ships

The first known Roman wrecks in Britain were twelve ships of Julius Caesar's invasion force in 55 BC. 'Now it was a full moon and we did not realise that this generally means high tides there; so the tide began to swamp the invasion craft which Caesar had beached while the storm battered the transports in the roads and there was nothing we could do about it,' he explained. Those used to the Mediterranean still find it something of a shock when they discover how closely all sea and undersea operations in the north are geared to the relative positions of the sun and moon; and that ignorance of the complicated tidal patterns which result must mean failure and may involve utter disaster. The phrase, 'the cruel sea', was coined for the Atlantic, not the Mediterranean. Although Atlantic wind and water can be bitter, the sea is powerful rather than cruel, and with knowledge this power can be used, but not defied. Many of the archaeological lessons learned in the Mediterranean are not applicable here, or require considerable modification. As, indeed, did the Roman ships. Caesar himself noted that the local vessels were of quite different construction to those used by the Romans, and the few Roman ships which have been found and excavated in Britain show how Mediterranean practice was altered to cope with very different conditions.

However, as only three examples have been found so far of Romano-British vessels, and as two of these were probably Thames barges, they serve only to hint at the patterns of Roman shipping, both merchant and naval, around the shores of Britain. All three discoveries were made in Londinium, the capital of Roman-occupied Britain, in 1910, 1958, and 1962 as a result of modern construction projects. The County Hall ship of 1910 is a supposed small merchant vessel of the late third century, A D. Her construction was entirely Roman (except for the materials, which were local), in so far, that is, as we know about Roman construction. Benito Mussolini is still the greatest benefactor of underwater archaeology, for Roman times, in that his project to drain Lake Nemi in the 1930s in order to expose Caligula's two great pleasure barges sunk there was entirely successful and that these vessels were of 'shell' construction, with the planks put in position first, the ribs, frames, and keel added later for strengthening purposes, and with lead sheathing on the wetted areas as protection against marine borers. Underwater discoveries made later have tended to bear out the idea that this represented general practice, but nevertheless the bulk of the evidence still rests on two highly-specialised ceremonial vessels. In 1910 so little was known of Roman methods that the ship was supposed to be a Viking galley until nautical experts ruled that the structure was too heavy, when she was classed as a small merchant vessel. More probably she was a horse ferry, such as that shown in a Roman MS in the British Museum—a kind of flat-bottomed bath tub poled by a man at each end and with the interior divided by a central plank into two horse compartments.

The other two discoveries were definitely barges, another highly-specialised type of vessel, designed to take the ground in a 'mud berth' but not to withstand the stress of open sea conditions. Both the Guy's Hospital vessel of 1958 (dated to around A D 200 and the Blackfriars

124

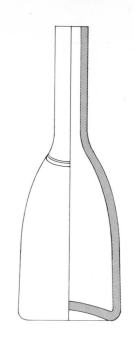

Roman tear drop flask recovered off Lulworth Cove Dorset, and dating from about A D 200.

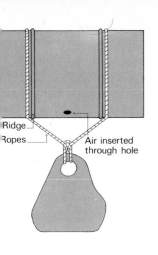

Roman stone anchor, also
covered off Lulworth
ve, the diagram (*left*)
ustrating the method of
covery.

Bridge barge of 1962 (dated to the second century A D) were found in
rivers; the former in what must have been a tributary of the Thames, the
latter in the Thames itself. Both were of similar construction: carvel-
built like Mediterranean ships, but with clenched nails holding the strakes
to the ribs and caulked with hazel twigs, and with the Blackfriars example
certainly having no keel, the other probably not. Northern ships of the
time tended to be clinker-built, that is, with the planks overlapping, and
for the skeleton of the ship to be erected first, instead of the shell, as with
Mediterranean ships. In short, these two vessels appear to have possessed
both Mediterranean and northern features of the time, judging by the
little we yet know. Peter Marsden, of the Guildhall Museum, who conducted the 1962 excavation, has described this aspect of all three vessels
very fully in *A Roman Ship from Blackfriars, London*.

The excavation was very similar to that of Pantano Longarini and
the London Fire Brigade did the pumping. But as the site was tidal and
covered by 20 feet of water at high tide, it could be worked on only at
low water, spring tides giving a $2\frac{1}{4}$-hours exposure, neap tides $1\frac{1}{2}$ hours.
Nothing of the ship showed above the bed of the Thames and parts of
it were buried to a depth of 6 feet. The barge had sunk at right angles to
the current at the south-east corner of Londinium, and must have been
an obstruction to Roman navigation of the river for some time. In 1963,
a coffer dam was to be built directly across the wreck as part of a new
embankment wall in course of construction, so the 1962 excavations were
concentrated on that portion of the vessel which would be cut off, and then,
after the coffer dam had been built, the remainder of the wreck was
excavated in the dry, without regard to tides. The top layers of gravel

125

were removed by mechanical grab, which got down very quickly to a point near the remains; and then a water pump was used to expose the actual timbers. With practice, this method proved to be more gentle than the picks, shovels and trowels used in a normal land excavation. A 'good luck' bronze coin of Domitian found in a recess at the bottom of the mast-step dated the barge, and a heap of Kentish ragstone showed that the cargo had been building material, brought probably up the Medway via Rochester into the Thames for the construction of the Londinium town wall. Among the artifacts recovered was a piece of leather bearing part of a dolphin design, and it could be shown that the oak timbers had been attacked by *Teredo* and *Limnoria*. The latter was evidence for the vessel having operated in the less brackish waters of the Thames estuary, particularly as 'during the Roman period the sea level in relation to the land in south-east England was considerably lower than at present'.
126

The 550-year-old wreck of King Henry v's 1,400-ton battle-ship *Grâce Dieu* being re-surveyed during the exceptionally low tide of 7 September 1967. Both Major-General Michael Prynne and Commander George Naish (*top left, with the tape*) of the National Maritime Museum took part in the original survey of 1933. Maurice Harknett, standing out in the river in white shirt and thigh-boots, marks the position of a large timber, possibly the sternpost of the ship.

mmander Naish and
jor-General Prynne
mine a find made among
ribs on the port side of
Grâce Dieu wreck.

It is this alteration of sea level, with its effect on river depths and coast-lines which makes deliberate search for Roman wrecks difficult. At any given point, where was the coastline in Roman times? The most famous enigma concerning this is the 'Pudding Pan Rock' in Herne Bay off the coast of Kent, only 7 feet down at low water, from which much pseudo-Samian ware has been brought up in oyster-dredges. Is this a Roman wreck or a submerged occupation site? Possibly it is both, for it is locally held that the Roman coastline was at that point two miles to seaward of the present shore, because not merely pottery but tiles, cisterns, and so on, also come up in the dredges. Possibly 'Pudding Pan Rock' was a Roman lighthouse, and perhaps a cargo ship from the Mediterranean was wrecked at the foot of it. The fact is it would be ridiculous to consider the three Roman vessels so far found in Britain as evidence of a trade pattern: two river barges and what may well be merely another

127

barge after all. Two related land sites will suffice to show it. At Fishbourne, near Chichester in Sussex, is a recently discovered but hitherto unknown Roman 'Palace' superimposed on an older military granary associated with the drive of Vespasian's Second Legion towards Dorset and Devon. The 'Palace' is built of Bembridge limestone from the Isle of Wight, Purbeck marble from Dorset, and other marbles from the Côte d'Or in France, from Tuscany and Carrara in Italy, and from Skiros in Greece. Just over the border into Hampshire is Portchester Castle, which is actually a Norman castle and church built inside the walls of a Roman naval and military base known as Portus Adurni, one of the Saxon Shore forts housing the equivalent of a Brigade Group with a mobile, anti-piracy role. The Saxons were noted sea-raiders. Of all this activity, which must have been reflected by many wrecks, the seabed so far has produced one broken pot brought up in the crane-grab of a shingle-dredger a mile or so outside Portsmouth Harbour.

Very recently, however, there have been two Roman finds off Lulworth Cove in Dorset, an area which must have seen a good deal of Roman mercantile traffic in stone and clays. Both were made by Mr. A. J. Greenland, an amateur diver from Bromley branch of the B.S.A.C. The first was a small pot which he thought unusual but did not recognise. On showing it to Miss Joan du Plat Taylor, he learned that it was a Roman unguent jar and, moreover, of a type not matched on land in the British Isles, where it is better known when made of glass. Possibly, although not certainly, this might indicate a ship coming from the Mediterranean direct. His second find was in the same area and may have come from the same vessel, and this time, having in the interval read a good deal about the subject, he did recognise it—the artifact was unmistakably a stone anchor of the type carried by Roman ships in the Mediterranean. With two friends, John Humphrey and Mick Greenhough, he raised it to the surface and it is now in the National Maritime Museum at Greenwich. The extraordinary thing about these discoveries is that both were made by the same man, and in an area which, because of its extremely good visibility—often 30 feet or more—attracts hordes of visiting divers from all over southern England. Indeed, it has been probably the best-known diving site in Great Britain for more than a dozen years. The number of people who must have swum over these relics from a Roman ship and failed to notice anything unusual, must be beyond computation. Un-doubtedly, there must be many more traces around the British Isles of the long period of Roman occupation.

However, the Romans eventually withdrew their forces and the present population of England arrived. The South Saxons stormed ashore at Selsey, near Chichester; they were certainly Frisians, their place-names betray it. Emden and Emsworth; Norderney and Northney. The Jutes took the Isle of Wight. What they had, they tried to hold against very similar invaders arriving in turn, very similarly equipped. Basically, they were double-ended 'longships'—galleys, in fact, but clinker-built and designed for the rougher waters of the north. In detail, they must certainly have differed, for the *Anglo-Saxon Chronicle* records for the year 897

excavation pit showing the peculiar 'three-skin clinker' method of hull construction which links the *Grâce Dieu* with the Vikings: she provides the only known evidence of this important stage of development.

Then bade King Alfred that long ships be built against the 'esks'; and they were full-nigh twice as long; some had sixty oars, some more; both swifter were they, and steadier, and eke higher than the other. Neither like the Danish were they shapen, nor the Fisian, but so as seemed him to be most worth.

Until recently, only fragments of such ships had come from the sea; whereas complete vessels had been found on land—the Viking ships of Gokstad and Oseberg (both ninth century and found near Oslo); and the Sutton Hoo ship found in East Anglia just before the war and reconstructed, not by her hull, which had rotted away, but by the imprint of the hull in the soil. The excavator, thinking the war would not last long, covered over his excavation with bracken; but the war lasted long enough for a German pilot to get a direct hit on the ship with a bomb (which did not explode, but had to be dealt with all the same) and for a heedless

British soldier to drive a tank across it. One or the other must surely have woken the Viking dead. Led by William, Duke of Normandy, the Vikings were eventually to conquer England, and with warships of the same design, but their renown as sea raiders has tended to obscure their very real achievements as sea traders—which took them to Russia, to the Mediterranean, to Britain and Ireland, and across the North Atlantic to Greenland and Canada, long before Colombus arrived at the West Indies. And, of course, they could not have done all this exclusively with specialised warboats, which is what a longship was.

Until the excavations in Roskilde Fiord during the years 1957 to 1959, ship-building of the Viking period, (AD 800–1050) had been represented by vessels used as tombs for a chieftain—that is, warships or ceremonial vessels. But here, from one site alone, came no less than five Viking ships—and, moreover, ships of five different types. Merchant ships as well as warships were included, and even the war vessels were interesting, because they were operational craft. Full-size replicas of Viking longships had been made and sailed from time to time; they sailed badly, and one of them sank with some loss of life. The reason now became plain—in the replicas, based on reconstructions of ceremonial ships, the figureheads at bow and stern had been grossly exaggerated in height and weight.

The investigations began with no great expectations. After all, the Mediterranean experts had repeatedly declared that there could be no valuable ship-finds in shallow water; and, further, that no wooden hulls could remain unless buried below the seabed. However, an unimportant site in shallow water would be ideal as a trial of underwater archaeological methods. The Danish National Museum at Copenhagen initiated the project as a result of some ship fragments removed from the fiord as long ago as 1920. They came from a site known to the local fishermen as a stone barrier which closed one of the narrow navigational channels to all shipping. The legend associated with the place was that a blockship filled with stones had been deliberately sunk to block the channel and so prevent an enemy fleet carrying on up the fiord to Roskilde itself, where in about AD 1400 the Danish Queen Margrethe had her palace. The fragments did not bear out this historical association, as they appeared to be from a ship not unlike those of Gokstad, Oseberg and Tune, and would date to some four centuries earlier, to around AD 1000. It took three years work to establish that there were five blockships filled with stone, not one, and that they did indeed date from the late Viking period. In short, the legend had proved a good, but not exact, guide. The connection with Queen Margrethe had proved mythical, and was probably due to the fact that she was a famous historical personage in the area. Otherwise, the story was basically true, although how much was deduction from observed facts and how much was word-of-mouth down the long centuries, is impossible to guess. It could also be seen that the timber was in good condition generally, and that the damage which had taken place had been caused by ice, by currents, or by human beings—but not by Mediterranean shipworms which found the water too brackish to support life. In this case, ship timbers had survived for nearly 1000 years under-

130

One of the Viking wrecks of Roskilde Fiord, Denmark. Inside the coffer dam part of the hull of Ship No. 1 is exposed—she was a heavy cargo vessel used for deep sea navigation, especially suitable for Atlantic voyages to the Greenland colonies, and further west to the coast of North America. This ship alters all theories based on the idea that the Vikings had only war galleys for their voyage of exploration, which would have imposed severe limitations both on range and ability to colonise— one might as well try to run a transatlantic airline with fleet of fighter planes.

water, as had the timbers in the 'barrows' built round the ceremonial ships on land in Scandinavia—but not in England. The timbers of the Sutton Hoo ship had not been preserved in conditions of land burial, whereas the timbers of these ships had survived their sea burial. This very important lesson was to be noted outside Denmark.

As soon as the importance of the find itself had been realised, it was decided to enclose the area inside a coffer dam and pump it out for an excavation in the dry. Up to now, the work had been done either by wading or by diving, the maximum depth being about 9 feet. The coffer dam prevented the further uncovering of the ships being turned into chaotic destruction by the current. This was another new factor to consider in underwater archaeology, and, indeed, almost the only debt owed to the Mediterranean divers was the air-lift, or suction apparatus, used to carry

131

out the initial stages of the 'dig'. Underwater, there are two alternatives to the pick and the shovel, which are crude, destructive implements, and these consist of the water-jet or the compressed-air suction tube. The former blows away the mud, clay, sand or gravel, whereas the latter sucks it up the tube, but will only operate where there is some depth of water present. For the final, delicate work of loosening the deposits found between the cargoes of stones and also between the timbers of the wrecks, the equivalent of a garden-spray was used, which proved to be superior to the trowels employed in a land 'dig'. The plans and measurements were carried out by untraditional methods also, by the process known as stereo-photogrammetry, which at its simplest consists of placing a measured object in the area to be photographed, and then just pressing the button. From the photograph, a draughtsman can make a scale plan far more quickly than if he had to measure tediously every object in sight. After being tagged and recorded in this manner, the various timbers were placed in polythene bags filled with water and welded tight. If allowed to dry out naturally the wood would both shrink and distort, and the longest and most expensive stage of the operation—the conservation of the timbers so that the ships can be rebuilt on land—has still to be completed. Indeed, the technique is still experimental to some extent, even in the north, and the early Mediterranean excavators did not know even that the problem existed; consequently, they were astonished to find that their Roman wood, perfect when brought up, rapidly became both smaller and unrecognisable in shape.

After the Viking-type ships of around AD 1000 occurs one of the most remarkable gaps in history. The period ends with the Norman invasion craft of 1066 as depicted in the Bayeux Tapestry. Up to this time, ships had one mast only, although the Roman cargo ships had a bowsprit, the artemon, which was almost a foremast; and the vessels were steered by oars fixed to the side near the stern. But by the fifteenth century, ships commonly had three masts and were steered by a rudder, not an oar. Of the transition period which gave rise to this revolutionary development, we have virtually no evidence at all. The historians were forced to consult the work of artists who depicted ships on the emblems and seals of medieval towns, which usually involved distorting the ship in order to fit a very awkward space indeed. In these circumstances, even the *graffiti* incised on medieval stonework are studied gratefully.

Literature has more to tell us than the seabed. For instance, William of Malmesbury, in his *Chronicle of the Kings of the English*, recounts the story of the loss of the White Ship on 25 November 1120. In her was Henry I's teenage son, William, heir to the throne. As the seventeen-year-old boy was being groomed for kingship, he was allowed a good deal of latitude by an indulgent father and had surrounded himself with a gang of irresponsible teenagers, or, as the chronicler more charitably expresses it, 'almost all the young nobility flocking around him, from similarity of youthful pursuits'. Henry I having sailed from Barfleur, in France, for England, the young William impulsively decided to follow his 'square' old father at the last moment, collected his cronies, commandeered a ship—of the latest modern construction—and, having allowed the crew to get drunk, put off into a dark night surrounded by the cream of swinging London, boasting that they would speedily overtake the old 'square' and reach England first. What they speedily overtook was a rock, and the solitary survivor gives us some of the detail we need at this point. The vessel used oars as well as sails, was decked, for the wild party ran up from below at the impact, and was large enough to carry a boat—this, by definition, making the vessel itself a ship rather than a boat, whereas the Viking warships are really boats, properly speaking. We know there was a boat, because the young prince escaped in it; and we know that the young man imprudently went back to save his illegitimate sister, the Countess of Perche, who was still aboard the sinking vessel, and that a stampede of would-be survivors into his boat drowned them all. Perhaps someone someday may find the White Ship, supposing that anything remains; but the possibility is still remote, because so few successes so far have resulted from deliberate search for a particular identified vessel. Even if found, she would be hard to identify, as the saga of the Bursledon Ship shows.

Bursledon is a village on the River Hamble, between Southampton and Portsmouth, lying above stream of the mooring place for large ships in medieval and Tudor times. Later, ships laid up 'in ordinary' between wars were moored at the back of Portsmouth Harbour, but even in Napoleonic times, there was a good deal of shipbuilding in the area. In one of the mud-berths above Bursledon, was a wreck, visible only very occasionally at low water of exceptionally high spring tides, and with a projection which resembled somewhat the figurehead of a Viking galley. Consequently a Danish galley she became—to wit, 'Sweyn's Longship'. Sweyn being a renowned Viking raider whose name had been recorded in local history. Sweyn's Longship held sway for many years, and in White's Directory of the Isle of Wight for 1859, she was 'supposed to have been burnt by the Saxons'. Twenty years later, in 1879, a marine 'archaeologist' named Crawshay undertook to examine the wreck, which had become more exposed because of a diversion of the river. It seemed to be a large ship, estimated at 130 feet long, and with three layers of planking. Crawshay's idea of identification procedures included the liberal use of high explosives and the wholesale, harmful and meaningless plundering of much of the timber. The Admiralty stepped in to prevent this destruction of our naval heritage, halted Crawshay, and commanded that the miscellaneous fragments be placed in protective custody in the local Coastguard hut, from where they vanished as completely as if Crawshay had been allowed to keep them. In 1899 the Hampshire Field Club crowded down and took away some timbers for Winchester Museum, as relics from a Danish war galley.

There the matter rested until 1932, when G. S. Laird Clowes, the naval expert and historian, visited Bursledon. It did not seem to him that this could be a Viking galley of around A D 990, it was much too large and of quite different build. So he suggested that the remains might be those of a 900-ton merchant ship of fairly recent date, perhaps 1845–50. He made one very bad, elementary error. There is a bridge across the Hamble, below the wreck, which would prevent any vessel as large as this from ascending to the wreck site, and consequently the date that bridge was built could be an important factor in dating the wreck. Laird Clowes forgot to check this, and as the bridge had been built prior to his suggested date of around 1845, the local antiquarians had no trouble in dismissing his analysis and standing up for Sweyn.

It is worth remarking that both these stories, more or less, are still current. I have been told that the vessel is a merchant ship, albeit medieval, and also that a University team recently descended on the site in the belief that it was Viking, and went away again with the same impression.

However, Laird Clowes' verdict, which he gave to the Society of Antiquaries in January, 1933, sparked an immediate and more thorough investigation of the remains with the object of a definite identification of the type of vessel. Not, of course, its name. The team involved included Mr. F. C. P. Naish, and his son George Naish, now of the National Maritime Museum, Greenwich, and among other appointments, head of the recently formed Committee for Nautical Archaeology of which Miss Joan du Plat Taylor is secretary. There was Dr. R. C. Anderson, the eminent authority on shipbuilding, and Mr. M. W. Prynne (now Major-General M. W. Prynne, CBE) to whose recent lecture on behalf of the Committee for Nautical Archaeology I am much indebted. Not least were Mr. Herbert Moody and his workmen from the local shipyard, who already knew a good deal about the wreck and were in a position to evaluate it. The wreck had been known to Mr. Moody's grandfather as 'antique', and clearly it must be very old, much older than Laird Clowes had suggested.

In some ways the conditions in which the work was undertaken were not unlike those which Peter Marsden met with in the Thames, only more so. The wreck appeared above the water, partially, during periods which occur only twice a year; and then, only for an hour at a time. This was during the equinoctial spring tides which occur in the spring and autumn. Spring tides have nothing apart from this to do with spring; the word is derived from a Saxon word meaning 'strong'—and that is what they are. Whereas neap tides are weak. The actual amount of water movement is much greater on 'springs' than it is on neaps, the currents run faster, the slacks are shorter, the high water level is higher, and the low water level lower. At the equinoxes, the effect is even more marked, and at low water one sees exposed enormous areas of seabed which are normally covered. As far as diving is concerned, the visibility at these times is perfectly horrible, and the currents run riot. Springs alternate with neaps once a week, so the Bursledon team worked only on the spring tides in March, April, and October of 1933. This meant, additionally, very dim light—dawn or dusk—because low water of extreme spring tides coincide with the fading or coming of darkness. One echoes Caesar, 'and there was nothing we could do about it'.

Consequently, with small resources available, there was no excavation; instead there was measurement and sampling. Rods were driven down

134

into the mud to mark the outlines of the wreck, and then plotted; it was not possible in the time available to secure the complete outline, but a number of cross sections were taken. Necessarily, these were of what had been the lower part of the hull only, so that the plotted results gave an apparently double-ended vessel of odd proportions. Hence, of course, Sweyn's Longship. The bow was located, plus the junction of the stem with the keel, showing that the wreck had her bows to land and her stern somewhere out in the river at a point too deep to be reached by wading. The mast-step was found and examined, plus portions of the planking still in place, which showed clearly the method of construction (an involved, three-piece 'clinker' hull). A number of stray timbers were also recovered, including a notched baulk of wood, which, if upright, would certainly resemble the popular idea of the prow of a Viking ship. Some of the wood was charred and showed that the ship had been burnt. The minimum length of keel was 125 feet, and this did not include the unsurveyed portion out in deeper water. Deductions made after a scrutiny of contemporary documents compared with various clues found in the wreck indicated that the ship had originally had a keel length of 175 feet, an overall length of perhaps as much as 200 feet, with a 50 feet beam, and a tonnage of around 1,400–1,500 tons. A very large ship indeed. Yet the method of construction meant that she must have been earlier than the sixteenth century. Further, she had been a real ship in the full meaning of the term; not a Viking war galley, no matter how large, for these were boats.

There was one apparent objection to the logic of this dating, and this was a report published in *The Graphic* of 27 November 1875, that there was 'cement between the keel and the timbers', a seemingly modern touch. Actually, as we know, this was what is today called a 'concretion' and is evidence of age, not modernity; but the directors of the 1933 project were forced to send a sample to the Geological Survey for analysis before their fears were set at rest.

With this objection disposed of, the logic of identification led to so obvious a conclusion that at first the team were wary of adapting it. The finger was being pointed, not at a type or a period, but at a fully identified, named ship. A very large warship named the *Grâce Dieu* was ordered by Henry v for his French wars. Construction was begun in Southampton in 1416, the vessel was launched in 1418, and then, because the crisis ended before she could see action, the great battleship was laid up in the Hamble river at Bursledon; later, in 1434, she was taken further up the river to a mud berth and there, in 1439, was struck by lightning and burnt. All this fitted. So, too, did her clinker-build, the caulking of moss and pitch, and the absence of a mast (known to have been removed). Her tonnage was given variously as either 400 or 1,400 tons, the latter figure agreeing very well with the reconstruction of the Bursledon ship. If all this was correct, she was 10 per cent larger than a ship known to have been built at Bayonne for Henry v, and of a size not again to be equalled, so far as we know, until 1682.

Major-General Prynne believes that she had two masts only, consisting of a very large main mast, the step of which was found, and a second mast near the stern in the area not investigated. He doubts that she had a foremast, because the general evidence for the period shows that battleships were of the 'Carrack' type, with enormous, overhanging forecastles which would make a sail near the bows quite superfluous. These forecastles, which were fighting platforms for soldiers and small artillery pieces, were at that time the main armament of a battleship, the equivalent of a land castle from which a shower of missiles could be hurled down onto the decks of a lower-built opponent. This, of course, makes quite logical the building of enormous specialised ships for fighting purposes; and makes this quite possible in combination with fairly light construction, because the structure would not have to bear the crushing weight and thunderous recoil of the complete batteries of heavy guns which were not introduced until much later.

The survey of the *Grâce Dieu* had been carried out more than thirty years ago, long before anyone knew that the Mediterranean experts would come to deny that wood could last more than twenty years in salt water, and that their findings were to be corroborated by research on Spanish 'galleon' wrecks thousands of miles away in the Caribbean. Henry v's battleship should not have lasted from 1933 to 1967, let alone from 1418 to 1967, and therefore I paid her a visit on the only possible date for me, 24 May 1967, when I calculated part of her would show at low water for a brief period. I wanted to see the surroundings and try to evaluate the corrosion and preservation aspect, of which much more was known than it had been in the 1930s. Indeed, I do not think any of the earlier investigators had then even asked this question. I had considered hiring a dinghy from Moody's boatyard, but, fortunately, as it turned out, decided to chance my arm on finding her by driving as far as possible and then wandering along the river bank in the region where I hoped she was, which was open country uninhabited except by bullocks. By extreme coincidence I stopped the car to ask what route I should take across the fields from two men standing chatting in the lane by the brickworks. One of them was actually going there, because he had his home in a houseboat overlooking the *Grâce Dieu* from a distance of about 100 yards, was a shipbuilder by trade, an expert on the corrosion of the local water and mud, and occasionally used his dinghy to take schoolmasters and their pupils out to see the wreck on the few occasions on which it was visible. He thought she might not uncover that day, but was able to tell me exactly the nearest point on the bank from her. She did uncover, the stem and about ten or twelve feet of the bow section rising just out of the water, but only after I had been there for forty minutes or so. I had plenty of time to study the landscape and made several abortive attempts to get through the mud to her.

Briefly, at this point there was a wide bay in the eastern bank of the Hamble River, which was cut by various natural drainage channels bringing down rain water from the surrounding fields which were muddy and waterlogged. There were the remains of piers or wooden platforms where boats could come alongside at high water, and I was told that

M.T.B.s were broken up here, that the Americans had a small naval base in the last war on the opposite bank, where also there was a V.2 crater still on view. Steel and iron corroded after a year, because of the large amounts of old brass, copper and iron lying in the mud, causing galvanic action. Certainly, it was no ordinary mud. I tried to cross the wide expanse of it, exposed by the 16 ft. tide, attempting to walk with flippers; I was unsuccessful, and my bare legs being encased in the stuff, I had first rate evidence of its unusual chemical properties from the tingling of my skin. Also, just alongside the *Grâce Dieu*, as she began to appear, was the exit of the main freshwater rivulet, still pouring down into the Hamble. By the time that a row of seabirds had settled on the protruding posts which were the ribs of the port bow, it was clear that, although the river was tidal and carried saltwater up here, the main supply was fresh. The important points it seemed to me were that, firstly the site was a boundary area supplied alternately with freshwater and saltwater, which would tend to discourage the growth of many organisms, and, secondly, that the highly corrosive mud, physically unpleasant to me, would be equally hostile to many other organisms. I was thickly caked in it up to the knees, so had a fair sample on me; indeed, it took a bath to get rid of it. To determine its organic content would require examination by a professional marine biologist, but I thought I had the outline answer as to why Henry v's great battleship had survived in part above the level of the bottom after 550 years, where of much more recent ships in other waters there was no visible trace, the remains being well below the bottom surface. Also, from the local M.T.B. record, the place had been in use for warships of one kind or another into modern times, and the wide bay into which the *Grâce Dieu* had poked her prow was the obvious place to mudberth a ship of size. Clearly, they would have moved her up here on one of the big spring tides, which still determine the dates on which our own diving boats go into the water in the spring and out of it in the autumn. On 7 September 1967 I made another reconnaissance coinciding with the re-survey by Major-General Prynne, under whose direction the integrated portion of the hull may later be salvaged entire, as a preliminary to the eventual, more difficult recovery of the *Mary Rose*.

The *Grâce Dieu* was an uninformative wreck in many ways, especially because she had aboard her at the last only a maintenance crew of eight men, and because extensive salvage operations were only possible after the fire had cut her down to the waterline or thereabouts. Not far away, however, must lie the remains of similar ships, for in 1419 there was a sea battle in Southampton Water:

The Duke of Bedford, the King's Brother, gaigned a signal victory over the French in a sea-fight in which he took three Carricks, one Halke, and four Ballingers; three Carricks fled, one of which was wreck'd on the sands, one other great carrick was sunk before Southampton in which there perished eight hundred men in light Harneys. Eight hundred infantrymen in armour, plus a crew of 200 sailors, would give a total complement of roughly 1,000 men, and would indeed require a large ship of at least 1,400 tons. The discovery of that sunken French carrack, with the men aboard her, would solve many questions; provided always that the modern dredgers have not destroyed the wreck. They would not do this unknowingly, of course, but they would not necessarily report the sort of wreckage which was coming up in their grabs. Some very interesting items indeed are rumoured to have come up recently in that and other nearby areas, but enquiries too often meet with a fog of vagueness as to the exact spot and as to what precisely was found there.

Such a wreck, if reported and excavated, would throw light on the process which changed the warship of 1050, merely a light war galley, into a towering sailing ship carrying a thousand men by 1400. Historically, this area is a blank. Also a blank is the next process, which by shortly after 1500, only a century later, had turned the carrack type from a floating castle into a four-masted floating gun battery. The *Mary Rose* of 1509 was the first of the latter type, which is some measure of her importance, but her success led to the building of a similar but very much larger ship, the *Harry Grâce à Dieu* of 1514, usually known as the *Great Harry* in order to distinguish her from the *Grâce Dieu* of 1416. By coincidence, the *Great Harry* also ended her career by being burnt—but at Woolwich instead of Bursledon. In 1912 the remains of a ship which might have been this vessel were uncovered at Woolwich and partly photographed and measured. Speculation is based on these incomplete records, because the expert called in at the time to pronounce a verdict was in fact no expert on Tudor warships, although a Naval Constructor. He blandly passed off the remains as unimportant, those of an eighteenth century ship.

The expert who will not admit that he does not know is always a menace; but so too is the specialist. For instance, the carrack-type of ship was developed in the Mediterranean or, more specifically, the Adriatic, but little interest is shown in wrecks of this type by the local divers or archaeologists or even, it must be admitted, English classical archaeologists who dive in the area. One of these latter took part in the exploration of a Mediterranean wreck carrying built-up iron guns, but said nothing whatever intelligible about it, while devoting reams of space to Roman and Greek ships and even to a tourist's eye view of Turkey. A classical archaeologist is quite likely to have a blind spot for anything so modern as the middle ages, besides possessing no real knowledge of ship development or armament. It is also apparent that legends must be approached with caution. At Roskilde, the legendary medieval ship turned out to be five Viking ships, while Bursledon reversed the process—the legendary Viking ship turned out to be a great medieval vessel. On the other hand, had the legends been ignored or dismissed as being without significance, two vital pieces of historical evidence would have been missed.

9

Intact to the upper deck

The Zuyder Zee Wrecks
The Vasa
Finds in the Gulf of Finland

Pitt Rivers had first formulated the principle that every detail must be recorded dispassionately, because the excavator is bound to have specialised interests and will tend to concentrate on them; and that what he ignored and possibly destroyed may seem far more important to later investigators. This is well illustrated by the next link in the historic chain, the reclamation of the Zuyder Zee, as described by Professor G. D. van der Heide in his *Zuyder Zee Archaeology*, which gives the results for that part of this former inland sea now known as the North-East Polder. In this small area some 150 wrecks were found, one at least being a medieval ship, plus a forest and fourteen villages. Earlier reclamation projects produced little of interest, because there was rarely complete collection and recording of the facts. In this case, the shipwrecks were probably the least important, being those of highly-specialised small craft, albeit unknown from paintings. The most significant fact about them was their dating—they spanned the period from modern times right back to about A D 1400, and then stopped. Because before that time the Zuyder Zee was dry land and the villages had been inhabited. What the Zuyder Zee told us about the process of submergence is so important that it will be described in the second section of this book. The wrecks, however, produced a number of object lessons in themselves. They caused van der Heide to distrust the accuracy of dating by details of construction, because although this was a rough guide, the habits and traditions of individual shipbuilders varied very much; he found that pottery, coins, pipes, and other artifacts, plus the process of sedimentation, a more reliable check. It was interesting also that the skeleton of a drowned sailor was found in the wreck of a seventeenth century vessel loaded with sandstone; hitherto it had been believed, on the evidence of Mediterranean 'experts', that bones lasted only a very few years.

Probably the most striking sight, when the water had been pumped away and the seabed became exposed to view for the first time in six centuries, was that there were no old wrecks on it. The bottom of this sea was a nearly featureless plain. The wrecks—and the 150 which were found can represent only a small proportion of the total—were all buried beneath it, vanished completely from sight. No diver would ever have found them by swimming over the seabed. Their discovery was largely accidental, occurring when drainage channels were dug and the land generally made ready for cultivation. When found below the soil, they varied in state of preservation from just the keel and ceiling boards to a fair way up the sides of the hull, beyond the turn of the bilge; and this of course represented the softness or otherwise of the original seabed and the depth to which it continued to be soft before reaching harder levels. In every case the soil profile had been much disturbed by the presence of the wreck, and Professor van der Heide developed an excavation technique which would show this process and indicate at what point the wreck had been completely overlaid with sediment. Even if the vessel proved to be unimportant in itself, it would, if dated, also date the sediments; and as the sediments themselves contained the biological clues as to whether the environment of the time was fresh water, salt water, or

140

Stages in the recovery of the *Vasa:* fig. 1 half sunk into the seabed with mud accumulated inside to a height *above* seabed level; fig. 2 raised clear of the seabed in a cradle of cables, but still heavy with mud on all decks; fig. 3 cradled in in her floating pontoon, as shown in the photograph on p. 157; and fig. 4 as she is supported now.

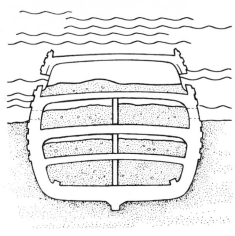

FIG. 1

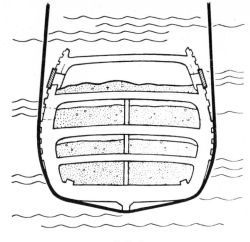

FIG. 2

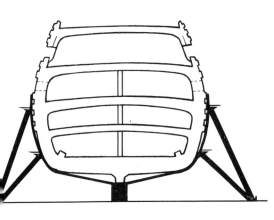

FIG. 3

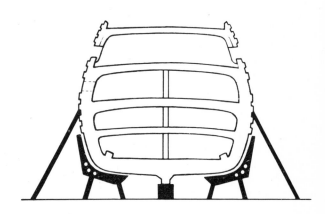

FIG. 4

brackish water, the process of inundation could be firmly reconstructed. This was necessary, because the Zuyder Zee proved to have been flooded with fresh water from the Swiss Glaciers as well as by salt water from the North Sea. The wrecks of the ships showed the latter part of this process.

This work was carried out some years before Throckmorton investigated the Methone wrecks in order to find out what happened to wooden hulls in Mediterranean conditions, and, partly because the number of wrecks examined was so much greater, it proved that the hulls were not always distorted or flattened out, although the sides were certainly cut off, as though sliced by a knife, at some level which must necessarily have been the point where they were permanently exposed to seawater. This, and its tie-up with the sedimentation pattern, was well brought out by van der Heide's method of excavation, which in its first stage left two 'walls' of unexcavated soil across the otherwise dug-out hull—one wall

141

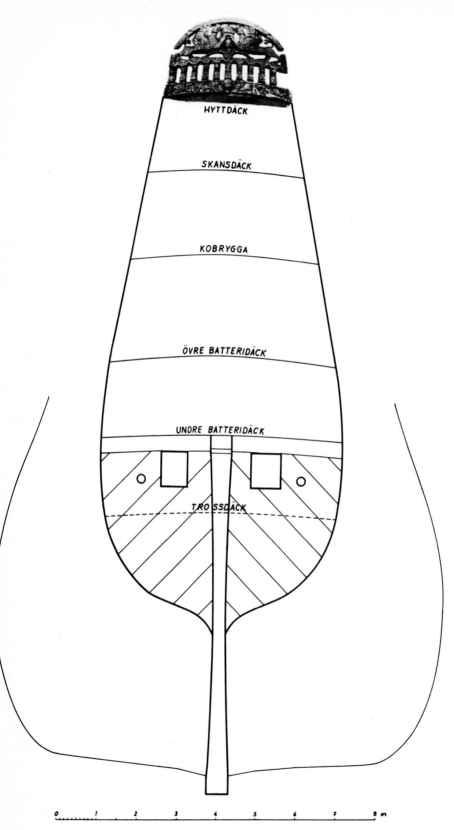

The narrow sterncastle of
the galleon *Vasa*—1,300 tons,
64 guns—with its six decks,
the midships beam being
indicated by single lines.
Only the three lower decks
and the hold ran the full
length of the vessel from
stem to stern: Upper
gundeck, Lower Gundeck,
Orlop deck, Hold.

HYTTDÄCK

SKANSDÄCK

KOBRYGGA

ÖVRE BATTERIDÄCK

UNDRE BATTERIDÄCK

TROSSDÄCK

0   1   2   3   4   5   6   7   8 m

running fore-and-aft down the line of the keel, the other wall running across the midships section, and both of course containing the visual record of the sedimentation process, like the layers of a sandwich.

A more recent discovery is the well-preserved 'cog' excavated 1962–1965, and dated by Dr. Siegfried Fliedner of the Focke-Museum, Bremen, A D 1250–1400. Never launched or even finished, she is thought to have been torn from the slips by one of the storm tides frequent in the fourteenth century and carried away from the town up the Weser, to disappear without trace beneath the sand and clay of the subsiding floods. The only survivor of the type of ship which carried the bulk of medieval seaborne commerce, she supports German theories as to the importance of the long-distance voyages of these cogs in building up the power of the Hanseatic League.

It is always tempting to postulate as a general principle what is in fact only a local phenomenon, and this is especially so in the field of underwater archaeology, because the sea itself, as an environment, is as yet almost completely unexplored and unknown; not merely in the literal sense of a quick look around, but in the basic structures of biology, chemistry, and so on, which will take centuries to explore. And it is precisely these factors which determine the preservation, or otherwise, of wrecked ships.

One man was largely responsible for awareness of this. Anders Franzén. He was also the first to develop a technique to solve the problems of how to find an important, identified ship known to have been lost long ago somewhere in a large stretch of very deep, dirty water. In his success, he still stands alone. Strictly speaking, he was neither archaeologist nor diver. The task he was performing is best thought of as the critical preliminary —archaeological reconnaissance. And, in effect, he found the *Vasa* on land. His interest in naval history went back to before the war and in particular to a discovery which had been made by a fisherman at Landsort in the Stockholm archipelago. This man was convinced that there was some interesting obstruction near there, because he tended to lose his anchors on it, and one day in 1920 there was a salvage vessel near by when he happened to get caught up again. For a bottle of gin, a diver agreed to go down and free his anchor. From the obstruction eventually came seven bronze cannon cast in Germany, Poland, and Sweden and an identification as the Swedish warship *Riksnyckeln*, sunk at that place in 1628. As the *Vasa* had been lost off Stockholm in the same year, interest in this great ship also was revived and a search programme mounted. The detection instruments employed included a divining-rod made of gold and operated by an experienced magician. Variations of this method are still suggested in modern times, except that the magic device is rationalised by calling it the 'X'-machine, or something similar. But all have their limitations and there is still no effective substitute for hard work, lengthy study, and original thought.

What this really involves can be shown by an analysis of what Franzén did. By research in the archives he selected about a dozen Swedish warships known to have been lost in the Baltic during the sixteenth and

seventeenth centuries, which for reasons apparent only to an historian would be of scientific interest. In short, he concentrated. He then concentrated his attention still further—to one specific ship, the *Vasa*. And he studied, not merely the ship and the conflicting information as to where it was lost, but also the environment in which it was lost. The earlier search for the *Vasa* had folded, partly because the magician did not come up to specifications, but also because of the alternative, easy theory that he had failed to find the wreck because the wreck was no longer there, having disintegrated after more than 300 years under the sea. This was of course a casual assumption, completely unproven; indeed, not even investigated. But it was commonly accepted and therefore required moral courage to probe. Franzén's great virtue was that he applied original thought throughout. He did test the assumption, and discovered a few simple facts, all that was known in those days. Wood submerged in water did not just disintegrate from old age; generally it vanished because it was eaten. There are not very many organisms which can subsist on a diet of timber, and these few require certain environmental factors to be

144

excavation of the *Vasa's*
lower gundeck. In all, 700
tons of mud had to be
removed from the decks
and carefully sieved for
artifacts. This accumulation
of mud throughout the hull
was one major reason for its
excellent state of
preservation. Another was
the fact that, when sunk,
she was a brand-new ship
fresh from the builder's
yard.

present also, among which are salt content, temperature, and light penetration. Even modern knowledge is woefully inadequate, but what
Anders Franzén hit on was the undoubted fact that the most famous of
the formidable shipeaters was the worm *Teredo navalis*, which flourished
in very warm, very salt water such as is found in the Mediterranean.
Indeed, a scientific report, over the name of Pliny the Elder, exists from
the first century A.D. The teredo was the reason the Romans sheathed the
wetted surfaces of their wooden ships with lead, and the cause also of
much experiment with brass and copper sheathing in England, and
resulting discoveries concerning the effects of various metals and materials
when in contact with each other in sea water.

Before the outbreak of World War II in 1939, Anders Franzén had
made his critical discovery, that the teredo was absent from the Baltic.
From this he drew the conclusion that the Baltic must be a unique
archaeological treasury of sunken ships. But he still had to prove it. In
1950, he prepared his wreck programme; in 1953, he started probing the
seabed for the *Vasa* and during the three summers of 1954, 1955, and 1956
was out every Saturday and Sunday on which the weather was suitable
for small boat operations; and in August that last year, 1956, he located
the wreck which proved to be the *Vasa*. Every place at which he probed
had been suggested to him by evidence of some sort, which he himself
had dug out of ancient documents, but as Commander Bengt Ohrelius
writes in his book *Vasa: The King's Ship* (Cassell, 1962), 'The path of the
marine archaeologist is beset with disappointed hopes, false conclusions
and misleading information'. Typical of the latter was the fact that, all
along, an echo-sounder chart existed which showed the *Vasa*, but when
Franzén enquired about it he was told by the authorities that the hump
plainly depicted at this point was in fact a heap of rock rubble dumped
there during the excavation of the Gustav V dock. Therefore he avoided
this clue and turned away to follow up other, false clues. Only in 1956,
after years of search, did he learn that the rubble from the Gustav V dock
had been deposited at a quite different spot. By this time, he had nar-
rowed down his search area, from documentary clues, to a workable
space which included that odd hump which now, after all, was known not
to be a heap of rubble and which, when he lowered down his core sampler,
provided a specimen of very old, black oak from a depth of about 100 feet.

Up to this point, it had been virtually a single-handed effort, the equivalent of Peter Throckmorton's years of going out with the Bodrum sponge-
divers to reconnoitre ancient wrecks, although that was still several years
in the future. But once the *Vasa* had been found, identified, and inspected,
there was all the difference in the world. The wreck did not lie off a
benighted Turkish coastline at the back of beyond, but in the protected
waters of a modern harbour within a mile or so of Sweden's main naval
base. Enormous resources were at hand—and they were to be needed. The
project has so far cost the equivalent of one million pounds, in spite of
the fact that neither the Neptune Salvage Company nor Anders Franzén
himself submitted a bill, and, according to his estimate (contained in a
personal letter to me), 'The future, permanent Vasa Museum, will cost

several million pounds, more. Conservation of the wooden hull, so as to prevent it shrinking and warping, forms a major item in these costs.'

But it was all thought well worthwhile, because the *Vasa* was a staggering discovery. She was generally intact to the line of the upper deck (although the deck planks had been ripped off by early salvage operators in a successful attempt to recover most of her cannon), and part of the foremast was standing well above that level. She had been damaged, especially at the stern, by later ships catching their anchors on her hull, but all this was really negligible. She had not been broken by being smashed against rocks in shallow water, she had not been scoured by ice or by fast currents, and she had not been attacked by voracious shipworms. Above all, she had been a brand-new ship when she sank, straight from the dockyard, never used; her hull had never undergone the stresses of long years at sea. Of course, some deterioration there had been, and from an unsuspected cause—fungi. Lars Barkman reported: 'The decay of the wood varied greatly, depending, among other factors, on its position in the mud on the harbour bottom, as well as the wood type. The wood surfaces that were not covered with mud, such as the upper parts of the deck planking and trimming, and the upper side of the deck, were greatly decayed up to one centimeter. Many of the experts attribute this decay to the presence of a certain fungi which lives underwater but was previously thought not to cause any decay in wood. Mycological research has shown that certain rot fungi do not attack timber that has a high iron content. The decay resistance of the different woods varies greatly, and in this case the oak has proved excellent. The 333 years under water would have been considerably harder on birch, for example.' This was of small account when compared, for instance, with the Zuyder Zee ships—sheered off at an older seabed level, so that nothing whatever showed above the mud; or the wrecks of Methone, preserved only below the mud and in a collapsed condition; and above all, the standard example for the Mediterranean, as described by Dumas, the wooden hull of the 3,900-ton *Panama*, sunk in 55 metres in 1896, and reduced to a mud mound only one metre high after a mere half century under the sea. The *Vasa* had sunk into the mud up to about the same level as her original waterline, but, instead of being destroyed above that level, as would normally be the case, had survived not merely intact to her upper deck but was still strong enough to be raised entire, pumped out, and then floated into a modern dock prepared specially to receive her. She sailed out of dock in 1628, and she sailed back again in 1961, having spent the interval under the sea. Thus, incidentally, avoiding all the bother of underwater excavation, although the site of the sinking had to be thoroughly searched for carvings and other items which had fallen or been broken off the hull.

Above all, it was what was found inside the mud-cloaked hull when the archaeologists had carefully examined it foot by foot, which was important. The traces of human occupation, including some of the corpses complete with shoes, hats, purses, and so on, was a part of the seventeenth century brought back into the present, even if not actually to life. Unfortunately, from the historical point of view, the soldiers had not yet joined when the

Seven hundred wooden sculptures have been recovered from the mud of the sea floor in the vicinity of the site where the *Vasa* lay before lifting, the largest nearly 5 metres or 16 ft. high, and the smallest just under 5 centimetres or 2 in. This impressive Coat of Arms consists of nineteen separate pieces.

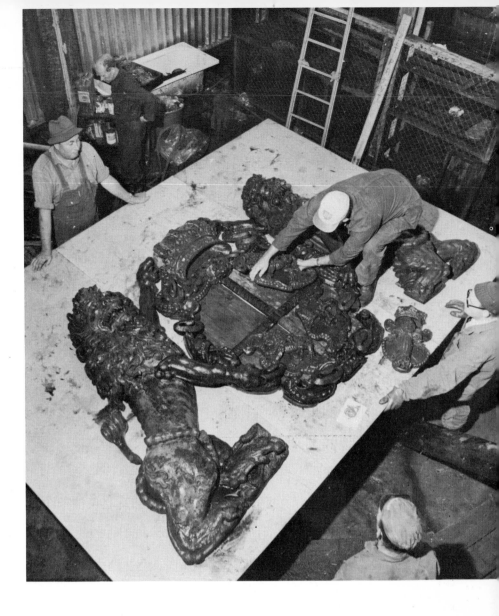

ship sank and the *Vasa* had not been properly lived in, nor had there been apparently great loss of life; nevertheless, few land sites could rival this one in its revealing details of a bygone age.

The carved statues and heads with which the ship had been liberally adorned were a field of study in themselves; of interest to the historian, with their relationship to similar carvings in the city of Stockholm, to the art-lover, and even to the anthropologist and sociologist, in that there could be conjectures as to their connection, if any, with similar practices among aboriginals. It will be recalled that the native Tahitians who joined the crew of the *Bounty* under Fletcher Christian wished to ring the ship with skulls in order to appear victoriously warlike and grim, and therefore frighten off or intimidate any attackers.

As part of the history of shipbuilding, or perhaps it would be better to

147

say the building of important ships, for too much can be made of dugout canoes, stone anchors, Tyne 'keels' and so on, the *Vasa* was priceless. She was a galleon, and virtually intact; and, in essentials, a Dutch galleon. Spanish galleons are only for schoolboys, who have not been taught that the word Spanish is put there to qualify the word galleon, as one would talk about, say, an American aircraft carrier to differentiate it from a Japanese or British aircraft carrier, without implication that they were invented in America, which they were not. Their importance is, however, that these were as important to the history of the world as the aircraft carrier, and similarly represented a definite development of the capital ship. To generalise briefly, the earliest known warship of the North was the Viking longship, which is very well known from a number of excellently preserved surviving examples. This was succeeded by the carrack, the great floating barracks with overhanging bows, possibly developed in the Mediterranean, of which the only known example is the Bursledon Ship, the *Grâce Dieu*, or what little is left of it. This was the first stage of the carrack which, with the development of more efficient artillery, flowered into the floating four-masted castle such as the *Mary Rose* and the *Great Harry*, via a possibly intermediate type which would be represented on the seabed by the English *Regent* and the French *Cordelière* which caught fire when locked together in battle off Brest in 1512, the revolutionary *Mary Rose* being present at this engagement. It is probable that these carracks were compartmented like castles, and although the later types had side guns from stem to stern, these represented in fact a number of separate batteries, on slightly different levels, and flanked by smaller, supporting weapons, rather than the continuous row of standardised cannon on a complete gundeck running the entire length of the ship, which we suppose is an innovation which came in with the galleon. A very wordy way of

148

putting it, but we cannot be specific because we do not know. No plans of a carrack exist, no scale model exists, no complete carrack has yet been found. And all we know of the galleon, the type of major warship which succeeded the carrack, is that the great overhanging fighting platform or castle at the bow had gone, to be superseded by a marked beakhead, and as this was a ship designed from the start, apparently, to have the gun as its primary weapon, instead of infantry backed by artillery as with the *Mary Rose* and *Great Harry*, we may suppose that this was perhaps also the place where the continuous gundeck was introduced. But we have very little to go on. No scale-models, a few fragmentary design drawings, some artists' representations of the ships afloat; no more than that. The only seabed example which would settle the matter, if sufficiently well preserved, is Drake's *Revenge*; the site, if poets are to be believed, is somewhere off 'Flores in the Azores'. After the galleon, no one is really bothered. There are plans and scale models in plenty, there are even surviving ships, such as the *Victory* in drydock and the *Foudroyant* afloat

Vasa soon after being ...ed from the seabed, ... the marks of the ...age divers' work still ...ent.

The lionhead carving, painted yellowish brown, white and red, is one of those decorating the *Vasa'* gunport lids. Such ornamentation was typical of the period. Later, warsh were strictly functional fighting machines and even the 'chequerboard' paintin of Nelson's ships was thought to smack of ostentation.

in Portsmouth Harbour to this day, apart from an American example of the American super-frigate or pocket-battleship of the early nineteenth century. They were so good that the British only managed to get one of them, the *Chesapeake*, which they turned into a mill at Wickham in Hampshire, although her anchor is still on view near one of the *Victory*'s on Southsea sea front. But there is no need to wonder how the *Chesapeake* was built, because the British Admiralty made plans of her after her capture by the *Shannon*.

No one would raise a million pounds to salvage or excavate one of those ships; not, at any rate, with the idea of gaining shipbuilding knowledge. The *Revenge* would be a totally different matter, as was the *Vasa*. She proved indeed to be a galleon; about 1,400 tons, length overall 165 feet, beam 40 feet, and with two complete gun-decks running nearly the full length of the ship. Not, like the *Mary Rose*, with a variety of armament ranging from 68-pounder downwards, but standardised batteries of much smaller guns. Those few remaining in her were all 24-pounders, and the early salvagers had spoilt the picture by removing the rest of the armament. By the standards of the *Victory*, she was a fourth-rate ship of the line with 64 guns, but the lack of positive information as to the calibre of all the guns must make us hesitate. Particularly as a really eminent nautical expert had proved on paper that the masts of such a ship could

150

not be raked, nor the decks cambered. The *Vasa* proved him perfectly wrong, and indeed a great deal of the scholarship put into ancient ship-wrightry is a waste of time, the evidence being as scant as it is. In one sense, however, the scholar may have been perfectly right and the ship-wright absolutely wrong, for when the *Vasa* went for her first gentle sail across the harbour, she simply lay down on her side and died. Indeed, galleons had a habit of doing this. A galleon built by Giovanni Maria Spuazza capsized while leaving the harbour of Malamocco on its maiden voyage in 1558, and another Venetian galleon launched about 1570 showed evidence of the same alarming tendency and was little used. The capsizes of the *Mary Rose* and *Royal George* arose from quite different causes and anyway were not comparable because both ships, so far from being on their maiden voyage, had completed many long years of hard service; indeed the *Royal George* had taken part in a victory over the French which was fought in a full gale and in shallow water. The mounting of the guns and their calibre would, of course, be critical for stability. An exact idea of how this problem of carrying excess weight high up in a ship was at length solved can be seen by visiting the *Victory* and looking at her in drydock bows on. It is at once seen that the bulk of the bulbous hull was below the waterline and that the sides of the ship above water sloped inwards very sharply, so bringing the weight towards the centre, and that the armament was allotted as follows: lower gundeck—30 32-pdrs, middle gundeck—28 24-pdrs, upper gundeck—30 12-pdrs; quarter-deck—12 12-pdrs, forecastle—2 12-pdrs and 2 68-pdr carronades (the carronade being a light gun for its large calibre—$1\frac{1}{2}$ tons against the 3 tons for a 32-pdr cannon). This was the 1805 armament, but although the armament of individual ships was often altered from time to time, the *Royal George* being a drastic example, the basic principle of having the lightest guns high up and the heaviest guns as low down as possible was adhered to.

If the *Vasa* had had 24-pounders on both gundecks, and in approximately equal numbers, that would be sufficient to explain her instability. The Swedes are trying to find the cause of the capsize by calculating all known weights and their distribution—from stores at the bottom to rigging at the top—and then feeding them into a computer. Their information on the guns, however, comes from old documents, because the early gun salvagers were so surprisingly successful. Consequently, we have the paper figures only, which were: 3 35-pdrs, 48 24-pdrs, 1 16-pdr, 8 3-pdrs, and 2 62-pdrs. The two latter were probably a light, mortar-type gun for sweeping an enemy's decks with anti-personnel shot at close range, similar in intention to the *Victory*'s carronades. The 35-pounders and the single 16-pounder may have been bow or stern chasers. The eight 3-pounders were almost certainly placed very high up, the equivalent of the *Victory*'s 12-pounders on forecastle and quarterdeck. The inescapable conclusion is that the *Vasa*'s basic broadside consisted of 48 24-pounder cannon mounted on two gundecks one above the other—a fatal contra-diction of the basic rule of armament distribution which had long been arrived at by the time the *Victory* was armed. The *Vasa* was not merely

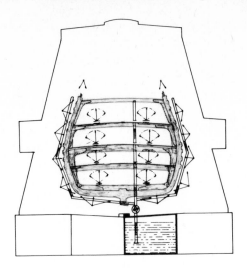

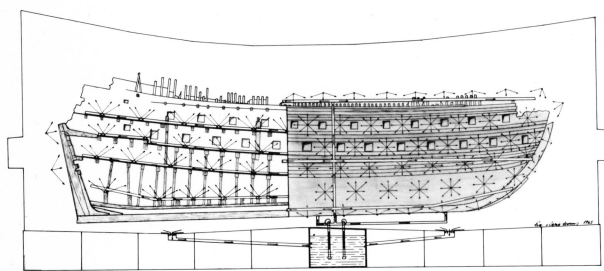

heavily over-gunned for her size, but far too much of the weight was emplaced far too high up, and too far out. Remembering that the *Victory* was a giant first-rate, a specially strong headquarters ship for an Admiral and his staff, while the *Vasa*, by size comparison, would have been barely fit to lie in the line of battle at Trafalgar. She would be the equivalent of Nelson's *Agamemnon*, 1,384 tons, 64 guns, a fourth-rate, but nearly flush-decked compared to the towering stern castle of the *Vasa*.

It is perhaps worth noting, however, that the English galleons of Elizabeth's time suffered no such disasters. Admiral Sir William Monson wrote in his *Naval Tracts: The marvel I speak of is, that notwithstanding the apparent dangers and casualties of the sea aforesaid, yet not one of her Majesty's ships ever miscarried, but only the* Revenge, *which I said, in her voyage of 1591, was taken by the Spaniards by the unadvised negligence and wilful obstinacy of her captain, Sir Richard Greynville. If we*

152

The change from mud-and-water to air-and-sun would have destroyed the *Vasa* in a short time, had not extensive conservation measures for the complete hull not been made in advance. The two diagrams illustrate the ship inside her metal 'house' and show details of of the sprinkler system which keeps the woodwork sprayed with preservative fluid. The final cost of her raising and restoration may amount to three million pounds.

compare these fortunes of the Queen's with those of her father's, who next to her had the greatest employment for his ships at sea, you will find great difference betwixt them, although we cannot properly call them voyages in King Henry VIII's time. For his ships were never so far from home but they might return again with a good wind in twenty-four hours' sail; as the others never expected to see the English shore, under four, five, or six months, and many times more.* Monson, being a veteran of the Armada Campaign of 1588, was a genuine expert on the difference between the carrack and the galleon. And he makes a valid point of vital importance which is obscured by Swedish and Venetian galleons which capsized in calm water and a light breeze on their maiden voyages. The difference between the English carracks and the English galleons was that the former were confined to operations in home waters, generally the English Channel, while the latter went raiding all over the world, into the Atlantic, down to the West Indies, and occasionally round Cape Horn and into the Pacific. The differences between them were undoubtedly those of speed and seaworthiness as well as armament, and yet we know very little of how this astounding revolution in performance was achieved. It must have been a matter of balancing the various requirements exactly: the *Vasa* certainly had the gun-power, she may have had the speed, but undoubtedly she lacked the seaworthiness; she was unbalanced in more senses than one.

But, as a result of the raising of the *Vasa*, the modern Swedes are the greatest experts in the new science of conservation of submerged relics, which can only be hinted at here. Where the hull had lain, searches so far have uncovered 2,500 articles, including 700 sculptures; and inside the dense masses of mud which had accumulated on every deck (including those *above* the level of the seabed) some 24,000 objects were recovered by the archaeologists; and all of these, plus the hull itself, have had to be treated to prevent deterioration. It should be added that no book of rules existed, and that the Swedish scientists had to start writing the first volume immediately, experimentally, and in a great hurry. Previously, the science was purely industrial: the demand was to give longer life to materials immersed in or exposed to water, not to preserve them for ever. To lessen the seriousness of mistakes and to allow for the invention of better techniques in the future, the Swedes sought to employ methods which were reversible, a wise step. There were many different materials involved—wood, leather, textiles, gold, silver, copper, bronze, brass, cast iron—each required a different technique and a different range of experiments. At one end of the scale, there were the ship's sails stored in the locker, large, very fragile objects; and at the other end, the bodies of the crew and their relatives, with in some cases most of their clothes nearly complete and even the hair on their heads preserved. Lars Barkman has described some of the measures taken in his booklet *On Resurrecting a Wreck*, written for the Preservation Exhibition in 1967. According to contemporary letters, 'some 30 people with sailors, wives and children who would sail to Vaxholm' perished in the disaster. Parts of the skeletons of 18 individuals were found, in all, a dozen of them in 1961. These were analysed.

153

The strangest thing was that when the mud was removed the skeletons rapidly changed colour from white to blue. This illustrated the basic principle that most materials suffer a chemical change which varies according to their final environment and finally arrives at stability. In this case the phosphate ions from the skeletons had reacted with the iron ions present in the surrounding water, and these were artificially present, occurring as a result of the rusting of iron, particularly forged iron, in the surrounding hull. When the bones were exposed to air, this was a new environment and the stability achieved underwater was destroyed by the oxygen content of the air, the outer sign of which was the colour change from white to blue.

Having women aboard warships seems weirdly strange to us, because, until the development of the latest type of capital ship, the nuclear submarine, warships generally spent no protracted periods at sea; even so, the women complained of the hardships of separation. In the days of sail, and especially when blockade duty was involved, as it frequently was in the Swedish Royal Navy, relatives were allowed on board until the ship actually sailed on operations. Consequently there were two female skeletons among the dozen examined from the 1961 recoveries. On the upper gundeck, now listed anonymously as Individual B, was: 'Woman, 25–30 years old, about 158 cm tall. Short cranium with obviously outward-bent arches and protruding cheekbones.' On the lower gundeck was Individual G: 'Woman, 25–30 years old, about 168 cm tall. Nordic type.' Among the men, the same two basic types were represented—the majority clearly Nordic, the minority probably Slavs, perhaps from the direction of Finland. In some cases, their medical history was revealed. Individual A had his 'right shin-bone broken in two places by the accident', while Individual I showed signs of 'pathological changes in the denture, left ear and arch areas and in some of the toe joints; health record includes bone enlargements symptomatic of syphilis'. Individual J, an older man of between 40 and 50 years of age, had 'a healed cut wound on the left shinbone and thigh'. Perhaps the most extraordinary survival was in connection with Individual H: 'Man, 30–35 years old, about 167 cm tall. Probably Nordic. The brain, dried in, remains in a greatly shrunk but fully recognisable form.' This was merely the medical report on him. The archaeological report clothed him, literally. 'The skeleton of a seaman was found under a gun carriage on the port side of the lower gundeck. His nails and dark hair, which he wore moderately long, had been preserved. The man's wearing apparel and the accessories he carried on his person were both well-preserved. He was dressed in a sweater of thick homespun cloth and fully-cut, knit wool pants that were amply pleated at the waist and probably tied under the knees. Over the sweater he had a jacket with long arms and short, pleated tails. Under the sweater was a linen shirt. A pair of sandals and sewn linen stockings completed his dress. A sheath with a bone or horn handle, and a leather coin purse were found at his waist. He had apparently had some coins in a pants pocket as well.' The dead were not quite brought back to life, but the discovery of a number of seamen's chests, containing personal possessions, including little stores

154

Items aboard the *Vasa* made of pewter, copper and bronze definitely belonged to the officers, including the bronze heating pan (*left*) for keeping food warm, the pewter plate, made in Stockholm, and the pewter stoop (*right*): stamps on the pewter show Swedish and German manufacture, and some pieces are possibly British. The tap in the foreground is bronze.

of private food for the voyage, mostly in a good state of preservation, bring them very close as human beings. And the presence of the wives, the tall Nordic girl and the shorter Slav, prolonging the parting to the last, before their men sailed away to war, is a scene neither young nor old.

After the *Vasa*, there were two points of view: that there was only one *Vasa*, the discovery was unique and could never be repeated; and that, on the contrary, where there was one *Vasa*, there must be many more—if only one looked for them with half the skill and diligence of Anders Franzén.

The latter view prevailed particularly in Finland, where the Sport Divers Federation had been formed in 1956. The prime mover on the archaeological side was Ora Patoharju, who lived at Helsinki on the Gulf of Finland. It had been shown that the Baltic, because of its brackish waters, was an exceptionally favourable environment for the preservation of sunken ships and their contents. But what wrecks were likely to be present, and what would be their importance historically? Firstly, there was commerce. The old sailing route (A D 800–1600) to Novgorod and Russia generally followed the sheltering archipelago of the north shore of the Gulf of Finland, as did the Hanseatic sea route from Tallinn and across the Gulf and thence to the East along the Finnish coast. Any of these merchant ships, with their cargoes, would be immensely interesting, if they could be found. Secondly, there was the Baltic considered as a battleground. Above all, there were the events of the Russo-Swedish War of 1788–1790. This opened with a naval attack by the Swedes on St. Petersburg, followed by a series of sea battles off Viborg in the first half of 1790, which ended with a heavy Swedish defeat, avenged a month later by a decisive Swedish repulse of a Russian massed attack. This latter battle took place off Ruotsinsalmi (Svensksund), the rulers concerned being Gustav iii of Sweden and Catherine ii of Russia. This was the greatest naval battle ever fought in the North and is claimed to be the third greatest sea battle of all time. It was supposed to have been fought under oar as well as sail, by galleys, and each side is supposed to have had more than 200 ships engaged, at one time or another. The losses appear to have been on an equivalent scale. But little is known about it, and it was the discoveries made by divers which inspired a current search into the Finnish archives, and also those of Stockholm and Leningrad, by two Finnish historians. This was to reverse the usual process, in which underwater excavations add to a large body of existing historical knowledge, but it is also true that almost every document you want exists somewhere, if only you know where to find it. In England, regarding research on this period for English ships, tempers rise to white heat only on such points as interior cabin decorations and the details of Nelson's cot, because virtually everything else is known. But this situation is nearly unique, and, clearly, a great many surprises are bound to come from Scandinavian research, both above and under water. For instance, we do know that the battles of Svenskund were directed from the Royal schooner *Amphion* (the stern of which is preserved in the Swedish National Maritime Museum in Stockholm). This vessel, virtually a Royal Yacht, compares strangely as headquarters ship with Nelson's *Victory* of the same date—a slow but strongly built and heavily armed monster designed to be virtually untakeable.

In the Gulf of Finland, underwater archaeology of a sort dated back to 1933, when eight helmet divers were employed by the Kotka museum to raise cannons and timber from the site of the naval battle of Svensksund. In 1935, a helmet diver was employed by the National Museum of Finland to study the wreck of a Russian 'gold galleon' at Pellinki, 15 miles east of Helsinki. This wreck, believed sunk in 1721, yielded cannon balls and one gold ring. Then, in 1948, there was another find in the Svensksund battle ground, when a survey ship located what was thought to be the wreck of a frigate sunk in the battles of 1789–1790. Helmet divers were employed for some years on what must have been a reasonably intact wreck to start with, but destroyed the superstructure and deck in bringing up 20 cannon, wine bottles and various small artifacts. This made a total of 22 cannons in all from this wreck, to which the working name of a known loss, the

At the same time as the *Vasa's* decks were excavated —in the summer of 1961— the aluminium 'house' in which she now stands was constructed: the humidity inside can be constantly controlled.

Russian frigate *Sankt Nikolai*, was assigned. The iron guns were conserved by removing the surface layer of rust and then brushed with paraffin wax after drying—and are now visibly disintegrating. It was a major error to have raised them in the first place, without knowing how to conserve them. On the other hand, this destructive operation was neither more nor less foolish than more lauded affairs in the Mediterranean carried out much later. It should be noted that both in the Baltic and the Mediterranean archaeologists and antiquarians were involved in such nonsenses, and even instigated them. Indeed, it was the amateur divers of the Finnish Sport Federation who helped put underwater archaeology in the area on a serious footing. The usual robbing of wrecks by one element of the amateur diving fraternity forced the more serious minded to approach museums; but the authorities were cagey. Then, in 1960, with press support, the Ruotsinsalmi Committee was formed, with Dr. Cleve, director of the State Archaeological Commission as chairman, and representatives of the Sports Divers Federation, Museums, and the press. By 1962, they had got a legal grip of the situation: all finds belonged to the state, all wrecks were placed under protection, and permits to dive on them could be obtained only from the State Archaeological Commission.

The main task of the divers initially was, of course, archaeological reconnaissance: to find, to assess, to report. Naturally, the major effort was made at Ruotsinsalmi, or Svensksund, with help from Finnish Navy divers. Careful measurements were made of the frigate *Sankt Nikolai*, in order to obtain a definite identification, and the result suggested that this wreck might be in fact that of the Russian chebek *Prozerpina*. The chebek was a Mediterranean type of vessel, not dissimilar in the hull to that of a frigate, especially when subject to the coarse Russian style of building, and was basically differentiated only by the sail and rigging plan, which was of the triangular lateen layout. This frigate or chebek presented a brand-new problem in underwater archaeology. The remains appeared

157

insufficiently strong for them to be raised complete, as with the *Vasa*, but at the same time, and in spite of the helmet divers, the ship was intact in places almost to the upper deck and had the stump of the mizzen mast still standing, after 170 years underwater following a battle in which she had received sufficient damage to sink her. There was no question of 'digging' the wreck, because it was upstanding above the seabed instead of buried, and therefore all the excellent precedents set by George Bass were quite useless. An orthodox archaeologist would, of course, advise that the hull be picked to pieces in some regular manner not yet clear or worked out, but the divers were loath to do this. They lacked the resources, for one thing, and there was also the possibility that rapid technical advances might make salvage of the hull intact a possibility. Therefore they concentrated on measuring the outside of the hull and thought hard about how to get inside to study the decks and the hold. The area was tideless, like the Mediterranean, but the visibility averaged only ten feet or so, and that would tend to drop to nil once they went inside. The real importance of this vessel, apart from showing that the *Vasa* was by no means an exceptional case of preservation, lay in the identification of it beyond doubt; if this could be achieved, then by comparing the location of a known vessel with the battle reports generally, there would be some indication of where to look for other, possibly more important, vessels. However, search in the vicinity disclosed only the badly broken remains, in shallower water, of the frigate *Maria*. The divers deliberately raised only very few objects, those which they had the resources to conserve properly. Two cannons were dealt with by electrolysis with the aid of local industry, and this was successful; whereas by no means whatsoever could the now 'dry' guns raised earlier by the helmet divers be prevented from continuing to fall to pieces. Ora Patoharju has described the conservation aspects in *Corrosion Problems in Marine Archaeology*, a reprint from the proceedings of the Scandinavian Corrosion Congress held in Helsinki during 1964.

The reconnaissance activities elsewhere were very successful in bringing to light a wide range of wrecks for consideration. The earliest vessel was discovered through dredging operations, however, in the harbour of Turku (Abo), and coins dating from 1629 came up in the grab; difficult diving conditions prevented any identification of the ship. At the scene of the naval battle at Riilahti (Rilax), which took place in 1714, three 'galleons' were found, badly damaged, and later on a fourth ship which was much better preserved, although lying in only 20 feet of water and therefore exposed to the destructive action of ice and waves. A peculiarity of the area is that the land mass of Finland is rising, especially along the north-west coast, and wreck remains there lying in only 10 to 15 feet of water today were of a ship, probably a Russian 'galleon', which sank in twice that depth off the city of Vaasa between the years 1713–1721, judging by the evidence of coins and artifacts recovered from it. The 'Gold Galleon' east of Helsinki was relocated and measured; it proved to be of very light construction and about 120 feet long; no gold objects were found.

158

The Gulf of Finland, with recent discoveries in the field of marine archaeology marked in by Ora Pataharju.

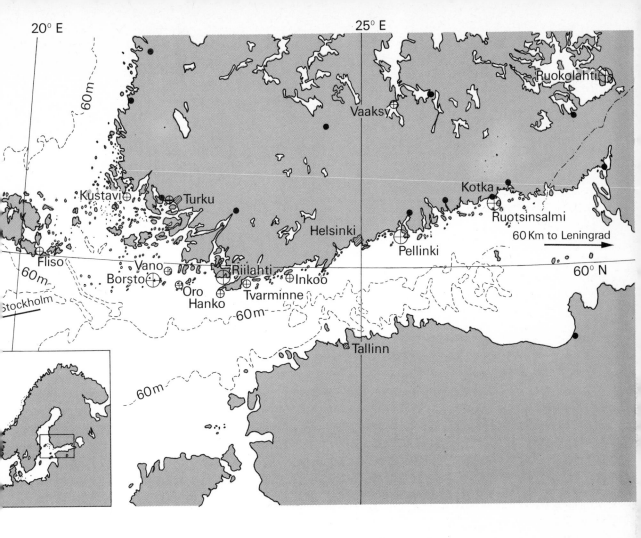

Probably the most interesting vessel found so far is that of a merchant ship lost off Borstö in 43 metres of water between 1746 and 1748. Swedish divers began to investigate her in 1960 and were joined by the Finns. The ship was 70 feet long, with a beam of 21 feet, and was probably bound for St. Petersburg with a cargo for the court of the Tsar. The after cabin held several beautifully engraved gold snuff boxes, silver and gold watches made in France, Holland and England, as well as gold ornaments decorated with rubies and diamonds. Additionally, there was a relief engraved on bone which, because of its subject matter, was not suitable for public exhibition. Most of the cargo in the hold has still to be removed, but this included a horse carriage. Unfortunately, the great depth, combined with darkness and an exposed position off the coast, have made the work difficult. These hazards offset the quite staggering realisation that here is a genuine treasure ship so completely preserved that divers can swim into the stern cabin and find the jewels where they were stored in the first place.

Nor is this standard of preservation exceptional or local, for other

Scandinavian divers have made similar discoveries around the Baltic coasts of Sweden and Denmark. Here also are wrecks that small boys dream about and divers never expect to see—seventeenth and eighteenth century vessels which still look like ships as they lie on the seabed, although their masts are stumps and their spars are fallen; with a little courage, the explorers can enter, swim down into the cable lockers and see the anchor ropes still coiled in place. One such ship, of the seventeenth century, was built of mahogany and no nails had been used in the construction of its hull, almost a throw-back to the cabinet-making techniques of the Roman shipbuilders in the Mediterranean. The Baltic is indeed, as Anders Franzén foresaw long ago, a unique treasure trove of wrecks; and the *Vasa* the first, but not the last, of the ghost ships to appear upon the surface again.

Blue plate from the *Vasa*, made in Holland in imitation of Chinese porcelain, and probably belonging to one of the officers.

Part Four
Hispaniola
AD 1555-1800

CARIBBEAN 1949-1967

10
The Plate Fleets

CEDAM:
El Mantanzero
The archives of the Indies

From the Tsar's treasure ship lying intact in 130 feet of murky, silt-laden brackish water in the Baltic, to the shattered treasure galleons of Spain sunk in the warm, clear, shallow, shark-haunted seas of the Caribbean area, there would seem to be an immense difference. And indeed there is. The most subtle is psychological. Most divers regard sharks as an acceptable and even exciting hazard; while some actually hunt them for amusement. After all, man is a predator, too, and carrying the war to the enemy is always sound strategy. But an equally ancient instinct is a sound and realistic fear of the dark, and this is immensely exaggerated underwater because man at present lacks almost all the sense organs which would enable him to operate with efficiency and safety in those conditions. The discovery of a treasure ship on a Florida Key is a matter of wild excitement, whereas the long descent into the cold, black depths of the Baltic is a deeply serious matter; the treasure ship, for practical purposes, is an unknown and therefore potentially deadly entanglement from which the diver, unless he is exceptionally careful, may never get free. It is the very fact of its excellent state of preservation which makes it so. In the Caribbean area, on the other hand, hardly any surface traces of the wrecks remain, and those which can on occasions be seen are invariably camouflaged by coral and other seagrowths, as well as sand and other bottom sediments.

One of the very best descriptions of this type of wreck, its environment, and the excitements and vicissitudes connected with the exploration of it, is Clay Blair's *Diving for Treasure*, in which he tells of the work he carried out with Robert F. Marx on a site off Cozumel Island which flanks the Yucatan Channel. It is a diving story, but it is also a detective story. For the fact is, that it is generally historians who find wrecks. Not necessarily professional historians, but those who are deeply interested in history and study in detail the particular period which fascinates them most. And this applies, even when it is treasure they are after, not historical knowledge. The chances of a bold, but relatively brainless, adventurer making a great discovery are remote. The wrecks are usually found on land, as a result of long and thorough research; the actual sea search reduced to a minimum. Nevertheless, almost always there is an interaction between treasure-hunting, history, and archaeology. Those who become successful at treasure-hunting inevitably become expert in the artifacts of the period being studied; armament, ship's gear, and above all, trade. They need the ability to assess a site rapidly and fit it into the trade pattern. They need to know where in the first place ships were likely to be wrecked (which means knowing the trade and convoy routes over several centuries); which sites are likely to be those of inward bound ships and therefore carrying—with the exception of one single commodity—goods of no present-day value; which sites are likely to be those of outward bound ships; and, of these, which were likely to be carrying cargoes still valuable today (timber, cochineal, indigo, cotton, and sugar, although expensive, tending to become worthless after a period of submergence). And also, which artifacts, although not necessarily especially valuable at the time, have since acquired many times their original value as 'period pieces'. If the treasure-hunter was not an historian originally, he most certainly is one by the time he has finished. It is also true that the treasure-hunter without method tends to miss a good deal of the riches in a rich wreck, and therefore where practical the exploiters of a treasure ship nowadays tend to mark it out on the bottom with measured, precisely aligned patterns of tape. This is only a refinement, after all, of every diver's first instinct, which is to establish the layout of the site, in an endeavour to understand it. When these methods become very refined, and are recorded stage by stage, then that is archaeology. And it is the least part of archaeology, for an archaeologist is primarily an historian who studies objects as well as documents, in order to recreate the past. For the treasure-hunter, the desirability of doing this is sometimes conditioned by the local presence of heavy surf, poor visibility, and pirates. Some of the latter do not even bother to fly the Divers Flag, let alone the skull-and-crossbones, which would be more appropriate. The rumours of night operations may well be correct. The point being that it is not necessary to approach a diving boat closely in order to establish its position, as this can be done very well at a considerable distance by taking bearings or sextant readings from two widely separated positions.

The concentration upon artifacts, particularly treasure, has tended to obscure the importance to the history of ship building and armament of some of these Spanish wrecks. The golden days of the treasure fleets are covered by the period 1555–1649. That is, from ten years after the sinking of the *Mary Rose* to about twenty years after the sinking of the *Vasa*. It should be borne in mind that the so-called treasure fleets actually represented a convoy system: merchant ships escorted by heavily-armed warships and with light ships for scouting and communications duties. On the whole it was an extremely successful system; what losses there were occurred from the normal hazards of the sea, rarely from enemy action. Occasionally, however, great risks had to be taken, especially when Spain was engaged in European naval wars. The most conspicuous early example of this is, of course, the Armada Campaign of 1588, when the entire battle squadron assigned to convoy duties in the New World was withdrawn to the Old for 'The Enterprise of England', or 'Operation England', as we would say nowadays. This was the Armada de la Guardia de las Indias, consisting of ten galleons—eight of them built in the Spanish Colonies overseas—plus three ships and two pataches, or fast scouts. Temporarily renamed the Armada of Castille, it formed, with the nine galleons of the Armada of Portugal, the only really formidable component of the Great Armada of 1588. Except for the galleon of the Duke of Florence, the remainder of that force is listed as consisting of ships, hulks, pataches, zabras, galleys, or galleasses. This point rather escaped Professor Galbraith recently when he made an eye-catching comparison of the time it would take nowadays to build up an equivalent force; he failed to mention, and probably did not know, that a great part of it was provided by the mobilisation of world-wide resources already in being, of which the 'Indian Guard' was a prime example. The real equivalent would be the recall of the British Mediterranean Fleet to join the

Home Fleet in British waters, in the days when Britain in fact had a Mediterranean Fleet, plus many detached squadrons all over the world. For Americans, today's equivalent would be the Sixth Fleet.

There were two famous disasters to Plate Fleets which occurred late in their development, when the system was already in decline—those of 1715 and 1733. Units of the former have certainly been found recently, and there are many claims to have found units of the latter. But of the really important period, when we know that the fleets were at their peak but badly lack detailed knowledge, there is a virtual blank. The possible exceptions all appear to have been found by 'Teddy' Tucker of Bermuda, whose list of discoveries includes what might be a Spanish merchantman of 1639 and what is claimed to be a vessel of uncertain nationality lost around 1595. In modern times, the first recorded discovery of a treasure ship of some kind appears to be a possible 1733 Fleet unit found by Arthur McKee Jr. east of Plantation Key, Florida in 1949. Tucker's first discovery dates from the following year, 1950. There have also been discoveries off the Bahamas, the Straits of Florida, and in Mexican waters. Underwater archaeologists of the Smithsonian Institution in Washington and C E D A M (Club de Exploraciones y Deportes Aquaticos de Mexico) have examined some of these sites, but nevertheless the melancholy fact seems to be that John Deane and William Edwards found a wreck fifty years older than the oldest known in the New World, and did it one hundred and thirteen years earlier.

To outward appearances, this must seem very odd, because McKee includes among his equipment a diving dress not dissimilar to that invented by the Deanes, as the shallow water makes this an efficient proposition. Most of the wrecks so far discovered are actually strandings rather than sinkings, and a fair number of them can be seen from the surface by a swimmer wearing facemask and flippers, and are within easy range of anyone who can hold his breath for 30 seconds or so. In any case, the greater part of the area is shallow, the outside of this sub-merged plateau being marked by a fringe of small islands, from the Bahamas in the north-west to the Leeward and Windward Islands in the south-east. Beyond this plateau, the seabed plunges abruptly to depths of around 6,000 feet. At Andros in the Bahamas, for instance, one of the favourite underwater tourist trips is to go 'Over the Wall', the wall being the reef which on the far side slopes gently to about 165 feet and then drops sheer for some 5,000 feet. Apparently, it is quite an experience to hang at 165 feet and look down into the depths as they change from light blue to dark blue and then to black. Any galleon sunk there would be gone for good, as far as this generation goes; but it is far more often in shallow water studded with reefs and banks which create heavy breaking seas, that ships are likely to suffer damage or to be simply blown ashore, quite apart from accidental strandings from navigational errors, un-suspected currents, and so on.

Consequently, it was no accident that most of the wrecks were found in the shallows of the Caribbean area, and that most of the finders found more than one; while the select few kept on making discovery after discovery, most treasure hunters found nothing at all. They did not know where to look, in the first place, nor what to look for, in the second, and if by chance they did find anything, they did not know how to assess the remains rapidly and accurately. Most of the wrecks were not of treasure ships, properly speaking, and many were not Spanish at all. Nevertheless, a great deal of fun was had and it was probably fortunate, from the point of view of archaeology, that little of real value was discovered in the early days. The happiest adventure of this kind is described in *Treasure-Diving Holidays* by Jane and Barney Crile. They found what they thought might be a Spanish 'treasure galleon' off the Florida Keys and were joined by Arthur McKee, Ed Link and Commander Mendel Peterson of the Smithsonian. The wreck was on Looe Key, a clue which would make any British diver laugh, because Looe in Cornwall is a famous diving area; in addition, there is a Looe Channel off Selsey in Sussex. Undoubtedly, however, the name is rather odd, and it was quite some time, and after they had at length discovered that they were dealing with a British warship, not a Spanish galleon, that they realised that few place names are entirely accidental. With the aid of a chart of the area and a National Maritime Museum list of ship losses, they connected first the Fowey Rocks with HMS *Fowey* (Fowey is also in Cornwall), then Carysfort Light with a ship of that name, and finally Looe Key with HMS *Looe*, a frigate lost in 1744. They had raised artifacts, including guns, indiscriminately and without any recording, but this now hardly mattered as the frigate was well inside the very-well-known area, historically speaking, and they had little trouble in obtaining a picture of the original ship. No doubt they could have had the builder's plans also, for the asking.

Blair and Marx, on the other hand, although dealing with a wreck of almost the same date, 1740, were convinced for the greater part of the time that they were investigating an English ship which, on account of the varied nature of its artifacts, they christened HMS *Woolworth*, but which eventually proved to be a Spanish merchantman from the Treasure Fleet period; as she was inward bound at the time of the disaster, she carried no treasure. In this case also, the clue was there all the time, in a place name, but more subtly disguised. What was left of the wreck—coral-encrusted anchors, cannon, and trade goods of many nationalities—lay near Punta Matanceros on the Yucatan peninsula. Just as Punta del Morto on Giglio can be translated as 'Headland of Death', so Punta Matanceros in Yucatan translates approximately as 'Slaughter Point' or 'Slaughters' Point'. They thought that this name described what happened to the unfortunate crew, at the hands of the natives ashore. Only after world-wide research and a visit to the archives in Spain, did the bizarre truth emerge. Their wreck had been the 270-ton navio, or small merchantman, the *Neustra Senora de los Milagros*. She had been built in the West Indies, not Spain, and her popular name, *Matanzero*, probably meant that the shipyard responsible had been sited at Matanzas in Cuba. This headland also had been named after a wreck, but who would have imagined anyone calling a ship the 'Slaughter', as the most obvious translation implied? Seamen give ships odd names, of course—

Nelson's men always referred to the *Bellerophon* as the 'Bally Ruffian', for instance—but in this case the name *Matanzeros* had been used in official documents, which is another matter altogether. Another cause of the difficulty they had in tracing her was that she was not in convoy, but sailing alone in an attempt to evade the British blockade directed by Admiral Vernon. Even so, the wreck was reported and the Spaniards were able to salvage a good deal of the cargo shortly afterwards. To mistake a cargo ship for a warship was particularly easy, especially when nothing of the hull was left, as merchantmen of the period were not greatly different from warships and were usually armed; quite apart from the confusion which could be caused by the possibility of wrecked pirates or privateers. Most modern ships are more specialised, of course; but although no one would mistake a liner for a battleship, nevertheless, the lower part of a liner's hull would not be too dissimilar to that of an aircraft carrier, once broken up and redistributed.

The main importance of the affair, however, lay in the cargo-identification lessons learned by Blair and Marx in the first place, by Pablo Bush Romero and his Mexican divers of C E D A M who joined in later, and at a distant remove, by the Smithsonian Institute. The ship had carried many items of definitely English manufacture which the researchers at first thought must rule out a Spanish vessel, because there was a trade embargo on Spanish merchants which forbade them to traffic with the 'enemy'. *El Matanzero* was the first archaeological, as distinct from documentary, proof that this rule was not enforceable; she had been carrying a good deal of contraband in addition to her officially listed cargo. In fact, it was possible to check her actual cargo with the declared cargo, and the differences made interesting reading. By this time also, the researchers had realised that many of the items thought to be English could equally well have been made in Germany or France, and that the number of artifacts which could be precisely placed as to country of origin was smaller than had originally been thought. From manufacturer's marks on artifacts and even scraps of newspaper preserved as padding inside a gold pocket watch, the names of people, famous and obscure at the time of the wreck, came to light: Johannes Esser Von Ach, Alexander Cleeve, David Baumer, James Cosack, William Webster, Count Seckendorff, Mrs. Clocker, the Prince of Wales, Mr. Lewis, and Mr. William Buckle. All these names, from under the sea, and from a Spanish ship wrecked 220 years previously. Furthermore, some of them could be traced, especially the manufacturers and merchants. Although not strictly speaking an 'excavation', which would have been hardly practical anyway, the recovery, conservation, cataloguing and investigation of some 15,000 artifacts recovered from a single, identified, dated ship was a valuable operation which marked a significant advance on previous unorganised scrambles for treasure. A good deal of credit is due to Pablo Bush Romero, who not only solved the logistic problems involved in carrying out large operations at such a remote place, but also took the opportunity simultaneously to put underwater archaeology in Mexican waters on a sound basis by using *El Matanzero* as a test case to obtain government decision and legislation on the status of historic wrecks. In this respect, Mexico and Finland, for instance, are far in advance of great maritime powers such as Britain, which have not progressed at all beyond the outdated concept of commercial marine salvage. If an intact Roman wreck was to be found tomorrow in British waters, it could quite legally be blown up in an attempt to salvage the cargo, and present regulations would ensure that most of the artifacts would either be destroyed by government agencies from lack of conservation or disposed of without any historical note being made.

The historic side of the enquiry, which is classic, was handled largely by Blair and Marx. They had met originally in connection with a carefully-researched hunt by Marx for the wreck of the *Monitor*, almost the only Civil War vessel likely to interest historians outside America. Marx, who had been a wanderer from the age of fourteen, and a diver from the age of fifteen, was at that time a corporal in the U.S. Marine Corps. He had located what he thought was the *Monitor* by the aerial search method, which can be an extremely effective way of finding wrecks; and a dive later had made him certain that a turret sticking out of the sand represented the remains of the first iron-clad. This was never confirmed, however, because the wreck vanished shortly afterwards, probably buried by a change in seabed level, and the requisite detection instruments were not then available. However, it was a very useful introduction to the inter-relation of history, documentary research, diving, and archaeology; and today Marx is a professional marine archaeologist employed by the Institute of Jamaica. Among his qualifications are a knowledge of Spanish which enabled him to undertake more than three years original research into the history of Spanish trade in the West Indies, working in the archives of Seville, Madrid, and the Vatican, among others, with the object eventually of writing a six-volume work on the subject. Up to now, most published works have come into the dual category of second-rate and second-hand, and some of the frantic copying which has been going on has been frankly hilarious. Partly, this has been the fault of editors, well illustrated by Throckmorton's tale of how he tried to interest a magazine in his discovery of the Bronze Age ship of Gelidonya and was told not to come back until he had found something really important, like a Spanish galleon. . . . A critical, factual study of the actual operation and organisation of the Spanish Plate Fleets is certainly long overdue, and particularly of the background, for essentially this is the story of a vast maritime empire, the development of which greatly affected European history. Very generously, Mr. Marx provided me with some preliminary notes on the basic points. Although, as he says:

'Thousands of books, and articles have been written on Columbus, Cortes, Pizarro and other famous men and events in American history, almost nothing exists in the English language concerning the "Spanish Treasure Fleets", which played a most important role in European and world history for nearly three full centuries. The fabulous treasures which came back to Europe on board these ships provided nearly 95 per cent of the precious metals on which the monetary systems of the major European powers were based. Before the discovery of America, very little

silver and gold was in circulation when compared with the period following the great discovery. The common conception is that Spain alone
benefited by the treasures brought back from the "New World". The
absolute opposite is true. Although Spain supposedly owned and controlled
the "New World" for a long time and organised and operated the treasure
fleet system, nevertheless she received little benefit from the lucrative
colonies and their mines. The reason is that both Spain and also her colonies
in the "New World" were totally dependent on other European nations
for the bulk of their manufactured goods and in return had to pay for
these items with almost all the gold and silver returning from the "New
World". The Spaniards used to refer to these treasures as "rain drops",
because when rain falls on land most of it filters down into the ground and
is totally lost to sight. Such was the case with the gold and silver returning
in the treasure fleets, because no sooner did it reach Spain than much of it
was transhipped to foreign vessels of other European nations to pay for
the manufactured products with which they had provided Spain and her
Colonies. It was also this same gold and silver that these other nations
used to finance their wars against Spain and her allies. About ten per cent
of the treasure returning with the fleets was consigned to the King of
Spain—that is, the state treasury—but this also quickly passed into
foreign hands as part of the great cost of maintaining Spanish military
forces in Europe and waging war there.

'In 1503, shortly after the discovery of America, the Spanish Monarch
ordered the establishment of the *Casa de Contratacion*, or House of Trade,
in Seville, which would have the responsibility for all shipping and commerce in connection with the new-found colonies. For the next two-and-
a-half centuries every aspect of Spanish commerce with the "New World"
was controlled by the officials of this "Ministry of Trade". The building
in which they worked still stands, and is now called the "Archives of the
Indies"; in it are 99 per cent of the documents concerning the Spanish
treasure fleets, and this is where I had the opportunity to spend more
than three years reading, copying, and translating thousands of them.

'Between 1503 and the middle of the 16th century very little treasure
returned to Spain; treasure fleets as such did not exist. A small amount
of gold was found on Hispaniola and other places the Spaniards had conquered, but the combined total did not equal in value that carried in a
single treasure galleon of the latter part of the same century. Most of the
ships plying from Spain to the Indies in this early period carried colonisers
and what was needed to establish settlements all over the New World.
Most of the treasure which came back in the ships consisted of gold taken
from the conquered Indians. It was true that every year many gold and
silver mines were discovered in the Indies, and that there were millions
of Indians available to work in them. But there was still no practical
profitable way in which the precious metals could be separated from the
other metals with which they were found. In around 1555, however,
such a process was discovered, involving the use of large amounts of
mercury to achieve separation of the minerals. At first, most of this mercury came from mines in Hungary, and had to be shipped to the Indies,
170

but very shortly afterwards a very productive mercury mine was discovered in Peru.

'It was at this period that the real "Spanish Treasure Fleets" first came into existence. Earlier, convoy systems had indeed been organised for groups of vessels going to and returning from the "New World", but as the amount of treasure carried was negligible, they certainly cannot be described as "treasure ships". It was at this time also that the "galleon" type of vessel was developed and brought into use; and, additionally, it was the time when other European nations began to set covetous eyes on the Spanish ships returning from the Indies. There was thus a clear need for a convoy system guarded by heavily-armed warships. In fact, there were three primary fleets which sailed from Spain to the "New World" every year, and this practice was maintained without exception for the next one hundred years until 1649, when some changes were made.'

Before going into the details researched by Bob Marx, it is first necessary to look at a world atlas. It will be noticed how much larger than Spain were the Spanish possessions in the 'New World'. It will be seen also that the narrow land bridge separating South from North America, flanking the semi-enclosed Caribbean, is near enough centrally placed between the Old World of Europe across the Atlantic in the one direction and the still older world of Japan, China, and India across the Pacific in the other direction. The Spanish 'New World' was in fact a very conveniently placed staging post for the interchange of materials and manufactured products between three continents. It is for this reason that the presence of, for instance, Chinese porcelain cups in a Caribbean wreck points to a Spanish ship. The distances covered by sea were of course enormous, in excess of 12,000 miles, and all under sail in unsophisticated wooden ships. Many of the ships were in fact built in the 'New World' and this was the hub of the trade system, five fleets in all converging on various points of the thin land bridge between South and North America, two from the Pacific side, three from the Atlantic. The conditions of the Pacific were exceptionally severe, but the operations of the three fleets on the Atlantic side were simplified by the discovery that the ocean currents and winds in that area are rotary. In the lower part of the North Atlantic basin the prevailing winds are the North-East Trades, blowing south-west with the current from Spain and North Africa towards the Caribbean. The currents flow round Cuba, past Florida and back towards Europe in association with the prevailing winds, the Westerlies, which trend to the north-east towards the English Channel. By riding these winds and currents, the fleets got a double-bonus from nature, and therefore all fleets outward bound from Spain dropped down to the Canary Islands off the coast of Morocco before turning out into the Atlantic on a course for the Spanish bases in the Leeward Islands—Dominica, or Guadeloupe. Having completed their business in the Caribbean, which took many months—and sometimes years—they would ride the current through the Straits of Florida, past the Bahamas, and thus step on to the other moving, invisible roadway in the sea, which together with the westerly winds in that area would take them swiftly back to Spain, with a last landfall for navigational purposes at Bermuda.

171

Economically, these were essentially trading enterprises of the 'middle-man' type, because the Spaniards were unlucky in their environment, living on top of rock and earth, instead of iron and coal like the English or the Germans. It is probably true to say that the Indians sadly cheated the trusting Spaniards by exchanging with them comparatively useless soft metals such as gold and silver for actual manufactured articles of priceless steel, as well as the luxury of the perfect mirror, made of glass, hitherto unknown.

The three Atlantic convoys were the *Nueva Espana Flota*, or New Spain Fleet, consisting of between 15 and 45 naos (or merchantmen) escorted by two galleons of the Spanish Navy and with two or three pataches for scouting and communications duties, which left Spain about March/April; the *Terra Firme Flota*, or 'Mainland Fleet', similar in composition to the first, which left Spain about April/May; and the *Armada de la Guardia de las Indias*, or 'Indian Guard', consisting entirely of warships, some eight or ten galleons, which left Spain about May/June. The latter were some-times known as the *galleons de Plata*, or 'Silver Galleons'. All three fleets followed the route down to the Canaries and then across the Atlantic with the N.E. Trades for the outlying Spanish bases in the Leeward Isles, among the Lesser Antilles chain, usually Guadeloupe or Dominica.

The naos, or navios (or naves, in Italian) differed very little in external appearance from the galleons, except for the galleons' higher castling at the stern—'tottering cagework', the Elizabethans called it—which was principally officers' accommodation. In the same way, a British East Indiaman outwardly resembled a British warship of the time, from a distance. The principal difference lay in numbers of personnel. A merchant ship was manned by the smallest possible crew, carried small guns only, and had her holds crammed with merchandise. On this outward trip, the cargoes would consist largely of European manufactured goods, from cloth to crucifixes, the sole item of present-day value being the mercury shipped out during the early period from Hungary for use in the mineral-separation process. The other items, such as wine, vinegar, olives, olive oil, cloth and clothing, although fetching high prices at the time if they reached the Indies safely, would be of no value at all if they did not and were to be salvaged today. The galleons, on the other hand, like all warships, were crammed with men instead of cargo. Many more sailors, to handle the ship and thus make fast manœuvres possible; many more gunners, to man the batteries of heavy guns; and a large contingent of fighting infantry, in armour and armed with swords and daggers, to defend the ship at close quarters. The headquarters ships, the flagship and the vice-flagship, called by the Spaniards respectively the *Capitana* and the *Almiranta*, which confusingly translates as Captain and Admiral (because the senior admiral held the appointment of Captain-General), were usually larger than the other galleons and had more elaborate accommodation for the flag officers, which included the equivalent of a present-day company boardroom for conferences and diplomatic recep-tions. The elaborate decorations so often associated with the galleries at this end of the ship, and so frequently admired and remarked on in popular works on the wonders of sail, were in fact art concealing, not art, but the officers' latrines. In a galleon, the openwork of the beakhead performed the same service, rather more uncomfortably, for the crew.

The formidable force of eight or ten battleships comprising the Indian Guard were the main escort for the two merchant convoys which had sailed earlier under the protection of two galleons only, when all three fleets joined together at the end of the season at Havana in Cuba for the return passage across the Atlantic. It is probable that the bulk of the specie and small valuables was entrusted to the warships for safer keeping; but in any event a large, armed convoy escorted by a full battle squadron would brush aside pirates or privateers and be perfectly capable of fighting a large-scale naval action. The number of ships involved in these convoys was sometimes hardly less than that of the Armada with which Phillip II challenged Elizabeth in 1588, although the manpower was not comparable. It is hardly surprising that for a long time rival powers rarely had any luck with attempted interceptions of the treasure fleets. Except, naturally, for that uncanny fellow, Francis Drake, who managed with frightening frequency to fall in with single and sometimes disabled Spaniards carrying rich cargoes. Whether the Spaniards or his brother admirals were the more annoyed at his successes, is hard to tell. Mexicans of Spanish descent addressing modern underwater archaeological conferences still speak with unfeigned bitterness of 'international pirates'.

The first two convoys, the *Nueva Espana Flota* and the *Terra Firme Flota*, left before the battleships and at timed intervals, because each had a rendezvous at a port on the Atlantic side of the narrow landbridge which gave overland access to a port on the Pacific side to which one of the two Pacific convoys was already heading. The *Nueva Espana Flota* was bound for the northern port of Veracruz, opposite the Pacific port of Acapulco, where the Manila Galleons, or China Squadron, of one to three ships, were expected to arrive. The *Terra Firme Flota* was bound for the southern port of Nombre de Dios (later Porto Bello), opposite Panama, which was the destination of the *Armada del Mar de Sud*, consisting of one to four galleons coming up the Pacific coast of South America from Callao, the port of Lima in Peru. These were the four main transhipment ports, the meeting places for the manufactured goods of East and West, and the sites of the official and commercial transactions and public fairs associated with them. Other centres were served by detaching part of the convoys en route. The northern fleet, the *Nueva Espana Flota*, naturally turned north after the first landfall in the Leeward Islands, skirted the Virgins and Silver Shoals, dropped off the detachment for Hispaniola (Haiti and Dominican Republic) south of San Domingo, and normally keeping north of Jamaica, headed for the Yucatan Channel between Mexico and Cuba, where any ships bound for Honduras would part company and sail due south past Cozumel and the place where *El Matanzero* was wrecked, while the main body bore on past the Isle of Pines and the shallows of Campeche for Veracruz. The southern fleet, the *Terra Firme Flota*, which left Spain later, had a shorter distance to cover on passage to Porto Bello, and would drop off some of its number

The routes of Spain's
Atlantic convoys.

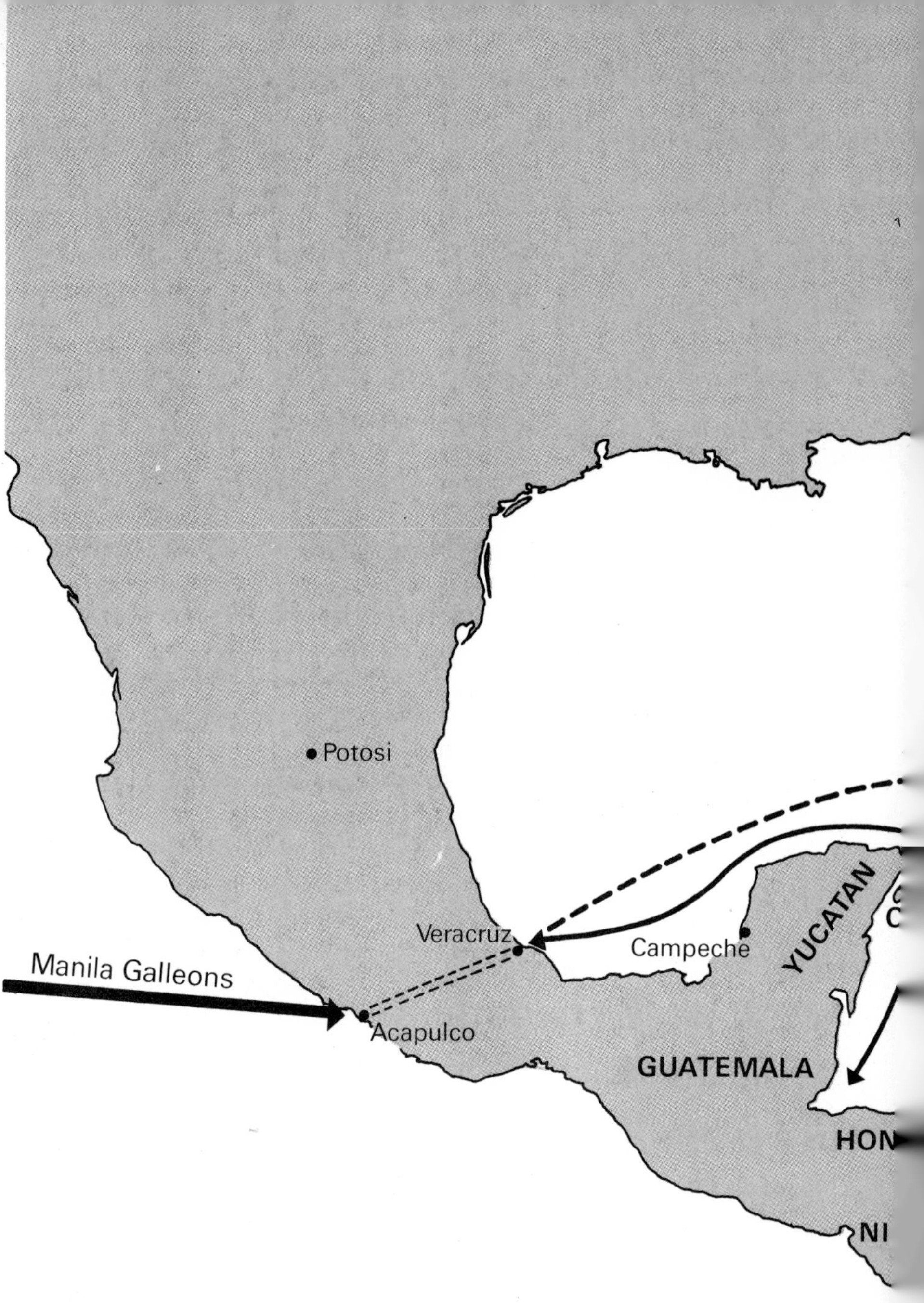

• Potosi

Manila Galleons

Veracruz

Campeche

YUCATAN

C

Acapulco

GUATEMALA

HON

NI

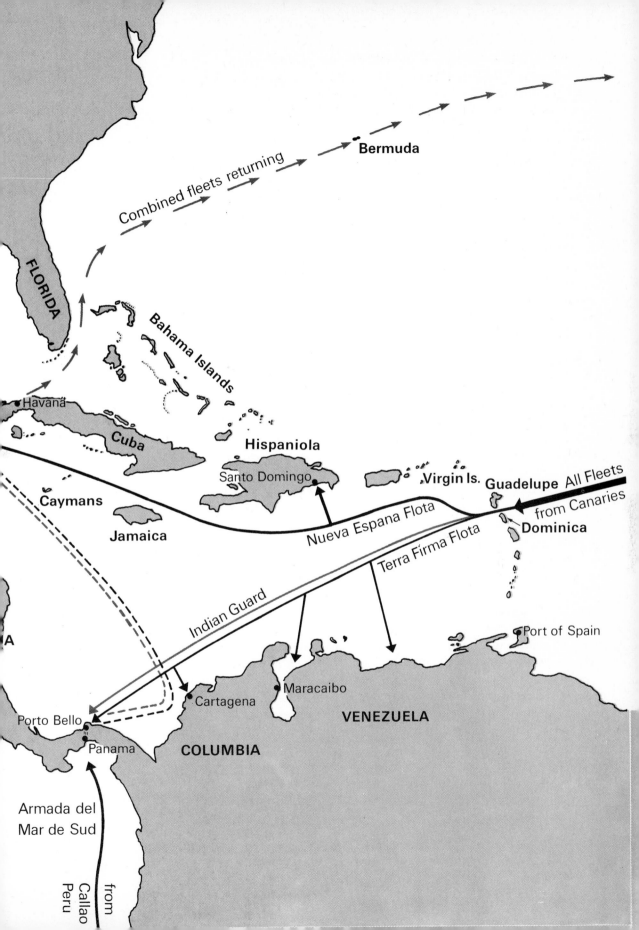

FLORIDA

Combined fleets returning

Bermuda

Bahama Islands

Havana

Cuba

Hispaniola

Santo Domingo

Virgin Is.

Guadelupe All Fleets

from Canaries

Caymans

Nueva Espana Flota

Dominica

Jamaica

Terra Firma Flota

Indian Guard

Port of Spain

A

Maracaibo

Cartagena

VENEZUELA

Porto Bello

Panama

COLUMBIA

Armada del
Mar de Sud

from
Callao
Peru

for ports in what is now Venezuela, while it put in to Cartagena for a short stay before taking the bulk of the merchandise on to Porto Bello. Some six weeks later, the galleons of the Indian Guard would follow this route exactly, only sending off a detached ship to pick up the yearly crop of pearls from the island of Margarita, where they were harvested by Negro and Indian divers.

These two fleets then returned in company to Cartagena, to load gold and emeralds as well as more mundane cargo, and finally made for Havana for the return rendezvous of all three Atlantic fleets. Many of the vessels were now genuinely treasure ships, particularly those which had taken on gold and silver at Porto Bello or Veracruz. The precious metals were often in the shape of bulk ingots, as we know from the evidence of wrecks, but there was also finished artwork in gold and silver from China and the Far East, as well as silks and other fabrics, from about 1560 onwards. The principal hazard now was the hurricane season, especially if the fleets were caught when passing northwards through the Straits of Florida on the first leg of the run to Bermuda.

This, basically, was the organisation during the period of Spanish supremacy 1555–1649. From 1620 onwards, however, Spain was increasingly being challenged; sometimes the fleets were bottled up, sometimes a single fleet would be required to risk the return passage alone and without adequate escort, and of course fast single ships were sometimes directed to make a run for it, depending on secrecy and speed. The only major disasters, however, were the shipwreck of a fleet off Padre Island, Texas, in 1555, without possibility of salvage, and the capture by the Dutch in 1628 of the complete *Nueva Espana Flota* before it reached Havana. From 1650 onwards, Spain was so hard-pressed that the *Terra Firma Flota* had to be dissolved and the warships of the Indian Guard had to take on part of their duties; from this time on, they were known simply as 'The Galleons'. Not only were their numbers reduced, but the sailings became more infrequent, on average every three to five years instead of annually. The year 1702 saw the Spanish treasure fleet under the protection of the French Navy in Vigo Bay, actually in Spanish waters, where it was attacked, captured or sunk by an Anglo-Dutch naval force. Two more major disasters shortly followed, the loss of exceptionally large treasure fleets off Florida in 1715 and 1733, in conditions of such severity that little salvage could be done. Normally, ships which fell victim to weather were stranded, not sunk, and salvage work not merely possible but promptly carried out. Exceptions were usually ships sailing alone when wrecked, so that the loss, or the exact position was never reported to the Spanish authorities. An instance of this was the early treasure galleon of 1641, wrecked on Silver Shoals, which was located and looted by William Phipps in 1687. However, over a period of three centuries, which includes the time of heavy losses by shipwreck or other causes, 93 per cent of the galleons made uneventful voyages and 91 per cent of the merchant ships and despatch vessels.

11
The stranded fleet

Caribbean and Bermuda Wrecks
The 'Combined Armada of 1715'

If a great deal of valuable information regarding the Plate Fleets has recently come from the archives, as a result of research by divers, it may be asked—what evidence has come from the sea itself, as a result of exploration by divers? And the honest answer must be: very little. Most of the evidence concerns trade goods and treasure; we can now see what this actually consisted of, with the important proviso that, generally speaking, what we are getting represents mainly the more durable items of cargo. Even so, this unrepresentative selection is in itself rarely complete. Only in a few cases has a system of systematic search and salvage been carried out; more usually, the wrecks have been picked over by the handful of lucky finders, and where they were unlucky, other treasure hunters moved in and picked away haphazardly also. Although there have been a few small-scale attempts at archaeology, after much of the damage has taken place, nothing has been published which even remotely compares to the work of the Pennsylvania University expeditions to Cape Gelidonya and Yassi Ada. This is not intended as criticism of individuals, because 'treasure ships', real or merely suspected, represent a special case. It is difficult enough on land to protect equivalent sites—the tombs of the Pharaohs are a case in point—but it is very much harder to guard an underwater site, and particularly when there is either no legal protection at all or, alternatively, the only laws available are those of ordinary commercial salvage. Further, the simple matter of logistics is frequently overlooked, but it is nevertheless true that any excavation of size, whether carried out on land or under the sea, requires far greater resources than two girls and a car or two men and a boat. Oddly enough, the basic reason why no treasure ship has ever been properly excavated, appears to be lack of funds. This seems so absurd that one feels inclined to suspect an excess of bureaucracy rather than a lack of normal business logic.

In Mexican waters, CEDAM probably possess the resources to excavate, when they find a sufficiently important wreck. In 1966, their ninth season, they found three cannon wrecks, one British, but all of the early eighteenth century. In the U.S.A., however, the organisation officially devoted to underwater archaeology consists of, as *Skin Diver Magazine* put it, 'Twenty per cent of Mendel Peterson and 100 per cent of Alan Albright'. Peterson is Chairman of the Department of Armed Forces History at the Smithsonian Institution in Washington, and can devote only 20 per cent of his time to dealing with reports of discoveries, visiting the sites, checking and conserving artifacts, and so on, and even with Albright as a full-time assistant, the set-up is adequate only for liaison and co-ordination, the preliminary—but only the preliminary—to the launching of a full-scale expedition. Consequently, the work done approximates to that of Pasley, Hall, Read, and Marsh at Spithead in 1840, long before land archaeology was on a sound footing; more is known about conservation of artifacts now, of course, but on the other hand colour photographs of them appear inferior in realism to the watercolours painted in 1840 with the help of the early camera obscura. The latter are so good, even after such a lapse of time, that they convey exactly the 'feel' of artifacts freshly

178

raised from the bottom of the sea. One can not merely identify most of the biological specimens but grasp the exact degree of corrosion of the materials to which they are attached. This is true also of the watercolour work done for the Deanes.

The situation has been summed up by Peterson as 'My plan is . . . to leave a legacy of information—an illustrated encyclopedia of artifacts, precisely dated, as a reference for later antiquarians.' In sum, the exact American equivalent, in 1967, of 'John Deane's Cabinet of Submarine recoveries, relics and antiquities' of 1839. The Smithsonian did indeed publish the first instalment in 1965. There is no archaeology in it; no site excavation drawings or reconstruction at all. The booklet is merely a collection of useful snippets of information, marred by minor errors. Laird Cloves for Laird Clowes, for instance, cannion-perrier for cannon-perrier, lombard for bombard,* and an indication that the carronades of a British First-Rate were 12-pounders. More important is that there is a kind of 'do it yourself' section for understanding and identifying various types of artifacts, and that devoted to cannon consists of five pages of photographs. This is to mislead the simple diver, or even the clever one. For instance, Major J. G. D. Elvin, mentioned in the book's Acknowledgments, is known to the present author as the world expert on naval armament of the Napoleonic war period. That is to say, the field of armament development is so vast that it has to be broken down into specialities, because no one man could possibly be expert over the entire area. Therefore, except in very simple cases, neither the underwater explorer nor the professional archaeologist should ever venture an identification; on the contrary, he needs to have access to a list of possibly relevant experts to whom the material may be submitted. Without such a list, and the organisation it implies, all but the most simple of identifications must be regarded as highly suspect—which is indeed the case for most of the 'Spanish treasure galleons' found so far. And on no account should an expert be consulted outside his field; the work of some land archaeologists in connection with ships, for instance, is a kind of permanent joke with the nautical experts and naval historians. The story of how a certain British archaeologist identified a Roman horseferry as a Viking galley is still recalled with unseemly mirth. And similarly, some suggestions by nautical experts as to how the Normans got their chargers into and out of their landing craft in 1066 cause even the most strait-laced of ex-cavalrymen to grin.

* 'Lombard' for 'bombard' is apparently not a typist's error, because it also occurs in Peterson's lecture to the Mexico City Conference organised by CEDAM in 1964. Although there is a Lombard Street in Old Portsmouth, it is associated with merchants instead of guns, and it is pertinent to quote an item from the Portsmouth *Evening News* of 28 February 1966: 'Councillor D. D. Connors, Chairman of the Royal Artillery Association Social Club, said that the history of artillery the world over began within the city, on Southsea Common, in 1346 when the English armies were drawn up for review before leaving for France and the battle of Crecy. Two "secret weapons" were on display on the common—"bombards", the earliest form of cannon. The men who worked them were "bombardiers", which is thus the oldest surviving rank in the world.' In the modern R.A., an N.C.O. with two stripes is a bombardier, not a corporal.

179

The work done by the Smithsonian tends to fall into the category of a 'rescue operation', one or two men being called in to examine an interesting wreck before it is destroyed, and to map what they can, if they can. Necessarily then, the information emerging is fragmentary. However, Peterson is of the opinion that Spanish ships were in general extremely strongly built, and cites the Bermuda wreck, supposedly Spanish of around 1595, as evidence. The timbers measured 12 inches on the edge, the planks were 15 inches wide and 3 inches thick; and below the turn of the bilge the vessel was solid timber. Another of Teddy Tucker's Bermuda wrecks, believed to be the *San Antonio* of 1621, had a keel 90 feet long and 3 feet deep; with 12-inch timbers and even thicker planking —nearly 4 inches—the width being about 15 inches. (The 'timbers' are the ribs and frames, the 'plank' is the skin). Mexican nautical experts agree that Spanish ships were very solid, and Jesús Bracamontes told the 1962 Conference: 'It could be said that they were highly reinforced throughout and that even the nails were applied prodigally, without stint. The ships of other nations, on the contrary, lightened their structure considerably, often jeopardising the durability of the vessel.' There is some literary evidence for Spanish solidity, dating from the Armada period, but nothing short of a thorough excavation of a well-preserved and definitely Spanish ship, properly dated, would tell the whole story, because the 'strength' of a ship's structure must not be considered as comparable to that of a building but rather thought of in relation to the stresses and strains imposed by awkward seas in conjunction with the action of the wind on the sails, transmitted through masts and rigging to the basic structure. Ships of other nations, especially those of the French, were designed from the start to be flexible, so that, for instance, the ship's structure would contract and expand when going into a nasty head sea and therefore absorb part of the strain. Flexibility in ships in fact dates back to the Ancient World and the principle can be taken forward into modern aviation and observed at any time by glancing out at the wingtips from the cabin of a jetliner.

More easily ascertainable points emerged from the many wrecks in the Caribbean. The presence of heaps of large ballast stones indicated a Spanish ship. Indeed, one of the more awkward elements of historic wreck identification in British waters is that the British, and the French also, tended largely to use shingle ballast; in fact, the word 'ballast' is still commercial English for shingle. Warships usually had fixed metal ballast as the basic weight, with adjustable amounts of shingle laid on top—and, of course, if a British diver sees shingle on the seabed, it does not immediately occur to him that this may indicate a broken-up wreck, whereas a mountain of large stones lying among Caribbean coral is immediately suspicious.

Nothing of great interest has emerged from a study of the main armament of Caribbean wrecks; nothing at all comparable to the finds from the *Mary Rose*, which still remain the greatest gun curiosity to come out of the sea. A few wrought-iron swivel guns, constructed on the built-up, breech-loading principle, with no particular context in most cases, but tending to show that the type, in the small sizes, lasted perhaps into the eighteenth century as secondary armament for the boarding phase of a battle; that is about all. The position as regards projectiles, especially for close-range fight, is more informative. The *San Antonio* produced a wooden cylinder loaded with scrap iron; and an incendiary shot; both for big guns. But this wreck also provided three new types of musket shot, which were in fact adaptations to the smaller sizes of anti-rigging missiles known to have been used with cannon—chain shot, sliding bar shot, and hinged shot. The idea in every case was to increase the 'spread' from a single muzzle so as to stand a better chance of hitting masts, spars, and rigging; the simplest being two cannon balls tied together with a short length of chain. Naturally the range would be short and the flight erratic, so these were close-quarter projectiles; indeed, in order to overcome part of these drawbacks, twin-barrel cannon were designed (although none has so far come from the sea, and one wonders what the unwary diver would make of the sight, if he saw it), and both barrels were fired simultaneously from a single touch-hole. None of this is really exotic, to the artillery-man at least, because modern guns have a wide range of available ammunition according to target: solid shot (armour piercing), hollow charge, explosive, air-burst, shrapnel, and so on. The old cannon man simply made the most of his opportunities to diversify, to obtain a wide range of capabilities from a single weapon.

A genuine curiosity appears to be brass hand grenades dated to the sixteenth century, if they are hand grenades. Cast iron shatters more easily and is cheaper than brass, so the material is curious, to start with. The idea that they were handthrown rather than hurled from guns is based merely on the presumed inaccuracy of the fuses of the time. The 'bomb', or 'bombshell', later 'shell', had been introduced into land warfare by this time, and it is only in very modern times that the word 'shell' has come to mean a cylindrical projectile fired from a rifled barrel. Up to and including the period of the Crimean War, a 'shell' meant a hollow sphere filled with gunpowder and fitted with a spluttering fuse. The projectile was literally only a 'shell', it was not solid. But, necessarily, there was no impact or proximity fuse, merely a crude time-device.

Most modern guides to guns and other artifacts, specially written for divers, are the equivalent of the epoch-making AD 1600 edition of William Camden's *Britannia*; this is the one to which he added illustrations of Stonehenge and Roman coins to a previously bare text, and thereby began the process of visual presentation in archaeology. But it is now AD 1968. Mediterranean amphorae types and other artifacts are reasonable fully dealt with in various works, so what is required is that the scholars produce, for the reasonably intelligent man and woman, thorough, illustrated guides to ship construction and armament, paying due regard to the fact that both are sciences. We need to know why, as well as how, and with what. For, with a warship, it is the battle we are out to recreate, not just the battleship. They should be able to answer the less erudite questions in the Gunnery Manuals, such as:

32. *State the Advantages and Disadvantages of Double Shotting a Gun.*

33. *Describe Grape Shot and Case, or Cannister Shot, and their use, either singly, or in conjunction with Round Shot.*

Any underwater archaeologist who cannot answer those questions is a joke, and a poor one; and therefore the simple facts should be readily available for study. At the moment, they are not. On the other hand, it would not be necessary to include the mass of technical and ballistic information which was primarily intended for the captain of a gun, such as:

51. *Give a Table of Horizontal Ranges corresponding to different Elevations, and also the Heights on the Enemy's Ship, measured from the Level of the Gun to be fired, at which it is necessary to Aim with the Point Blank Line, in order to Strike the Enemy's Ship nearly at a Point on a level with the Gun to be fired.*

53. *How far can Long Guns and Carronades be Trained Fore and Aft from a position square with the point, that is, from an Athwartship Position.*

The above are quotations from *An Introduction to Naval Gunnery*, by James Inman, D.D. (Woodward, The Hard, Portsea, 1828), prepared especially 'for the use of very Young Persons'. That is, a midshipman of Nelson's day would have had to know all the answers, and so, for that matter, would the commissioned and non-commissioned officers of the earlier Spanish fleets. Additionally, where the earlier, infantry-armed ships were in question, the archaeologist should know what is meant by the *Hallebarde, Pertuisane, Hache d'Armes, Faulx, Fourches à crochet,* and *Fleux de fer*, as well as a fairly fearsome array of missiles described in *Histoire de la Milice Francoise*, now a very rare book indeed.

As far as purely Plate Fleet wrecks are concerned, the cargoes were diverse. But there was a universal container, the large olive jar, which while not quite the same shape as an amphora served much the same purpose; fortunately, it did not come in so many sizes and patterns, nor cover so great a span of time, as its equivalent from the Ancient World, and therefore there is less need for a recognition book. In any event, pottery generally, while extremely useful for dating purposes, is a well and widely understood subject and expert advice is easy to obtain in most localities. Generally, Chinese porcelain is believed to represent cargo, while Talavera ware is normally taken to be ship's equipment. The dyes—red cochineal and blue indigo—are cargo; and Petersen has described how he saw from the surface, in 25 feet of water, a blue rectangle on the bottom which proved to be a rotted case of indigo. There were also mother-of-pearl, pearls, tortoiseshell, cowrie shells, and trade beads among the durable items; plus Indian figures which could be souvenirs or gifts being brought home by the sailors for their children. The almost completely random ransacking of the wreck sites normally prevents any differentiation between the cargo and goods belonging to the officers, passengers, and crew.

And, of course, there is treasure. Gold in bar form, ingot form, and coinage, the coins often being square. Silver also, badly oxidised, especially in the later fleets. One rumour concerning the Plate Fleet, was, that coins were frequently packed in jars of pitch, to prevent pilfering; and one day Tucker, diving on the *San Antonio*, found part of an olive jar with pieces-of-eight corroded to it, apparent proof that the story was true. For the smuggling of contraband we have literary evidence as well. When Shelvocke in the *Success* took the *Concepcion* of Callao, he found that her cargo consisted largely of sweetmeats, which were divided among the British crew. 'But one of the fellows', reported Shelvocke, 'complained he had a box of marmalade he could not stick his knife into, and desired it might be changed. I opened it, and found a cake of virgin silver in it, moulded on purpose to fill such boxes, and being very porous, was of near the same weight of so much marmalade, the weight being two hundred pieces of eight; in overhauling the rest, we found five more. This deceit serv'd them in a double capacity, of wronging their King and blinding their enemies.' Another captured cargo, apparently of sun-dried bricks, proved to be not what it appeared.

Regarded purely as a brilliantly successful treasure hunt, but also a first-rate example of historical and practical detective work, the recent discoveries of 'Kip' Wagner and his associates cap all others. He went after, not a treasure ship, but a treasure fleet—and got it. Some of the discoveries—a part of the seabed literally 'carpeted' with gold, large 'rocks' which turned out to be stacked silver coins solidified into lumps—by far exceeded the flights of the fiction writers who have helped to make the field of treasure hunting appear ludicrous. Generally, it is because lost treasure is almost always salvaged at once; and because the bulk of the world's seaborne trade has never consisted of treasure but of objects such as coal and 'cheap tin trays'. It is clearly not of much use to look for treasure ships off a coast where all the convoys consisted of colliers, unless of course one has a taste for 'black diamonds'. It was Wagner's luck to live beside a beach on which a complete treasure fleet, and one of the richest, had been wrecked by stranding, and where coins and other artifacts from it were continually turning up after gales. The problem of discovering the wrecks was not nearly so difficult as that set Anders Franzén by the location of the *Vasa*, sunk somewhere in a wide area of dark, deep water with only literary clues to go by. Even so, it was not easy and a decade of long study and hard work divided Wagner's initial enquiries in 1949 from the sale in New York during 1967 of a small part of the treasure which alone amounted to £80,000 on the open auction market. A single morning of the sale brought in $104,195 (£37,212).

Wagner's work is instructive, because there are in fact many such sites, to which the same principles apply, and about which nobody has done anything, probably because the treasure seemed of little value, or was actually valueless, or did not seem worth the effort, or the technical knowledge and equipment was lacking. Some of these sites, however, may well be of archaeological or historic value, and this department of the wreck-finding and excavation business well merits consideration. Broadly, the subject may be defined as that of the Stranded Wreck, as opposed to the Sunken Ship; the vessel blown on to a lee shore by a gale, possibly

because of prior damage to her motive power. There are other reasons, of course, but this is the main one and was the case with the fleet overwhelmed by a hurricane which made Kip Wagner's fortune. Associated with the subject, and an integral part of it, is the highly technical and as yet not very well understood process of sand and shingle transport in the sea and the resulting fluctuations in beach and sand bar patterns. Perhaps because there are very few real beaches in the Mediterranean areas inhabited by the early aqualung pioneers, the dictum that ships wrecked in shallow water break up so quickly and so completely that there is nothing left worth looking for, has secured world-wide acceptance. Some of the Cousteau team, notably Dumas, have propagated it and have been helped by the more uncritical of their admirers. It should be realised that the dictum is true, more or less, only for shallow, rocky seabeds; it has no relevance to mud, sand, clay, or shingle. Here, other factors determine the degree of preservation. Furthermore, it should be understood that although many of the Mediterranean pioneers and their uncritical admirers blithely chant that the reason for the break-up of shallow water wrecks is largely to be found in wave action, they have never studied wave action. Very few people have; and it is truly a formidably complicated problem. Indeed, it is only apparent when the seabed is loose and the

A contemporary sketch of a typical nineteenth-century sailing ship wreck on the coast of Sussex. The ship is a small coaster, possibly a collier, and has been stranded, rather than sunk, on a lee shore.

184

There were five wrecks within ten miles of my home between 8 January and 3 May 1967—the 2,155-ton East German freighter *Saale* (on fire as a result of a collision, later salvaged); the 500-ton Danish coaster *Bettann* (sprang a leak); the large powerboat *Tramontana* II (hit the wreck of the *Bettann*, later salvaged); a speedboat (capsized in a gale, salvaged by Maurice Harknett and myself in a night operation); and the 120-ton crane-dredger *Roway* (shift of shingle cargo). This shows the *Bettann* which, two-and-a-half months after her loss, was already part-covered with a 'fur' of algae and occupied by small spider crabs. The progressive assimilation of a wreck by the sea has never been exhaustively studied.

forces contained in waves, swells, and currents have the requisite materials with which to mould and sculpt and modify.

Five years is about the minimum time required to understand approximately some but not all of the factors acting regularly on any particular beach. That is, assuming a fairly intelligent study of it. There is no possibility of anyone descending on a treasure beach, scientific manual in hand, and making accurate deductions, largely because the manual has yet to be written. Consequently, the locals start with a cruel advantage. This will not for ever be true, because scientific investigation has been going on for some years, both with mechanical models and with real beaches. Wind direction plays a very real part in the sculpture process, but this is certainly tied in with geographic features, above water or sub-surface, which protect a beach from certain directions but not from others. The point at which waves break is certainly another, and this is a very variable factor. The action inside waves, and especially breaking waves, has never been explained to my satisfaction, although there are plenty of diagrams purporting to show it, with the particles moving in a circle. In order to establish the effect of a breaking sea on my own particular beach, I used an aqualung in Force 5 in about 4 feet minimum of water—that is, at the point where the waves were then breaking. The sand pattern was diamond-shaped—that is, it was sculpted into ridges which outline a diamond, with a depression in the centre. A knife was then driven into one of the ridges of a diamond and maintained there over a period of some minutes, while the waves continued to break. The effect on the body, with each wave, was of a violent backwards and forwards motion, with more forwards then backwards; there was no up-and-down movement at all, the motion was entirely on the horizontal plane. But as each wave crest passed directly overhead (registered by the eyes as increased darkness and by the ears as increased pressure) so the sand went momentarily into suspension—it looked just like a carpet of flak bursts, with puffs of sand appearing and then dissolving. After some minutes had elapsed, it could be seen that the sand ridges forming

the diamond around the knife blade had advanced. The pattern had not changed, but the place had. In short, each wave caused a successive advance of the sand ridges towards the beach; achieving this effect by a difference in force between the forward and the backward motion. That is—a pebble lying on the sand would oscillate under the wave crest, as the crest rolled over the top, moving first towards the shore, then back towards deeper water, but the forward movement taking it further than the backward movement. Stones too heavy to be moved by Force 5 broke up the front of the ridges as they advanced, and also formed reference points by which the process could be studied. In effect, the top layer of sand was being moved shorewards and up the beach in successive short rushes. But the pattern of diamonds never changed.

Other studies showed that beach contours could produce an undertow which took material back out to sea at an oblique angle to the beach; they were associated, in certain conditions, with two lines of waves meeting and tripping over each other, causing a crisp explosive sound like the loud crack of a whip; quite startling, when heard at night.

While Force 5 was the strongest onshore wind in which it was thought advisable to walk down the beach and into the sea while wearing a heavy aqualung and weights, the experiment was tried in Force 10 wearing merely snorkel diving gear—neoprene suit (it was November), mask, flippers and 12 lb. of lead. The conditions were the easiest possible, the wind from the west, blowing almost directly along the beach—not at it —but meeting head-on a fast westbound current, and with the lines of breakers stretching out to sea for about half-a-mile instead of 50 yards or so. There was no visibility at all and the water going everywhichway resulted in the experimenter spending most of his time submerged without actually intending to be underwater. A short trip back to shore to remove the weightbelt made it possible to swim out and take pictures of the

Spring-tide storm, Force 10, seen from seaward of Hayling beach, November 1963, while I was using snorkel gear. Although the westerly wind is blowing at 60 m.p.h. nearly parallel to the shore, the waves are riding in nearly on a level with the top of the beach defences and many feet above the height of the low-lying land immediately behind them. Had the wind been southerly, blowing directly onshore, an inundation would have followed; and had there been a previous rise of sea-level the submerged foundations at any rate would probably have been preserved in an un-eroded state.

breakers riding in with their crests appearing to be higher than the back of the beach, an awe-inspiring sight, and to establish two definite facts: the whole of the surface water at least was being moved very fast in towards the beach and at the same time was slanting west at a speed of about one knot to meet the 60 m.p.h. wind blowing from that direction. What was happening to the seabed material, it was impossible to say, but the definite shoreward trend of the watermass was very noticeable. Undoubtedly the shingle of the upper beach, which was roaring somewhat, was being thrown up, back and over, to help build the typical back-of-the-beach ridge. One way and another, it was an excellent demonstration of the sheer power inherent in wind, tide and water. Speech was almost impossible. Nevertheless, the wind was in a 'safe' direction, blowing almost along the beach, not directly at it. Had it been a southerly gale the sea would have been right over and it would have been quite impossible to get into the water at all in face of the breakers which would have resulted.

This would lead one to suspect that the Mediterranean men were right in their casual assumptions as to the actual effects of wave motion. But it is not so: 150 yards due west of the point at which this swim was undertaken, are the broken-up remains of a concrete pillbox hurriedly built in 1940 and eroded after the war. They are always in the same position, about 6 feet below the height of extreme high water, and for the greater part of the year are never visible; they show only around January and February, after the winter gales have cut down the beach by between 3 and 4 feet; that November, they were out of the reach of some three or four days of continuous Force 10 winds. Further to the east, in an area badly affected by heavy swells, coins turn up with fair regularity after spring tide gales, opposite the old Smugglers Inn. As they are of the reign of James II, and some are church tokens rather than coins proper, it has not so far been thought worthwhile to check whether they represent a buried hoard in process of being eroded out or a wreck. One snorkel dive there in a Force 8 gale which gave a visibility of half a foot or so was enough to demonstrate that only expensive instruments on a calm day would solve the mystery.

This was exactly the situation at the time when Kip Wagner found his first coin on the beach at San Sebastian in Florida; except that this coin was a silver *reale*—one of the legendary Spanish 'pieces of eight' associated with the treasure fleets. Not that he thought very much about it at the time, because everyone knew that such coins did turn up on the beach from time to time, especially after severe gales from the north-east. Then, one day in the mid-1950s, in the calm following two day's of hurricane-strength winds—Force 12—he walked down to the lonely beach near Sebastian Inlet and recognised nothing. The entire beach and foreshore had altered. The private path by which he usually made his way to the beach was gone, fifteen feet of the low cliff swept completely away. And his secret 'money beach', where up to now he had found some forty coins after gales, was deep in new material, shells and seaweed. He saw there something too bright to be a seashell, and picked it up. It was another

187

silver *reale*, perhaps no. 41 or 42. Hardly likely that it had come from the usual source, deep under matted debris now. He looked out to sea, where the aftermath of the hurricane was pounding the shallows. Where had the new material come from, the sand, the shells, the debris, the seaweed? From out there, of course. And the coin, too? Was there a source for the treasure, perhaps only a few hundred yards away, still in the shallows?

That question—which turned out to be the right question—began a quiet querying of the records, in co-operation with a friend, the family doctor, Dr. Kelso, and a well-known expert on coins and Spanish treasure, Robert I. Nesmith. At first, records was hardly the right expression for the evidence, which consisted of local tales and rumours of the coast and second-hand stories from second-rate historians. There was a Spanish treasure fleet which had been destroyed off Florida in 1715, but the location was given variously, either at a point 50 miles to the north of them, beyond Cape Kennedy, or at a point 150 miles south of them, along the Keys. There was no indication of San Sebastian as the site at all. Wagner brought out all the coins to show Dr. Kelso, and then it dawned on both men that the bulk of the coins were dated 1714, and that there were none whatever after that date. Further, those marked 1714 appeared to be in mint condition, literally, unused. This was the only armour they had with which to plough their way through the errors of historians, past and present. While this process was going on, Wagner turned to land archaeology and located a Spanish camp site just inland from the beach, and by using a war-surplus mine detector mapped it out on paper and then dug. Cutlasses, cannonballs, bricks, some fragments of silver, and a gold ring inset with a diamond, all turned up; and pointed to one thing: the work of Spanish military salvage operators, perhaps interrupted in their work by an onrush of yelling British pirates. This fitted a documented story concerning the immediate and partially successful efforts of the Spanish to recover the treasure of the 'Combined Armada of 1715'.

'All the evidence you want exists, if only you know where to look for it.' Dr. Kelso tried the Library of Congress, in Washington, where he found his Treasure Map, the one all treasure-hunters have had, since Long John Silver. It was an illustration to *A Concise Natural History of East and West Florida*, a book by the English cartographer Bernard Romans published in 1775. The site of the treasure was not marked by a 'X', nor was it a cryptogram, just a note: *Opposite this river, perished the Admiral commanding the Plate Fleet of 1715, the rest of the fleet, 14 in number, between there and ye bleach yard.* The river indicated was the San Sebastian River, and the site of the old bleach yard was easily located. There was not just one treasure trove lying off shore; there were fourteen of them. . . . Fourteen treasure ships lying along fourteen miles of coast. In defiance of the historians.

Of course, according to the serried ranks of Mediterranean underwater archaeologists, there could be nothing left. Wagner got a pilot friend to fly him over the spot to find out. He had no idea what to look for and at first saw only a featureless tangle of greys and blacks down through the water. This went on and on until, after signalling a turn, Wagner saw a long dark shadow down in the water. From it protruded rows of tube-like objects. The next day, Wagner went out to the site in a skiff and then put on a facemask. It was October and the sea was shallow enough and the visibility good enough to see the bottom from the surface and to make search easy. There were no timbers to be seen, just a heap of weed-fringed ballast stones with encrusted cannon, eighteen of them, lying along the edges of the ballast patch. A treasure ship, certainly. . . . Not a very rich one, as it turned out, but it made excellent practice for the later wrecks, as Wagner appreciated at the time.

The next step was not to dive in and come up, yelling, with treasure; but to see to the administration and organisation: the finance and the legal protection. Wagner and his friends formed a company, Real '8' Co., Inc. They were in business. They then negotiated with the relevant authority, the Trustees of the Florida Internal Improvement Fund, for a permit to recover sunken treasure: 75 per cent to them, 25 per cent to the State fund. Through the same authority, they came to an archaeological understanding, that if anything of historical value was found, they would notify the museums and the State would grant them legal protection against 'piratical interlopers'. Boats and equipment had to be bought or built, methods worked out and improved, but what it boiled down to was expressed by the slogan, 'We've got to move sand'. The remaining treasure trove was buried between the turn of the bilge and the keel, around and under the ballast stones, under many feet of sand. The sea had buried the treasure and thus preserved it from further hurricanes; and now they had to dig it up. Visually, there was virtually no trace on the seabed of the riches beneath. The digging machine they built was basically a pipe fed with fast-moving water from a hose, which set up a suction effect. The ballast heap was marked out and mapped by squares, to start with; then the stones were removed; then the suction pump was used to dig a trench. Archaeologically, it was awful; but as the timbers seem to have been nearly in a liquid state, and as the ships themselves were of no great historical importance, perhaps not a great deal was lost. It would have been difficult to carry out an orthodox 'dig' anyway. Sometimes there was calm weather and good visibility, but generally divers were rubbing shoulders before they could see each other. Often, there was such a remarkable swell, that some divers tended to be seasick when submerged, a highly critical matter when you are using your mouth to breath with. A swell is a kind of submarine wave which is very broad. Whereas the oscillation of an ordinary surface wave only covers a few feet horizontally and vertically, a swell often cannot be made out from the surface but will swing a diver back and forth twenty feet across the seabed; the sign on land is a perfectly calm sea but with heavy waves suddenly rising at shore level. Also, and completely destructive of all known underwater archaeological methods, was the fact that gales continued to occur, stopping work for as much as two months at a time, and covering up the excavations by producing a new seabed three or even four feet above the level previously reached.

In turn, they dealt with the *Nuestra Senora de la Regla*, in which the

Spanish salvagers had left little treasure; the *Nuestra Senora del Carmen y San Antonio*, which produced about 2,000 silver coins; the *Hampton Court*, a captured British warship which the Spanish Admiral was using as flagship of the Plate Fleet, and which produced 60,000 silver and gold coins, plus priceless jewelry, ingots, and a Chinese K'ang Hsi porcelain tea service intact; and a treasure nearly as great from the *San Francisco Xavier*, including 2,500 pieces-of-eight and 9,000 gold coins, some of which were individually worth £5,000. The remainder of the fleet has still to be found. One is known to have been cast clear up the beach, of which nothing may now remain, and two are known to have been overwhelmed further out in deeper water, so that they sank instead of stranding.

Apart from the use of metal detectors (primarily for non-ferrous metals such as gold and silver) and a magnetometer (for ferrous metals such as iron), there is no essential difference between these salvage operations and those of the Deanes in 1836. The gunpowder bomb shells the latter used for excavating mud, sand and clay were probably no more destructive than the suction pump. It is contact with history, certainly, but it is not archaeology. The real triumph was that of detection; of initiative; and the business-like approach. Everyone knew about the coins which were cast up on the shore by storms. Only Kip Wagner asked the right question, and then tried to answer it. And succeeded—beyond anybody's wildest dreams.

Part Five
Solent area
AD 1500-1800

ENGLISH CHANNEL
1965-1967

12
Return to the
Royal George

Royal George and *Boyne*
1965

I found the *Royal George* in my darkroom. It was on the evening of Christmas Day, 1964, just as I was coming through the door after a stiff bout of long-overdue printing. I think possibly because I had been re-reading Desmond Young's *The Man in the Helmet* during my last tea-break. But also, certainly, because the *Royal George* had been in the local news for several months, as a result of the setting up of a committee under the Presidency of His Grace, the Duke of Wellington, K.G., Governor of the Isle of Wight, to raise funds for the erection of a memorial at Ryde for the 300-odd victims of the disaster believed to have been buried there. It was just a flash of inspiration, on the lines of 'Now is the hour' and 'why not?' Why not, indeed? I am a fanatic for recording developments, and I see that I noted in my diary that night: 'Fixed Chart position of *Royal George* from 6 points—the OLD CHART OK—exact intersect.' And that was that, more or less. The rest was just stage development of a finicky, technical nature.

The old chart, which had been hanging, framed, on my wall for years, showed the *Royal George* buoy and, judging by the railway development, had been made in about 1842/3. Although the intersect was nice the scale was too small to be really accurate. I wrote to Mr. Francis L. Welch, honorary organiser of The 'Royal George' Memorial Appeal, and noted the same day: 'Intended to get *Boyne* at the same time, make it a double.' On 4 January, Mr. Welch sent the position information obtained by the Committee from documents and fishermen. This consisted of the wreck position marked in on medium-scale Admiralty Chart No. 394, plus the supporting information: Wreck lies $189\frac{1}{2}$ degrees, 1.94 sea miles from Portsmouth Cathedral (a prominent local landmark). This enabled me to transfer, with check, the position to large-scale modern Admiralty Chart No. 2625, gnomonic projection, i.e., the scale increases from the centre. I had been fond of maps and charts ever since I learned to fly light aeroplanes while still a schoolboy, and was well aware that there is no such thing as an absolutely accurate map or chart; but this would be good enough, considering how much the poor old *George* had been spread around by Pasley. The wreck area must be at least the size of a football pitch. The *Boyne*, of course, was a stone cold certainty; but nevertheless I wrote to the angling correspondent of the Portsmouth *Evening News* for the relation of wreck to buoy (only simpletons imagine that wreck buoys are invariably attached to the wrecks they mark). This was as well because he replied: 'The *Boyne* buoy lies 170 ft. W $\frac{3}{4}$ N of the wreck of the *Boyne* in 30 feet of water and serves to mark the western edge of the Horse sand. There is only 19 ft. of water on the wreck itself.' The other boats I pushed out, apart from kites flown, were an enquiry to Messrs. Seely & Paget, the architects then working on Portsmouth cathedral, for the heights to various parts of the tower above Newlyn Datum (in case we could get hold of a sextant); an order for photostats of Mackenzie's Chart of Spithead, 1784 (made two years after the sinking of the *Royal George*); and an essay in pin-pointing all the old landmarks of Old Portsmouth which still remained, in order to be able to relate the old charts to the new charts. The latter was fairly easy in one direction, because

194

Old Portsmouth was one of the very few heavily fortified towns in England and no one moves a bastion in a hurry, even with a bulldozer. In fact, most main points could be related even to charts of the sixteenth century, by means of key buildings—Southsea Castle, Square Tower, Round Tower, Cathedral, and so on. Even those buildings which had been demolished could sometimes be put back, because the original sites were known. On the other hand, efforts to find convenient and accurate 'marks' (or 'transits', as the intelligentsia call them) were severely hampered by the fact that Admiralty charts showed the built-up area of Portsmouth sometime in the 1920s or 1930s, without the bulk of the quite substantial alterations which had occurred as a result of the period of confrontation between Britain and Germany from May, 1940 to May, 1941, when on occasions the radar simply gave up, the operator reporting '300 plus, we can't count 'em, good luck'. In addition, new blocks of flats were going up like mushrooms throughout 1965 and 1966 and masking old landmarks.

The most significant kite flown was for information regarding the Deanes (at that time I did not even know that there were two of them, and had only Davis for a guide), and this took some months to take effect; indeed, I did not have the full, documented story in my hands until November, 1966. I thought the *Mary Rose* very much of an off-chance at that time, and said so, but considered that the way to her must lead through the developments of diving apparatus and the deeds of the early pioneers. Regarding the *George* and the *Boyne*, I had by 4 January 1965, set a crisp target: 'Now privately aiming at 90 second search. i.e., 90 seconds to elapse from divers hitting water to success buoy hitting surface. . . . May be optimistic, but we ought to aim at that standard of efficiency.' It was optimistic, the *George* took ten minutes, the *Boyne* three minutes. But I am unrepentant. However, I had no illusions concerning the *Mary Rose*; there was no really reliable position information, she could be anywhere, and in difficulty and importance was directly comparable to Anders Franzén's feat with the finding of the *Vasa*, which has yet to be duplicated.

While boats were still being pushed out, and kites hurriedly flown, there were politics and propaganda to be undertaken. The project I had in mind was miles beyond my own unaided resources, and would require a team and boat support, which meant making friends and influencing people. On 2 January 1965, a little over a week after emerging from the darkroom, the decisive conference took place. Present were John Towse and John Baldry, Diving Officer and Scientific Officer respectively of Southsea Branch of the British Sub-Aqua Club, and Mr. R. V. Wells, M A, a marine biologist who had done underwater work with a cut-down dustbin on the Deane pattern in the 1930s and with whom we had collaborated before. What resulted was agreement to two, interlocking projects. We had in fact been doing archaeology for four years, concentrating exclusively on a submerged building site and by concentration, getting results. Necessarily, we had had to study geology also, and had dabbled in the much more demanding field of marine biology, not because we felt up to it, but because no properly-qualified person would then take it on. Baldly stated, we would now leave the work on submerged sites and concentrate all resources on the ships. It was needling to have to read all about the *Royal George* in books on diving written by Americans and Frenchmen (much of it cribbed from Davis, as it happened), while we ourselves had never seen our most famous local wreck. But a mere return to the *Royal George* by itself would be no more than a combined schoolboy lark cum publicity stunt, which is why no one had suggested it before. Any fool can dive, and many of them do. We did not wish to be associated. Had we but known it, we were representative of a good deal of parallel thinking in other branches at this time, for Kingston were about to concentrate everything on a long-range effort to study the Eddystone reef, making a large-scale model of it and studying all aspects—archaeological, geological and biological; while our next-door neighbours at Southampton were laying plans to dive the Needles for H M S *Assurance*, a project which their friends condemned as suicidal and which the team concerned were later to admit meant going into what they had begun to term 'Sea Area Clammy Death'.

In fact, the *Assurance* was on my list, too, and as a possible 'treasure ship' to boot. Briefly, we had a baker's dozen of reasonably interesting identified wrecks, plus many more unidentified, about which nobody had done anything. Directly off Portsmouth, in and around Spithead, there was a rectangle containing five big ships, four of them certainly battleships. The rectangle was about a mile long by roughly half-a-mile wide. The battleships spanned the period roughly 1500–1800. To the east were two more. To the west, an East Indiaman and the site where the Roman pottery had come up in the dredger's grab. To the south, possibly the French flagship of 1545. To the north-west, two great French carracks of 1419, with the *Grace Dieu* of 1418 tucked away round the corner at Bursledon. Around the Isle of Wight were two wrecks dived by the Deanes, *Guernsey Lily* of 1799, *Carnbrea Castle* of 1829, and a host of others ranging from the *St. Mary* of 1314 to the *Assurance*, 40 guns, of 1753. Plus reports of Roman ship nails washed up on a beach, and at the other end of the scale, four or five U-boats if you wanted them. And lots of aircraft. What we called Project 'Solent Ships' was intended to locate some of the more important of the historic wrecks, starting with the *Royal George* which, having been demolished, would make an excellent training ground and should absorb any early mistakes due to ignorance, and to discover how much remained. In fact, a preliminary 'sounding'. At the time I wrote: 'We are not thinking in terms of an excavation, because present methods are too primitive and might damage the remains, but merely of an inspection and assessment of the problems.'

One of those problems was biological. And this tied in with the weather and tidal pattern problem which meant that, on some occasions, the main objective could not be attained and we must have a diversionary target. That target was to be achieved by taking part, through Mr. Wells, in the current Marine Mollusca Survey then being conducted on a nation-wide basis in the U.K. In short, we should go looking for sea shells. What did this have to do with wrecks? Everything. The biologists were interested in shellfish because they are most sensitive to the slightest variations of water content, temperature, light, and so on; because they are in fact what are called 'indicator animals'. The presence, or absence, of certain mollusca provide the necessary clues to deductions about the full range of animal and plant life in a given area, and of the 'vitamin' content of the water itself. Sea areas vary very much, and, specifically, one of the better-known frontiers was along Bembridge Ledge on the Isle of Wight, the famous Isle of Wight 'cut off'. A wide range of plant and animal life is different on one side of the ledge from what it is on the other side, and one can see this simply by swimming along it with facemask and snorkel. The type of seashell present is the quickest and simplest way of telling where the frontier lies. And as sunken ships are literally eaten by some creatures, while being protected by others, to ascertain the biological range of the area is the first, not the last, feat the underwater archaeologist should attempt. But, of course, this was a new principle, which to date only Anders Franzén had grasped and then only in one special application. It was not then generally understood, nor is it generally understood even now, that there is no such thing as a homogeneous ocean. 'We had reason to believe,' as the policeman says, that the preservation of wrecks inside the Solent area east of Bembridge Ledge would be far better than that of those ships which had been wrecked west of the ledge in water of higher vitamin content, superior light penetration, lower temperature, and so on; and that there would be further variations still actually within this special area of the Solent. Quite apart from the other variations caused by depth, type of seabed, exposure to geographical factors and items of that sort. The reports of the pioneer divers showed clearly that we might expect in some cases a degree of preservation about midway between that of the Zuyder Zee wrecks, cut clean off just above the turn of the bilge, and those of the Baltic, intact to the upper deck. Subject, of course, to the unfortunate fact that most of the large Solent area wrecks had been 'blown'; deliberately demolished by explosives. This would add yet another new factor to be investigated. In short, we should be mad to consider any precedent from the Mediterranean or elsewhere, even where we respected the work of the individuals concerned; it would be better by far mentally to file the lot for future reference and start with a clean slate and no preconceptions.

This was a viciously heretical decision to take at the time, because British underwater archaeology was then very much Mediterranean-oriented; but it paid large and decisive dividends, especially as it coincided with the less rigid attitudes of the North Americans now working in the Mediterranean, whom we all agreed to be the undisputed leaders.

One point not generally grasped, and still to be considered in the future, before the first actual excavation is planned, is that of sheer size. The Bronze Age 'ship' of Cape Gelidonya, 28 feet long, was not a ship but a boat, and a ship-of-the-line, like the *Victory* or the *Royal George* carried four of them on deck, and so small are they in comparison with the great hull of the battleship that most people do not notice them.

Indeed, this effect of sheer size and bulk is the one which strikes even knowledgeable people when they see the *Victory* for the first time. Many of the Greek and Roman wrecks are not ships either, but the equivalent of small schooners; and even those which are genuinely ships are cargo ships. They were not built to be shot at. The *Victory* was. Whichever way one looks at it, either as a matter of costs, or of time, or of manpower, the genuine excavation of a ship-of-the-line must add up to a sum nearer to the *Vasa* than to Yassi Ada. Say nearer £3 million than £30,000. Consequently, one would have to be sure that the ship was worth it before recommending such a procedure, and here the very peculiar nature of British nautical history had to be considered. In Portsmouth at this time there were only two historic ships, the rebuilt *Victory* of which only the lower parts are genuinely Nelsonic, the rest having fallen victim to beetles, and the fake *Foudroyant* afloat in the harbour. The intense English interest in maritime history led to the preservation for about a century of Drake's *Golden Hind*, and later to the preservation as a sail training ship of Nelson's *Foudroyant*. It was a gallant private effort by a lone individual but, like so many scholarly enthusiasts for maritime affairs, he really knew very little about it; and he piled her up off Blackpool. The present *Foudroyant* is her substitute. She is really the *Trincomalee*, one of a class of 33 frigates built in Bombay around 1815 because the enormous Royal Navy of the Napoleonic Wars period had denuded England of oak. For instance, Nelson's little 64-gun *Agamemnon*, launched at Beaulieu in 1781, consisted essentially of 2,000 trees, 200 tons of wrought iron, and 30 tons of nails and copper rivets, before fitting out at Portsmouth where her anti-corrosion copper sheathing was added. Wood could be saved by making many of the reinforcings, such as the 'knees', of iron instead of wood. Another way to save oak was to use Indian teak in India, hence the 33 frigates, and, although teak is very heavy, nevertheless it is much safer in battle than oak because the shot went through like butter instead of splintering. It is heresy perhaps to mention this, but the *Trincomalee* was built in 1817 and there is a vessel of the same class built two years earlier still afloat in Scottish waters.

The existence of these and earlier vessels—the *Victory* was laid down in 1759—rather take the steam out of ordinary nautical archaeology. This point is better and bitterly made by the fate of the unfortunate HMS *Implacable*, a 74-gun ship-of-the-line built at Toulon in 1797 and sunk off the Owers, not far from Portsmouth, in 1949. For the sake of the printer, I will write that again. 1949. 19, not 18, or 17. During 1965/6 she started to break up and parts of her timbers began to come ashore opposite the author's home. She was deliberately scuttled. Not by the Royal Navy but at the instigation of the people responsible for preserving her. They had insufficient money to keep up both the fake *Foudroyant* and the *Implacable*, and they chose to sacrifice the latter irreparably. Her crime was that she had fought at Trafalgar on the wrong side, as the *Duguay Trouin*, against Nelson, and with three consorts been captured shortly afterwards by Strachan's squadron, after, according to the British Admiral's despatch, 'having fought to admiration, and not

The *Trincomalee* (a 46-gun frigate) was built in Bombay of Indian teak in 1817, and renamed *Foudroyant* in 1912, when she was taken over as a boys' training ship. She is still employed for this purpose after having been afloat for 150 years.

surrendering until the ships were unmanageable'. Under British management, she took the Russian 74-gun *Sevolod* in the Baltic, 1808, and waged war against Hitler as a Royal Navy storeship, 1939–1945. After that, for the lack of rather less than £250,000, she was towed out to sea and sunk.

It will be appreciated that, even if it was possible to raise, say, the remains of the *Boyne*, with the fingers of one hand—which is undoubtedly the popular conception of the mechanics of marine salvage—the only result would be an order to sink her even deeper, on the grounds that she had no connection with Nelson. This situation must surely be peculiar to the British Isles.

On the other hand, such liberality with historic ships did imply very considerable knowledge of them, and this was probably unique, too. If the careful reader scrutinises books on Mediterranean underwater archaeology, he or she will obtain the useful tip that the present 'in' word is 'keelson'; all authors use it, but as they almost never use any other word which one would naturally associate with it, one assumes it is the only

The *Foudroyant*, moored in Portsmouth Harbour, attracts the expert eye of Peter Throckmorton.

word they do know. Similarly, a British 'archaeological' team investigating a ship-of-the-line lifted artifacts right, left and centre and when they did not understand them, produced elaborate and entirely imaginative theories in order to explain them. These were very simple fittings, such as many modern wooden boats still have, and the cause of all the theorising was that they had mistaken the purpose of a fitting: it was the bit that fits round the sternpost to take the rudder, not, as they thought, the bit that fits round the rudder to take the sternpost. Consequently, they were performing exotic mental exercises in order to explain why the piece was curved. In Portsmouth, however, every child is familiar almost from birth with an actual ship-of-the-line, as well as more modern constructions, and good care was taken to see that the diving teams taking part in Project 'Solent Ships' had a range of knowledge which, when combined, at least eliminated the possibility of embarrassing errors. This need not, and did not, mean that we were all world authorities. It will be recalled that Colonel Pasley had employed a naval officer expert in naval architecture to pronounce upon all ship fittings and gear, in spite of the fact that similar ships were not merely still in service but one was actually being used by him as a floating base on the site; and that more erudite questions were passed for comment to the leading physicist of the day. If this procedure was correct then, it is doubly so now. But as a large number of experts into a small boat will not go, we merely ensured that the reconnaissance teams were carefully selected for range of knowledge and a list of back-up experts was available for an authoritative evaluation if that should prove necessary —one for guns, one for bones, one for biology, and so on. The most pressing requirement was for conservation, as some materials will deteriorate markedly within a very short time of being removed from the water, and on almost every occasion we managed to have a professional conservation expert actually in the boat, so that conservation began on site. This was Mrs. Margaret Rule, an archaeologist in charge of on-site conservation

Project 'Solent Ships', showing the main area of operations—also the battleground of the English and French fleets in 1545. Basically shallow, with a low water depth of 10 ft., the area goes down steeply in places to about 100 ft. on the bed of the drowned Solent River Valley, now the transatlantic liner route to Southampton. Since there is still no protection for historic wrecks in British waters, the exact positions of the *Mary Rose* and another possibly important wreck have been omitted. The 'Swashway' is indicated by the wreck of the *Portsdown*, which was mined when traversing it, a tribute to the accuracy of the minelaying Heinkels of the ix Flieger Corps.

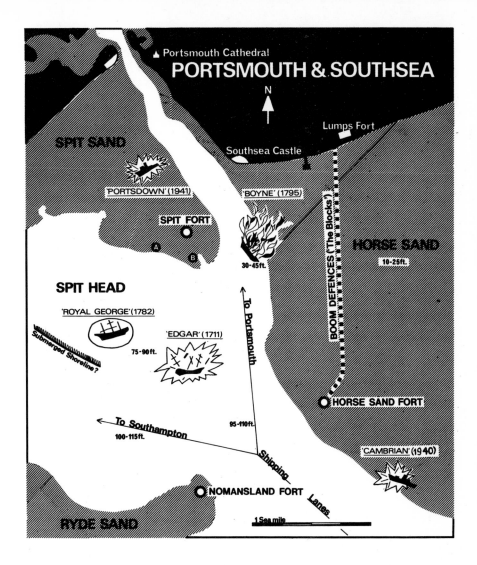

at the current land 'dig' at Fishbourne; even in land archaeology to have on-site conservation is unusual and ahead-of-the-herd, a refinement, but in submarine archaeology it is a necessity.

But the role of Mrs. Rule went well beyond this. As a professional archaeologist, she could follow each step we made, check it, and argue it out. Even among professionals, a second opinion is vitally necessary, because archaeology is not an exact science, if indeed it is a science at all. Mostly, it is just commonsense, but also it is a certain way of looking at evidence and evaluating it. At this stage, we had no diving archaeologist for a second opinion on the seabed, and although Mrs. Rule could snorkel dive, Spithead was no place to learn aqualung diving.

Indeed, it could be said that our trouble was, that we wanted to live for ever. That first conference, back in January, had been a sober affair. Mediterranean diving can be exciting and adventurous, but excitement and adventure were precisely what we planned to avoid at Spithead, if possible. The depths, by Mediterranean standards, were laughable—

ranging from 5½ feet to about 115 feet at low water. But the water ran quite fast through the deep channels, at one point, on spring ebbs, at 6¾ knots. Only about 4 knots for the *Boyne*, but as a 2-knot current underwater equals a hurricane-force wind on land, anything like that would have to be avoided. Of course, a single hazard is easily dealt with. It is not so easy to out-calculate a combination of hazards, and this precisely was what we believed we had. The second hazard was ably expressed by a friend who refused to be pressurised into diving Spithead by stating that he'd heard that the 'gash' lying around on the bottom included barbed wire. We did not doubt it. The junk of many fleets and many wars must lie there still, and especially the assorted unexploded armament of 1940–1941. One young diver did once ask me if anything had happened here during the war, were there any wartime wrecks, or anything? It is therefore best to explain that there were daylight visits by up to 90 bombers with a large fighter escort and that on some nights, at midnight, the sky over Portsmouth was a bright daylight blue, as the first fires took hold, after which the whole was more or less covered in a molten cloud of smoke which might last for some days. By later standards— Caen, Cassino, Cologne, Dresden—these were mere pinpricks, but nevertheless there was likely to be a great deal of lethal junk lying around in the sea, from cannon shells to bombs. We trusted that all the magnetic/accoustic/pressure mines which the Luftwaffe used to lay by night had long since been exploded. Combined with this, we might expect poor visibility because of the mud brought out from the harbours, also Southampton Water, by the fast currents. So what it amounted to was: fast water plus entanglements plus high explosives plus poor visibility. To which the answer was, theoretically: neap tides only, slack water only, or current just beginning to flood in from the Channel.

So far, so good, providing there was nothing we had not thought of. The fourth complicating factor was a little more difficult. Spithead, it is true, is theoretically a fleet anchorage; but most of the time there are no ships anchored there and it is merely an extension of the main shipping roadways. The *Boyne*, of course, was within a few feet of the main navigational channel leading to Portsmouth Harbour. The *Mary Rose* eventually turned out to be underneath the 600-ton 15-knot Isle of Wight packets half the time. A large, modern steel vessel in drydock is an impressive sight, especially the screws. The vessels using the area we intended to explore ranged from Hovercraft to 100,000-ton supertankers, from nuclear submarines to Atlantic liners, from pleasure yachts to naval squadrons. We were to have most of them, some merely near, others right overhead, occasionally with only about 25 feet clearance between their keels and the back of our necks. Some of us got very expert at judging their distance by the changing note—a high, shrill whine superimposed on the sound of several express trains meant dead above, and at least 600 tons. The sound of Asdic we liked even less, particularly as we had not thought of that one in advance; close enough, it can kill you stone dead. For the ship problem, we had devised several answers; all of which have worked, so far. In defence of our cowardly shilly-shallying, it should be

202

said that the British Sub-Aqua Club takes a poor view of fatal casualties, and that it was not death we feared, so much as the obituary in their magazine, *Triton*. Additionally, however, as we discovered, in the shallower water the passage of a vessel over your back creates a disturbance of the bottom which has been observed to reduce visibility, on one occasion, from 8 feet down to 2 inches, thus considerably obstructing the search procedure.

But better safe than sorry, and in comparison with the research and careful planning that went into the project, the actual operations were brief indeed. Each one was carried out in a particular place at a particular time for a particular purpose; the briefings had been very thorough; and whether triumph or failure resulted, it was all over very quickly. 'Triumph' and 'failure' are hardly correct: positive or negative was how we regarded it, and a negative could be as important as a positive, although no excuse for a celebration. The de-briefings were the weak point; one was too tired, and too relieved to be still alive, and one's head too full of mental notes and new impressions, to write it all down at once. To locate and assess the *Royal George* and the *Boyne* took three days only, three widely separated days—24 April, 22 May, and 7 June— because this was a part-time amateur effort and there was also the requirement that good weather must coincide with favourable tidal conditions. Numbers were available, if necessary, but were not used. The *Boyne* was assessed in one dive by one lone diver actually in the water (but with another standing by in the boat and the boat captain on the alert, because surface protection was vital at this site). The *Royal George* was more complicated and required six dives (normally by pairs) before a valid picture had been built up and the required critical information obtained—was or was not the *Mary Rose* lying next to her, as Sir Robert Davis had implied? Due to the depth and the old-fashioned cylinders in use, the average duration of a dive was 20 minutes only. Two dives per day would bring a diver to the brink of the point where he would require to do stage decompression; so he stopped completely at that point, thus avoiding yet another complication altogether, for which in any case we lacked adequate supplies of air. No diver with less than three years' experience of Solent area conditions was used, and most had between seven and ten years' experience. From the standpoint of economy of effort, or cost/efficiency, this stage was satisfactory. We learned a lot for very little, and, it must be said, from very little; for the evidence was remarkably undramatic, the signposts being of a subtle nature.

The 'target' time of 90 seconds for visual location and discovery had been based on the chain: accurate chart position of the wrecks; reasonably good 'marks' to bring the boat almost to the exact spot; and a recording echo-sounder to show the presence of a mound. We were unable to beg, borrow, or steal an echo-sounder, and as the hire fee for one day would be £50, the third part of the chain was gone. Indeed, on the first tidally favourable weekend it looked as if we should be without even a boat, most people not putting their boats into the water until May, but at the last moment Alan Lee very kindly offered the use of his craft, which was about 15 feet long and entirely open; too small in fact to take five people and at the same time allow them to suit-up on site. We had to get into our suits on the beach, in the rain, before setting out on 24 April for the first operation. April in England is not warm, and out at sea it is cold at all times, even during a heatwave in August, but winds were light and the morning intermittently sunny and we had no cause to complain. Clearly, there was going to be visibility of a sort on the bottom which, apart from eliminating half the hazards to life would also eliminate the archaeological hazards, especially the difficulty of recognising a wreck mound as a mound at all. We knew the *Royal George* was a mound, because we had the reports of Pasley's divers from start to finish (this was part of the briefing); and if these were correct, then it was only 2 to 3 feet high and with a very gradual slope because they had scattered the debris over an area at least four times the size of the original hull, and Pasley had reported the anchorage clear. I felt this could not be true because, by his own arithmetic, he had left nineteen guns unaccounted for; but we had to plan for the most difficult eventuality—a low, gradually-sloping mound. I had had files on all these ships for 25 years, and had written and broadcast about the *Royal George* on television at about the time I had started to dive regularly, 1958 and 1959, so we were probably the best-briefed divers ever. As it turned out, we needed to be.

Instead of having a smart command post craft making a bomber-style run-up to the target with instruments, we arrived at Spithead only after a painfully slow journey of two hours, because Alan's Bass Boat had very little freeboard, and finally anchored after trying out the 'marks' and discussing them. Fixing the 'marks' of a site you have found is easy, and you may return usually with an error of no more than 20 feet; but the reverse process—finding a site you want by searching a chart for suitable 'marks'—is a different matter; partly because the chart is an inaccurate representation on a flat surface of what is in fact a curved surface, and partly because many 'marks' which look good on the chart are less so, or useless, or totally obscured when you actually get out there. We cruised round slowly and eventually selected two 'marks' which intersected at an angle of about 70 degrees—Blockhouse Point touching Dockyard Wall and Gilkicker Point Beach in line with the back of Stokes Bay Pier where it bulged out (that needed to be checked by a visit to the pier, because at this distance it was not crisp enough). These 'marks' had been selected by the 'double-check' method—that is, John Towse, who was doing Site Secretary, had worked out 'marks' of his own, while I had worked out 'marks' of my own; the more obvious ones coincided.

John Baldry and Roger Hale (due to instruct at Giglio later in the year) went first. They towed a large surface buoy as protection against ships, to the end of which was attached a large reel for the line and an artifact bag, and, even if the visibility was very bad, both would be in contact by means of the line in the region of reel and artifact bag. Archaeologists rightly tut-tut at artifact collection, but in the reconnaissance stage it is quite definitely necessary to take selected artifacts for identification purposes. In my report I wrote: 'I saw the buoy move ahead of the boat

204

for 5 minutes or so; then start moving at right-angles towards the North, harbour entrance in background; then stop. Air began to bubble around the stopped buoy, and we knew they had got something. After some minutes, they surfaced in a perfect frenzy of bubbles, and began to swim back towards the boat, heads down, side by side, obviously carrying something heavy between them. As they came closer, we could see that Baldry had inflated his life jacket. Getting the object in the boat so rocked it that I had to lean over to the other, port, side, to compensate and did not photograph the great moment. Object was a perfectly obvious 32-pdr. iron cannonball, heavily concreted except for a little bald patch. I think they emptied the artifact bag into the boat at this time, and that the carving and the two bones came out of it; anyway, I photographed them all together, with the grey slime from the seabed still wet in the bottom of the boat.' (The photos later showed that I had in fact remembered the artifact-order correctly). 'They then completed the square search by coming back to the anchor, near which Baldry reported seeing a large round stone, the same size and shape as the iron 32-pdr. cannonball—obviously (to me, at any rate), a heavy stone shot, possibly *Mary Rose* or the battle of 1545; also a nest of twisted ironwork, probably modern, a piece of standing rigging (identified by Towse as a shroud), a small floppy thing (identified by Towse as a slab of anti-fouling paint), and misc. items of no particular import. These were, of course, exactly the sort of artifacts one would expect to find on a site of this sort. The depth was right—varied between 75 and 80 feet. Baldry said that the bones were two samples taken out of six; all being the same kind of bone—which suggests leg-of-mutton in cask sort of thing, which is right, because from the orlop.'

Now, all this had to be noted and appraised in between putting on my own gear ready for my dive and making the critical decision as to what I should do, and in what direction I should go. My reason for being happy to let Baldry go first and have all the glory if there was any, was that only the leader of the second team out of two teams can really affect the issue—in effect, he has the power to commit the reserves, acting upon the information brought back by the first team. The iron cannonball and standing rigging were quite clearly 'right' for the *Royal George*, or similar ship. The whalebone carving looked like 'scrimshaw' work, the typical product of a seaman's idle moments—but needed expert appraisal (which eventually postulated an alternative theory, that it could also be a native 'totem' brought home as a souvenir). The bones, there having been six in all and all of the same type clustered together, did suggest meat in cask from low down in the ship; but on expert appraisal proved to be immature sheep's tibia, unbutchered—which was to suggest live sheep, and these were certainly on board the *George* at the time; indeed, one got out of the ship and was observed to be swimming round with a small boy frantically clinging on to it (when picked up, he could say only that his name was Jack, and, his parents having drowned, never did discover his own surname). The bricks were 'right', theoretically, as the galley was virtually a brick-lined room inside the ship, but they did not look as though they had been down long, and, as I knew already, there was no way of dating

them by design. The position in which the iron cannonball had been found was, by observation of the buoy, about 60 to 70 feet north of our boat; and the stone cannonball had been found around our anchor. That was the sum of the information I had to go on, apart from a claim by Baldry that he had had his ears cleared for free by the asdic of a frigate which was cruising up and down, apparently calibrating. We had the diving flag up (NATO '4'), but as the Bass Boat had no mast, it was not exactly conspicuous.

My decision was: to turn away from the chance of souvenir-collection in what Baldry termed the area of the 'mother lode', around the buoy to the north, and go in the opposite direction, south and trending west, in order to first, establish what the natural seabed consisted of, secondly, to note what artifacts it contained, and thirdly, to look for the *Mary Rose*, in case Davis was right and the stone cannonball had come from her, although of course it could have been fired at her, or even been fired from Southsea Castle, about two miles away.

Lee and I dived together, and my report read: 'Lovely vis. up top, clear as a bell, but got pea-soupish 20 feet down, and the last 15 feet or so were black until the seabed came into focus around the anchor. Baldry came with us for the first five minutes or so, until his air ran out; stated he could see us 10 feet away, but effective vis. looking down at seabed 6 feet or so. Very, very good. Of course, essential we turn back so as to run out of air roughly in line with boat; do that or die. The surface party observed half the NATO navy—four frigates in line ahead—pass directly over us. I didn't hear them, Lee thought he did. I heard no asdic. The seabed was pretty level; layers of small shingle and dead slipper-limpet on grey clay-mud-ooze; with doubtless hard clay underneath, not far down. Hermit crabs, anemones, a possible seamouse. No fish. No weed. Very dead. No colours, no contrast. Enormous amount of mostly modern 'gash', including motor car tyre, tube of toothpaste, 1957 spoon—all lying largely 'proud', or entirely so. Like an old, forgotten museum half a century after the last atom bomb has fallen. In prospect, 40 million years on, what we were watching was the formation of the Solent 'Beds' with their famous limpet and NAAFI tea-mug fossils! Baldry had reported undulations, or mounds, up to 18 inches high. There was none here. Results NEGATIVE until near end of last leg of 'V' (i.e., almost back to boat line); then I went past a very old large lump of iron, heavily concreted, 60 per cent buried, but with a little tide trough round it, and all faintly dusted with grey ooze. Didn't look very promising, but turned back to examine, the burial contrast being so marked with the wide-range samples I had taken. These small samples appeared to be modern or semi-recent (and in fact were), i.e., the NEGATIVE was *definite.*'

For my pains I had a shell-encrusted ginger beer bottle circa 1900, the knowledge that while the area north of our anchoring position held many artifacts consistent with the wreck of the *Royal George* the area south of it held none whatever, and the idea, implicit in the geological joke, of stratification of artifacts. But what should we claim we had found? A brief conference on the beach produced the formula: 'The area of the wreck of the *Royal George*' (but most published accounts deleted the qualification-word 'area'). Not that it mattered, for nothing we had noted made sense without full knowledge of what Pasley had done to the ship during 1839–1843. The artifacts I had collected during the delimitation to the south had all been lying on the surface (apart from the large, heavily concreted ironwork), and when expertly examined proved to date from around the turn of the century to a precise dating of 1957. All of them came under the heading of 'anchorage gash', the maritime equivalent of dustbin refuse, enshrined in the traditional lines:

> Tinkle, tinkle little spoon,
> Knife and Fork will follow soon.

And the heavy concentration around 1900 clearly represented the gigantic fleets, and some of the fleet reviews, prior to 1914 (when the big ships went north to Scapa and Scotland). It remained to test the stratification idea, and this we proceeded to do on 22 May.

Maurice Harknett's fast and manœuvrable 25-foot cruiser *Gina-Anne* was now in the water, equipped with non-recording echo-sounder; and Mrs. Rule was available to come out with us. I decided to drop off and have a look at the *Boyne* on the way to Spithead. Because of the presence of seabed cables, anchoring is forbidden in this area and the Portsmouth approach channel lies directly to one side of the wreck. In my report I wrote: 'The well-thought-out procedure was: To avoid breaking the letter of the law, the boat was allowed to drift, unanchored, but positioned in line with and close to the *Boyne* Buoy, so that any ship which collided with it would also collide with the buoy itself (and therefore be clearly in the wrong). Wind and tide being opposed, the boat in fact held position very well without use of engine, though wallowing in the heavy seas heaped up at that point by ebb versus S.E. wind. To avoid breaking the intention of the law, I dived solo and towing a red surface buoy (so that the boat would not lose sight of me, but not have to follow), and very careful u/w navigation to ensure when out of air that surfacing was to eastward of ship channel. The largest ship which passed was a minesweeper (the smaller the ship the closer it will come to the buoy). It will be appreciated that if the diving boat had to follow an erring diver merely by his bubbles into the ship channel and thereby caused any ship to run aground, legal action and very heavy damages would follow; but this might be the alternative to losing the diver. No boat-owner should be faced with this dilemma.'

The visibility was three feet and black with it, depth the expected 30 feet. I followed exactly the delimitation procedure thought up on the spur of the moment for the *George*, on the principle of first inspect the natural seabed, where you know no ship is, before you turn in towards the wreck, so that you may recognise it when you see it. I did a zig by compass towards the deep channel, finding a light shingle bottom covered by many dead oyster valves, no weed, hardly any modern 'gash', and a few odd, tiny splinters of wood. There were no sharks, although large tope and a small thresher had been caught here by anglers; indeed, no fish at all. I then did a zag towards where the wreck mound ought to be, and was surprised and pleased to note that I could see the definite shape of it, plus some lightening of my darkness. My report read:

'Indications that this was the wreck area were: (a) the steep rise of the seabed could be visually distinguished; (b) the light got noticeably brighter (c) odd and unnatural patches of small weed began to show up, attached to great dollops of immovable, heavily-concreted ironwork sticking out of the mound, and virtually sign-posting them. (Example of the practical use of biological principles to establish archaeological or geological points). Two closely examined were: (a) a cannon-appearing hollow tube, mouth uppermost—with crabs evacuating in panic from the knife-scrapings; (b) cannonball-appearing lump. Both so heavily concreted that no identification possible; do not wish to suggest these were in fact a cannon and cannonball. Ran out of air before I had time to cruise along the other, eastern side of the shipmound. I conclude: the *Boyne* has not been abolished. The results of a perfunctory demolition, leaving an enormous shipmound some ten feet high and probably 200 feet long, encapsuling the lower hull and the artifacts inside. In effect, has become a large shoal, part of the seabed. Recommendation: leave this wreck alone until equipment and technique further advanced.'

The tide being favourable for the *Boyne*, it was necessarily unfavourable for the *George*, by the time we got there, and getting worse, steadily. On the basis of what we had found, and where, last time, I now altered the 'marks' slightly to put us north of that anchoring site and sweep it left to right. Harknett and the late Jim Dipnall did the first tide-ride. I reported: 'The tide was really running so Harknett decided to do an anchor-ride in reverse. This way he would lose neither Dipnall nor the boat. Technique: Underweight, climb down anchor cable, lift anchor one man to a fluke, let the boat drift back across the site (in this case from West to East, along the axis of the *Royal George*), drift till you see something, then dig in anchor and inspect. In effect, using a cabin cruiser as a marker buoy (and also as a safety measure for surfacing, for you just nip up the cable). An old, and quite popular, technique actually. That it was very necessary, was shown when the surface party heard a booming noise close on the port side, and saw 3,000 tons of dirty black nuclear submarine (HMS *Dreadnought*, bound from Southampton to Pompey) slide past at what seemed 100 feet away, but was probably more, this "boat" (the size of a pre-war light cruiser) being so large.' Harknett and Dipnall, who were underneath it, were quite safe using the anchor-ride technique, but could claim they had shared the same water with the biggest, blackest sea monster of all. Dipnall reported:

'The bottom was undulating, with scattered mounds littered with wreckage debris. I took sample of period pottery and a bone, colour dark grey. I picked this up with one hand, holding pottery also, and holding on to anchor. Dropped some of the pottery and in an attempt to retrieve it, dropped the bone. The strong tidal conditions were sweeping us across the bottom, the boat above was pulling the anchor through the mud, which went into suspension, although it settled quickly. Because of all this, I could not find the bone again. There were valleys in between mounds which indicated they were not natural mounds. However, the visibility was 3–4 feet or so, and as we were dragged at speed across the bottom, there was not much time to assimilate the surroundings.'

Having recovered them, we then drove back to the original start point and re-anchored. As there were only three of us, the next was mine alone, but although I had intended an anchor-ride it proved impossible at one diverpower, the anchor just skidding with the pull of the boat, kicking up boiling clouds of muck 'in a landscape almost without light in any case. . . . I should have to bore ahead into pouring current and veer to East by compass, so as to surface in line with boat and on safe side. Gulped, and decided to risk it. But shaken to find I could hardly read compass even when close to mask.' This was the ebb, faster than the flood, and bearing all the silt of Southampton Water out to sea. In my report, under the heading 'Intention', I wrote: 'Close in on "mother lode" area and get artifacts for *Royal George* dating only (i.e. ignore modern and semi-modern "gash" by patent method, still on trial). A gold guinea would be nice, but object was to go for pottery which was definitely, either by burial-appearance or by significant relationship, of very long-standing in that place. Discriminating by new, theoretical methods between this material and the later pieces which are present in super-abundance.' As

I knew nothing whatever about pottery types and datings, this was quite a good test. Finning fast, but nevertheless only creeping slowly ahead across the floor, I had a good opportunity to evaluate. There were mounds all right here, about 6–8 inches in height, like oases in a desert, with a higher shingle content and a higher proportion of static and semi-static life than the ooze desert in between. These mounds had been absent from the landscape of my April dive, so clearly we were on to something new. I wrote: 'The amount of "gash", mainly pottery and sherds, was extraordinary, one per square yard approx.—also one drifting newspaper and some drifting weed which wrapped itself affectionately round my window. Ignoring the barren clay-mud areas, I bored ahead and inspected mounds only. Near end of air, which took me out barely 50 feet, I saw an obvious item about 60 per cent buried in a mound. Grasped this thankfully. It was a nice little bowl, and looked right. The rest of the pottery was certainly gash and I did not bother with it. Surfaced as intended, ahead of boat to east; knife-point first, Excalibur fashion (having no marker buoy).' This is a dirty-water drill to ensure that if you hit something on the way up, you don't do it with your head. 'Mrs. Rule took the bowl from my hand directly from the stern ladder, and whipped it straight into a polythene bag. On the evening of Monday 24 May, exhibited it at meeting of archaeologists, but without revealing where it had come from. Barry Cunliffe, Director of the Fishbourne Palace excavation, dated it as late eighteenth century.' Both Mrs. Rule and myself were pleased with this performance, as it was quite convincing, but to achieve standards of strict legal proof it would of course have to be repeated. The reasons for selecting this bowl out of the hundreds of pieces of pottery seen will bear repeating: it had a high degree of burial; it had a significant relationship with a mound containing a high degree of shingle. Nevertheless, Mrs. Rule noted that my recording had been inadequate, and that I should have noted and memorised also exactly how the bowl was lying. She had

210

a number of other, detailed criticisms, equally justified, and I wrote: 'We agree. Indeed, one reason for inviting her out was that we should learn, from someone who can see at first hand the difficulties but won't take excuses. However, she was most impressed by the obvious discipline shown in general, so different to widespread impression in academic circles that diving is all a bit of a lark (so it is, sometimes).' The opinion of the archaeologists was that the type of evidence which was being put before them, although neither so exciting nor romantic as the usual conception of a wreck, with half-buried cannon, etc., was far more acceptable in this context of demolition following by raking, half-anchor creeping and grapnel dragging for dispersal of the hull debris known to have been carried out by Pasley.

Consequently, I now thought it was time to check the famous statement by Sir Robert Davis: 'The wreck (of the *Mary Rose*) was abandoned and forgotten until, during the *Royal George* operations, divers came accidentally upon the remains of the ship sunk 237 years earlier, lying but a short distance away.' In the context, this appeared to imply Pasley's operations; and by 'accidentally', implied a matter of a few hundred feet only. But it was all implication, none of it direct statement. An equally eminent authority, Oppenheim, appears to have been the source of a statement that the *Mary Rose* sank off Brading or St. Helens, Isle of Wight, five miles from the *Royal George*, and this was repeated in certain local histories and even in the inscription on the *Mary Rose* gun at the *Victory* Museum in Portsmouth Dockyard. This was contradicted by the contemporary painting of the battle of 1545, and I had long since dismissed it; but the painting, the accuracy of which was not that of a modern chart, did not contradict Davis. The 'line' appeared to be right, but the distance out from shore rather too far; on the other hand the work had been a perspective drawing, not a map, and all that remained was an engraved copy, the original painting having burnt in a fire at Cowdray House in Sussex. But it was Monson, with his statement that he had seen the ribs of the ship with his own eyes, who really threw doubt on Davis; the *George* was really too deep to allow that, unless one postulated that he had seen the upper works of the *Mary Rose* down through the water on a day of exceptionally good visibility.

This does happen, and indeed it was happening now. A mist, obscuring the 'marks', made us abandon an operation planned for 5 June, but at the various points where we did dive that day, visibility was up to 25 feet, and at the base of No Man's Land Fort Harknett found a cannonball. For sheer size, it made Baldry's 32-pdr. look like a shrunken pea, and, indeed, if we could get it up would undoubtedly be the largest cannonball in captivity. I told Maurice to check if it was explosive or not, but found that he already had a fluke of his grapnel inserted in the empty fuse hole. This was the type of projectile used in the mortars mounted by the Bomb Ketches, and it took three of us to haul it into the dinghy. In spite of being hollow, it weighed about 200 lb. and nearly sank the dinghy.

We obviously could not afford to waste this absolutely fabulous visibility and so laid on a maximum-with-one-boat effort for 7 June, with five divers plus Mrs. Rule and her husband, who was an amateur archaeologist. The plan was basic delimitation: to dive a series of parallel lines, A, B, and C, 100 feet apart, approximately on the line of the current. Line A would start on what we hoped would be the southern part of the *Royal George* wreck area, and artifacts would be taken to establish this, continuing on towards the shallow water of Spitsand. Line B would repeat this procedure 100 feet further out, Line C, would be 100 feet further out still. Thus a very large rectangle would be scanned for remains of the *Mary Rose*, with the direction of dive being towards Spitsand, which would bring us to her, if at all, on the broadside according to the Cowdray engraving, which, if accurate, did not allow her to be in any other arc from the *George*. The dive of Team A was to be timed for slack water, to allow for the checking of artifacts which would in fact establish the start point as part of the *Royal George* wreck area. Before starting their run, they would wait two minutes at the anchor to accustom their eyes to the gloom and make a methodical check of the seabed.

Dipnall and I were Team A. Visibility was very good, at least 15 feet, and the light bright. The ordinary seabed was sparsely scattered with small shingle, but the small mounds had a much higher shingle content and were biologically profuse. We had been finning slowly over the small mounds for a minute or so, widely spaced out, with the end of the buoy line between us, when we found ourselves coming to a very large mound at an angle. As we rose up over it we could see that it was enormous in extent, going on far out of sight in breadth as well as length, and, Dipnall estimated, some 5 or 6 feet high. Clumps of dark laminaria weed marked heavily-concreted ironwork protruding from it; we saw two simultaneously, and divided to examine them. For one wild moment, I thought we had found the *Mary Rose*. Then I knew we hadn't. This was exactly the *Royal George* mound as Pasley's divers had described it, but higher and more definite. Possibly it had built up in the years since 1843. There was certainly a lot of what looked like old driftwood around the base, where the lateral current would tend to deposit it. On the other hand, it fitted with precision the description shortly before, it had been claimed, the final explosions had caused the last dispersal which had enabled Pasley to declare the anchorage clear of obstructions. I had always been doubtful of this, because Pasley was under considerable pressure at the time, from many directions, both to declare the *Royal George* operations at an end (he had given 1840 as the final year, then 1841, then 1842, and at last 1843) and also to protect the authorities from fishermen's claims for torn nets; indeed, an irate Mr. Beale had already fished up a destructive piece of timber which he claimed was from the supposedly demolished *Royal George*. I was sorry for Pasley, because he had got himself into a false position: he had not made the distinction between freeing an anchorage of an obstruction to large warships and of making it safe for trawling: two very different things. Here was the proof that he had been manœuvred by inexperience into over-stating his case. In modern times, after a wreck has been explosively demolished, the area is marked, not clear, but 'foul', as a warning to trawlermen. This is realistic. Certainly, considering his equipment, he had done wonders: the *George* was no longer a ship, but rather a compost heap of mud, clay, shingle, buried and half-buried artifacts and fragments—bits of wood attached to ironwork, broken bottles, bones, etc., some of the ironwork being so deeply buried that it was impossible to move it. The alignment of the mound appeared to be a little south of west, as far as could be judged, which fitted the *George*. It did not fit the *Mary Rose*, nor did the scene before me fit a diver's description of the latter ship, which I had now unearthed. All the documents and descriptions were, of course, in my head at the time; and the only amendment made as an afterthought was the hypothesis that some of the shingle in the mound might be ballast rather than driftstone.

It occurred to none of us to stay on the *George* and look for the guns, as very probably they were buried; in any case, even had we found one, and tried to haul it up, we should in fact have winched the boat down to the gun, instead of the gun up to the boat. We single-mindedly carried on with the search pattern and Team B, Maurice Harknett and Tony Bye, did a long tide-ride. They were asked to report *Mary Rose* or nothing. 'The answer was nothing. Flat bottom, no mounds, no old artifacts, no bones, no cannonballs. Complete and definite negative.' Team C consisted of Bye, Dipnall and myself doing a buoy-ride with a fast-running tide; spread out in line as we were, 15 feet visibility gave a coverage from flank to flank of 40 to 50 feet. Indeed, the light was bright enough for Tony Bye to shoot a colour sequence with his cine camera. This was very, very easy, lazily finning and yet, because of the tide, really sweeping effortlessly over the bottom at a rapid rate. But before we set off I did the usual two minutes study around the anchor, reporting: 'No shingle. Lot of mostly dead light shells. No laminaria. No mounds. Flat. Clay/mud/ooze. Then off we went, peering ahead into the fog. Negative *Royal George*, negative *Mary Rose*. Some gash about and all of it modern. With such good lighting, no mistake was possible. The difference between the *Royal George* wreck area and the barren area to the south was made perfectly clear.' In this case, we went a long way and the boat had to follow our marker buoy in order to prevent our being over-ridden by ships. One thing puzzled me. This was the presence of occasional very large items, obviously modern, because they were lying flat on the bottom with no burial at all. Typical of these was a steel plate from a ship's hull, in isolation, with no hint of a wreck.

The inevitable intellectual's interjection, when asked to explain anything he does not already understand, is to retort, 'Oh, it must have fallen overboard.' This would hardly do, in the case of a hull plate. In fact, it is rare for an artifact, or even a body, to fall overboard. Usually, they are pushed. The bulk of the anchorage artifacts we had seen at Spithead was explainable and datable as modern garbage; the equivalent of the contents of dustbins. That the dating of these in the *Royal George* area was rarely earlier than late nineteenth century was most plausibly explained by the fact that no ship could anchor anywhere near the site between 1782 and 1843. The single motor car tyre was most probably a lost boat fender, but

213

did not in any event require careful explanation. Whereas the heavy modern metalwork most certainly did. The answer was obtained during the next stage, when I was questioning a professional trawlerman about the area, in the hope of some clue to the actual position of the *Mary Rose*. He pointed out on the chart two areas of 'fasty ground', where trawls or anchors were likely to be fouled by seabed obstructions. Then added, that if any heavy junk came up in the trawl, they took it over to the *Royal George* and dumped it. They knew perfectly well where she was, because they deliberately avoided that area owing to the risk of fouling their nets; therefore, it was a convenient dumping ground. From this, I judged that the hull plate probably came from the wreck of the *Portsdown*, mined in a Spitsand trawl area in 1941 and afterwards largely, but not entirely demolished. In any event we had an explanation for a complete category of artifacts. This was well worth knowing, because every problem we dealt with was new to underwater archaeology. The explosive category of artifact did not show up until later, when the first proved to be an aircraft bomb.

As a result of what we had seen on 7 June, I was convinced that the *Mary Rose* was nowhere near the *Royal George*; and decided to rely only on contemporary evidence, which amounted to a number of small and not very definite hints. The Cowdray engraving and Monson taken together, and taken as literally accurate, put the wreck in the arc north-east from the *Royal George* and in much shallower water. That is, off the Tail of the Spit. With a very soft seabed indeed, according to the diver's report (which was John Deane's, describing how he excavated a hole for the gunpowder using a spade). This area was very large indeed, but much of it too shallow to allow for the sinking there of the *Mary Rose*. The problem of reducing the possible areas boiled down to: What routes around and across this area are there today? What routes were open to the *Mary Rose* in 1545? Which one did she take? And that meant studying the battle, in order to find out exactly what she had been doing when she sank. And this proved not to be a case of consulting the historians, but of upsetting their applecart. The best one could say, if charitably inclined, was that none had given much thought to the matter. Therefore, what eventually emerged, as a result of underwater archaeology, was a clarification of what had happened during the Battle of Portsmouth, 1545; based, not on spectacular underwater discoveries, but on the contemporary evidence which had been in existence for 420 years already, re-interpreted in terms of the actual seabed contours and actual sea conditions of the area as we now knew them to be.

13
Battles long ago

Mary Rose, 'Convict Ship'
collier wrecks 1965 - 1967

The documentary research took much longer than the seabed reconnaissances into the new, suspected *Mary Rose* area, which for convenience I dubbed Spitsand, to differentiate from the deeper water of Spithead. Just as I had argued out the archaeological evidence step by step with an archaeologist, Mrs. Rule, so at intervals I argued this out with Tom Glasgow, Jr., of Charlotte, North Carolina, a specialist in Tudor history and especially Tudor nautical history, with whom I had been corresponding for some years as a result of a book I had written on the Armada Campaign. Other people whose current research had a bearing were both local —Mr. A. Corney of Portsmouth Libraries and Museums Department, who was about to publish a booklet on the history of the fortifications of Portsmouth; and Mr. C. T. Witherby, author of the booklet, *The Battle of Bonchurch*, and an unpublished work entitled *Invasion of England, 1545*, both mainly concerned with the land fighting, from the standpoint of an author who knew the Isle of Wight extremely well. Towards the end Mr. Ian Morrison, of Edinburgh University, the expert in photogrammetry, was briefly involved, as by then I had amassed sufficient information, I thought, to enable him to produce a chart by this method from the Cowdray engraving. What would have been a most interesting experiment was cut short by the discovery of the decisive evidence as to the actual position of the *Mary Rose*.

This step could not have been contemplated without the aid of the nobleman who ordered the Cowdray painting. Close analysis had shown that he had, as was customary in the days before photographic recording, demanded a most accurate delineation, not merely of the ships but of the landscape. Not art, but accuracy, must have been his instruction, and although the viewpoint could only be exactly duplicated by means of a helicopter hovering over Southsea, the artist had probably been required to sit on Portsdown Hill and make preliminary sketches of the landmarks; he must also have studied the ships themselves and been given a wealth of other information. In sum, the analysis showed that the Cowdray engraving was far more reliable than at first appeared. It was documentary evidence of the first importance.

The other historical personage to whom I am deeply indebted was Martin du Bellay, a senior officer of the contingent of light horsemen in the French fleet during the battle, who published his Memoirs in 1580. Through the courtesy of Mr. J. D. Jones, Curator of Carisbrooke Castle Museum, Isle of Wight, I was able to obtain a typed copy of the original French narrative, and promptly had this translated into late Middle English. I find it hard to believe that British naval historians have ever studied this, because du Bellay gives an 'appreciation of the situation' from the French viewpoint which chimes exactly with the one I had already made, based on very accurate knowledge of the area. The French knew the area very well, and had in addition sent out boats to reconnoitre the channels further, whereas modern British naval historians must have entirely neglected to study the 'ground', which the military historian invariably takes as his basic start point. Many illustrious names have made this startling error which, unfortunately, makes Harry VIII and his

216

Admirals undeservedly look like fools and therefore demands sharp correction. Briefly, say the nautical sages, 'The English were then commanded by John Dudley, Lord Lisle, whose tactics were no more advanced than those of his luckless predecessor. The English attacked in two divisions, line abreast. . . . Henry's larger ships mounted "great guns", but his commanders had not yet learnt effective battle tactics. . . .' What all the sages wanted King Harry to do, was to attack in line ahead so as to employ the power of the 'new' broadside (which was not in fact new, as it had first been built in to the *Mary Rose* in 1510, thirty-five years earlier). They wished him to attack in line ahead because, during a long, but not noticeably successful period far ahead into the future, that is what most navies did. Nelson in fact made his name by disregarding or modifying this impossibly rigid requirement. Lord Lisle, of course, had never heard of Nelson, nor of the 'Line'; he did what Harry VIII told him to do, and those instructions were both sensible and successful. Had 'line ahead' tactics been employed by the contestants of 1545, they would have wrecked both fleets in an astounding series of mass strandings, because there simply was not room; the modern naval historians gave the impression that the first and only view they had of the area was from the bridge of a pre-1914 battleship ginned to the eyebrows, but the real explanation is likely to be that they too formed 'line ahead', each one copying his predecessor without bothering to give the matter any original thought. We did, but only because we were forced to, in an attempt to find the *Mary Rose*. And if she was where we thought she ought to be, that would be strong corroboration of the validity of our reading of the battle also.

Briefly, battle aims were limited. English troops, depending on sea-borne supply, had captured Boulogne and were holding it against French besiegers. The French riposte was to try to take Portsmouth, the English naval base, and destroy the English battlefleet. If they succeeded, Boulogne must fall to them. For their part, the English only needed to stonewall; and as the French invasion force, when it arrived off the Isle of Wight on 18 July, 1545, consisted of 235 ships (150 large 'roundships', 60 'flutes', 25 galleys) against the English 60, due to be reinforced by another group from the west, they were obliged to adopt an aggressive defensive. Not even Nelson, who was a genius, could have carried out a successful offensive battle against those odds, quite apart from the fact that his dictum was, that only numbers can annihilate. The English problem was, to prevent themselves being annihilated by the sheer numbers of the French. And they did this very cleverly, by making the utmost use of 'ground', whether land surface or seabed, and never over-reaching in their counter-attacks. The strong, walled defences of Portsmouth were extended east along the Southsea beaches by the main field army, with Southsea Castle as a strongpoint and other strong gun-points built up eastwards. The fortifications on the west flank of the harbour, from present Blockhouse to Gilkicker, were armed and manned. The line Southsea Castle/Round Tower forms almost a right-angle with the line Blockhouse/Gilkicker, the point of the angle being the entrance to the harbour, normally capable of being blocked by a heavy chain boom. Into this wide-mouth 'V', covered by cannon mounted in strong fortifications, they placed their battlefleet, leaving open only the main navigational channel with its fast currents of up to $6\frac{3}{4}$ knots. Any enemy fleet advancing this way would have to do so nearly in single line ahead, under a double-fire from both sides, and at the mercy of the fast current, which was capable of driving them back or of bringing them on so fast that they would be unable to stop, even by anchoring. The French appreciation mentions this and details the chaos that must ensue; and, of course, they knew a good deal more than we do about the actual sailing and handling qualities of their vessels. The nature of the shallows of Spitsand and the Hamilton Bank, where the English anchored their ships, again would simply put the attacking force through the 'mincer', if they tried any route further west. It might well also put them aground. Furthermore, and this is important, there is no single current in the area, but a number of them, which flow nearly at right-angles; and this complex would enable the English fleet, by using either single or double anchor, to turn their broadsides to an attacker, almost regardless of the wind.

Provided one knows the area, the Cowdray engraving can be read at a glance. The time is two or three hours after high water, on the ebb; and, to overcome the lack of wind, the last of the English vessels, small ones, are using it to come out of Portsmouth Harbour and turn S.W. to take up position with the rest on Spitsand. They will be current-borne all the way, for they are using a minor channel across the Hamilton Bank known today as the Inner Swashway and used by shallow-draft vessels such as car-ferries around the time of high water, which lasts for an unnaturally long time at this point and is sometimes referred to as 'double highwater' or the 'highwater stand'. The water comes up the beach, and stays up, regardless of what the current is doing. The heavier ships of the English fleet are moored along the northern edge of another channel, the main Swashway, which leads off at $47\frac{1}{2}$ degrees towards Ryde, Isle of Wight, which at points to the south is covered by sandbanks which are less than 6 feet down at low water. The *Great Harry*, commanded by the Admiral, Lord Lisle, has clearly just gone down the Swashway with the current, in very light airs, and is engaging with her bow-chasers four French galleys which have been firing into the English fleet at long range from the No Man's Land area, which is shallow (12 feet or so), but borders the main navigational channel (90 feet). The seabed slope here is very steep, the transition from shallows to great depth most abrupt. In the background, in the St. Helens anchorage off Brading, and around Bembridge, the main French battlefleet is drawn up, with the big ships on its right wing (the east). The four galleys were sent forward to harass the anchored English with long-range fire and tempt them out in a counter-attack which, if it over-reached, would enable the French battlefleet to crush them with odds of four to one. Lord Lisle did make a lunge forward, leading off in the *Great Harry* and supported by Carew, the Vice-Admiral, in the *Mary Rose*; the latter being shown sunk, but mainyards still showing, heeled to port on course to No Man's Land but well to port of the *Great Harry*. This lunge of Lisle's is criticised on the grounds that the *Great Harry* is using her bow guns, not her broadside against the galleys, which ignores the elementary fact that, especially in a light wind such as this, she could only deliver a broadside against the much faster and more manœuvrable oared vessels by special permission of the galley commander, which he was unlikely to give. This is a lunge, an attempt to squash the wasps by sheer weight of tonnage, infantry, and artillery; and dangerous, because the *Great Harry* was built to take punishment and the galleys were not. Nelson won Trafalgar by just such a twin-pronged head-on attack, but has not, to my knowledge, been criticised for it. The English big ships were also supported by 'wasps', the cannon-armed oared vessels which the French called 'Ramberges'; and this enticement action, which lasted about an hour was a close call for the galley force commander, Leone Strozzi, Prior of Capua, Knight of Malta (whose brother, Pietro Strozzi, was also with the fleet). This day he achieved nothing, because the English withdrew their lunge with excellent timing, enough to damage Strozzi, insufficient to fall into the trap laid for them.

Their success was marred, however, by the capsizing of the *Mary Rose* while under long-range fire at the beginning of the action, which the French naturally enough thought had been caused by their own excellent aim. We knew that this occurred primarily as the result of a turn very badly executed, because the mariners were all so experienced and status-conscious that they would not take orders among themselves; presumably the yards were in an awful tangle and the ship heeling and falling away from the wind, which was from the north at that time. We know that Sir George Carew's uncle, Sir Gawen, drove past the *Mary Rose* in his own ship at this point and called out, the Vice-Admiral shouting back that he 'had the sort of knaves he could not rule'. Apparently also, the heavy artillery had been carelessly secured, or not secured at all, and then the heel became so extreme that those on the high side ran down the deck to the low side. With this extra weight on one side, the lee gunports, open for firing, with their batteries run out, dipped below the level of the water and the ship went down. Accounts vary as to how many were lost—400 to 700; but all agree that only about three-dozen men survived. The Cowdray engraving shows some being rescued, and other, lifeless bodies floating in the water. Most, however, must have gone down inside the ship, or with it, the armoured infantry standing very little chance, even if on the upper decks. The engraving shows also that the *Mary Rose* lay heeled over on her port side, masts and yards above the waves. The turn she executed was therefore a turn to port. Where, considering the channels and the position of Strozzi's galleys, would the *Mary Rose* have been likely to make such a turn?

That was the essence of the location problem. How did Carew intend to get from A to B—via X or Y? And if Y, via Y (a) or Y (b)?

'B' being No Man's Land, there were two main choices: follow the main Portsmouth deep channel to the East of Spitbank and go round the Tail of the Spit that way. Or, more probably, follow the *Great Harry* down the Swashway towards Ryde, and then, like her, turn to port for

No Man's Land as soon as there was enough water under the keel. This still gave two choices. The *Great Harry* has clearly gone to the western end of the Swashway and into the Southampton deepwater channel before making her turn to port; but the *Great Harry* was a very big battleship. It may have been open to the smaller *Mary Rose* to short-circuit that, and reach the galleys more quickly, by taking a channel, 10 feet deeper than the surrounding banks, which has no name, but which I will call the Sub-Swashway. Its angle is 23 degrees and today one merely drives down the Swashway until the Guildhall Tower touches the eastern corner of Clarence Pier, and then you make your turn. This cuts a corner, but a further alteration of course to port would be eventually required to bring you on a heading for No Man's Land. A wide area, seemingly, but there was a terrible logic in this process. If the ships would go then by the routes the ships go now, we should have to go underneath where the ships go now. Before, we had had ships over us from time to time. But what this meant was that entire operations would have to be carried out underneath a traffic stream of steamers, one every 5 minutes or so. And in shallow water, for we must now take Monson literally. Further, the Isle of Wight packets not merely cut the corners, they shave them. They are prepared to touch bottom briefly in order to save time, and I had seen them do it; seen the shudder as the vessel driving at 15 knots ran her keel through the mud. Any diver underneath one when it did that, was going to get cost-free and instant burial.

Stage Two of Project 'Solent Ships' was therefore aimed primarily (but not entirely) at the *Mary Rose* and consisted of visual surveys without instruments of points within the logically-indicated area which, judging from markings on large-scale charts, might be wrecks or wreck mounds. I numbered these A, B, C, D, and W. The first four were all off the Tail of the Spit, and B was actually marked 'Obstruction'; whereas W stood for the large stranded wreck near Spitbank indicated on the 1784 Chart. In the event, D was 200 yards from the *Mary Rose*. At the time, however, we could not know that; and were simply snooping into a new search area, hoping for visual clues. Site A proved to be no mound at all, but merely a pattern of clay ridges with alternate ridges deep in slipper limpet and mussel. On that basis, C was not worth looking at, but we persevered at Site B in an attempt to find out what the 'Obstruction' really was.

An anchor ride showed me a decided slope, which could be part of a mound or, alternatively, part of the natural slope of Spitbank, or even a submerged beach; and large clumps of laminaria, which had signposted both the *Boyne* and the *Royal George* launched me into space to investigate. They proved all to be attached to long chains of encrusting slipper limpet. At that point, however, Harknett's echo-sounder jumped, to show either a mound some 13 feet high, or, alternatively registering my swim back to the surface; which it was, we did not know. On 7 August a determined effort was made to clear up the matter, with two boats. The

Southsea Branch storm boat held John Baldry and his echo-sounder, Tony Bye, Jim Dipnall, Roy Abbott, and John Millerchip. John Towse's smaller *Miranda* held the owner and myself as divers, plus Mrs. Rule and, for the first time, Miss Joan du Plat Taylor, who had worked at Cape Gelidonya with George Bass and was now Secretary of the newly formed Committee for Nautical Archaeology, which tied in London University with the National Maritime Museum, the Science Museum, the Guildhall Museum, the British Sub-Aqua Club, and various other interested bodies at London level.

As usual, Towse and myself had independently worked out 'marks' and so were able to double-check each other on site. One 'mark' proved to be spot on, the other in practice a little blurred by trees, which introduced an element of guesswork. We anchored, however, as it proved 40 yards from the 'Obstruction' we were aiming at, one mile out from shore, which was not too bad in the circumstances. The 'Obstruction' itself proved to be a mere pin-point in the sea; a kind of metal dustbin mounted on tripod legs spanning at their base no more than a dozen feet or so, which had us looking around for Dr. Who and was immediately christened the 'Dalek'. After nosing round the seabed for some time, I found that it consisted of a series of terraces, and carried out a quick trial 'dig' in a number of them with a trowel-type implement. I reported: 'Went down the first foot with ease, the grey clay covering giving way to thick, sticky black mud. The next foot was harder work. With this composition, there may be no mound.' On this, as on other occasions, we obtained a great many biological samples for Mr. Wells; but I distinctly remember my mood of black depression as I discussed the matter later with Miss Taylor. With her, I had gone over my evidence for the shallow water area off the Tail of the Spit, including the tone of the salvage operations of 1545 which pointed at a shallow site, but did not expressly say so; and now, it looked as if the wreck might be completely buried, without any mound at all, judging from the seabed there. At this, Miss Taylor produced a copy of ·Throckmorton's paper on the wrecks at Methone, then new to me, which showed exactly the same type of wreck formation as I had now postulated. Considering how large a suspect area we had, this was the reverse of cheering news. We should need either a pin-point position or, alternatively, the use of a detecting instrument. In the event, we were to need, and to get, both.

The formative year for underwater archaeology round Britain was 1965, with Miss Taylor sitting at the centre and lightly holding all the reins. At Swanage in Dorset Dr. Waechter of London University had sunk an artifact-laden barge under the old pier as a submerged classroom for archaeological students, aimed mainly at the diver interested in archaeology. But London University had also formed a diving group among the University members and students who had read, or were reading, archaeology; for them, Swanage was an easy introduction to diving, rather than archaeology. Also associated with the Swanage 'School'

221

was the Scientific & Technical Group of the British Sub-Aqua Club; and this Group, in association with the new Committee for Nautical Archaeology, had conceived and were carrying out, with considerable assistance from the Royal Navy at Portsmouth, a *Mary Rose* project of their own. The timing was coincidence, but the target was happenstance; everyone knew she was the most important identified wreck in British waters. This was one reason why I had planned a much more general reconnaissance, into wreck formations as a whole, complete with biological background, instead of just trying to find the *Mary Rose*. Roman wrecks in the Mediterranean are ten a penny; if one is destroyed from archaeological inexperience, it is sad, rather than tragic. But there was only one *Mary Rose*. The effects of poor technique, let alone wanton destruction, could never be undone. To my mind, it was not a site for trial excavations based on experience with a barge under Swanage Pier.

Because the operational leader of the S. & T.G. team at Spithead was a charming serving officer, Lieutenant-Commander Alan Bax, RN, we kept in contact but did not work in co-operation. This would, in fact, have been impossible as, quite apart from the basic approaches to the subject being incompatible, both search and diving procedures were quite different, and could by no means be integrated. They were carrying out a methodical pattern search by sextant angle and echo-sounder, to seaward of the 10-fathom line, looking for the *Royal George* and *Edgar* in between 13 and 14 fathoms. Much of their diving was in the range 95–105 feet, whereas according to our information, both historic and as regards actual position, the depth was 12 fathoms at low water, or just under 90 feet at high water. This was a very odd discrepancy, and it caused Bax and me to check our theoretical positions for the *Royal George*; and as far as we could make out, their chart position for her was 650 feet south-west of ours. They had found nothing at this position, whereas we had a selection of the right sort of artifacts, plus the great shipmound, at our position. They were sure, and continued to be sure, right to the end, that the *Mary Rose* was next door to the *Royal George* in deep water. Of course, it was true that, if we had been mistaken in our identification of the *Royal George* and the mound was of some other ship, then our careful delimitation from it for traces of the *Mary Rose* was valueless.

Therefore the Committee for Nautical Archaeology, to whom we had both been submitting reports independently, called a meeting at Guildford on 5 February 1966, to organise co-operation and resolve the disputed positions, both of the *Royal George* and of the *Mary Rose*. Nothing would resolve the dispute about the *Mary Rose*. They were certain she was in deep water by the *George*. I was sure she was in shallower water to the north-east off Tail of the Spit. Therefore, for the 1966 season, we divided the area; they to continue their search to seaward of the 10-fathom line; we to search within that depth, closer to Spitsand. Neither Bax nor I nor anyone else could establish the reason for the discrepancy between the two different *Royal George* positions; there was no navigational error involved, the difference must lie in the charts. Bax therefore promised to arrange with the Hydrographer of the Navy for us all to examine the

222

original chart from which the S. & T.G. had taken their *Royal George* and *Edgar* positions. Unfortunately, on the day appointed he could not make it in time and John Towse and I carried on alone, Bax having made all the arrangements for us.

What happened next is still, for me, the highlight of the entire series of operations. As Kip Wagner has remarked, every treasure hunter traditionally has his old treasure chart with an 'X' marking the spot. A small and yellowing piece of parchment. We, however, were given a chart and a cup of tea by a charming girl in the department, plus heavy weights to keep the enormous stiff canvas unrolled when we had succeeded in unrolling it. Its scale was so large that this took us at least ten seconds. The actual scrutiny of the chart took less than five seconds because, of course, we knew that area north, south, east and west. Our eyes went to a red cross marked '*Royal George*', in 12 fathoms, then moved down the line of the anchorage to a red cross marked '*Edgar*', in 13 fathoms. Then, quite automatically, we both looked up towards the Tail of the Spit, into our own search area, and—there was a red cross marked '*Mary Rose*'! (I will not divulge the number of fathoms, nor the name of the chart, for security reasons, but the depth indicated was a lot less than 10 fathoms). We swallowed the tea as we frantically went to work to transfer this position to our own charts, working separately and by individual methods in accordance with our normal double-check procedure. Towse used the scientific instruments available in the department, I did a quick off-the-cuff comparison learned while navigating light aeroplanes, where you have no chart table. But our transfer of the position was so close there was scarcely a millimetre of difference. We had her! The *Mary Rose* was in our hands at last, and near enough where we thought she would be. I ordered photostats of the chart, and then we went off for a quick conference with Bax at Waterloo Station. Our long detective work had proved accurate, but without Bax's help we would never have obtained access to the chart, so we could hardly act dog-in-the-manger and stick to the letter of the agreement dividing up Spithead and Spitsand into separate spheres of influence. We should have to co-operate. C.N.A. neatly solved the situation by making Mrs. Rule director of the project, with Bax and myself as representatives of S. & T.G. and Southsea Branch respectively.

There was still the chart discrepancy, and neither Towse nor myself believed literally in the *Mary Rose* position we had taken; there was what looked like a scour mark some hundreds of feet to the north-east, which both of us thought significant. When I got the photostat, I was able to see that there was a discrepancy for every wreck, in the southern arc, when the charts were compared. I suspected the reason lay in the methods of map projection used. Bax settled the matter by asking the Hydrographer of the Navy to transfer the position from the old chart to the current one, using station pointer. And this corrected position was exactly on the edge of the scour mark! Now we were all happy. The next stage was to work out 'marks' to pin-point this position in actual fact, on the real sea, which proved difficult due to lack of good 'marks', and also to examine the actual seabed in the area. It never occurred to me at first

223

that we might find the *Mary Rose*. I knew the seabed would be soft and
as I was now aware that the Deanes had found the wreck by clearing a
fisherman's net, it was perfectly obvious that he would have taken care
to leave nothing protruding. We would be dealing with a completely
buried, totally invisible wreck; for the final location, detection instruments would be required, and Miss Joan du Plat Taylor set out to try
to obtain them for us. For our part, we had already begun to take a
stage further her plan of introducing archaeological students at London
University to operational diving conditions in the Solent area, after they
had been given initial training by Brian Booth, the national coach of
the B.S.–A.C. They included three Americans, Miss Gayle Wever, a
conservation expert, Miss Helena Wylde, who had worked with Throckmorton, and Mr. Robert Hurst, a graduate of Florida State University,
as well as Miss Margot Varese, who was on the staff of the Institute of
Archaeology at London University. Only the two latter managed to make
it that year, and their introduction, unfortunately, was of such a nature
that it may have offput the others.

I chose the most favourable tide of the year, the weekend of 13/14
April, and a quick dive from the beach on to the 'Convict Ship' at Langstone as the opener. This wreck had been found by Pete Cope a year or
so previously, and was a standing contradiction of all previous theories
as to wreck formations and wreck deterioration, which was why, apart
from easy access, I had chosen it. First, it was shallow; only about 6 feet
down at normal low water, and on the 'Spring Tide of the Century' in
1967 actually showed above water; it was intact to the cleats on the bulwarks; it was marked by weed; it didn't look like a wreck; sometimes
it was completely hidden by sand; I had already had the woodwork
checked by Mr. Wells, getting a clear negative for teredo, there being only
the comparatively harmless gribble present; and very probably it was
indeed, as the Harbour Master believed, a convict ship, because the prison
hulks were moored only a few hundred yards away during the period
1750–1850. In that case, it had lasted more than a century in shallow
water. Anything less like a Mediterranean wreck, or for that matter, the
barge under Swanage Pier would be hard to imagine. In fact, both Margot
and Bob found it hard to believe that it was indeed the remains of a ship,
which was the first lesson learned. The second lesson, the unpredictability
of English Channel weather, the inaccuracy of weather forecasts, and the
impossibility of firm planning, was learned in connection with the boat
trip laid on for the following day. The forecast for that morning was simply
very cold, which it was, but it was absolutely calm as we drove down to
the Ferryboat Inn to rendezvous with Maurice Harknett's boat. As
Gina Anne ran her bows ashore for the pick-up, it began to snow, and
the wind went right round from N.E. to E., increasing in velocity. Mr.
Spraggs, the Harbour Master, had already implied that he would like to
know the name and address of next-of-kin, and it was clearly impossible
to go out of the harbour, as heavy seas were already raging on the Winners.
We therefore drove over to the lee side of the 'Mulberry', a Phoenix
Caisson which broke its back before it could cross to Normandy in 1944,

The wreck of the 'Convict Ship' in the Langstone Channel exposed above the surface for once by the spring tide of the century' 27 March 1967. A cleat I removed from this bulwark on 20 March 1966 had suffered damage from the gribble, but there was no trace of teredo.

where Miss Varese and I had first to undress before suiting up. By this time, most of the surrounding scenery had vanished in driving snow, in what the local papers reported as BLIZZARDS LASH PORTSMOUTH—COLDEST MID-APRIL THIS CENTURY, with notes that the hover-craft service was suspended and the rescue helicopters grounded. For Margot, this was appropriately her 13th lung dive, and Maurice commented that it was the shortest dive he had ever seen me make! Even so, visibility was about 4 feet, though black in the lee of the Mulberry. The only gain was represented by some surface photographs of the scene, which could be used as evidence back at the University that underwater archaeology was not always a merry lark for the lads and lasses. It reminded Bob of his home waters back in Florida, they were so different.

Margot's next dive with us was on 11 June, when it was so hot that the women were sunbathing in the boat, and we were able to get surface pictures suitable for use at the University as recruiting material among the students—bikinis at Spithead! The object of this operation was to test whether or not a wrist-compass could be used as a metal-detector. On my first look at the actual site, with Towse, on 14 May I had suspected my compass of behaving erratically, as if there was a mass of metal in the vicinity, but with no landmarks to go by could not be sure. On this occasion, Margot and I were to dive and hang on to the anchor of *Gina Anne's* dinghy, which, rowed by Pete Cope, would contain also Mrs. Rule with a bearing compass. They, on the surface, would take a straight

225

course which should land us over the scour-mark or 'depression', if this in fact existed, while I should note any sudden deviations or oscillations shown by my compass. The time chosen to give the dinghy some help from the tide, as towing behind you two divers at depth is no light matter for the oarsman. We waited momentarily for an Isle of Wight packet to roar past, before jumping off; we should have a short, clear space before the next one. Visibility on the bottom was 8 feet and Margot took up station as planned, stepped up to the right in echelon, in a deliberate copy of the fighter formation for pairs which gives the best view to the pilots. We drifted slowly over the bottom, eyes down on my compass, Margot prodding with a 3 ft. handspear. Seabed was the unusual combination described by Deane—with sand patches among the mud and clay; and extremely soft—push a finger into it, and you go in up to the armpits. My compass remained steady on its original heading, then veered; but as the dinghy anchor-rope was doing peculiar things, I guessed it was trouble on top. No great surmise to guess what that was. On the next occasion, the needle swung right round to east, but without the oscillation I had expected; and Margot came close, making signals I could not understand, there being no recognised diver's code for: 'I can hear a noise like an express train, can't you?' Shortly afterwards, the needle came back on course, and then the bottom dropped away beneath us about 6 feet or so—in short, we were going across a depression. Normally, I would have released my hold on the anchor and had a prod around, but it seemed inadvisable, so we surfaced up the anchor rope and swam back to *Gina Anne*, covered by the dinghy. The dive had lasted 20 minutes, and in that time the dinghy had been forced four times to row frantically out of the path of Isle of Wight boats approaching at 15 knots. This view shows just how broad and squat most ships really are, no matter how lean and rakish they may appear from the side.

We first obtained the loan of a Wardle & Davenport proton magneto-meter on 1 September, through the good offices of the company and of George Cooke, of the S. & T.G., an aeronautical engineer at Farnborough who had built his own one-man submarine. We had no option about the date. It was a spring tide and the weather forecast for that morning was: 'Force 6, Gusting to Force 7, with Force 8 Imminent'. For once, the forecast was dead accurate. We hoped to get away with it by a quick run out, before Force 8 Imminent became Force 8 actual. That is, a 'whole gale', or full gale force. Fortunately, a magnetometer is not affected by bad weather. The Wardle & Davenport version is very compact—transistorised—and consists of a box like a small radio set, linked by cable to a wooden stick with a jar at each end. Provided it is not used in a built-up area, or near power sources, it will detect the presence of buried ferrous metals such as iron. That is, when in their vicinity, a needle on a dial will give a double signal which can be interpreted as either positive or negative. It will detect over a considerable distance, and down through water, as well as under the seabed; but there must be no other metal near it. We went out of harbour at ten o'clock, in driving rain, the seas breaking clean over Eastney and Southsea promenades, and much

226

drifting wreckage visible on the wave crests. Maurice Harknett was boat-handler, Mrs. Rule and Mr. Cooke were to observe the reactions of the magnetometer, I was to do the diving. But first we had to calibrate the gadget, to get an idea of what the readings actually meant, after rigging it. We found that the bottles had to go in the fibreglass dinghy, in order to get a clear reading, the dinghy towed well astern, because *Gina Anne* has a heavy iron keel, apart from diesel engine and metal fittings.

We did a simple test, by switching it on in the lee of Spit Fort, which is ringed by metal 'gash' of all kinds, and then letting the boat drift off with the wind for a few hundred yards until it was over a clear area. The needle duly indicated the change. We then moved over to the *Boyne*, for a really severe test, the wreck being close to seabed cables, and we got, as we expected, no clear indication. That showed the limitation. But the *Mary Rose* area contained very little gash and, according to the charts, no cables at all. We went on to the Southsea side 'marks' for the standard run-up to the target, and I signalled 'stand-by' about one minute before the not-very-good Gosport side 'marks' became critical. Nothing much happened, then there was a tremendous agitation of the needle, which continued for a suspiciously long time; we turned and ran back, drop-ping a buoy during a strong reaction. By the time I had suited up, the buoy was a little distance away, and it looked as if wind and current combined, coming from the west, were driving *Gina Anne* east. At 1.20 p.m., I jumped over, with marker buoy and metal prodder. My report began:

'Swam slowly down the anchor rope, unrolling buoy line, the anchor rope pulling and plucking violently all the way to the bottom. Green pea soup turning to black, with a tinge of grey. I didn't like the tinge of grey, which was observed when the anchor rope gave way to the chain which is attached to the anchor. I concluded that either the Loch Ness Monster was out there, stirring it up, or, alternatively, the anchor was dragging wildly across the bottom (which would be hardly surprising for soft clay with Force 6 or more on top). It was not the Loch Ness Monster.'

In that muck, I did not see the whole anchor, only part of a fluke, but dived down over it and found a narrow furrow beyond which it had cut as it dragged. The current was running 80 per cent of maximum, and the object detected by the magnetometer was somewhere along that furrow to the west. By finning very hard and digging in my prodder to help me forward, like an old man doing dot-and-carry-one, I followed up the line of the furrow. Presumably *Gina Anne* was dragging farther away from me all the time, but I had my marker up top and great faith in Harknett. Light was poor, but I could see three feet now. Eventually, I sensed rather than saw a solidity in the furrow; prodded at it; found it did not dissolve; and thankfully hooked on to it and rested, while with one hand I felt around it, cautiously in case it was explosive, excitedly, because it was far too solid to be a mere piece of 'gash'. Then I found I could get my hand under it, that it was round, and extended some distance in two directions, and that the alignment was between ten and twenty degrees east of north by magnetic reading. It was, beyond doubt, a buried cable approximately four inches in diameter, lying generally some two or three inches under the clay, and not the barrel of a swivel gun! That it ought not to be there was beside the point. It explained why the magnetometer reading had gone on for such a distance.

I swam on briefly until my air ran out, then surfaced and found that I was looking up at the sky along the inclined surfaces of the waves, which were somewhat steep. Their tops were tending to collapse now, or to be blown off. As I rose up on one, I saw three heads and the top of *Gina Anne's* cabin above the waves some distance to the east. I held my prodder vertically, to mark my position, then waved it slowly from side to side. One of the heads raised an attached arm and waved slowly back in acknowledgement. The pick-up was made without anchoring, so that there was no relative movement of boat and diver.

We then turned and ran for it, with the wind behind us. This introduced the only moment of real danger, for off South Parade Pier *Gina Anne* began to surf, just like the Beach Boys, which meant that the rudder momentarily ceased to have any effect—and ahead of us lay the 'Blocks', the wartime boom with its narrow gaps. However, Maurice went through between them in the most skilful manner. Approaching the Langstone Channel, he altered course slightly to investigate a yacht lying there under bare pole, but it then got under way with a small storm jib up and followed us in. When it was in the troughs of the waves, all one could see was the tip of its mast, and the crew of the Eastney inshore lifeboat, warned by the Harbour Master to stand by for us, said that we disappeared completely from sight when in the troughs. However, Maurice avoided being 'pooped' by the following seas, and we went on to calibrate the magnetometer on two more known wrecks—the dredger *Withern* and the tug *Irishman*. The needle reacted in the right way at the right places, but it was now clearly a full Force 8, so we went home to tea at 4 p.m.

At the Brighton Conference of the B.S.–A.C., which began next day further down the coast, I met Peter Throckmorton, who was present in England to lecture on Pantano Longarini. Miss Taylor wanted him to see the *Mary Rose* site for an authoritative assessment from the angles of burial and preservation. Throckmorton had excavated, whereas we had not, and therefore his opinion was worth something. Our opinion was that, considering the seabed material and the heel to port of the hull, she should be preserved up to at least the line of the lower gundeck. This was tentative, of course. On the other hand, we were able to say that we had decisively downgraded the teredo and other shipworms; the shallow water factor also. We had obtained exact figures for shipworm damage which had resulted from a study of materials in artificial fishing reefs carried out by the California Department of Fish and Game. Off Southern California, wood lasted about three years and never more than five years by which time it had been eaten to a shell by various types of shipworm, including *Teredo navalis* and *Bankia cetacea*. These were the findings of a scientific study deliberately undertaken, and very much more precise than anything done previously. For our part, we could now produce a range of datable submerged wood which proved a substantially different picture for the Solent area. During 1965 and 1966, Maurice Harknett and

228

Section of 4-in. × 4-in. timber from a streetcar after fifteen months exposed submergence off Redondo Beach, California, showing severe teredo damage.

I had located and examined a number of new wrecks. 'New' in the sense of either our being the first divers to see them, or being the first people to think of taking a look at what was obviously on offer. They were in date order, the *Monte Grand*, a French sailing ship carrying coal and wrecked in Bracklesham Bay, Sussex, in 1920; a few hundred yards from her, also off Wittering, another French sailing vessel, the topsail schooner *Blanche*, wrecked in 1910; the bucket dredger *Withern* in Langstone Harbour, a metal ship but with a good deal of woodwork in her construction, sunk in 1909; the 'composite' barque *Caduceus*, another collier, sunk off Hayling in 1881; and Pete Cope's 'Convict Ship' which I had deliberately re-examined for biological specimens, but for which we had no definite date, merely the suspicion that she was more than a century old. In 1966, these gave test survivals for wood of 46, 56, 57, and 85 years, in respect of *Monte Grand*, *Blanche*, *Withern*, and *Caduceus*, which we managed to identify to the strictest standards of legal proof. Between them they gave a depth range at low water of spring tides between nil

and 30 feet. This was the really harrowing thing. The two wooden vessels in Bracklesham Bay were so shallow on ordinary tides that both had buoys attached to them to prevent paddlers spraining their ankles or breaking their legs on the wreckage, and indeed I had been forced to reconnoitre the *Monte Grand* first of all by snorkelling over her in 18 inches of water. An even more dreadful fact, elicited from the inhabitants of houses overlooking her, was that the local authority had repeatedly tried to remove her by explosive demolition, without much success, as I could see. What now remained of the Mediterranean dictum; that wrecks in shallow water break up quickly and that, in any case, shipworms will destroy the wood within twenty years?

The oldest definitely identified wreck among them, the *Caduceus*, was farther out to sea but still fairly shallow; she was in an area which was regularly pounded by gales every winter and had indeed broken up. But there was still a lot left: the decks were still obviously decks, the ribs ribs, the keel keel, the rudder post, the rudder post; and, of course, under the sand and shingle the buried woodwork was perfect. We had found her as the Deanes had found the *Mary Rose*, by a fisherman getting his net hung up on an obstruction and asking us to free it. She also gave us a date for the survival of iron which, according to the Mediterranean pioneers, lasted no longer than sixty years there, because she was of that peculiar build known as composite construction, introduced in 1851, which lasted some ten years only. Her frame was of iron, which was now in process of building up a shingle concretion, while her hull and decks were of wood. The reason for this method was that copper sheathing was believed to be essential for protection against underwater corrosion, and copper and iron do not mix well in seawater, setting up galvanic action.

230

After forty-seven years in shallow water, plus explosive demolition, part of the *Monte Grand* still remains and probably always will. The seaweed vanishing into sand marks parts of the wreck which have been temporarily covered by a change in beach contour. But, if the archaeological diver did not know his biology, he might easily assume the impossible— that seaweed can grow on sand—and therefore miss plain evidence of a buried structure.

A typical wreck of the Second World War—the buoy marking the armed trawler *Cambrian* blown in two by a magnetic ground mine laid by aircraft in 1940 on the Horse Sand off Portsmouth. The trawler's ammunition has not been salvaged and is still dangerous. By 1965 the survival intact of wood, canvas, and bedding in this wreck showed that Mediterranean dogma did not apply to Spithead.

Therefore, a wooden hull on an iron skeleton was proposed, and in the case of the *Caduceus*, they had sheathed the wood with brass, not copper. As she was of no historical importance, we had turned her into a lobster farm. Her destination had been Salerno, not unexpectedly, because this type of construction had been intended for use in areas of specially high corrosion; the China Clippers often employed it. Apparently the old-time shipbuilders had known what we were now discovering, that corrosion from various causes varies very much with the actual sea areas involved. Our studies of the biological pattern of the Solent area—how it is different, where it is different, and why (so far as we know) it is different—were to take up several chapters of my next book *Farming the Sea* (Souvenir Press, 1967), and cannot be repeated in detail here. Suffice it to say that this wide range of enquiries had a distinct bearing on Project 'Solent Ships', and were indeed part of it, programmed in from the start in co-operation with Mr. Wells.

Of course, we were not terribly surprised. There was still plenty of woodwork in good condition in that very well-known wreck, the armed trawler *Cambrian* on the Horse Sands, one of the compulsory stops on the itinerary of the local underwater tourist. She had been mined in 1940, twenty-five years previously, but I had seen a wooden armchair with canvas strappings, and even a mattress, lying among the wreckage. Of course, an intellectual would have interjected that they 'must have fallen overboard' from something or other (an angler's dinghy, perhaps?), but I guessed they had been washed out of the poor old *Cambrian* and had never taken the Mediterranean verdicts as applicable to anywhere except the Mediterranean.

Another point made by the *Caduceus* was that, judging by the dimensions of various components such as part of the keel, rudder posts and

metal braces, she was more than 120 feet long; and her actual length indeed turned out to be 124 feet, when we got hold of her specifications. We later discovered that there existed at the Science Museum tables giving such proportions exactly.

In the very brief time available at the Conference, I tried to give Throckmorton a summary of our findings; while quizzing him on the costs of full-scale excavation, of which we had no experience. He replied that these varied very much, from £5 to £35 a diver per hour underwater. That is, if one diver was employed to do three hours work per day, that could cost £100 per day, in transport to site, boat costs, equipment, and so on. Using North American personnel in the Aegean was clearly an expensive basic proposition, much more than using Portsmouth personnel on the *Mary Rose*, but even so I stood most of the boat costs and consequently, out of the 70 aqualung dives I did in 1966, seven only were expensive ones on the *Mary Rose*. Fortunately, the Committee for Nautical Archaeology paid the costs of the *Mary Rose* site sounding by Peter Throckmorton. As Miss Joan du Plat Taylor was also in the boat, we only needed George Bass to complete the Cape Gelidonya trio. We were forced to charter a large, beamy commercial boat called the *Mary*, a coincidence, because the Deanes had operated from a smack called the *Mary*, and I earnestly hoped that we should get typical Solent area conditions for Throckmorton, so that he would be able to make a just assessment of the facts. We did not need a gale, because Peter had had plenty of gale diving experience off

232

The topsail schooner *Blanche* wrecked at Wittering in 1910 and partly uncovered during an exceptional spring tide in 1966. She is still well preserved to above the turn of the bilge after fifty-six years' exposed submergence in shallow water. The photograph is taken from the bow, looking towards the stern.

is close-up view of a
ction of the *Blanche*
early shows the degree of
eservation.

Bodrum, where the weather was just as temperamental. In fact on 7
September the bad weather ended, and we had a flat calm sunny day, with
U.S. Navy ships in port and at Spithead, and the Stars and Stripes flying
to and fro. We might have laid it on on purpose for an American visitor.
The Isle of Wight boats turned up exactly on cue, as if prompted, and
as the first one came bearing down on our anchored position Peter looked
at it thoughtfully and commented '15 knots?'

I carried a camera in the hope of getting a frankly cheating picture of
Peter about 2 feet down below the surface, which I could then title
'Throckmorton dives Spithead'; but even that was impossible as you
couldn't see two feet even up top, and as we went down the anchor rope
the water darkened steadily until it became absolutely black. Peter was
fresh from diving off Sicily and in the Gulf of Taranto, and I don't know
what he thought of it, but it was certainly the worst I had ever experienced in the Spithead area. On the bottom, we could see a little, but a
matter of inches only, and it was clear that the gales had put the entire
seabed into suspension: that is, it was a matter of argument which part
was largely seawater mixed with sediment and which part was largely
sediment mixed with seawater. There could not have been a better
demonstration of the extraordinary lightness of the bottom at this point.
Peter prodded around in darkness for ten minutes or so, and after that,
had obtained all the evidence he required. From much comparative
experience of wreck burials he judged that the *Mary Rose* would have been

233

deeply embedded almost at once and that the interior would very quickly have filled with sediments. This, he thought, would have preserved most of the port side and lower part of the hull and might even have preserved documents inside her. We had not gone so far as to say that, and had we done so would have exceeded our experience; but Peter was the man who had found the 3,000-year-old wreck of Gelidonya and seen the wicker basket come up intact from it, preserved from the Bronze Age to modern times.

Also, while we tended to be obsessed with the limitations of small teams and tiny budgets, to which we were accustomed, Peter could look at the excavation prospects with fresh eyes; note how sheltered the site was, how close to the Dockyard, and how we might use Spit Fort as a base, or even moor a large landing craft on top permanently, which would give real protection against the Isle of Wight packets and also 'pirate' divers.

All this, of course, depended on the Deanes having done little damage to the hull and the paragraph about Pasley having blown her up being false. Part of my research that year had been to try to track down every gun and every artifact ever recovered from the *Mary Rose* by the Deanes. Eventually, I was able to produce a list of salvaged guns which, when compared to the ship's armament as listed in the Anthony Roll, showed that they had raised less than half of it. This very much implied that it was the starboard side guns, lying on the wreck, which they had salvaged; and that the other half of the armament was still intact and in its original siting on the deeply buried port side. It was this siting that I was interested

Relics of the 405-ton barque *Caduceus* sunk in shallow water off Hayling Island on 28 November 1881 and found by Maurice Harknett and myself on 23 August 1966. To the left, a wooden rudder post and brass fittings (pintle and brace), the protected woodwork being perfect after eighty-four years under the sea, and the exposed woodwork only partly decayed; on the right, a recovered plank, still recognisable and with only minor damage from marine borers.

in, having come to the conclusion that these early warships were armed like castles and on military lines, instead of with rows of identical battery guns. I was sure that they and the ships that carried them were employed on principles similar to those in use on land at the time; and that it was useless and misleading ever to think of them in terms of Nelson. The only disturbing item which cropped up was in consequent correspondence and conversation with Mr. B. W. Bathe, of the Department of Sailing Ships at the Science Museum and a member of the Committee for Nautical Archaeology. He had come across references to payments made during the years 1545 to 1549 to the Italian diver Peter Paul for recovering guns from the wreck of the *Mary Rose*. This was subsequent to the work of the Venetian salvage experts, which I had already followed up. These payments amounted only to about £100, however, and might have been in respect of the guns in the castles and on the upper deck, which should have been easy to recover at the time. Considering the type of seabed and also the fact that the Deane correspondence contains several references to the guns being found 'lying on top' of woodwork, there was still a better than even chance that half of the *Mary Rose* and half of her armament was still there; and this of course, if properly dealt with by salvage or excavation, would enable the main hull to be reconstructed, with almost her full armament.

Even if the magnetometer had worked on this site, it would not have given us this information. Whereas a sub-bottom sonar device should enable an electronic sounding to be made, giving us answers quickly and without disturbing the wreck. We did not want to air-lift the sediments away at this stage, because we knew now for certain that an immediate biological and chemical deterioration would set in, once they were exposed to oxygen-impregnated seawater. Indeed, for some time Miss Joan du Plat Taylor had been in touch with Mr. John Mills, the British representative of E.G. & G. International, an American company handling some of the products devised by Professor Harold E. Edgerton of Massachusetts Institute of Technology. These included a range of sub-bottom sonar devices of the 'pinger' and 'boomer' types. In effect, they sliced down through the seabed by means of sound waves and produced on what looked very like a large roll of toilet paper a continuous profile of the seabed and what lay below it, just like a cut sandwich. These instruments were hard to get hold of, when you wanted them on loan, because they were in continuous demand all over the world by cash customers. They were currently being used both in connection with planning for the Channel Tunnel and in the North Sea in connection with the 'Gas Bonanza' now in progress there; but their worth had never been proved for archaeology. Professor Edgerton was personally interested in this application for his device, and had let John Mills try for the Tobermory 'Treasure Galleon', which had been the object of search and salvage, some of it successful, from the days of the early diving bells. There had been a largely abortive attempt, using brutally powerful airlifts to dig trenches, in the early 1950s, carried out by the Royal Navy and Lieutenant-Commander 'Buster' Crabb, killed later in Portsmouth Harbour. Judging by

Registering the magnetometer near the *Boyne* buoy on 1 September 1966. Still only Force 6, with the worst to come, but George Cooke and Margaret Rule are already soaked and weary. Miss Joan du Plat Taylor and Peter Throckmorton (*below*) discuss a magnetometer 'contact' on 7 September 1966, shortly before he made his reconnaissance dive on the *Mary Rose* site.

the ballast stones they came upon, I thought there was little left of the wreck, but one tracing by the Edgerton instrument had shown the trenches, and, some 8 feet below them, a litter of large, unidentified objects. It was highly inconclusive because, although the machine worked perfectly away from the wreck and produced very sharp profiles of what lay below the seabed, something was upsetting it in the 'Galleon' area, possibly an organic layer acting as a screen. Would our slipper

limpets act in the same way, and would it be possible, by recognising their pattern, to unscramble the profile?

We first expected the one-day loan of this instrument in the autumn of 1966, but because of further commercial commitments, it did not in fact become available until the first week of January, 1967. The weather was so unnaturally calm and sunny that week that John Mills telephoned me from Hull, where they were doing a job in connection with the North Sea oil rigs, just as I was making up my mind to get in touch with him. We agreed to meet at the Ferryboat Inn, on Hayling Island, at 10.00 hours on Saturday, 7 January. We both checked the weather independently. John rang the Air Ministry, who forecast Force 3 N.W.; I walked along the beach, where the bay was like an inland pond without a whisper of wind, and then watched Southern Television. Their forecast was Force 3–4 N.W. This meant light breezes from the land direction, which always gives calm water in the area; it is, in fact, the best possible direction;

237

S.W. is next best, because this gives the protection of the Isle of Wight; the worst is a wind from the south-east, as this brings a swell directly into the area. We had to be so careful, because E.G. & G. were sending two scientists and an engineer, apart from thousands of pounds worth of equipment, and, the sonar principle being employed, too much wave noise would make an operation pointless. As matters turned out, we were approximately twelve hours too late. The Friday afternoon would have been perfect; but on the Saturday morning, when we were already committed, the wind although light was veering madly before settling down to a steady light blow from the south-east, which still did not explain the tremendous seas breaking on the Winners. Temperature had been down to freezing point by dawn, but everyone was assembled, and the boat hired, and we had to chance our arm. In fact, we might just have done it, if we had been able to get away sooner, on the high water slack; but there was a great deal of very heavy equipment to be offloaded, carried 100 yards, then stowed in the boat. But it was still millpond calm with excellent visibility inside the harbour, as we cast off and carried on down the channel towards the Winners.

The gadget was the 'boomer', not the 12 Kcs. 'pinger' used at Tobermory, and to test all connections, the generator in the stern was started up, and the machine began to emit a healthy tapping noise as it produced the roll of large toilet paper just like a ticket machine at a railway station. What we were getting, however, was the seabed and a slice of the cake right down through it. It certainly was an extremely rapid method of probing and was working well in spite of increasing wave noise. Harknett

238

w we found the *Mary
se*—with £20,000 worth
electronic gear crammed
o the saloon of the
ent Queen. John Mills
reground) watches the
ording paper coming
m the seismic sub-bottom
ar device—the pinger—
ich shows the vertical
nposition of the seabed
terials. Bob Henderson
ckground) watches the
ording paper coming
m the sidescan sonar,
ich shows the horizontal
terns of the seabed. In
ct, sidescan looks
eways up to 1,000 ft.
ay, while the pinger
be cuts vertically
wnward beneath the keel
a depth of up to 100 ft.
ow the seabed. The
ht-hand illustration shows
towfish—the torpedo-
ped container holding
instruments attached to
sidescan sonar—
dy for lowering into a
ry rough sea, off the
e of Wight. The 'fish' is
ved at varying depths
hind the boat, preferably
l down to avoid the
ise of the screws.

and I were missing the subtleties, because we were unused to reading such profiles, but we saw it register the mysterious 'deep hole' beyond the Eastney 'Bunnies', which, like a number of other similar formations in both Langstone and Chichester channels, had long puzzled us. But at that moment we had no time to study the new information we were getting, and indeed the trace of the seabed profile recorded progress to the end with awful finality. The seabed rose beyond the 70 ft. 'deep hole' to the Bar, very shallow; the tide was now ebbing from north to south, against a heavy swell sweeping in from the south-east. But even this combination did not explain the height of the wave which rose up at us off the Bar. It was so enormous that Bert Knight, who was driving, turned *Teal* off course and headed directly at it, so as to take it with the bow and not the broadside. I was unable to photograph it, because I was using both hands to hang on, but I saw a white wall of water sweep the stern, where the petrol generator was firing away, and saw it stop in a cloud of steam. Rather dazed, we simply hung on until we were out beyond the Langstone Buoy and in slightly deeper and calmer water. There is a mathematical progression to the height of waves, and that one was the sort of monster that occurs only about once a week. A freezing veil should be drawn over the rest of that winter day, except that Dr. Paul Marke and his assistant laboured on the wildly heaving stern to repair the generator, succeeded, and as we settled down for the final run-up to the *Mary Rose*, it stopped again. We even tried to dive, but it was impossible, the boat would insist on hanging along the line of the wave-crests and almost rolling her gunwales under. Rounding the Langstone Buoy on the return, the wind I think still below Force 5, but the average wave was six feet high and we had to keep turning off course to take the larger ones over the bows. It was at this point that we were seen from the land.

My family had checked with a friend at Hayling Island Yacht Club, and in his opinion conditions outside would be so bad that we would abandon the operation. Consequently, they had gone down to the ferry to meet us, and when we did not turn up, walked out along the East Winner bank as it dried. From here, they first caught sight of the top of *Teal's* unmistakable mast and derrick, out beyond the buoy, between one wave and the next. Donald Campbell had been killed a few days previously and a friend had been up there taking underwater pictures for television. It was this which prompted my eldest daughter to say, 'At least let's hope that it's not like Campbell, and they've found him.' They were waiting for us at the pontoon as *Teal* slid alongside, very wet, decks in chaos from fallen gear, everyone very cold, very bitter, very blue, but all undeniably present. Dusk was just about to bring the next snow-storm, and I remember just sitting there, idly watching an exposed gear wheel revolving; and John Mills suggesting that I put the cover back to save people from losing their toes. In vain, for I just sat there, not ever wanting to move again. This scene I remember, when people remark: 'What fun you must have with your underwater archaeology!'

I did not, however, forget to salvage the long roll of sea-soiled toilet paper which recorded a profile of the Langstone Channel up to the point

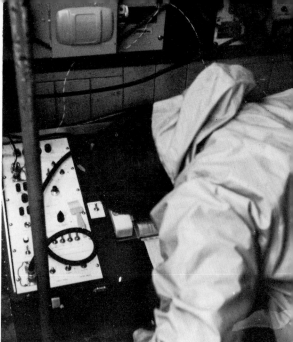

where we met that wave. Wave noise or no wave noise, it had certainly demolished one difficult theory as to the cause of the 'deep hole' phenomenon. A wreck found by the Towse team off the Isle of Wight had presented a new, Norman Castle with motte-and-bailey formation; it was burying itself in clay and was surrounded by an underwater, water-filled moat. Was it possible that these deep holes were caused by wreck scour? The 'boomer' profile proved conclusively that this was not so; there was no solid obstruction anywhere beneath the seabed at this point. On the other hand . . . to the south of it were two deeply buried objects which suggested bombs, and just off the Eastney 'Bunnies', buried 20 feet down under the bed of the channel, was what looked remarkably like the cross-section of a large ship. John Mills was not present to interpret the profile with skill, but we had a mystery of long-standing at this point. Further out, near the buoy, John Eberhard had found a solitary cannon and heavy chain. Off these 'Bunnies', Maurice Harknett had found what looked remarkably like a nest of cannon, some of them of odd design. The only breech which was not buried, was square. I did not see this one, but I saw others which certainly appeared to be 32-pounder cannon, and one which was similar but doubtful. I showed a sketch of the latter to Major J. G. D. Elvin, the cannon authority, who lives in Portsmouth, and he ruled it out as a possible cannon, but in a search made by the Fort Cumberland Preservation Society, of which we were both members, they found a genuine cannon half-buried in the beach. There were also reports of a large wooden hull on the beach at that point many years ago, and all this possibly tied in with the loss of HMS *Impregnable*, 98 guns, a similar ship to the *Boyne*, which had stranded off the harbour mouth. The possibility that the cannon were the supports to the sewage pipes

The Wardle and Davenport magnetometer (*left*) being successfully tested in gale force condition at Spithead on 1 September 1966, and (*right*) the recorder used with the 'pinger' and 'boomer' sonar devices being installed under cover in the diving boat before the *Mary Rose* trip.

240

had occurred to us, but technical opinion was against this hypothesis at first and there was no formal proof—like so many documents, they had fallen victim to the fire bombs of 1940 and 1941. As two dives off the sewage outfalls had put Harknett in hospital and me off sewage for life, we had abandoned the mystery. Now, the 'boomer' had posed the problem again, and of course the gain was enormous. We had unanimously reported the seabed clear of all heavy hull wreckage; we had been perfectly truthful; we could not detect an anomaly between 10 and 20 feet below the sand. But the 'boomer' could.

Consequently, although the purchase of such an instrument was beyond us, it was clear that potentially here was a most important new tool for archaeological research, which might well solve the problem of where those Roman wrecks had got to. And we began to consider, very critically indeed, its operational relationship to the *Mary Rose*. Just how could we get the utmost information out of it, supposing that Mr. Mills could be persuaded to try again? Archaeologists, both on land and in the sea, work basically to get their information by literally and physically 'trenching' through the construction they are studying; and this necessarily means partial destruction of it. It seemed to us that a 'boomer' or 'pinger' might, if realistically handled, produce the equivalent to trenching by non-destructive sonar profiling, and of course in a fraction of the time. We were very anxious to try it.

In the event, both the Edgerton personnel and myself had a startling surprise; and an archaeological technique which none of us had dreamed of was experimentally established. And this at the very end of yet another persistent run of bad luck. During the hot, calm summer months of 1967 the instrument was not available for non-cash customers, but a four-day period of trials and demonstrations to potential buyers was planned for the autumn, and John Mills arranged for this to take place in the Solent area, so that there might be a chance of doing a run or two over the *Mary Rose* site. If the weather was very bad indeed, the tests of E.G. & G. International could still take place in the sheltered space of Southampton Water. In fact, there were winds of up to full gale force during most of the first three days, combined with one of the most powerful spring tides of the year.

Two instruments were to be tested and demonstrated, both of them sonar devices vulnerable to excessive underwater noise. There was the sidescanner, which is sonar aligned both sides of the ship in the horizontal plane, throwing out narrow sound beams like invisible searchlights to illuminate and record the contours and patterns of the surface of the seabed, together with any disturbances of it or objects lying upon it. The extreme range of the beam was 1000 feet, but resolution of the objects improved as range was reduced. At average search setting, this instrument gave in effect an underwater visibility of 500 feet and recorded on graph paper what it saw, thus enabling measurements to be caculated. In addition, there was a pinger probe, which investigates and records vertically downwards through the seabed below the keel, penetrating as much as 100 feet of sediments, thereby showing the composition of the seabed and the sub-surface layers and also measuring them. Essentially, the two instruments are complementary, are set up side by side, and record simultaneously. But for a buried wreck we placed our faith in the pinger only, although the sidescanner would also be tried.

This is not the place to tell the interesting story of the four days of trials and demonstrations carried out during the period 2nd to 5th October in the small 45-ton steamer *Solent Queen*. On the 3rd, however, there were no customers aboard, just Bob Henderson, an American engineer and executive of E.G. & G. International, John Mills, their British representative, myself, and the three-man crew of the *Solent Queen*. As we had now charted Southampton Water extensively and the Needles Channel was impossible, because the wind was blowing Force 7 to 8 from the wrong direction, Bob said we could try a run down to Spithead to see if that area was workable. They therefore streamed alongside the hydrophone hose of the pinger probe, which was so badly affected by the excessive wave noise and screw turbulence that it was thought best to pay out more towline and stream the hydrophone further astern. All went well until the vessel turned out of the Hamble River to set course for Spithead, then, simultaneously, the pinger stopped recording and there was an ominous, rapid clanking from under the stern. Some object was caught in the screw or propeller shaft, and it did not require a first-rate detective to work out what it was. Apart from the probable destruction or loss of the hydrophone, it was possible that the tangle of metal-tipped hose and towline might stop the screw revolving and so put the vessel completely out of control. As the tide was then ebbing fast at 3 knots and a full gale was blowing, the consequences might be alarming.

Still clanking, we moved slowly across Southampton Water and tied up to a buoy by the Fawley oil refinery. There was only one set of diving gear on board—mine. I had brought it just in case we located the *Mary Rose* not too deeply buried, but unless the hydrophone could be recovered reasonably intact, I could say goodbye to any hopes at all. There were two critical points only to consider—how to get in and out of the water from a high-sided steamer, and how to prevent myself from being swept far astern by the three knot current, the equivalent in water of a good average hurricane on land. With the steamer crippled, there would be no pick-up, and I certainly could not swim against the mass of water rushing seaward.

I suited up, a light ladder was lowered, and John tied securely round the belt of my aqualung harness the nylon line of my marker buoy. I refused the insistent offer of a much stronger line, for fear of becoming entangled in a tangle which I could not cut my way out of inside thirty seconds or so. In the conditions of turbulence under the stern of the vessel, such a line might well remove both facemask and mouthpiece, and if so, I would not have long to live. I preferred to take the chance of the nylon line breaking from the force of the current, which would at least leave me alive, if alone and a long way out from shore on a fast-ebbing tide.

With Bob and John holding the other end of the nylon line, I jumped into the water. They took the strain of the racing torrent against my body, and let me be carried slowly towards the stern. I grabbed the rudder with my left hand and hung on, being violently buffeted by the turbulent water eddying round the stern and screw, but relieved to find that the visibility was a clear $2\frac{1}{2}$ to three feet. To my surprise, I could see that the hydrophone hose, which we had feared lost, was wrapped round both the propeller shaft and the blades of the screw, although cut and twisted into a rough triangle. The towline attached to it had taken rather less than a dozen tight turns round the propeller shaft and several more round the boss and blades of the screw. I decided that two strategic cuts of the tangled towline would probably free the vital hose, and I made the first, nearest and easiest by holding on to the rudder with one hand, while I tried to use the saw-edge of my diver's knife on the line and at the same time keeping it taught against a screw blade, as this was the only way I could obtain sufficient leverage to achieve a cut. The difficulty was, that I was being bobbed about, weightless, like a cork, my aqualung cylinder being banged against the hull of the *Solent Queen* and my facemask being almost torn off and repeatedly half-flooded with water.

It took many minutes of hard sawing to cut through the stout line, but that achieved, I moved forward and tried to get a grip with my left hand and elbow on a blade of the screw itself, while I severed the line where it was wrapped round the propeller shaft. This afforded another insecure and painful grip on a number of barnacles, although I could not see the blood and felt nothing until afterwards. Stopping occasionally to get my breath back or to clear my mask of blinding water, I cut down to the last strand, and then considered the final act. If I cut right through, the hose would immediately be plucked from my grasp and whirled away forever astern. I therefore had to fight the rushing water in order to get forward, still maintaining a grip on one blade of the screw, and then try to get my left arm through the triangle into which the hydrophone hose had been most conveniently bent. I at last managed to do this, then made the final cut. The hose came free, securely locked under my left arm and shoulder, and with a little effort I was able to thread it firmly through the loop in a line lowered to me. It was swiftly drawn up on deck, but I could not get out of the water so easily. The entire task, so simple on land, had taken twenty-five minutes of hard, high-speed work underwater and, at the age of forty-nine, not nineteen, I was too exhausted to heave myself up the unsuitably short and narrow ladder. Eventually, after having taken off both aqualung and weightbelt in the water, I was hauled on board by main force and refreshed with a rum-and-coke. Next day the hydrophone was working again, after a fashion, but something short of its normal efficiency; and I suppose that much the same could be said of me.

On the fourth and final day, 5th October, we had perfect weather, a light breeze from the north-west, and a full score of customers—representatives of oil companies, a geological team from the Netherlands, personnel from the Home Office and the Police, and many others. In mid-afternoon, when we had shown the geologists the unique features of the underwater

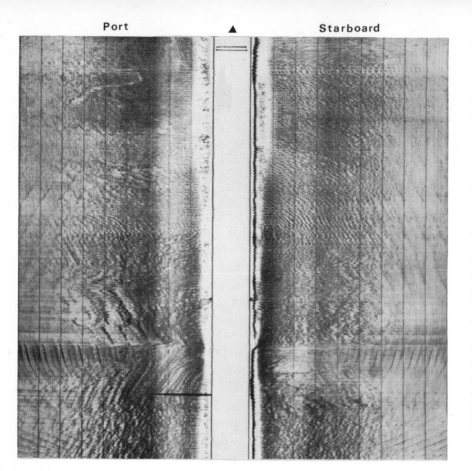

Port   ▲   Starboard

An historic sonar picture. The first run on 5 October 1967, with the sidescanner recording a large anomaly 200 ft. away on the port side at the estimated position of the *Mary Rose*. From the course of the boat, indicated by the white central band, the alignment of the buried anomaly (*top left*) can be worked out; the dimensions are recorded by the scale lines. Sidescanners are designed to record the surface patterns of the seabed only and this is believed to be the first occasion on which such an instrument has detected a buried wreck. Scour and disturbance of the sediments created by the wreck originally, together with the presence of a mound above it, may be responsible.

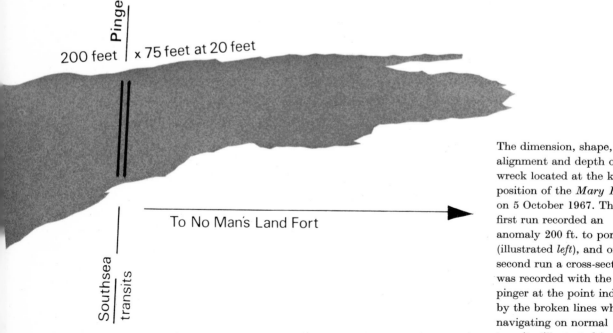

Pinger

200 feet | x 75 feet at 20 feet

To No Man's Land Fort

Southsea transits

The dimension, shape, alignment and depth of a wreck located at the known position of the *Mary Rose* on 5 October 1967. The first run recorded an anomaly 200 ft. to port (illustrated *left*), and on the second run a cross-section was recorded with the pinger at the point indicated by the broken lines while navigating on normal transits (illustrated in section *top right*).

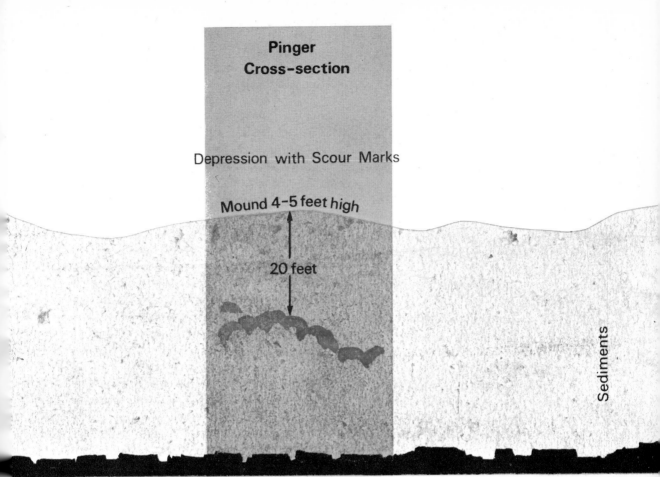

Pinger Cross-section

Depression with Scour Marks

Mound 4–5 feet high

20 feet

Sediments

Geological feature (continuous) at 35–40 feet

Bembridge Ledge, off the south-eastern tip of the Isle of Wight, Spithead lay to one side of our return route to Southampton, and John said that there was just sufficient time, perhaps ten minutes, to make a quick run or two over the *Mary Rose*, with both instruments recording. So many expert witnesses were present that I nearly had an attack of 'first night nerves'. Any failure would be very public. But the long hours we had spent during 1966 in navigational exercises in the area, coupled with underwater investigations, gave me great confidence. I had, however, spent too much time conning motor boats over the various navigational 'transits' for the site, and failed to take sufficiently into account the larger turning circle and reduced manœuvring powers of a 45-ton steamer. For this vessel I had allowed insufficient space for the approach and we passed to starboard of the site on the first run, instead of right over it. And then the incredible happened.

As we came abeam the sidescanner, the seabed surface instrument, picked up a large, buried anomaly 200 feet to port—startlingly clear and accurate. I doubt that any of the international experts present realised that I had muffed the approach badly, and by all accounts they were trying to scramble on each other's backs in the tiny saloon in order to see what the graph papers were recording. The pinger located nothing, because it registers only what is directly below the keel of the ship.

I made quite sure we were well past the site before asking the helmsman, Colin Barkham, to turn slowly to port and line up properly on the navigational 'marks'. This time we came straight down the intended, long-practised line, and as the Gosport side intersecting 'mark', not a very good one, began to close up I leaned down and told John to stand by the pinger. Five seconds later came his shout, 'We're right on top of it!' A crew member threw my marker buoy overboard and simultaneously the sidescanner registered the same anomaly as had the pinger—a double, corroborative check. With pencil and paper I took two new, excellent transits right and left, plus a sextant angle. Then we turned round for the third run and came up to hover by the marker buoy. Again, simultaneously, both instruments registered an anomaly. I took more marks and another sextant angle, and then allowed the vessel to drift unobtrusively off the site. It was all far too quick for anyone who did not know the local skylines to find his way back to the place, so the necessary security was preserved. In fifteen minutes, from a comparatively large and clumsy vessel, we had obtained measured sound pictures of an anomaly almost exactly where we had expected to find it—had in fact crossed it. But what puzzled us all was the way the sidescanner had shown up a deeply buried object, better from the side than from directly above it, in fact. The subsequent post-mortem examination of the recordings appeared to demonstrate a new principle in the detection of artificial, manmade objects sunk in a natural, otherwise undisturbed seabed.

Both instruments showed, in their varying ways, an anomaly, and in their varying ways told us something about it; a great deal more in fact than one would learn from diving to an unburied wreck. The object was an anomaly because it was unique to the area; it was not repeated anywhere in the recognisable patterns which were revealed. That conclusion was shown by both instruments, which would argue for a manmade object rather than a solitary piece of rock strata. When their evidence was put together, it showed us this: the slope of the seabed was interrupted by a large depression. In this depression there were two mounds surrounded by clear scour marks. Obviously, some large 'foreign body, had at one time disturbed the natural patterns of the area, leaving clear traces of its presence. The most prominent of the two mounds was some 4 to 5 feet high and the buried anomaly lay 20 feet below the crest of this mound, and about the same distance above a continuous geological feature, possibly rock strata, which lay under the entire sedimentary layers. By scanner measurement this object was approximately 200 feet long by 75 feet wide and as we had intersected it almost at right-angles to its greatest length, this length was aligned roughly towards No Mans Land Fort. We had intersected it near the north-west end. What the pinger showed, in addition to depth of burial, but not very clearly, was a cross section of the object at that point, where it appeared to be at

246

salvaged hydrophone
—a vital component
he pinger probe—lying
deck almost cut in two,
r it had wrapped itself
nd the screw and
peller shaft of the
nt Queen during a
ce 8 gale. It took me
nty-five minutes of hard
erwater work to free
recover it, thus helping
make possible the
ection of the *Mary Rose*
days later.

least several feet thick. Closely examined, the section through the shape was roughly that of a ship hull which had flattened out like a dying rose, resembling closely the cross-section cuts through actual wrecks made physically by Peter Throckmorton in the Mediterranean.

Certainly this was a wreck, and the instruments gave at least 75 per cent of the proof that it was the *Mary Rose*. We had a very good chart position, well worked out on the water as well as on paper, and this wreck was at that position—indeed, the Southsea side transit intersected it. We had estimated the *Mary Rose* to be at least 150 feet long overall, and both the dimensions and the shape of the wreckage agreed closely with that estimate. We knew from the Cowdray Engraving that the *Mary Rose* sank heeled to port on course approximately to No Man's Land, and this wreck lay aligned a shade north of No Man's Land Fort, accurate to a tolerance of five degrees or so. I could be fairly sure that the

247

pinger had cut an electronic cross-section through the afterpart of the *Mary Rose* remains, and that when Margot Varese and I had been forced to abandon our dive at the start of a deep depression in the seabed, we were in fact almost over Henry VIII's vice-flagship, nearly 450 years after she had been built.

The remaining items of proof for the full, formal identification, sufficient to launch a multi-million pound operation to raise and restore the *Mary Rose* as the Swedes had raised and restored the much-later *Vasa*, would mean air-lifting the clay and mud off part of the hull and selecting a few strategic artifacts for recovery; not too many, for we should have to place numbered tags to mark the places from which they had been removed. But before this can be done, the most important battle of all will have to be fought—the fight to obtain legal protection for underwater sites of historic value, so that these areas may be declared prohibited for both diving and dredging; in effect, to put up a 'Trespassers will be prosecuted' notice, and enforce it. This campaign has now been launched, with the *Mary Rose* as a 'key' test case, and not before time.

Up till now, the Ministry has been selling the rights to blow up and plunder the wrecks of historic warships to anyone who cares to apply, and the recent discovery of two 'treasure ships' and their subsequent drastic treatment, has come perilously close to discrediting totally underwater archaeology around the British coasts.

The use of £20,000 worth of electronic equipment to locate and survey a wreck thoroughly in advance, therefore strikes a distinctly odd twentieth century note; but this is what we will have to do shortly. Obtain the loan of both instruments for a full day instead of a quarter-of-an-hour, and with the pinger working at full efficiency, use sonar to cut invisible and undestructive trial trenches through the remains until detailed, measured plans can be produced as a guide to the great operation which may follow.

As the Committee for Nautical Archaeology had failed to obtain legal protection, even after years of negotiation, at their suggestion we formed the *Mary Rose* (1967) Committee, consisting of Mrs. Rule, myself, Mr. W. O. B. Majer, a Trustee of the Society for Nautical Research, and Lt.-Cdr. Alan Bax, R.N. Our first meeting on 27 November decided the strategy. Instead of merely applying to the Ministry of Defence (Navy) for a salvage contract to the wreck, we would apply to the Crown Estate Commissioners for a lease of the *seabed surrounding the wreck*. In drafting our application, I studied the Law of the Continental Shelf, 1964, and the precedents involved in North Sea gas. Whitehall gave us a favourable decision in the short time of two months, and on 1 April, 1968, we became the 'tenants' of 1,200 square feet of seabed at Spithead, holding the deeds to these 'demised premises' from our landlord, HM the Queen. The *Mary Rose* was protected from both commercial salvage and casual plunder, and perhaps a precedent had been established for the preservation of other valuable underwater sites.

Part Six
Submerged land surfaces

14

'Twenty Canutes and a plasticene elephant'

Submerged caves, coastlines and 'cities'

Nothing so arouses the savage beast within the human breast as the contemplation of submerged cities, unless it be the mention of legends concerning church bells ringing under the waves. In the past, scholars have turned and rent each other like wolves in the conflict between belief and non-belief in the existence of any factual basis for these stories. That struggle, terrible to witness, is over, although it has left its scars; and has been succeeded by a struggle even more ghastly and far fiercer, waged to decide an issue far more difficult to decide—what were the causes of submergence? I was engaged very early in my amateur diving career in the first stage of the enquiry, and was slightly astonished to discover the heat engendered by the subject; and not merely astonished, but amused. Either it was so, or it was not so; there was no need for scholarly tantrums. Later, the psychology of the contenders became a study of almost equally absorbing interest. The root trouble seemed to be that underwater archaeological discoveries, together with the standard of work done on them, are extremely difficult to check. Such checks are necessary and are indeed a commonplace on land, the reason being that there is no such thing as the one hundred per cent scientist using some infallible scientific method. Scientists are fallible humans, and their methods are only as good, or as bad, as the humans employing them. And in any profession, only the top ten per cent are really any good. In underwater archaeology generally there are hardly any professionals at all; virtually everyone is a part-time amateur of no particular standing, which increases the necessity for checking. The Atlantis myth was probably responsible for much of the psychological disorder obviously present; no one much cared to be associated with an enquiry dangerously open to ridicule, and particularly not the professionals, with reputations to lose. There were also, for those with longer memories, the stories of the archaeological hoaxes of the late nineteenth century—some strictly commercial, but others purely mischievous, where the jokers sowed sites with false clues in order deliberately to mislead the excavators. But also, and more intriguing, there was in some quarters a quite definite feeling that submerged cities and sunken churchbells were dangerously romantic, and ought not to be allowed.

It ought therefore to be stated at the outset that all genuine submerged landsites examined so far have been comparatively shallow, and that where 'sunken cities' are concerned, such a 'city' would not merit that title nowadays.

For the subsequent conflict as to causes of submergence, there are also charitable explanations. Some scholars can regard theories as expendable tools with which to work, to be scrapped when disproved; but others fall in love with them and cannot bear to be parted from their dead offspring, still less to adopt another man's child. That is to say only, that archaeology, like any other science or semi-science, is basically a creative act.

One other thing needs to be said. An archaeologist without active and expert nautical advice should never be allowed anywhere near a sunken ship, as he or she is a menace; from ignorance rather than malice. For

252

submerged buildings, however, the ordinary rules of the game apply: the excavator of a bell barrow knows not merely the particular excavation technique which is applicable to that type of structure, but has considerable knowledge of the people who built it and the tools and other implements they made and used. For later periods, where literary sources are available, he should know these.

We are, however, now operating in a different time scale. Up to now, a ship wrecked two or three thousand years ago was very old. In terms of submerged land sites, however, the artifacts found on board the ships would be regarded as very recent. An artifact 100,000 years old is fairly recent. We are now forced to think in terms of one to one-and-a-half million years ago. To the beginnings of the world as we know it today, and to the entry of man onto the stage, so far as we know. Naturally, at this remove in time the evidence is by no means precise, and a great many of today's theories are bound to be modified or overthrown, regardless of whether they are held tentatively or dogmatically. With that vital proviso, we may sketch the outline of today's beliefs. The oldest rocks, the Pre-Cambrian of the Eozoic Era are supposed to have formed approximately 1,200 million years ago. The youngest rocks, the Recent Pleistocene of the Quaternary Era, are supposed to date from 1 million years ago. It was in this Era that man is believed to have first appeared, co-habiting the earth with beasts and plants not essentially different from those existing today (except for those which man himself has exterminated), and there is archaeological proof that he preyed on beasts far more powerful and massive than he was, and how he did it continues to puzzle archaeologists. Being for the most part scholarly men and women, they do not fully appreciate how vicious, cunning and aggressive this two-legged meat-eater really is. For a modern tribal group, assembled round its television set, a hairy mammoth is a thing of pleasurable horror, made of rubber, usually in the U.S.A. For a prehistoric tribal group, assembled to consider the pressing food situation, a hairy mammoth was meat on the hoof (or pad, or whatever). And therefore doomed.

Now these hunting communities, which can hardly have known where the next meal was coming from, had from time to time much larger hunting areas available than we have today which, combined with their small numbers, may have made their existence less precarious than it seems to us. The reason was a peculiar and basically unexplained fluctuation pattern in sea levels during the period from 1 million to 10,000 years ago. The immediate and obvious cause of the fluctuations was that, periodically, much of the moisture which falls as rain and so enters the sea by one route or another, was temporarily locked up in vast ice sheets which spread out from the poles. The level of water in the oceans was therefore very much lower, at those times when a larger part of the earth's surface was covered by ice and the climate was exceptionally severe. The greater part of the continental shelves would have been exposed as the sea retreated, and vast areas of new land would have become available for occupation by the hunting communities. Because of the severe climate they probably did make much use of caves and other forms of natural shelter, whereas prehistoric communities which have survived into the twentieth century, with some exceptions such as the Eskimoes, are sited in warm and often wet regions. There are believed to have been at least four main Ice Ages, the first starting about one million years ago, the last ending about 10,000 years ago, and presumably we at present are in an Interglacial period, with another Ice Age ahead of us in the fairly remote future. The greatest drop in sea level caused by an Ice Age is believed to have been in the region of 300 to 400 feet below present levels. If this occurred today it would expose all the English Channel and most of the North Sea, and neither England nor Ireland would be islands any more, but merely highlands of the continental land mass. The coast of California would be a few miles seaward of its present position, whereas the coast of New England would extend for an immense distance out into the Atlantic, for even 250 miles out the water today is only some 600 feet deep.

Therefore, much of the archaeology of the Palaeolithic and Mesolithic periods, usually known as the Old Stone Age and the Middle Stone Age, lies below present sea levels and in some cases, many miles out to sea. The Neolithic, or New Stone Age, is taken to coincide with the end of the last Ice Age some 10,000 years ago, and some investigators believe that even in 6000 BC (or 8,000 years ago) the coastlines lay at around the present 100 feet contour below the seas. In short, a great part of man's early history is submerged. To discover it would be of service to geology as well as to archaeology, for there is still a great deal of conjecture as to the patterns of the Ice Ages and the complicated causes of submergence. It has even been postulated that 'race memories' of these events are responsible for flood and inundation legends which have lasted into modern times; these suppositions being put forward by geologists, geomorphologists, and even archaeologists, but not by historians. The survey of submerged prehistoric land surfaces is a fairly new study carried out, literally, at different levels.

An excellent example of such surveys at present beach level, or slightly below, is afforded by a number of investigations along the Selsey peninsula in Sussex, as this, literally, has everything—from submergence by inundation to the highest rate of horizontal erosion in Great Britain (5 yards per year until recent sea defence works), plus submerged sites dating from prehistoric times to the present. The earliest known site was last excavated by Dr. G. de G. Sieveking of the British Museum at low water of the big spring tides of mid-March, 1965. The site was actually a submerged marsh or peat-bog dating from the Pleistocene Inter-Glacial of about 120,000 to 180,000 years ago, covered under beach material south-west of the new Lifeboat Station, and exposed by gales. Officially, it was the 'Ebbsfleet' excavation, although ribald helpers dubbed it 'Twenty Canutes and a Plasticene Elephant'. King Canute was, of course, a local character who achieved world fame at nearby Bosham by confounding his ever-flattering courtiers with scientific proof that the Channel tides were not subject to Royal Command. The parallel was very close, because, when the low spring tides should have exposed the peat bog for the score or so of would-be excavators, they refused for the first days to do so, thus

254

illustrating the fact that local sea levels depend also upon barometric pressures plus the strength and direction of the wind, and that predicted tidal heights according to the tables are not to be taken literally. The 'Plasticene Elephant' was a reference to the fact that, from this bog a few years previously, the bones of an elephant and a rhinoceros of the Pleistocene period had been discovered and excavated, the surface of the bog being about 15 feet below present high sea level. Two flint flakes and a core were found in the peat, but it was impossible to thereby associate prehistoric Selsey Man with the bones of the elephant and the rhino. But, as I saw for myself, some of the wood from the trees and a piece of tree bark in mint condition was recovered from the submerged bog and these of course must have been considerably older than the animal bones, possibly a million years older. Pollen analysis and also a search for prehistoric insects were part of the project, but the site being neither sea nor land, but more sea than land, was in a peculiarly difficult location and these difficulties were not overcome that year. The previous year, when diving in deeper water, both John Baldry and John Silver had seen bones, the former a 'cow-like' type in Bracklesham Bay, the latter a horse's legs type off the Shoal of Lead on the Owers; but it had not occurred to them that these might be the remains of semi-tropical prehistoric beasts.

In January, 1967, the winter gales which were cutting back the actual tip of Selsey Bill, and threatening to destroy modern houses, actually produced a Roman well and the first Roman land level for the area, before destroying them. Up to this time, a number of Roman wells had been discovered on land in the area, usually by bulldozer, and on the only occasion when the discovery was intact, a gang of small boys stole the well cover before it could be seen by an archaeologist, thus destroying the critical piece of evidence. In this case, however, the sea uncovered the well vertically, by bringing down the cliff in front of and around it, and a local antiquarian immediately informed Mrs. Rule, who informed me, and we both went along to photograph it. The top of the well coincided with a dark line in the cliff between 8 and 10 inches below the top soil, which was obviously the Roman land surface, perhaps 1500 years ago. The wall was built of uncut stones obtainable locally, which can be found on the beach and under the sea; when, two weeks later, the sea had taken the Roman stonework completely, there would be no hint in the locality that any Roman structure had ever existed there. This is the typical effect of beach-cutting horizontal erosion. There are, somewhere under the sea off Selsey, one Saxon Monastery, one Saxon Cathedral, one Norman hunting estate, one Saxon quarry, three Saxon villages, one Belgic Capital City, complete with mint (the coins and raw gold from which are sometimes washed ashore over a wide area), probably a Roman seaside suburb, possibly three prehistoric barrows, definitely the submerged Looe River, and most certainly the place where three Saxon longships rode to shore for the conquest of the peninsula, where they 'slew many Welsh'. And, of course, the bones of prehistoric beasts, but all we have seen so far are the fossilised palm trees of 40 million years ago and the huge fossil seashells of 65 million years ago. Of all the sites, by far the most important

Horizontal erosion at Selsey. The Roman well uncovered by a cliff fall in January 1967 and already half eroded. Within two weeks it had gone completely, and as the stones were local, natural, and uncut, no evident trace of the structure remains even on the seabed. This total destruction is typical of an eroded site, as distinct from an inundated structure, some part of which may well remain intact under the sea.

is the Belgic Capital, almost certainly built nearly entirely of wood. Probably the three barrows had interior structures of wood also; we have swum around one of three related hills, in excellent visibility, and regretfully decided that, with present meagre resources, the chances of successful detection are small. But this will not always be so. However, a detailed survey of the entire area to seaward of Selsey would certainly cost lives; not from the sharks which must cruise the underwater cliffs, but from the prodigious tides which scour them. These cliffs may represent a former coastline, below 15 feet, but the currents and the gales which smash the area make recognition difficult.

Going deeper into prehistory—indeed, making a conducted tour of it in a small area—are various scientific divers in California, including those from Scripps Institution of Oceangraphy and the University itself. There, the saying is, that if you dive in certain places to 100 feet, you go back 8,000 years in time. The evidence, which required a good deal of thought and careful investigation to collect, is in the form of Indian artifacts, some quite well known on land; these could be dated by their land associations. Then, by noting where the various types were found in the sea, datings for the rise of sea levels were achieved. The material was found to seaward of a 200 mile long coastline, from the Mexican border to Santa Barbara, and in association with lagoons or river mouths and a prolific shellfish population in shallow water; good places for prehistoric settlements, in other words. The artifacts are found only after the winter gales have cleared away the deep summer deposits of sand, exposing a stony bottom. Of course, in the beginning the usual red herrings were suggested. As the first finds were made in shallow water, a ceremony was postulated: the Indians simply cast their offerings into the sea. As the offerings included very many heavy stone mortars, some weighing up to 75 lb., plus a lot of other household junk of a non-religious nature, this represented merely an interesting variation of the intellectual's "Oh, it must have fallen overboard" gambit. When, as time went on, very heavy stone objects were found at distances out from shore which would have postulated Indians of super-Samson strength of arm and shoulder to physically propel them that distance, the main battery was fired and, clearly, the artifacts must indeed have "fallen overboard" from an Indian canoe. But when the whole picture was pieced together, with graded and dated artifacts at definite distances and depths from shore along a coastline of nearly 200 miles, it became perfectly clear that the heavy stone artifacts were the sole remaining solid survivors of prehistoric settlements on former coastlines now submerged at varying depths down to 100 feet. Like most prehistoric implements, they required an expert to recognise them as the work of man, particularly after being rolled around and battered on the seabed for thousands of years. Apart from the stone mortars, corn grinders, choppers, scrapers, and hammerstones were recognised and recovered by the thousand.

In 1960, a geological investigation off the Cornish coast by R. H. T. Garnett revealed a submerged cliff with its top 66 feet down and its foot in 102 feet; and Kingston Branch under Major Hume Wallace have studied changing sea levels off Plymouth by means of the Eddystone Rock on which the lighthouse stands. The rock rises steeply from great depths with the record of the various sea levels notched in it, and as England is not subject to severe earthquakes, they are fairly confident that they can indicate on their scale model how much showed above water when, say, Pythias sailed up the channel in 400–300 BC. Indeed one of the drift searches by the Scientific & Technical Group for the *Royal George* produced a plot of a steep ledge in the seabed to seaward of her, which, if correct, would appear to me to be a submerged beach, as it followed exactly the extension of the land contours. Reported depth was 80 feet. It is likely to be an estuary beach, part of the submerged Solent River.

For a more immediately clear-cut answer, other people have gone to the Mediterranean to study steep rock faces, and they have gone very deep. Gibraltar and related sites have been studied by a group including Dr. John Waechter, of the Institute of Archaeology, London University, Dr. N. C. Flemming, of Cambridge, and Dr. John Woods, of Imperial College, London. Their object was to locate old sea levels and, if possible, to date them. Recognition is fairly easy, because there are many 'raised beaches' on land, evidence of much higher sea levels than exist today. Indeed, there is a famous one cut into the chalk of Portsdown Hill at the back of Portsmouth, and elsewhere on the South Downs they are, where appropriate, 'mined' for shingle commercially by open-cast methods. Those of us who live on the low-lying coast of southern England are in fact dwelling on a seabed. But the easiest of all from the recognition aspect are where a tideless sea coincides with a hard cliff which drops steeply into great depths. If the sea remains at a certain level for a comparatively short space of time, the beating of the waves cuts a 'notch' into the rock face at that level—a permanent mark worked in stone. If, however, the sea remains at that level for a long time, or, alternatively, if the rock is soft and the time short, then the undercut portion of the rock face collapses and another notch is begun, resulting eventually in a kind of step or platform being excavated in the cliff. Dives were made down to 280 feet and at Gibraltar clear evidence was found for old sea levels at 13 feet, 65 feet, 81 feet, and 117 feet. That is, below present sea level. There were other beaches above present sea level, in air.

By itself, this meant very little. Two further factors had to be considered, and the first was dating. Apart from scientific methods involving costly laboratory techniques which work only with certain types of rock, the main clues to dating are provided by submerged caves which were formerly occupied by prehistoric man, possibly over a long period of time. Dr. Waechter had first studied this problem at Gibraltar in 1948, in the case of a cave which was now only half-submerged but which showed traces of two periods of human occupation, probably by prehistoric family groups, separated by a period of submergence. The evidence normally is slight and by no means obvious. The floor of such a cave will contain occupation debris, plus wind-blown sand, which tends to raise the height of the floor. When sea level rises, most of this loose material is swept out to sea by wave action, which is extremely violent inside caves, but there is often a significant concretion left, where the floor material has been in contact with the rocks at the sides of the cave, and this may contain datable human artifacts. Where a cave has been occupied, and then submerged and occupied again, and again submerged, there may be two layers of concretion around the sides, at different levels and not necessarily at the level of the present floor. The most spectacular cave was that located by John Woods and his team under the island of Gozo, near Malta, in 1963. It was very carefully mapped and modelled, and Woods estimated that it held a quarter of a million tons of seawater. The entrance to the cave, at 30 metres, or around 90 feet, is related to a wavecut platform at the same depth; and inside the cave are notches representing three different sea levels, at 29, 20, and 16 metres respectively. Woods thinks the cave may be about 40,000 years old.

But Malta, like much of the Mediterranean, is subject to severe earthquake effect, which technically comes under the broad heading of *tectonic* movement of the earth's crust. I can well remember, as a boy, standing on a swaying balcony in Malta, while inside the bedroom the ceiling plaster rained down like snow, so that the sleepers' hair turned white overnight (not that anyone actually slept through that experience). Any English town subjected to a similar series of violent tremors would have largely collapsed in ruins, but the house was built to withstand earthquakes, being of stone blocks on a steel girder framework. For this rather vivid reason, among others, I cannot accept most Mediterranean figures, as discovered and presented to date, as representing anything in
258

particular. The area is far too erratic, geologically speaking, for a cursory examination to be anything but misleading.

In addition to earthquakes, which are a result of stresses within the earth's crust, slow warping of the strata for the same basic reason also takes place. Additionally, there are sometimes external stresses, such as that imposed by a heavy ice covering and its removal, which are technically known as *isostatic* movements. There is also the possibility of recent sediments being compressed by the weight above, of either land or water, and of emerging sediments drying out and thus also becoming more compact and so lowering land level. In short, the crust of the earth is far from being static; it fractures, warps, tilts, rises and falls either very abruptly, as in an earthquake, or very slowly and almost imperceptibly. Geologists have known this for a long time, and until recently tended to measure the alterations with reference to sea level, which they regarded as static. Whereas the oceanographers, who believed that the land was relatively static, tended to measure sea level, which they knew to be subject to fluctuations for a variety of reasons, by reference to the land level. As Dr. G. E. R. Deacon, the oceanographer, has remarked, they have now bumped into each other going backwards! A rise or fall of sea level due to an absolute increase or decrease in the volume of water present in the oceans is known technically as a *eustatic* change.

Therefore, those who set out to identify the eustatic changes of sea level during the past one million years or so, during which there were at least four Ice Ages, know in advance that the cycle of accumulating ice/ melting ice must mean not merely a series of variations in absolute sea level but also alterations in relative land levels because of the stresses set up on the land strata first by the weight of the ice, then by its removal. When, as in the Mediterranean area, the existence of geological faults and also of violent volcanic action are known to be present, the problems of matching a wave-cut notch in a cliff face with any particular period in time and of stating what the sea level was at that particular time, appear virtually insoluble by present techniques. If the notch is 60 feet down, this does not mean necessarily that sea level was actually at that point when the notch was cut, because the cliff itself may have been either elevated or depressed by any of, or even a combination of, the other causes. There could hardly be a more uncontrollable field of study.

One of the methods used is to take submarine cores from a wide area of the continental shelf in order to plot the entire Quaternary, or Ice Age era, from $1\frac{1}{2}$ million years ago to the present, and so establish at least an outline pattern. Such outlines have been constructed, notably by David Ericson and Goesta Wollin on the one hand and by Dr. Kenneth Oakley on the other. These outlines, while not basically dissimilar, do not precisely match; do not interlock. The reason is plain as far as submarine coring is concerned, where the evidence is based on climate, and the climate is established by the type of fossils found in the strata, especially the sea shells, or mollusca, the 'indicator animals'. But, as we have seen in the comparatively tiny Solent area, and particularly with regard to the Isle of Wight 'cut off', quite different ranges of species can exist literally side by side at precisely the same point of time. Possibly other parts of the chain of evidence, such as the 'erratics' and other rock debris carried along by the moving ice sheets in their expansionist phases, may perhaps be more reliable; but 'erratic' would be the correct description of the pictures resulting at the moment. Of course, this is only the beginning, when one should not expect too much. For instance, by June, 1966, a team of six led by Ian Morrison had been tackling this problem under-water in the estuaries of the Forth and the Tay and on the intervening open sea coast of Scotland, full time and for a period of four years. By that time they had accumulated over 10,000 accurately measured heights on former shorelines, literally hundreds of boreholes and numerous radiocarbon dates, and realised that they were still short of a good deal of necessary evidence, the problems being so complicated. By January, 1967, after they had analysed over 500 Carbon 14 datings, the earth metaphorically shifted under their feet, when many of the datings on which they had relied were modified in the laboratory lists. Consequently, it is still necessary to be extremely cautious regarding the patterns of sea level change in prehistoric times. The bulk of the work has still to be done.

In historic times, the position is better, but still confused by the fact that the unique Mediterranean area has absorbed most of the effort. The number of submerged sites is very great—nearly 200 have come to light so far—but the causes of submergence are still hotly disputed. Waechter and Flemming virtually rule out eustatic change during the last 1,500 years or so; although Flemming goes so far as to admit a barely possible rise of 2 feet. Basically, they believe the causes of submergence of the harbours, seaside suburbs, and cities, are to be found in movements of the earth's crust, because the depths to which the remains are submerged vary so greatly, from 2 feet to 30 feet, and with several cases of uplifting, the reverse process; and because those sites about which data was obtained are near active volcanoes, in known earthquake zones, or in the deltas of great rivers which bring, by degrees, the land into the sea. They have not, however, assembled any dating evidence from literary sources which, when combined with the regional evidence, might give a more definitive picture. This is important, because of the time element: an earthquake is almost instantaneous, a geological movement is so slow as to be almost imperceptible, whereas a eustatic movement comes plainly in the middle.

Precisely the opposite view to that of Waechter and Flemming is taken by Dr. Dietrich Hafemann, of Mainz, in his *Die Niveauveränderungen an den Küsten Kretas seit dem Altertum* published in 1965. A position midway between these two extremes is taken by Anton Bammer in his *Zum jungeren Artemison von Ephesos* published almost simultaneously. Off the Cape of Artemision one of the statue-cargo ships was found, it will be recalled; but the point of Bammer's study was on land, with the rebuilding at successively higher points of the Temple of Ephesus, a structure to which there are references in literature. The gentleman whose family cave was excavated by Dr. Waechter was, so far as we may judge, illiterate;

260

he was certainly a creature of prehistory. But when we come to deal with historic times, it pays to examine first those sites concerning which there is contemporary documentary evidence and also existing archaeological evidence. We are then on very much surer ground than when considering a notch in a cliff face or a submerged wave-cut platform without context. The Artemesium, or temple of the goddess Diana at Ephesus, is on the coast of Asia Minor which was colonised by the Greeks, north of Halicarnassus (which is now called Bodrum), and excavated by Woods in the late nineteenth century and then by Hogarth. It was then a semi-waterlogged site and its central point was what Woods took to be the 'Great Altar', but which Hogarth believed was the pedestal upon which the statue of the goddess had stood; and on digging there he discovered the treasure of Diana, amounting to about 3,000 items. This pedestal is Bammer's central reference point, because the English archaeologists gave its height above sea level as 2.45 metres at a site so close to the sea that any gale would batter it. The temple was later rebuilt on a wide, level platform 2.68 metres higher, which seemed odd. The dimensions of the foundations fit those given by Pliny, which serves to identify, and a description of the final evacuation of Ephesus in Roman times and the building of a new town on very much higher ground, given by Strabo, fit a rise in sea level which would explain both the abandonment of the early temple, the building of the new one on a platform which would serve to protect it from the sea, and a still remorselessly rising sea which caused the town itself to be re-sited. Previously, it had been suggested that the re-siting of the town had been caused by river-deposition of sediments. To arrive at his conclusion, Bammer interlocked his historical dates and data with rises and falls of sea level charted by other workers, notably A. von Gerkan and R. W. Fairbridge.

Bammer was unable to find evidence of any recent geological movements or violent displacement by volcanic activity in the Mediterranean; so he ruled out those causes. Nor did he believe in an alternative theory, almost standard in the geological textbooks, of a small but steady rise of sea level for eustatic reasons in association with geological movements. He came to the conclusion that all factors were subordinate to a broad pattern of eustatic oscillation, although they would certainly serve to modify the effect of this to a certain extent. That is, that actual sea level rose and fell alternately within the Interglacials, with a period of about 1,760 years; in other words, the great fluctuations of the great Ice Ages repeated between them on a comparatively minute scale; or, put another way, superimposed on the broad pattern. Theoretically, if all the ice at the Poles thawed away, sea level would rise 150 feet all over the world; and a water temperature rise of only 1° C. would melt sufficient ice to raise the height of the seas by 2 metres, or 6 feet. These theories are complicated because the system being examined is complicated; the easy one-factor solution will not serve.

A contrary view is taken by William Newman, of the Department of Natural Sciences, Northeastern University, Boston, who cites evidence at another temple; evidence very similar, in fact. Bammer, considering the Temple of Diana, the original of which was built about 550 B C in an emergence (or low sea level) phase, saw evidence that the peak of the submergence (or high sea level) phase had brought sea level to 6 feet above its present height, as part of the eustatic oscillation process. He did this by comparing historic data with the work of von Girkan and Fairbridge in charting these oscillations from other evidence. Newman, however, considering the Temple of Jupiter, near Naples, built in the first century A D, points out that the base of this temple is only just above present sea level (a point it has in common with the Ephesus site), and decides that this must mean that it was once at a higher level relative to the sea (another point in common with Ephesus); and that the columns of the temple show borings by marine creatures to a height of 18 feet above the floor, from which it followed that at a time subsequent to the first century A D it must have been submerged by not less than that amount (yet another point in common with Ephesus, except that the 'peak' of submergence was 6 feet instead of 18 feet). Newman does not make these parallels with Ephesus, nor does he co-relate historical data. He simply assumes that the process is entirely geological and has nothing to do with eustatic change. But evidence from North-West Europe, which we shall deal with later, show both submergence and emergence phases after the building of this temple; and as this can have nothing to do with geological movements in the Mediterranean, it is clear that eustatic oscillation is a major factor, modified probably by geological movements of various kinds, which would amply explain the variations in depth or height of the submerged or emerged sites. With fluctuations of both land and sea taking place simultaneously, and not merely one-directional but, taken over a long period of time, an up and down movement, it is little wonder that confusion and speculation still exist.

But these disagreements as to causes are a far cry from the previous derision of all 'sunken city' myths, which took its first knock in about 1900 when some geologists began to suspect that the sea was not static after all, in an Interglacial. Why they should ever have thought it was, is the large mystery. Their entire craft, when considering the period from $1\frac{1}{2}$ million to 10,000 years ago, is devoted to explaining the truly dramatic effects of eustatic changes of sea level of the order, they say, of as much as 600 feet. Then, at 8000 B C, or very shortly after, down comes the blind and eustatic change is laughed out of court. The root cause probably is, that geologists hate to have to consider anything more recent than that, because of the difficulties; and so they take the easy way out, instead of asking whether other directions of enquiry, such as historic evidence, might help them to a conclusion. However, they do not deny the existence of recently submerged sites. They merely see a different cause. Newman, for instance, quotes the case of Disenchantment Bay in Alaska where, in 1899, a geological fracture produced a displacement of 47 feet. As he very rightly points out, such an occurence underneath a seaside city would be so sudden that 'there will be no removal of individuals not to mention artifacts'. It would be like Pompeii, only much quicker. And, as he further points out, the Mediterranean is located in an earthquake belt where just such displacements may occur. By the computation of Flemming, who is an anti-eustatic man, there are some 50 submerged cities in the Mediterranean, of which only a dozen or so have been properly surveyed. With some, only the harbour areas or parts of the harbour works are submerged, and the investigators therefore have to differentiate carefully between harbour walls, quays and seaside suburbs completely submerged and what, on the other hand, may simply be ruined harbour works, the foundations of which were in the sea anyway. David Blackman, Bristol University, points out that, even in the sixth century BC, it had been possible to build harbour moles in 100 feet of water, and that some of these still exist and have been examined by divers. This was before concrete had been introduced by the Romans and really massive underwater engineering was possible. Other harbours, however, have silted up and today are as much as ten miles inland. He has described recent excavations at a modern port which revealed that an effluent pipe had been built on a handy BC foundation which, on examination, proved to be one of a number of parallel slipways for triremes. These slipways led to rows of covered buildings on shore, rather like aircraft hangars. Their dimensions gave a badly-needed clue to the dimensions of the larger triremes, and measured 35 × 5 metres, giving a length to beam ratio of seven to one. As the ordinary cargo ship of the time was probably only about $2\frac{1}{2}$ times as long as she was broad, the galleys were clearly long, light, narrow vessels, more nearly resembling the racing 'shells' associated with the Oxford and Cambridge Boat Race than a ship. No remains of ancient shipyards have yet been found, but many of the Greek harbours are still viable, because, as Blackman says, the Greeks had the scientific approach and thought out the matter of silting, whereas the Romans had the engineering approach—'It will be *there*, because that is the shortest distance from A to B'—and consequently their harbours, like modern ones, tended to silt up.

The pioneer of ancient harbour survey was Father Poidebard, who first noticed the submerged structures from an aeroplane and during 1934–1936 carried out the first archaeological work, using helmet divers, on the old port of Tyre; and after the Second World War went on to survey Sidon, where he found that the harbour built by the ancient Greeks had endured as an efficient unit rather longer than the new French-built harbour there, which silted up after four months, convincing proof that modern science is not always superior. Those interested in the detailed technical arrangements of what one might call free-flowing and self-flushing harbours will find the subject more than adequately covered in *Marine Archaeology*, edited by Miss Joan du Plat Taylor, *Under the Mediterranean*, by Miss Honor Frost, and *4000 Years Under the Sea*, by Philippe Diolé. More recently, Guildford Branch of the B.S.–A.C., led by R. Kingsford-Curram, have located a harbour of similar, Mediterranean design, submerged off the Scilly Isles, which have a maritime connection with the Mediterranean probably ante-dating the Bronze Age craft of Cape Gelidonya; and Bronze Age wrecks in British waters there must be, an 'ox-hide' shaped block of tin being dredged up off Falmouth to prove it. The more elaborate harbours of the actual Mediterranean were usually double—a large outer harbour for merchant shipping enclosing a small harbour, within the fortifications, for war craft. The entrances to these inner harbours were narrow, 80 yards across at the most, from which Blackman assumes that the effective range of the ballistas mounted on the towers commanding the entrances can have been no more than 50 yards. These inner harbours were little more than shallow ponds, adequate for the light and manœuvrable war galleys.

Until recently, land archaeologists never thought of what might be learned from submerged harbours; nor did they ever consider that a land excavation of a city which was part submerged was incomplete without at least a survey of the inundated area. Nor had they given a thought as to how exactly the former sea level could be ascertained, and many were not even interested in alterations of sea level. Probably the great difficulty of the undertaking, as it appeared to them, was sufficient obstacle. The situation now is very different: a substantial part of the survey work involved can be done by any person, lying on the surface and wearing face mask, snorkel and flippers; the visibility is usually good, the depth generally negligible, the water warm. In 1966, for instance, the Cambridge Expedition to Sabratha carried out searches and surveys at no less than eighteen different sites along the coasts of Tunisia and Libya with eight divers, who made 100 aqualung dives in depths between 6 and 75 feet, compared with 500 man-hours of snorkel diving by breath-holding alone. The most interesting discovery was at Thapsus, thought to have been a large port in Roman times, where a concrete mole can be observed running out from shore for a distance of 130 metres. By carrying on underwater search from the 130 metre point, the team discovered that the mole continued, submerged, for a further 870 metres in 30 feet of water with the top of the concrete and squared blocks being between 10 and 15 feet down. This is believed to be the longest free-standing Roman harbour mole ever discovered and in its original state is estimated to have contained 1/5 million cubic yards of cut stone and rubble, equal to one quarter of the volume of the great pyramid of Gizeh. But this is probably only part of the structure; there were indications of a second mole to complete the harbour.

Lightly-equipped expeditions such as this still have a great deal of scope for discovery and survey, but at the same time a number of full-scale, University-backed excavations are taking place, where the remains, both on the land surface and submerged beneath the adjacent water, are being simultaneously worked. For instance, the Phoenician trading settlement at Motya in Sicily has for some years been in process of excavation by combined teams from Leeds and London Universities. It was besieged and destroyed by Dionysius in 397 BC and is a typical example of a site favoured by the Phoenicians: an island or promontory for ease of defence in association with a bay or lagoon for their trading ships. The inner harbour at Motya was found on land, being merely a small rectangular area which had been dug out of the soil and then joined to the sea by a narrow channel faced by stone quays. The specifically

The landward part of the site at Kenchreai, Greece, with church walls in foreground. In the background—where the man in the white shirt and shorts is standing—is the makeshift coffer dam enclosing the area where the glass panels were found and excavated in 1964.

underwater side of the enquiry rather pointed to an increase of sea level, because if the level was lowered the approach channel to the outer harbour would become extremely narrow and therefore difficult for a seaborne assault force, while the flow of water through this channel would be very much faster than it is today and would tend to scour it clear of silt; and indeed the besiegers complained that whenever they tried to block the channel by dumping stones into it, the current swept them away. The divers also investigated a causeway which leads from the island to the mainland; although submerged, it is still usable by high-wheeled carts. Pottery found during the excavation matched with that in some of the wrecks off Giglio, previously mentioned, so that gradually the studies of ancient ports and the studies of the shipwrecks associated with the periods at which they flourished, are converging to build up a coherent picture.

One of the most interesting large-scale combined excavations to be undertaken as a result of the findings of a preliminary survey is that of Kenchreai, part of the port facilities of ancient Corinth, a meeting and mixing place of cultures in the ancient world. The inhabitants were basically pagan Greek, but the international set built their own churches according to their own beliefs. We know a good deal about the cult of

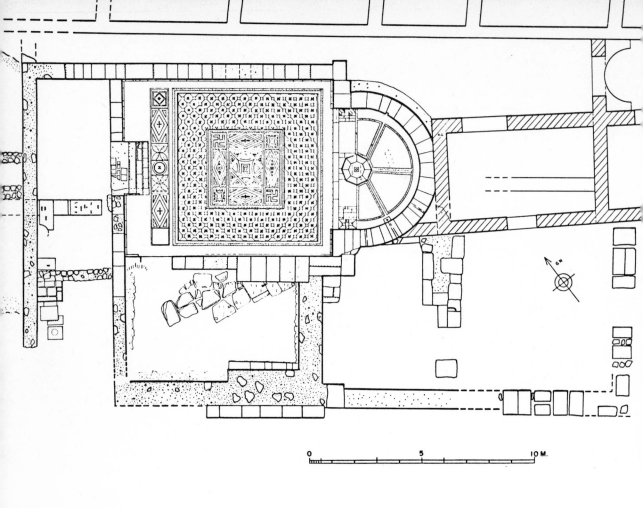

0   5   10 M.

Isis at Kenchreai, because there is a detailed description contained in
a well-known novel, *The Golden Ass*, by Lucius Apuleius, author of
Discourse on Magic and *God of Socrates*. The former, however, as with
some of the works of D. H. Lawrence and Henry James, has acquired a
notoriety which masks the writer's serious intentions and, indeed, his
qualifications, for in professional life he was a priest of Isis and Osiris.
The tale of the man transformed into an ass, in spite of the bawdy jests,
has basically a religious theme: God is Love. His was a more exclusive
religion than Christianity, which was oriented towards the lowly and the
slave, although the rich and well-born were not absolutely excluded, for
which there is ample evidence in the works of its chief representative at
Corinth, St. Paul, who mentions a certain Phebe as 'deaconess' of the
Christian congregation at Kenchreai (sometimes spelt Cenchrea). This
must therefore have been one of the earliest Christian communities in
the world, and we know also, on the word of a Roman traveller, Pausanias,
that there was a sanctuary of Isis at one end of the harbour at Kenchreai.
With these two facts in mind, the situation in 1963 when the preliminary
searches were made, was that there were largely unexcavated ruins on land
at both ends of the harbour, and that these continued out into and under

Kenchreai, the submerged
temple area.

266

the sea. One of the buildings on land was a church, and one of the buildings washed by the sea appeared to be another. Its floor was only just below the surface. At the north-east end of the harbour there appeared to be a broad mole with remains of buildings on it, and at the south-west end of the harbour there appeared to be another mole, with the remains of warehouses and the 'church', continued out to sea on some form of pier structure.

The survey was undertaken by the University of Chicago and Indiana University, on behalf of the American School of Classical Studies at Athens. The greater part of the initial effort was concentrated on the south-western structures, the mole and the pier. As the site was mostly shallow, swimming on the surface with a face mask was the first stage of reconnaissance; for those who could not swim, a sponge-diver's glass used from a boat proved adequate. The searchers were totally confused and soon lost their bearings. They were looking at 15,000 square metres of sunken ruins, distorted to larger than life size by the masks, and, with an average visibility of 8 metres, seen only in small sections. In the beginning, the only real reference point was a huge, upturned granite bowl which was popular as a resting point, because when standing

on it, the tired swimmer's head was just above water. As the remains were entered on a drawing, the arrangement became clearer; and later a large map was constructed, both of land and of water, with a long baseline on land extended in due course out into the water. More than a mile of rope was laid underwater to mark the centres of walls, with numbered markers attached at important points and surface-buoyed if necessary. Although the area had been submerged for 1600 years, it was relatively protected and the most surprising finds came to light.

In 1963, the foundations of a large rectangular room with an apse at the east end could be seen barely submerged, and it was possible to paddle about on it when the sea was calm; and the hypothesis was, that this was the original church site, abandoned when the sea rose, or the land fell. In 1964, the theory was tested and found to be not the whole story: the visible floor, at sea level, was on top of the floor of an earlier building at a lower level, about three feet below the water. The earlier floor was covered with rubble and debris, on which the later floor had been laid; and this debris was rich in extraordinary antiquities, of wood, ivory, and glass. In 1965, the area was sand-bagged around the perimeter and so made water-tight; and the superimposed floor removed. This uncovered

268

Joseph W. Shaw explores one of the trenches at Kenchreai. At a depth of 4 to 5 metres, these contain a great deal of Roman pottery expected to help date the remains of the mole, and the rubbish dump proved interesting enough to justify a second season's work.

the earlier mosaic floor and a fountain. It is conjectured that the later building was erected during the fifth century A D, and that some of the debris was laid down then as a basis for its floors; and that the building below this debris was a structure of the first century A D. The real puzzle was, how to explain the neat piles of stained-glass sheets stacked immediately on top of the lower, mosaic floor? It looked as if they had been packed in crates, ready for removal; and that this operation had been interrupted; that they had been forgotten and covered with debris; and that the builders of the later structure had sealed them in, unaware, under the protection of their own floor, long before the water rose to submerge both floors. Had they been taken down during an orderly dismantling of the earlier building? Or were they to be associated with the later building in some way? And what was the purpose of the building with which they had been associated—a rich man's dwelling, a public building, or a religious structure? The point being that they were pictures, and that they were also art. But of a most curious mixture. There are formal floral patterns of Roman aspect, and there were also Egyptian scenes—ibis birds in a swamp of lotus and papyrus, a man riding a crocodile; and another depicting curious buildings and also a ship, which could be a scene set

269

in an Egyptian town, or a Roman town, or a Greek town. The style suggested early Christian art, with its fusing of cultures, and therefore a possible contact with the Corinth of St. Paul; but equally the contact might be with that other temple, the sanctuary of Isis connected with Apuleius. Or it could be neither.

In this sunken room there were found also a great many fragments of wooden furniture; some were fragments merely, others appeared to represent complete items which had been broken; and many had carvings or engraved designs. They were of a type which could be Roman, but could also be Christian from the time of the catacombs. They have not yet yielded anything like their full potential of information, because conservation is not complete: the wood requires the usual treatment and the glass has suffered chemical change. Neither the co-directors of the project, Robert Scranton and Edwin Ramage, nor Joseph W. Shaw, of the University Museum, Philadelphia, who served as architect, have yet been able to come to firm conclusions. This also applies to sea level change. It would seem that there has been a relative alteration of at least six feet, but Corinth is in a seismic area and there is an indication from one of the warehouse walls that the land level has tilted since the structure was built, provided that the tilt is not explained as the settling of an artificial structure.

A similar sunken room, but with contents of a quite different type, and also in association with harbour works, was discovered by the Anglo-Israeli Underwater Archaeological Expedition, 1966, in the 'Tower of Flies' at Acre, now called Akko, on the Bay of Haifa. In 1799, Acre was besieged by elements of Bonaparte's Egyptian expedition and defended by Sir Sidney Smith. The 'Tower of Flies' certainly controlled the entrance to the harbour, but little was known about the history of it, and the object of the investigation was to try to establish the age of the original foundations, their extent, and the purpose of the building. This part of the work was jointly directed by Alexander Flinder, a London architect who is also a member of the Committee for Nautical Archaeology, and Elisha Linder, who was appointed by the Israeli Government Department of Antiquities to head the Israeli team. Submerged walls were found in depths of 5 to 7 metres, and laid in an astonishingly precise manner, considering the present depth. It was thought that these might have been foundations for the west wall of the tower, which would indicate that the building had once been twice as large as the present remains. Even more intriguing was the discovery of a room inside the tower, which was below present sea level, and completely filled up with boulders. Divers removed these, to reveal a staircase leading down below water into a domed room, with signs of fire apparent at one point, and at the lowest level, neat rows of cannon balls and quantities of lead musket balls. Clearly, the room had been an arsenal, and the 'Tower of Flies' a fortress.

A prominent member of this expedition was Dr. E. T. Hall, Director of the Laboratory for Archaeological Research at the University of Oxford, and pioneer of the proton magnetometer. This instrument was used to survey the area around the 'Tower of Flies' and also the harbour and its

otya, the channel to the othon' or inner harbour.

approaches, an extremely difficult proposition for an instrument which merely records anomalies in the earth's magnetic field, but not what they are, or precisely where they are. Therefore Dr. Hall devised a navigational system based on a pattern of sonar buoys in order to plot the exact position of all anomalies relative to each other. The anomalies indicated by the recording instrument proved, on inspection by divers, to cover an impressively wide range of submerged artifacts: at one end of the scale, the wreck of a copper-sheathed wooden ship about 150 feet long, and at the other end of the scale, some metal bedsprings somewhat less antique. The wreck was thought to be of an eighteenth century warship, possibly associated with the siege of Acre, but in any case an excellent subject on which the Israeli divers could practise survey and excavation techniques. A particularly large anomaly was indicated at a point where there were no surface seabed remains at all, but from which preliminary soundings produced Roman pottery and large pieces of unrecognisable metal which had been completely buried. This could be a more important wreck.

The electronic part of the equipment worked very well, especially where there were large masses of metal to be located. Earlier, Dr. Hall had found two battleships sunk off Gallipoli in 1915, the *Ocean* and the *Bouvet*; and he was able to repeat this performance off Haifa by detecting the wreck of the Italian submarine *Scire*, 620 tons, sunk on 10 August 1942 with the loss of all 50 of the crew, plus ten 'frogmen'. The *Scire* was the 'assault craft transport' of the 10th Flotilla used in many of the underwater attacks on shipping off Gibraltar as well as the famous affair at Alexandria when the battleships *Queen Elizabeth* and *Valiant* were put out of action. Defects in Dr. Hall's apparatus did show up, but these concerned the sonar buoys mainly and were of a mundane sort, for the corrosion which attacks sunken wrecks operates even on swimming trunks, which deteriorate rapidly when immersed in water. As a well-known underwater archaeologist has remarked, 'The trouble with all this sea machinery seems to be the sea itself, with pieces of things falling off or getting leaked into or eaten up by large fish. It looks to me like the success of all archaeological and most scientific endeavours depends principally on enormous amounts of strong string'.

One of the most dramatic proofs of coastal alterations, and in an area moreover where no new finds could be expected, was the recovery in 1964 of a number of statues from the famous Blue Grotto of Capri by two Italian divers, Raniero Maltini and Piero Solaini. The area of Naples generally, with its submerged Roman seaside resorts at Pozzuoli, Baia, and elsewhere, lying at depths down to 18 metres and some distance from shore, has been partly surveyed by teams working from the archaeological frigate *Daino*. That the famous Blue Grotto itself owed its weird blue lighting to a submerged entrance further down, which was probably the one used by the Romans, was accepted; but for statues to remain unseen inside such a popular tourist item was amazing. What had protected them from discovery previously proved to be the fact that, part broken, covered in concretion and sea growth, and seen in the flat, no-contrast lighting of an underwater landscape, they looked like rocks. Maltini and Solaini looked a little closer than had all their predecessors.

The whole area, overlooked by Pompeii on the slopes of Vesuvius, could provide evidence for relative alterations of sea level; but not for a measured estimate of the various causes. For that, it is necessary to study earthquake-free sites, and the most informative of these so far are all located in north-west Europe, on the shores of the English Channel and the North Sea.

15
Church bells under the sea

HAYLING BAY
1960~1966

The first investigation of a sunken church legend in British waters began with a bang on 16 July 1960. Two bangs, actually. Dead overhead at about 15,000 feet. That sorted out the age groups—those who had been in the war and those who had not. The former, looking up at the twin white puffs of smoke, knew it for heavy A.A. directly above the three diving boats tossing over Church Rocks in Hayling Bay, and knew what they were about to receive, and also that there was nothing to be done about it. There was an indignant howl from the boat next to us, as a light fragment clattered on to their cabin top and an ominously large boiling of water appeared ten feet from our starboard bow, a nose-cap or base-plate, perhaps. In 1966, when the average age of the divers was much younger than in 1960, we found an unexploded 3.7 shell just north of the site. Significantly, like most of the divers who explored the Blue Grotto of Capri, most of the youngsters made the elementary error of mistaking an artifact for a rock, and even those few who recognised it for what it really was, were innocently sure that it must be harmless, and so I made a mental note of yet another addition to that already long list of famous last words which begins with, 'I think it's one of ours.' On the 1960 occasion, however, the Club Chairman was an ex-Captain of the Royal Artillery, and our boat up anchored and turned out of line to make for the beach two miles to the north and the nearest telephone box. His opening words to the battery commander were brief and to the point. He was hardly at all mollified by the explanation that the Royal Marines were not responsible, the guns on this occasion being manned by an Army unit who were sure that they had been firing ten degrees off the point at which our three boats were clustered, with an underwater reporter from a television station aboard.

It was a brisk opening to our campaign to investigate a sunken church legend, and it had an ending just as sharp when the reporter, who had learned to dive in the Mediterranean, became unable to cope with rough English Channel conditions and would have drowned but for some split-second rescue work. Nevertheless, all honour to him, when the water had been poured out of him he made a coherent report of having seen among the rocks below 'a sort of ditch in a straight line, with pillars or columns down it, hard to describe'. It was to be some years before I was to see such ditches, and later still before I knew what they were. To conclude the occasion, the television cameraman who was also present took out his handkerchief to blow his nose and scattered pound notes all over the sea. The looks on people's faces as they saw good paper money waving about in the waves while proceeding astern at about two knots cannot be described; but they were all in the water after it in a second or two, and it may therefore be claimed that we also have recovered treasure from the sea.

Although this was the first planned expedition of a campaign which was to be pressed hard for many years, it was not the actual beginning. That was a casual and indeed accidental discovery made two weeks before, on 3 July 1960. It was more of a suspicion than a discovery, and as I made it, I shall here have to be autobiographical; and looking back on it, I was extraordinarily lucky, for it seems much more dramatic

274

in retrospect than it did at the time. I had done three dives in Siebe-type gear in 1951–1952 for a radio feature concerning the underwater work of the Royal Engineers, but this gear is too heavy to make a hobby out of it. In 1958, I bought mask and flippers and taught myself to snorkel dive around Portsmouth and also in the Möhne-see in Germany, the site of the famous 'Dam Buster's' raid. In 1959, aged forty, I joined the Southsea Branch of the British Sub-Aqua Club, and during a club visit to H M S *Vernon* got in a dive with oxygen breathing gear and Navy suit, mask and flippers, none of which fitted. But because the B.S.–A.C. required certain snorkel diving tests to be completed before training with their aqualungs in a swimming pool could begin, I still had not used an aqualung when, on 3 July 1960, I went out for my first boat trip with the Club. Indeed, my object was to carry out three witnessed, breath-holding dives to 21 feet in order to complete the pre-aqualung schedule of training. The main point of this requirement is, that if you know you can swim to that depth and back again without breathing gear, the failure of an aqualung (a rare occurrence) would not be unduly disconcerting. I was therefore very much the novice of the party and when we anchored alongside another boat some two miles out from shore in Hayling Bay, I was first into the water long before anyone else was ready; they had to put their rubber suits on, whereas all I had were bathing trunks. Not that I thought I would reach the bottom. Two miles out to sea seemed an incredible distance, implying a depth well beyond my capacity, so I took one deep breath and dived, finning down rapidly. About three seconds later, a startled fish took fright under my nose and there was a mass of seaweed and some very odd-looking rocks with mustard-coloured, orange-shaped growths attached to them. I was too ignorant to recognise them as sponges, or even to know that you had sponges in British waters; but I did see that the visibility was 4 feet and the depth about 14 feet. Even as ignorant as I was, there seemed something very odd about those rocks, and I reported this. When, with the rising tide, the water got deep enough for me to take my test, I slipped overboard again, made the three required dives, and during one of these saw what I noted at the time as 'a rock which was right-angled—like the corner of a house foundation; reminded me of something I had seen; remembered later it was the foundations of a building in the Möhne valley swept away by the flood when the dam was broken'. It was impossible to inspect, because the visibility was now down to 3 feet and the tide was running, so that you were carried away while you were finning back up to the surface. For this reason, although our suspicions were aroused, we left the area and went over to Seaview where the visibility was 25 feet. This contrast was to prove the rule rather than the exception throughout the investigation.

Almost the first thing I did after stepping ashore was to check whether there was any 'sunken church' story attached to Church Rocks. There was indeed, and I recall a Portsmouth librarian, as he looked up the references for me, remarking that there had been a correspondence about this in the local press recently, and it was remarkable how heated people became on this subject. As I learned later, we were not the first to find the rocks. They had been located in 1955 as part of a general survey made by the Hayling sculptor Frank Martin, a pioneer of the aqualung in England. He was advised by a local historian, Major F. G. S. Thomas, who described the first, negative results in his book *The King Holds Hayling* (Pelham, 1961). On the basis that he had seen no walls, Mr. Martin now stated in the local press:

'I find the "Church Rocks" natural and presenting a variety of formations covering a considerable area in two distinct groups. Samples of these rocks reveal nothing of sound building quality and certainly no Caen stone, the main building material used.'

At this stage, there were two broad arguments. All previous local historians, and also the author of the *Victoria County History*, pointed out that there were records of three medieval churches on Hayling Island, of which two still existed—the oldest being St. Peter's at North Hayling, known to have been built as a subsidiary to the original church, and the present senior, but later, Church of St. Mary's at South Hayling. The original church was gone and this, from documents which they quoted or paraphrased, was two miles out to sea at Church Rocks, having been overwhelmed by inundations in the early part of the fourteenth century. They could all point to various structures on land which had clearly been constructed from salvaged materials, some of it of a clearly religious kind, and assumed that much of the inundated structure had been removed at low tides soon after the disaster. The only important point on which the latest local historian, Major Thomas, took issue with them was on the location of Church Rocks. There were no less than two different historical references to the inundated church as having stood formerly 'in the centre of the island', and if that site was now two miles out to sea on Church Rocks, then pre-inundation Hayling must have been a good deal larger than twice its present size. Thinking solely in terms of horizontal coastal erosion, without consideration of changing sea levels, he considered this impossible and looked for a site nearer to the present shore. The makers of old charts obliged him, showing no less than three 'Church Rocks' sites close inshore, just off my house. Frank Martin had also found genuine building material at a point close inshore. Who was right—the chart makers or the fishermen? Here, I was biased; I had lived in a fishing village for some years, Bembridge in the Isle of Wight, and knew how much they knew. But I also snorkelled out to check two out of the three chart-marked sites, located them by noting the difference in wave action, and saw that, although there might be something underneath the sand, at neither could it be a church and village. Also, both were in the wrong place. It was recorded that 'almost all the hamlet of Eastoke' and been lost around 1300, and the modern village of Eastoke was further east, almost opposite Church Rocks, in fact.

By now, I was not only deep in local history but laying down the main lines of the enquiry. Strictly speaking, it was not archaeology at all, and certainly I had no intention of excavating a ruin for information when two perfectly good churches of the same period, associated with the inundated structure, moreover, were available on land. Briefly, I wanted answers

276

to two questions: Were there remains of buildings on Church Rocks, two miles out to sea, and if so, how and why were they inundated? The year was 1960, remember, when nothing was certain and many conflicting views were being published. On the one hand, there was James Dugan, in his *Man Explores the Sea*, published by Hamilton in 1966, re-issued as a Pelican paperback in 1960, who adopted the cynical attitude:

'... the old handicap, the belief that the Mediterranean rose and drowned cities. The idea is a variant of "Atlantis" and "Lemuria" lost-continent superstitions which have no scientific support. The American version is the sunken pirate city of Port Royal, supposed to have slid into the Caribbean when an earthquake and fire struck the wicked down. Diving expeditions to walk the streets of Port Royal are a traditional hot-weather newspaper item in the United States. There are architectural remains in the Mediterranean, but serious scholars deny that the sea drowned them. They fell off ships, they are parts of buildings that crumbled and fell in or people pushed them in ...'

On the other hand, there were scientific writers such as Maurice Burton, who wrote in *Under the Sea* (Vista, 1960):

'There are other traces of former cultures and civilisations than those contained in sunken ships. There are sunken harbours and submerged villages and towns. These require the organised attentions of trained archaeologists rather than those who dive for sport, although the two must eventually combine to make the ideal teams. . . . The results of such work belong to the future.'

Did they indeed?

It was of course presumptuous of me even to attempt the problem, because so far I had not even had a lesson in the aqualung, let alone used one, although I had read the theory. There didn't seem to be anything to it, and there wasn't. A group of Club conspirators decided to lend me one for ten minutes on Church Rocks, for a good long look around, on the grounds that I knew more than they did. Which was true, but at that time I was barely keeping one jump ahead. To square matters with the regulations, they officially declared it a 'non-Club trip', so that if there was an accident, no blame could attach to the B.S.–A.C. Diving tragedies were then so infrequent that they attracted a good deal of unfavourable publicity. Although it was a calm day, there was a fair sea running at Church Rocks, the current was fairly fast, the visibility 4 or 5 feet. I had no suit yet, but was wearing three jerseys instead. I was literally in good hands, because an experienced diver, Jack Millgate, literally held me by the hand so as to keep in touch, but in fact it was delightful, far easier than snorkelling, and you could take your time. I had hardly begun to enjoy it, when I saw a right-angled rock and hauled Jack round in a 180 degree turn to get at it. I reported: 'Looked like a table-top in size and shape—perfectly straight, top and sides.' Owing to the current and sand we kicked up while trying to stay in one position and stay together we lost it, being swept away. But not to worry, a few minutes later we found another one. This was a large rectangular slab of much the same dimensions as a coffin; ruler-straight sides, when you discounted the organic growth and borings, and quite flat on top. I concluded: 'These two rocks too regular to be natural, when their different sizes and shapes considered. I was so fascinated I didn't want to come up—indeed, I had forgotten about coming up; but I was, after all, living on borrowed air!'

In retrospect, making one's first aqualung dive on to what was probably a sunken church, is the sort of thing which appears only in books, and schoolboys' adventure books at that. At the time, however, and for several years afterwards, my main emotion was overwhelming curiosity as to what we would find next; and an intense desire to learn more about medieval structures and building methods, so that I might understand whatever it was I found. At first, my knowledge lagged just that vital bit behind, and I had to show drawings or photographs to an expert before the piece could be identified, and then I knew what I should have done at the time of discovery to continue the investigation further. On the other hand, I never had any trouble in finding building material: I could see the straight sides and the right-angles through the camouflage and despite the no-contrast lighting, and worked out simple tests early on. No more than one diver in ten proved able to do this consistently. And only when one of these reported a particular area as 'negative' could you believe him; far too many took everything underwater for granted just because it was underwater, most strikingly illustrated by those who could swim over a live A.A. shell and assume it was a 'rock'. If you ask no questions, you will get no answers. There was another basic reason also, so important it will bear repeating. I wrote in *Triton:* 'I concluded—and this may be of help to others—that if even half your mind is on lobsters, you are likely to find lobsters. But no building material. To find building material, you have to "think" building material; and better still, go and look at some of the stuff in air.' Later, I discovered that this was not an original thought. David Hogarth, the excavator of the Temple of Diana at Ephesus, had written long before: 'In digging, you only find if you care to find, and according to the measure of your caring; or, as a famous and fortunate explorer once put it, you find what you go out to find.' Later still, the matter had been put clinically, in a different context, by the naturalist, W. H. Hudson: 'He must have a quick-seeing, ever-searching eye, and behind the eye a mind intent on the object. The sharpest sight is useless if he falls to thinking of something else, since it is not possible for him to be in two places at once.'

The lobsters and the flatfish were the main distractions on Church Rocks, from the very beginning, as Major Thomas makes clear; but especially the lobsters, as they break any search pattern. In point of fact, an inexperienced diver will see no building material, and no lobsters or flatfish either, although he may pass within inches of them. When I went looking for lobsters on Church Rocks, that meant that my part of the investigation was concluded; there were buildings there, a number of them, and I felt that I understood exactly how and why they were inundated and what were the various forces at work. To go on from there to a complete mapping of the entire area was beyond my resources, and

278

anyway would not materially add to knowledge, except to make certain that what appeared to be the church complex was in fact the church complex—for it was nothing so simple as a single building, or even a single village. But old habits die hard. One day in 1966, I boxed the compass. Looking for food for the family, I spotted an enormous excavated dustbin area which could only mean the residence of a gigantic lobster; and surely such a monster would long since have been taken by some other diver from such a popular spot as Church Rocks? As I turned in to make sure, I saw that the occupant had built himself a barricade, and that it was composed of one large brick and one large flint, carefully laid. Clearly lobster or crab work. But these were human artifacts they were using, and I removed the brick for a closer examination and then, to clear it of encrustations, banged it repeatedly on top of the entrance to the cave. Two blue-black claws the size of garden-shears came moving out at me. For a moment, archaeologically-oriented, I was disconcerted. The beast was more than two feet long which, underwater, looks like three feet and, moreover, as I was lying down, I was looking at him at eye-level. Then, all science forgotten, I could think only that here was a meal for my entire family, plus the cat. By coming out of cover, he was just asking for it. I moved left, under cover of my own smokescreen, came in behind him, saw the stupid beast peering out at where I had been, but was now not, both antennae forward, and two seconds later I had both hands round his head at the base of the claws. I had to go to a restaurant to borrow a big enough pot to cook him in, but it was worth it. This sort of surprise—or bonus—one never gets in orthodox land excavations, which, I must confess, bore me, apart from being dirty and far too much like hard work.

The Church Rocks investigation is the most appalling subject to describe, because it is not one subject, but half-a-dozen related subjects investigated in parallel; and moreover it was undertaken while we were ourselves learning to dive as well as trying to follow up the parallel lines of enquiry, which in some cases meant undertaking study courses, particularly in geology and archaeology. It was also an historical enquiry from the documents relating to Hayling and similar sites. It included an enquiry into oceanography, a study of the theories relating to changes of sea level, a study of the relevant buildings on land, a study of the coast-line, both above and below water, and of the effects of horizontal erosion. And also, of course, of the currents and conditions of Hayling Bay, plus some skill in underwater navigation, in order that we might stay alive while doing it. From several land excavations in which I took part, in order to further my knowledge, I discovered that an orthodox archaeologist simply drives his car up to the nearest pub and parks it there. Even if he does forget where he left it, there is no real harm done. But if, with the tide running fast, we went out too far to one side of our boat, or dropped astern of it, while still on the seabed and navigating by means of current-direction, compass and an ability to solve triangle-of-velocity problems in our heads; if, in these circumstances, we made any error, we were in very serious hazard and most probably dead. It is not the diving which is dangerous; it is the limited air supply and the vulnerability of a heavily weighted diver on the surface in an area of large tides, fast currents, and cold, murky water. As Solent Area waters go, Church Rocks was not especially hazardous, being safer than many other sites, but it was no Kenchreai. And we were amateurs in every direction, we were learning all the time.

Adequately to brief a diver for Church Rocks nowadays takes forty-eight hours as a minimum; less than that, and the man or woman does not know enough to operate efficiently. No adequate account of this intricate investigation could be given at less than book length. It is necessary to summarise fairly savagely. Also to remember that we took no advice from anybody, except on technical detail; with the experts divided as they were, a thoroughly independent check was what we planned. Nothing else could be of value. That we knew nothing to start with, was probably an advantage.

A general hunt by many people for information in 1960, laid the groundwork. Four days after my first aqualung dive on Church Rocks I hired an Auster to fly over the entire area from Southsea to Selsey, because if the documentary story was true, the inundations could not possibly be local to Hayling, and, from observation, were certainly not due to horizontal erosion. The aviation approach was second nature, because I was flying light aeroplanes solo at the age of fifteen, and unlike those who hit on the same bright idea later, I had the great advantage of being at the controls myself. I could put the machine just exactly where I wanted it, at the height I wanted it, and at the best angle of bank in the turns consistent with safety. Land archaeologists normally try to conduct a screaming technical dialogue with the pilot while hanging out of the door, and fail to understand the reasons why some types of light aircraft will not hold their height in what used to be called a 'split arc' turn, or anything like it, and that some will spin out of it, particularly with the door open and half an archaeologist hanging out. I came over the wreck of the tug *Irishman* in Langstone Harbour, and was staggered by how much I could see of it down through the water, then I put the aircraft on the right line for Church Rocks and waited for the western sea 'marks' to come on, approximately. There was nothing of interest to be seen close to shore and when I got out to Church Rocks, I duly reported: 'Short, choppy sea and some tiny white horses visible on grey-green sea. Impossible to see down through it—remarkably black.' I then flew east to Selsey and circled the Mixon. Here you could see the weed on the bottom. I was trying to fix the pattern to a description of the lost monastery given by the Venerable Bede; several submerged areas of high ground fitted, unfortunately, right out to Boulder Bank, but there was a yacht still using the course of the submerged Looe River to pass through the Owers. I then flew back towards Wittering where I saw a great growth of weed, ship-shaped, in the shallows. 'Wreck or rocks probably,' I noted; it was in fact, a wreck. I had a final look at Church Rocks from 600 feet and then from 100 feet, plus the inshore area, and of the outer site noted: 'Dark, choppy sea stained with small streaks of white from breaking waves.'

280

Short circuiting much seabed and documentary proof, this was in itself clear evidence of a former coast line, and I was to take the view that of the two main inundations, the first around 1300 ended at Church Rocks, submerged the priory church complex and 'almost all the hamlet of Eastoke'; and that the second inundation in the 1330s flooded most of the area between Church Rocks and the shore. I have not seen the principle of seabed contour changes detected by wave indication stated previously in an archaeological connection, but it is a good guide. I had used it in the sea as well as above it, of course, and it was the double view which was most informative. The overall view of the flat, indented coastline with a shallow, gently sloping seabed to the south, intersected by a network of deep channels which were 'drowned river valleys' was extremely useful. It was to explain later why the shallow wrecks suffered much less damage than one would expect. The force of the waves began to be broken many miles to seaward instead of, as in the West Country and also the Mediterranean, close to a steep rock face.

There was also a useful contrast to the very similar, low-lying indented coast of East and North Frisia. I had flown over Sylt at the junction of Schleswig with Denmark, but in a Meteor jet-fighter trainer instead of a poor old Auster, so that we covered a lot of ground. I had also taken holidays in Sylt and on Norderney, and visited Heligoland, and possessed among my baggage brought back from Germany in 1952 a number of historical studies, both in English and in German, of the long record of inundations by the sea which those areas also had suffered. The disadvantage peculiar to all the local historians was they that were indeed local, whereas from the start I thought it best to consider the coasts both of the English Channel and the North Sea as a unity, and a peculiar one. The other advantage was, of course, what turned out to be many years' close study of the submerged areas. Even so, I did not differ materially from their findings in the end; and claim only that my detailed interpretation of the events of the period A D 1250–1425 was more precise. The significantly new contribution proved to be regarding the causes of the events, not the events themselves.

I broke a leg in Anglesey in the autumn of 1960, which considerably upset my aqualung training schedule, apart from the fact that a number of the pool tests gave me trouble, particularly the pointless performance of 'backward and forward rolls'. My wife had no difficulty in doing these, because she had learned them as a child, but I tended to fall off the top of the loop, which was enough to fail one. As first designed by the Club, to meet the original problem of how to train divers when no trained instructors existed, they were admirable, as the subsequent safety record proved. Now, they were a hindrance to operations, tying down the by now experienced instructors to the routine of pool training and retarding the pupils' progress. This explains why for some years the Church Rocks investigation stood almost alone as a single project pressed with determination. I had to buy my own aqualung and break all the safety regulations to do it, but in fact it was perfectly safe, comparatively speaking; nothing to do with the sea (or for that matter the roads) is absolutely

Church Rocks, off Hayling
Island: John Towse and
John Powell with the
flagstone raised in 1961
which matched with a
quarry in the Mendips,
Somerset.

safe. But I seriously doubt whether anyone who takes up underwater
exploration does so in the belief that it is safe; the hazard is part of the
attraction, and by the time it is realised that the dangers have been grossly
over-rated, the diver is so fascinated by the scene that he cannot give up.

Nevertheless 1961 was a good year, because the rocks were showing
more prominently; clearly much of the sand, shingle, and slipper limpet
had been removed. In these conditions, even an idiot child could find building material without really trying. On 18 June, for instance, John Powell
and I found a piece of 'long and short work' which matched precisely
with salvaged stones in the medieval Dovecote ashore, this building having
been constructed mainly of debris, including a piscina and Norman sliding shutters. The piscina, the drainage bowl for an altar, was upside down
as the roof of a dove's home. A few feet away from our stone lay a flagstone which John Towse found and raised. This was matched later with a
Mendip quarry, and it was the first visible proof we brought to the surface. We were mistakenly rather wary at first of lifting small items, for
fear of disturbing the evidence, not realising then that only the larger
blocks and, later, the foundations, were good position evidence. The
smaller pieces were subject to trawls as well as wave action, and it turned
out that many local fishermen had at one time or another caught dressed
stone in their nets in the area. We had no idea where the finds were, and

never could locate them again, so 'sampling' was kept to a minimum. This would have been a splendid year, if we had had a large force available for a proper survey, but the bulk of the Club's time was devoted to the cumbersome training programme and, with my inexperience, I was in no position to launch expeditions, quite apart from the fact that I had no boat.

In 1962, everything changed. Three of us got together to attempt to crack the problem, all of us novices. Roger Hutchins, who was the boat owner, Tony Segrave, and myself. We made a pact to go out every week-end, regardless of weather, on Sundays as well as Saturdays, if we could get air; that we would search alone, to cover larger areas and because of the low visibility; and that if one of us failed to surface, no search would be made by the others for the body, not even a token one, as a rescue, if made, must take place within four minutes of the accident. Action must be taken instantaneously, or not at all. This would not look good in the coroner's court; but then, none of us expected to appear there. The division of responsibility was that I handled the historical side and the local contacts, including the Vicar, the Reverend John Beaumont, who, having two medieval churches in his charge already was both interested in, and knowledgeable about, the third and oldest, and also the local archaeological society through Mr. H. J. Earney, representing other

283

informed local sources and opinion. We would also make a geological check on the area and I would submit the samples to the Geological Survey in London. This was necessary, because the building material was on a reef of natural rock which, as we were subsequently to discover, had been levelled in places for building and itself used also as a quarry. Roger and Tony would handle the archaeological side; they had constructed a base-line and grid for a methodical survey.

Even at Kenchreai later, the divers were to be confused. Their confusion was nothing to ours. Their average visibility was 25 feet, ours less than five. We had quarried rock mixed with natural rock. The area was tidal, and biologically fertile, and when the current changed direction the great weed carpet changed with it, and altered the entire landscape. There was no question of laying out a pattern of ropes in straight lines, with all main items tagged and buoyed. Church Rocks was a popular fishing 'mark', and attracted clusters of boats, all of them with anchors. They were secretive too, and buoys we had previously laid to mark important finds permanently, had disappeared within twenty-four hours. Also, we were three people working part-time at weekends, and with limited supplies of compressed air, whereas a land excavation of such a site would require a six-year campaign employing a labour force of at least sixty people eight hours a day for six days a week for three months each year. Hence, we planned only to survey, if possible, not to excavate. The base line was to consist of numbered stakes driven into the seabed along a line temporarily marked out by a rope stretched taut; with the grid used for making detailed drawings. No photographs had at that time ever been taken underwater in the Solent area, not even in places where the visibility was much better, and photography at Church Rocks was thought impossible. But I bought myself an underwater camera case and hoped for the best, spurred on, I must admit, by scepticism about my descriptions of building material. I eventually succeeded, through being able to control the whole photographic process from exposure to print; but the results were not, and were not intended to be, art. They were factual records merely.

The base line did not go right. The rope simply would not lie on the bottom, and this turned out to be because it was across the top of a large steel cylinder, bobbing about upright on the seabed and in shape like a small magnetic mine. Jack Milgate had twice reported this object over the years, but few could believe, because he also said that it was not moored—and how could a semi-buoyant, unmoored cylinder stay in one place in a tideway? But he was right, all right, for its tail was trapped in a rock crevice. Almost my first successful underwater photographs and drawings were of this object, made as guides to the Royal Naval Bomb & Mine Disposal team who would have to deal with it. It was not a mine, capable of destroying every boat over a wide area, but merely a compressed air cylinder, potentially capable of killing a diver, but having no fuse. But once the rope was laid flat and hauled taut on an east-west axis, the numbered stakes could by no means be driven in, and were therefore merely placed on the bottom. The grid failed, because when it was moved a cloud of smoke welled up, obscuring everything. Nevertheless, the base line, for as long as it lasted, which was until the winter gales, did give a reference point for finds and by its aid we achieved what we had never succeeded in before—seeing the same object twice. Neither Roger nor Tony saw it unfortunately; all their discoveries were of small pieces, including two more flagstones, which many people thought could be merely boat ballast. Towse made the discovery on 29 May, showing it to me the same day; and I found it again on 9 June; but that is the last I have seen of it. It was a massive block, with what looked like a hole on top and a quite definite 6-inch cut-out at one corner. I had to show the photographs and drawings to a builder, Mr. A. Gregory, for an opinion as to its purpose in a building. Why the cut-out? Normal practice to interlock heavy stonework, was the reply. Why the hole on top, if it was a hole? To pass an iron rod through, so as to strengthen a heavy load-bearing point, was the answer. But the block could also be part of a window, he pointed out. People did not cut holes in heavy stones in order to make windows, they would either cut-out the corners of four blocks, or cut-out rectangles in two, joining them together edge to edge. The original windows in medieval buildings were small, because of primitive technology in glass-making. This block weighed many tons, but other discoveries by Towse were of small white blocks, which just possibly were Caen stone. I found a 2 ft. square block with a moulding at the bottom, and a lobster underneath; but still hoping for a survey, we raised none of this evidence.

The natural rock samples and fossils were much appreciated by the Geological Survey in London, as the seabed in this area was not known. The findings were definite. Church Rocks, which is a long narrow reef running nearly parallel to shore on a near east-west alignment, was, not

n explosive artifact: a ry-suited naval diver rapes the Church Rocks nine' after it had been xamined and lifted by the N Bomb and Mine isposal Unit of HMS *Vernon*. proved to be a huge ompressed air cylinder, a otentially explosive object ut nowhere near as deadly s a ground mine.

unexpectedly, part of the Bracklesham Beds which take their name from neighbouring Bracklesham Bay. This is a very crumbly rock, which possibly had led Mr. Martin, the architect, to believe it unsuitable for building. But Mr. Gregory, the builder, stated that it would be perfectly usable, when weathered, and he would not mind having a few hundred tons for his business; and the Geological Survey confirmed this, stating that they knew of cases where it had been so used in buildings. What we had, therefore, was a reef of rock in its natural state, used as foundation ground for heavy buildings which could be constructed partly of this natural rock; plus 'foreign' rock from far-off quarries imported for building purposes; plus debris rock brought down by an Ice Age, known as 'erratic blocks', but more usually called 'erotic blacks'. These were in fact dark, very hard, and had some naturally straight and polished sides. Most people dismissed them, but this really was not possible. Certainly, they are natural rock in their natural state, but are they naturally placed? Later, part of the briefing for newcomers included a visit to St. Mary's Church, contemporary with the submerged church, and the pointing out of two large erratic blocks, one on either side of the south porch. Natural blocks, in their natural state, but deliberately placed by some persons unknown in the distant past in association with a religious structure. The next stage is a visit to St. Peter's Church, built to take the overflow congregation from the submerged church. This has no foundations of the normal sort, but instead the most peculiar supports for all the load-bearing points— corner walls, pillars, and so on. These are erratic blocks. Natural blocks, in their natural state, employed for a most unnatural purpose; indeed this type of construction is very rare.

286

Another explosive artifact: an AA shell near the North Site on Church Rocks. Almost certainly it is still 'live' but some divers, misled by the organic growth, thought it was a rock. The lack of contrast in underwater lighting, as shown here, makes such mistakes easy.

riangular block *in situ* on
he North Site on Church
ocks, in 1963, with part
f the encrusting sponge
nd algae scraped off to
how that the top and side
re two flat surfaces
orming a right angle.

In 1963, we found its counterpart in a building under the sea; and in 1966 yet another team found an additional building of this sort. This was a very close connection indeed with the construction of two medieval churches on land. Roger and Tony found their results of 1962 inconclusive, and dropped out; but Maurice Harknett, another boat owner, took over. He knew Church Rocks well, visiting it mainly for lobsters, but he had seen several features which he regarded as suspicious and wanted to investigate further. One of these features was what he called 'Harknett's Pillar'. It was probably the 'dome' reported by many divers who had thought nothing more about it. It was a substantial rock, apparently erratic, standing between two and four feet high, depending on the amount of sand/shingle cover, somewhat pillar-shaped, and about 3 feet inside the beginnings of the reef; sometimes lobsters perched on top. What Harknett had noticed, and nobody else had, was that about 15 feet due south of the 'Pillar', out on the sand was a smaller rock, and about 15 feet from that, due south again, a large, long rock with a crevice right down the middle. One dead straight line, apparently, judging purely by eye when blundering along in poor visibility. But, nevertheless, the best sort of seabed marker; and Harknett had been using it for precisely that purpose, in order that his searches should always start from a known point. In short, a natural baseline not to be destroyed by any gale or interfered with by any anchor or trawlerman's net. Up to now, all our searches had started actually on the reef, with rock all around: Roger's position finding was extremely good, and on one occasion he actually put the anchor on the base line—accurate to inches two miles out to sea. But once you got down, you didn't know if you were coming or going, once

Scale $\frac{1}{2}$ inch = 1 foot

away from the baseline. Harknett's method with his 'Pillar', however, was to anchor 20 feet or so south of the rocks, on sand; then swim to the southern edge of the reef and tour along it, first one way, then the other, looking for the 'Pillar', and then checking that it was this rock and no other by swimming south in a straight line, past the small rock to the crevice rock. If you started by buoying 'Harknett's Pillar', and buoyed any finds temporarily, they could all be related to the 'Pillar', roughly.

Now the foundations began to be seen and recognised and we were also able to raise medium-heavy blocks for examination, their approximate positions being known. And one day in August, we got 35 feet visibility! After that, the area of 'Harknett's Pillar' was dubbed the 'South Building'. Simply by snorkelling on the surface, one could see clearly that the three suspicious stones were spaced equally apart and in a straight line. This pattern was repeated to the west, but with the third stone missing. If these were the foundations for the east and west walls of a building, nothing showed this to the south, but to the north, where logically the ruins of a north wall might be, there were many 'foreign'-appearing blocks, two being twins. We raised two, including one of the pair. This latter required four men to lift into the boat, one being the Vicar, who was able to come out on occasion (Sunday was not his best day) to give snorkel cover to the lung divers working below. Chips proved both blocks to be of Weald Sandstone, the nearest outcrop of which is more than 20 miles away; both, therefore, were indeed 'foreigners' and, moreover, typical of what I had all along thought to be building material, even when very rough, as these were. They had probably been rough-cut, but the only proof was by implication—the existence of a pair (later, this turned into

289

a foursome). To the Vicar, they suggested coping stones. Flat base, sides curved, tops rounded. Mr. Gregory pointed out that such rough blocks were also used for doorways. All the indications were for a massive building of Saxon or Norman type, but not necessarily a church.

At other points, actually on the rock reef, two other types of foundation were recognised. An apparent plinth block with a three-foot-wide gap (for a door?), cut from the natural rock. In two other places, the opposite—those ditches which the unfortunate television reporter had claimed to have seen. I called them 'pathways' until I knew what they were. The two I saw this year were three feet wide, filled with sand and shingle, and ran ruler-straight through the reef. 'Robber trenches'—that is, ditches cut to take wall foundations, from which the useful material has been 'robbed out' later for re-use in other buildings. These were both just to the north of the 'South Building' and presumably formed part of a more important structure, or a later one. Further north still, just clear of the northern edge of the rock reef was an enormous single plinth in association with a small triangular block and a larger piece, which I called the 'North Site'.

Elated by the 35 feet visibility, we laid plans to plot Pathway 'B', just north-west of the South Building, which, from photographs, appeared to have a floor on its west side. Five weeks of gales and half-gales prevented any work at all being done for more than a month, and the season petered out with no more than a check of the reef which showed that it

Close-up detail of the 'pathway' complex at Church Rocks. The scraped area (*top left*) is obviously a floor, the 'ditch' on the right being a 'robber trench'—the linear feature left after a wall has been 'robbed out' with the object of re-using the salvaged material elsewhere. See diagram on p. 291.

rt of the complex of
thways' up to 1 ft. wide
nd near the 'Pillar' at
urch Rocks in 1966 and
otographed in detail
e illustration on p. 290),
t necessarily in close-up
a range of 2 ft. with
de-angle lens. The
ttern indicates trenches
t in the natural rock
ata to 'key' in the wall
ndations; as they are
ly 1 ft. wide at most,
ssibly there were interior
lls.

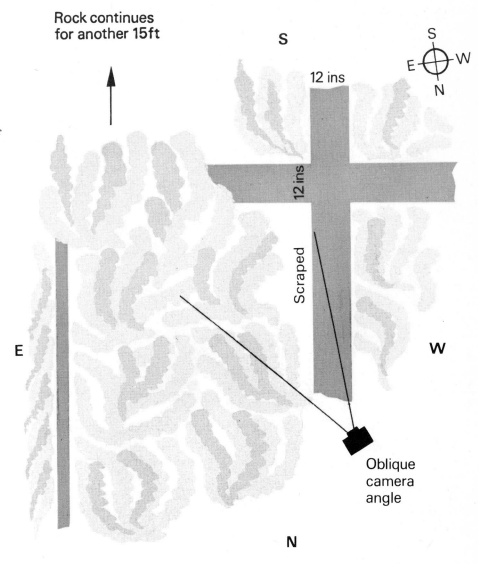

Rock continues
for another 15ft

S

12 ins

12 ins

Scraped

E

W

Oblique
camera
angle

N

disappeared a few hundred yards to the east, while continuing for a great
distance to the west. So we planned for 1964, and went out to Church
Rocks seven times—on 16th, 23rd and 30th May, 4th and 19th June,
5th and 25th July, all favourable tidal periods. Average visibility throughout was 2½ feet, with heavy or very wild weed growth. We gave up, and
instead carried out a geological and biological survey of Bracklesham Bay.

Up to that time, two other possible archaeological sites in Hayling
Bay had been reported: to the north-west, the so-called 'Big Rocks',

described as looking rather like Stonehenge; to the south-east, fallen 'columns' (but these could be fossil trees). The first year of Project 'Solent Ships' was 1965, but in 1966 there were a number of other discoveries in Hayling Bay. The Millgate team came across parallel stone pathways about a mile south of Church Rocks in deeper water. Colin Watts and Colin Porter reported finding a new site just south-east of Church Rocks, with regularly placed boulders, one with a square-cut hole in the top, plus various pieces or shaped masonry; apparently the remains of a structure similar to the 'South Building'. In the same area, Peter Cope found what looked like a wall with a section cut out of it. I had only a quick look at this area, found small 'foreign' stones lying about and a buried ridge which might repay excavation with an airlift. As part of Miss Varese's introduction to the area, we showed her Church Rocks, and in poor visibility picked up 'Harknett's Pillar', and a few minutes later found what proved to be a complete 'robbed wall complex'. The weed was then very wild and all she saw was a pathway with a straight-edged rock alongside it, the top of the rock being flat and disappearing under the weed and into the gloom. I thought it might be footings, she preferred a 'robbed wall' explanation. Soon after, I saw it again in ten feet visibility, with much less weed, and it was in fact a complex of robbed walls one foot wide meeting at a junction and with a lobster-infested 6-inch ditch further east. Later, I was lucky enough to see this area twice in about twenty feet visibility, and find more of this complex, plus two further items which matched with the 'pair' of possible coping stones and a coffin-slab shaped block with clear biological evidence that the sand and shingle had temporarily been eroded away from the area—below a certain 'tide mark' the surface of the stone was clean, smooth and perfectly flat. It was perfectly obvious by now that mapping must mean clearing the weed and keeping it clear and that the force involved would number at least 50, and, because of the tides and weather, these 50 might have to be kept hanging about playing ping-pong for weeks, or even months on end. Only a rich University could tackle it. I did not greatly care. The investigation was concluded: sewn up.

My original questions had been: Are there buildings on Church Rocks, and, if so, how and why were they inundated? I felt that I had the answers. But I had had to go pretty far afield, throughout Europe, to get them.

16

'In the time of the King, your Father...'

Historical exploration and evidence

We had made a dead set at the Church Rocks problem when the trend was in quite the opposite direction. The prevailing pattern of Club diving was neither concentration nor yet exploration; excellent for training, useless where results were concerned. It was true that the University groups did concentrate: on the Mediterranean. And they talked so much of their 'serious scientific purpose' that one suspected 'free holiday in the sun' immediately. There is nothing against this, of course, and it has indeed been an established archaeological gambit among the northern nations for almost a century. But as far as establishing the causes of relative alterations in sea level was concerned, it had almost nothing to commend it. The answers lay in the north.

The choice of Hayling Bay was partly a matter of logistics. It could be studied closely all the year round, year after year, checked and re-checked. It was not a fly-by-night economy-fare fleeting visit of an investigation; and indeed, I must guiltily admit that, when among the congregation of St. Peter's or St. Mary's, my attention sometimes wandered from the sermon to consider the stones, in a subconscious effort to memorise the entire structure piece by piece, so that I would be able to recognise them in a dismantled state underwater: A D 1324 seems a very long time ago, considered as a date in a history book, but not when you look at the list of Priors and Vicars on the wall of St. Mary's. Between Prior Reynard, who gave evidence in that year to the King's Commissioners regarding the loss of church land by inundation, to the last name on the list, the Rev. John Beaumont, M B E, ex-prisoner of Colditz, who had helped recover building material from the land the sea had taken, there were not a great many names. The very brevity of that list showed how close we were to those times, comparatively speaking. This was the second fact: there was documentary evidence—names, dates, testimony, and above all prices, for the bulk of our information lay in the surviving tax returns; they were State Papers, official documents. The third fact was elimination: although England is occasionally subject to slight seismic tremors, it is hardly an earthquake zone, and therefore violent displacement or warping by volcanic action, faults, fractures, and so on could be ruled out. One major factor eliminated. But also, although there was still *isostatic* depression and recovery to be taken into calculation, its general direction was reasonably well established. As a result of the thawing of the heavy weight of ice on the highlands of Britain, and indeed all around the shores of the North Sea and Channel, the mountainous areas were believed to be rising; and as the weight of frozen water so removed was now in the sea, the effect was thereby increased. Very gradually, the mountainous areas in the west of the British Isles were rising and the low-lying coastal strips along the North Sea and English Channel were sinking. Tilting would be a better description. And if at the same time the *eustatic* sea level was rising, the process of inundation would be accelerated in the south-east of England; but if the amount of water in the sea was decreasing, then the process of inundation would be slowed and partially masked. The reverse would be true, of course, for the north-west.

294

I looked in the documents for a number of clues, apart from the mere fact of inundation. Firstly, for evidence of climatic change, for this would be one obvious effect of a *eustatic* change. Secondly, for the time-scale involved—the dates. *Tectonic* change is very rapid, *isostatic* change very gradual; anything in between would probably be *eustatic* in origin. Above all, I wanted to know in as much detail as possible, exactly what had happened. Naturally, horizontal erosion came into the pattern, but it is a truism that erosional effect is necessarily at its maximum during a rise in comparative sea levels; at its minimum, or absent altogether, during a fall in comparative sea levels.

Without going into medieval history, it may be said that the fourteenth century was a period of disaster without parallel. Firstly, great inundations all round the coasts of north-west Europe; then war; then the devastation of the Black Death, bubonic plague; and odd happenings, wolves crossing the frozen Baltic over the ice, the herring no longer entering the Baltic towards the end of the century, and, an extraordinary fact only recently discovered in the Archaeological Research Laboratory at Oxford—the difference between true north and magnetic north being virtually nil at the beginning of the century, whereas in about A D 1000 it was known to have been between 25 and 30 degrees east. The outline period covering most of this was roughly A D 1250–1425. A period both too short and also too long to have any significant geological cause. Too short to be *isostatic* in origin, too long to be *tectonic*. By a remarkable chance, the Hayling documents contained the time and depth-scales, not exact, but near enough, in far greater detail than one could have expected; and there was even a 'control' present. All this hidden among the price of prime hoggerels. Of course, I did not get all the evidence I wanted from the one document or even the one site; the 'big picture' was the thing. And anyway the Norman fact-finding had not been devised to produce the statistics I wanted. Here, we were not dealing with a novelist, as at Kenchreai, or historians, as at Ephesus, but with the bold Baron Fitz-Bloodsucker. Not Apuleius, nor Pliny, nor Strabo, but the King's Commissioners in the persons of Ralph de Bereford and Richard de Westcote. What brought them down to Hayling was another French war.

They arrived and held their inquest on the Wednesday after the Vigil of St. Katherine in the 18th of Edward II. Which makes the date sometime in either November or December of 1324 (Edward having been crowned in July, 1307). It must have been an interesting confrontation between the Norman administrators and the Prior, Henry Reynard, representing the French religious foundation of Jumièges which owned much of the agricultural land of Hayling. The outbreak of war had made the Hayling estates an 'Alien Priory', which had to be taken into custody of the crown, and therefore its current value assessed. This was done, and, when the statisticians, at Westminster put it through their equivalent of a computer, a most extraordinary and suspicious set of figures popped out. There had been a general survey of land values on the lines set by that pioneering administrative project known popularly as 'Domesday' in the year 1294, and the value of the property held by the Priory of Hayling was then

£144 8s. 3½d. But the inquest of 1324 showed a value of only £42 4s. 7d. A drop in land, crop and cattle values of over £100 since 1294. No doubt the administrators could guess the reason, but the opportunities for a 'fiddle' were obvious and Reynard now technically an enemy alien. This would have to be enquired into very closely.

The two Crown Commissioners for the Alien Priories therefore returned for a full 'field' investigation, which was held on the Friday before the feast of the annunciation of the Blessed Virgin Mary in the 18th Edward II (8 March, 1325), with the Prior making his case to the Commissioners in front of a jury consisting of Nicholas Stak, Simon le Rous, Geoffrey de Brockhampton, Simon Ingel, Simon Michel, Thomas Stak, William Stuteville, John the son of Ralph Clark, John de Hursi, John de Longe, Richard Thomas, and Robert le Eyr, who, being on oath, were to decide on the question: *as to whether the possessions of the priory of Hailyngge were submersed and destroyed by the sea, as had been asserted by the prior, there or not; and if so, then what possessions were then so submersed, and of what yearly value those possessions were at the time in which the house was in the hands of the Lord Edward I, by reason of the war then existing between him and the King of France; and also what and how much the possessions which he then had there were worth by the year in all issues.*

Being on oath, and present in person on the land at the time, the jurors found: *that 206 acres of arable land of the demesnes of the priory had been inundated and destroyed by the sea, since the house was in the hands of the Lord Edward, father of the lord the then king, on account of the war; and that they were worth at that time £10 6s. 0d. by the year, because the better land of Hayling was nearest the sea; that fourscore acres of pasture, which belonged to the priory, had been submersed by the sea since the time aforesaid, which were worth by the year twenty shillings; that six virgates of the land of the customary tenants of the priory had been submersed by the sea and destroyed since the time aforesaid, from which the prior was in the habit of receiving 48s. rent by the year; that nearly the whole hamlet of Eastoke, with the lands pertaining to the same, as well as a great part of the larger hamlet of Northwood, and the greater part of the lands of the same, which hamlets and lands were belonging to the parish church of Hayling, and which the prior had for his own proper use, were submersed and destroyed by the sea . . . .*

This document, which is in the Public Record Office (PRO E. 106/8/9 Sect 5), is not so detailed as we should like, nor so full. It is technical, because it is a tax enquiry on agricultural values according to the Norman system; and it is limited to the agricultural property held by the Abbey of Jumièges in Hayling; it is not a complete record of land losses, because there were other land owners on the island apart from the French foundation; and it does not record the loss of buildings which were not connected with agriculture and therefore profit-making. Nor does it give a precise date to the inundations, merely the statement by the Prior that it had occurred 'in the time of the King your father, during the late wars with France'. That is, between 1294 and 1307. Nobody pushed the question of a precise date, for the very obvious reason that the great inundations had begun in about 1250 and by 1300 were widespread all round the coasts of Europe. The significant point is, that the Prior was pushed to defend his case for losses by inundation in front of two commissioners and a jury, and made it good.

The modern equivalent would be a Government enquiry set up to consider the claim by a County Council as to damages caused to beaches by the oil pollution from the *Torrey Canyon*, with the enquiry being held a mile or so from the beaches in question. The checks and balances would be considerable. However, Major Thomas, thinking in terms of horizontal erosion, considered the Prior might have exaggerated; and there was certainly a loophole, from the purely tax point of view, in the claim that the best land had been near the sea, and that therefore the value of what was lost was, acre for acre, higher than that of what now remained. But this is a purely historical conjecture and does not concern us, and we must be grateful to Major Thomas for extending his own enquiries to Jumièges in search of fresh documentary evidence, unfortunately without result. More recently, another amateur historian, the schoolmaster A. C. Reger, has stated much the same view, that Prior Reynard 'foxed' both commissioners and the jury, but this is to imply an almost superhuman cleverness, in that the Prior was able to fool the authorities of his own day but not someone re-examining the case more than 600 years afterwards. Mr. Reger was, however, the only local historian among a very great number who was able to examine the evidence and find no hint of a submerged church; his view was that the missing third church, the original one, was probably underneath a present building on land and that the stories concerning Church Rocks had no foundation. By mischance, he arrived at this conclusion almost at the same time as we began to find building material there.

In fact, Reger's argument was really with C. J. Longcroft, the best-known and most detailed of the earlier historians, who was a local solicitor and landowner and author of the *Hundred of Bosmere*, published in 1856. Longcroft had, or had access to, original documents which Mr. Reger's searcher was unable to find in modern times in the Public Record Office (with some exceptions, including the extracts above quoted, which are from Longcroft's translation, not Reger's). Reger was therefore unable to check these or his translations of them. But this was rather to trifle with detail, or so it appeared to me, as I was scrutinising the evidence in a different light—what I had seen on the seabed; and with a different intention—to establish the factors involved in the inundations. The critical quotation concerning the church itself (translated, of course, from the original medieval Latin) refers to a petition for relief of tax which was investigated for the Crown by John Roches and William Brockhurst in the 14th of Edward III (1341/2). They found: 'that there were the towns of Stoke, Estoke, Northwode, Southwode, Myngham, Westiton, and Hayling, within the island of Hayling; and that the greater part of the same island, in the fourteenth year aforesaid, was nearly destroyed and submerged by the inundation of the sea; that the place where the parish church of the same island was first erected and built was in the centre of the island; and being so built within the time of living memory of some coming thither, it stood by the seashore in good preservation, and at that moment was so deep in the sea that an English vessel of the larger class could pass along there, and that it was then distant from the land about two miles; and so from day to day, on every side towards the sea, the land was destroyed and submerged by the inundation of the sea . . .' Scrutinised in our light, this ruled out horizontal erosion and showed two large-scale inundations at least; the submersion of a church built originally in the centre of the island, which stood for a time by the seashore, and was then deeply submerged after the next phase. But there was corroboration of Longcroft's translation in Major Thomas' book, where this author referred to another lost document held by another former Hayling historian and solicitor, Padwick. 'I have a map of William Padwick's', wrote Thomas, 'which boldly marks an area between one and two miles seaward from West Town as "Hayling Church" and "Rocks". A footnote to the map which I would say was in Padwick's own handwriting runs, "This church stood in the centre of the Island as appears by an office copy of a petition from the inhabitants of the then Town in the Island in Mr. Padwick's possession which was presented to the King 1st Richard II 1377 praying to be relieved from certain 15th and 10th in consequence of inundations that took place 14th Edward III 1341 which was granted." '

Both from their occupations, as members of the legal profession, and from their interests, which concerned local history, Longcroft and Padwick were likely to lay their hands on documents, or copies of documents, not now to be found in the Public Record Office—or perhaps it would be better to say, not easily found, for in some ways this institution is not unlike the Archives of the Indies. Their own copies may still exist, or may have been destroyed during the war.

The next document quoted by Longcroft is the critical one from the causation point of view, and it follows on from the petition mentioned by Padwick for the 'reign year' 1st Richard II (1377) and is dated 2nd Richard II (1378 or 9). It is the findings of the jurors resulting from the enquiry which followed the petition for tax relief:

That the men of Hayling, on account of the great destruction of their lands in the island of Hayling, and the flux of the sea, and by reason of other disasters to which they had before that time been subject, as well as from the expense and charges which they had been put to for the defence of the island against the attacks of the enemy, were brought to such poverty that they had not sufficient to pay (the tax of) the tenth. And they found that the men of the island had made divers walls of piles, earth, and turf, for the preservation of their lands in various places within the island aforesaid, at the cost of the men of the island of forty marks, which by the inundation of the sea were entirely broken down, destroyed, and submerged; that three hundred acres of arable land, which used to be ploughed and sown, were submerged by the sea and entirely destroyed within forty-three years then last past; that there was then deep water there, and that at every flux of the tide some part of the lands of the island was destroyed and overflown, which land, so overflown by the tide for five or six years then last past, could not be sown nor any profit be taken by feeding of the same land, or in any other manner; and that the premises having been seen by the Barons, it was considered that a part of the taxation should be remitted.

And there you have it. The dates, the process, everything. The land area inundated forty-three years previously—in the mid-1330s—was now 'deep in the sea'; the land areas inundated during the five or six years previous to the petition, were merely being 'overflown'—that is, were still shallow and uncovered at low water. Only a large eustatic rise of sea level could explain how an overflowing by the tide could be converted to a deep water submergence after a period of around forty years. Much too slow to be a violent tectonic effect, much too rapid for gradual iso-static change. This process has now stopped and may even have been reversed, and the proof of that is a visual proof. There are accurate maps of Hayling dating from the first half of the nineteenth century, which show a narrow channel at the Chichester Harbour entrance side of Hayling, and on that land a watchtower. This is now a very broad channel, with no sign of the watchtower, but the lost land has not disappeared 'deep in the sea'; any wind at high water shows its outline clearly by the breaking effect of the waves on it, and at low water the greater part of it uncovers. In short, after more than a century of being 'overflown', it is still 'over-flown'; it has failed to submerge 'deep in the sea'. At low water, one can walk on the lost land.

A minor, but still important point, also arising from this document is the proof that sea defence walls were erected, the design stated, their fate indicated. But, again, for the full implications to be realised, present local knowledge is required. Where present land level on Hayling lies below sea level at high water (which it does at parts of Eastoke), it is defended by high concrete walls, sadly cracked. Where there is only horizontal erosion to worry about, as on the stretch directly opposite my house, wooden piles have recently been driven in to form a complex of walls which hold the winter shingle and have proved far more efficient than concrete breakwaters which, in living memory (the late 1950s, as attested by photographs of my children climbing on the wreckage), were disinte-grated and dispersed. The pile method appears to be the same as that employed by the medieval inhabitants of Hayling, reinforced by walls; but although this is a proved method of holding horizontal coastal ero-sion, it will be useless against a rising sea level; it will in fact only make the resulting disaster more catastrophic and complete–and would com-pletely explain the peculiar nature of the remains of the buildings on Church Rocks. All the local historians, but especially the modern ones, endured the disadvantage of seeing only the modern effects of horizontal coastal movement by erosion, and therefore assumed that this was the only factor to be taken into account. But, as I knew from the first, hori-zontal erosion could have played only a tiny, subordinate part in the submergence of the Church Rock buildings. Flatly, it was inundation and not erosion. Because most of the stone blocks were lying flat on the reef or on the shingle, very few were tilted; and the foundations were quite unaffected, being in their original, largely unbroken state. Having kept a continuous photographic record of what happens to pillboxes and concrete breakwaters subject to horizontal erosion, no one could ever convince me otherwise. The result is a complete break up of the structure and the scattering of fragments, usually wildly tilted, all over a large area. An inundated area may be preserved, an eroded area never. The formal proof lies in the photographic files: underwater on Church Rocks and above water on the present coastline.

The cause of the inundations was therefore a rise in the level of the actual sea, occurring fairly rapidly, and continuing into the first part of the fifteenth century, as attested by the various petitions which were made up to 1407. From this time on, there is no reference to great disasters from submergence. The movement had stopped. It may be compared to a high tide much prolonged. The very cessation of the movement also helped to rule out isostatic change, as this would have tended to continue the process of submergence. But it did not do so, and it has not done so.

The next point to consider was: What did the alteration of sea level amount to? This is very difficult to determine with exactitude. We do not know what the relationship of land to sea was before the inundations began. Today, Hayling is low-lying and parts of it are below sea level. But what is sea level—high tide or low tide? Spring tide or neap tide? And what is seabed level? There isn't one. Like the tides, the local seabed varies its height, although not so frequently or regularly. Changes of between 2 and 4 feet are common, changes of up to 8 feet are reported. What is the original land level at Church Rocks? On the level of the floors? Or are these cellars? What is the depth at Church Rocks? That depends on where and when you measure. It is not level ground now, and I have seen quite a deep depression, almost a pit, in the sand and shingle among the rocks. Do you measure to the top of the rocks? Or to their base? To the top of the highest rock? Or the lowest? I once amused myself by doing a depth-gauge check on an average, in-between tide at high water to the base of an average rock and got a reading of 28 feet. Unfortunately, depth gauges are inaccurate. An average low-water reading would be about 14 feet. Taking all factors into consideration, but still purely as a guess, the rise of sea level could be anywhere between 15 and 25 feet.

And one example, one solitary submerged site, is insufficient evidence; so far, generally speaking, we have only historical evidence to go on, which tells us little of depth and nothing of what now remains, but almost all of what we otherwise want to know: the question I first asked myself in 1960—could such a disaster possibly be local to Hayling?

Almost the first thing which takes the eye when studying the widespread historical evidence is the surely significant grouping of the dates. This never seems to concern most of the Mediterranean enquirers, the Germans excepted, of course; for most, one date appears to be as good as another, on those very few occasions when they even remember to put the date in. This must result from the generally geological, non-historical approach generally adopted so far, when a million years out one way or the other is of little moment. Trying to fix a geomorphologist to a date is like trying to pin a wasp to a board, under the impression that it is a butterfly. But dates are important, to the archaeologist no less than the historian, and nowhere more valuable than here.

And the tone of it, that was important too. Starting with the Solent area, with the answer to the petition of 1401, when the inhabitants of Hayling had suffered for a century and had been refused a certain tax relief by the Barons of the Exchequer, King Henry ɪᴠ had intervened 'with pious affection, pitying the miserable state of the same men, of his special grace, in reverance of God'. They don't give you a medal for under-going isostatic change. Language like that, from the Government, means downright disaster, not a little cliff erosion. The inundations had been compounded by French sea raiders and by bubonic plague, but the inundations were always mentioned first in the tax petitions, heading the disaster list.

One of my first discoveries, and one of the most important, was that no one had ever properly studied the subject, by collecting the documenta-tion. One of my later discoveries, just as important, was that no one ever would: it was beyond the knowledge and capabilities of one man. Little fragments of evidence, sometimes hints merely, turning up in the most unlikely places, as accidental by-products of other research, for instance. In 1966, I turned to the memoirs of Sir John Oglander, for eye-witness evidence at secondhand of the *Mary Rose* battle of 1545, which went on long after the point where I left it in Chapter 13, and culminated in the invasion of the Isle of Wight; and I found an inundation reference instead. Sir John, who was Deputy-Lieutenant of the Island 1595–1648, described the 'inning' of Brading Harbour during his tenure of office. That is, part of the seabed was reclaimed for agriculture by damming. And on the bed of the harbour, now dry, they found a stone-lined well! Sir John conjectured that this was the result of an inundation around 1300. This was most important evidence indeed, for it was an intact, inundated, uneroded well; in complete contrast to the horizontally-eroded Roman well which I was to see in process of complete destruction at Selsey a year later.

The only practical method would be to collect all the local works and follow up the references in the Rolls, which is really the province of a medievalist. But, running rapidly from left to right along the coastline from Hayling we come to Bracklesham Bay. Again, the petitioners requested to state upon oath the reasons why they should not pay the tax of the tenth. In 1340, for the little benefice of West Wittering, the causes were divided into three; firstly, 'much arable land which had been absorbed or laid waste by the waves of the sea'; secondly, 'much arable land devastated by the sand near the sea'; thirdly, 'the grass devoured by the Bishop of Chichester's rabbits lessened the valuation'. Only the date is important; no great disaster has occurred, if you can add rabbits. But the overall picture for that part of Sussex, covering the period 1291 to 1340, showed the loss of 5,500 acres, of which nearly half, 2,700, was at Pagham, on Selsey peninsula. One village, Rumbrugge, believed to be a derivation from the Saxon *thrim beorgum* (Three Barrows) gave up the ghost without a fight. The last reference to it is in 1398, when a diocesan register records that Cecily Rumbrug rendered homage to the Bishop for land called Rumbrug in Manewode. After that a silence, presumably of the sea, intervenes and the records stop. 'Three Barrows' is the only clue, not a very good one, to Commius and the lost Belgic capital, lost long before this; not in the Middle Ages at all, but in Roman times, or before. Two great inundations; not one. As for Selsey Bill itself, the chart speaks as well as the documents and the old maps: the whole stretch of the Owers, where the South Saxons first landed, was once above water. And here we are getting very close. Why did the Saxons come to England? Land hunger, reply the historians. Why was this? Partly because their population was increasing, partly because they had less land. Why did they have less land? Because the sea took it. Where was this? Friesland. When? The landings began in 477, in Sussex, but Kent had already fallen to Vortigern after a campaign lasting from 449. So we have the same process going on in the fifth century as we did in the fourteenth. Only, the events of the fourteenth century are better documented.

Move to Shoreham, the documentation tidily collected in a little church guide by the Reverend F. S. W. Simpson, MA, FSA. Shoreham was a port in Roman times, and after the Norman conquest rose to a status comparable to that of Southampton and Portsmouth combined. But on 16 January, 1404, against its name in Bishop Rede's Register was the laconic entry: 'one of the benefices destroyed by the sea'. By 1432, it had a population of only 200, and in Camden's *Britannia* published in 1586, appears the description: *Upon the shore, a little lower, appears Shoreham (anciently Scoreham), which by little and little has dwindled into a poor village, now called Old Shoreham; having given rise to another Town of the same name, the greatest part whereof is ruin'd and under water, and the commodiousness of its Port, by reason of the banks of sand cast up at the mouth of the river, wholly taken away; whereas in former ages it was wont to carry ships under sail as high as Bramber, at a pretty distance from the sea.* This phenomenon, the blocking of harbours in conjunction with inundation, no longer puzzles us. At Church Rocks, the former land surface has been clearly cut down by the scour of the currents, the topsoil completely removed; all this new material, in suspension, would go up and down Channel with the lateral run of the tides and be liable to be sucked into the nearest harbour mouth by the much faster currents to be found there on the flood. With sea level continually rising, a high proportion of it would tend to stay there. Of the known number of important medieval buildings, three only now remain at Shoreham; a Carmelite Priory and the Hospitals of St. Katherine, St. James and St. Saviour have vanished. Need anyone wonder where they are?

Further east is Hastings, affected by much the same forces at much the same time. The significant recorded dates are 1325—bursting of the sea defences; 1331—large part of the castle fallen into the sea; 1412—abandonment of the priory; 1440—neighbouring parishes of St. Leonards and St. Margarets severely affected. There was lesser damage during the great flood of 1333, of which Holinshed's Chronicle records:

This yeare, on Saint Clement's daie at night, which fell on the three and twentieth of November, through a marvellous inundation and rising of the sea all along the coasts of this realme, but especiallie about the Thames, the sea bankes or walles were broken and borne down with violence of the water, and infinite number of beasts and cattell drowned, fruitfull grounds and pastures were made salt marshes, so as there was no hope that in long time they should recouer againe their former fruitfulnesse. The effect of this storm tide on a town like Hastings, where the original sea defences had already been destroyed, would have been less catastrophic.

Further east still is Winchelsea, high up on a hill. Built to a grid design, it is the first example of town planning in England (by the English, at least), and for a very good reason. The writing was on the wall by 1251, in which year Matthew Paris, a monk of St. Albans, wrote: *At the time of the Equinox the sea overflowed its usual bonds, causing no small injury in the provinces of England lying near the coast, and the shore was inundated six feet higher than it had ever been before. . . .* In the following year, 1252, he noted an east wind swinging to south (the really dangerous, but most unusual, direction) on 13 January, which resulted in a sea which 'covered the places adjoining the shores, took possession of the mills and houses and drowned and washed away a great many of the inhabitants'. A Charter Roll of 1271 reported that St. Thomas's Church was partly washed away; and a Patent Roll of 1280 stated that the town was now partially submerged and in danger of total immersion. By Patent Roll of 13 October, 1283, the King appointed Stephen de Pencenstre, Henry le Walys and Gregory de Rokesle to design a new Winchelsea to replace the obviously doomed old town, which was finally lost in 1287, the site now being thought to be on Camber Sands, two miles to seaward of the present coast. Holinshed's description of these events is most valuable:

On the first day of October the moon upon the change appearing exceeding red and swelled, began to show tokens of the great tempest of wind that followed which was so huge and mighty, both by land and sea, that the like had not been lightly known and seldom or rather never heard by men then alive. The sea, forced contrary to his natural course, flowed twice without ebbing, yielded such a roaring that the same was heard (not without wonder) a far distance from the shore. Moreover the same sea, appeared in the dark of the night to burn, as it had been on fire and the waves to strive and fight together after a marvellous sort, so that the mariners could not devise how to save their ships where they lay at anchor, by no cunning or shift that they could devise at Hestbourne three tall ships perished beyond hope of recovery besides smaller vessels at Winchelsea, besides other hurt that was done in bridges, mills, breaks, and banks, there were some 300 houses drowned and some churches with the high rising of the water course. We shall probably never get nearer than that in vivid description of what these appalling and unprecedented events looked like and felt like to the participants in the disasters.

This must suffice for England, for the same story, with the same dates, occurs all along the coast, town by town, along the Channel coast and up both sides of the North Sea. Charles Green, Archaeological Consultant to the Ministry of Works, published in *Antiquity*, March 1961, a study of alterations in *East Anglian Coast-line Levels Since Roman Times*. This was a pioneer work, contradicting the previous unthinking assumption that sea level had risen in a simple progression. To avoid entanglement in arguments concerning causes, he preferred to use the neutral terms 'emergence' and 'submergence', 'marine transgression' and 'marine regression', but in spite of his caution what he is talking about is a series of very long-term up-and-down movements. In terms of the English coast, it is impossible to explain this by any other cause except *eustatic* change basically. He refers specifically to Yarmouth, where a beach was closely investigated by previous researchers, who showed that, even after the great flood of 1287, 'the coast here still stood some 13 feet higher in relation to the sea than it does today.' Work done in the Thames Estuary showed a submergence-phase beginning soon after 500 BC, reaching maximum probably in the first century BC (which probably put paid to the Belgic Capital of Commius). Then the reverse process set in and the land began slowly to emerge to close to its present level. This lasted until after the Norman Conquest. Evidence largely depended on excavating below low water mark, by coffer-damming, which was expensive, but he concluded that, 'It seems probable that, during the 13th century, a submergence-phase had begun, at first of trifling magnitude, but after the great flood of 1287, it certainly progressed with increased rapidity'. This is beach evidence, reinforcing and agreeing with the documentary evidence.

But evidence is found in the oddest places. For instance, an article 'The North-Frisian Outlands', which appeared in the *Cornhill Magazine* during 1868, deals with Sylt in very great detail. It lists the villages of Wenningstedt, List, Eydum, and Rantum as being some miles to seaward, with the same process as for Hayling, the new village taking the name of the old, except in the case of Eydum, the only trace of which is an old altar-screen in Westerland Church said to have been salvaged from it. This story also has its counterparts on Hayling, the artifacts being a bell and a font. The evidence cited for this area is not in the form of tax returns, but the 'registers of extinct churches and parishes, in which there is every reason to confide'. Knowing Sylt and other Frisian Islands from the ground, the air, and the sea, I have no reason to doubt it. There are legends, of course, principally that of a supposedly very extensive peninsula called Süderstrand stretching out almost as far as Heligoland, which in turn boasts old maps, the most reliable being those of Johannes Meijers in the seventeenth century, showing a very much greater island where there are now two small islands only, one of rock, one of sand. And there is the tale of how Klaus Störtebecker, the fourteenth-century pirate, was able to sail his ships right up to the town of Marienhafe in Ost-Friesland and moor them to the church tower, the water level being so high. Another oddly-placed but interesting article on this side of the North Sea, opposite East Anglia, is 'Ost-Friesland Floods', which appeared

304

in *British Zone Review*, the magazine of the Control Commission, for 20 January 1949. As the author explains, 'The only records of the early floods were kept by the monasteries and the names of the more serious floods were usually taken from the Saint's day or the proximity of some Saint's day on which they occurred. Thus we have the St. Lucia Flut of 1287, the St. Clement's Flut of 1334, the St. Antoni Flut of 1511 and the St. Martin Flut of 1685.' The two latter were temporary in effect, the two former being much the more serious. In 1287, fifty villages in the Emden district were destroyed, and in 1334 the seas reached Norden and destroyed the village and church of Westeel, besides enabling Störtebecker to take up a religious mooring. The coincidence of the dates was so striking that this made clear from the first that there must exist a common factor absent from the Mediterranean and in fact peculiar to the North Sea and adjacent areas. This is, of course, the 'Storm Tide', the build-up of gale water in the North Sea and English Channel which can raise sea level temporarily far beyond its normal height and so bring down man-made defences of low-lying areas in one terrible catastrophe. Where no sea level rise has taken place, however, there is normally a recovery; but in a period of rising sea level—a 'submergence-phase'—the effect can be fatal and permanent. For instance, the casualties for the St. Lucia Flut of 1287 are given as 20,000 persons, whereas later floods were merely inconvenient. The very building of sea defences, by postponing catastrophe until sea level had risen dangerously would make large areas exceptionally vulnerable to 'Storm Tides'. As the writer remarks, 'It is fairly well established that by the beginning of the 12th century progress had been made in some form of sea defence work', and concludes that 'The following three centuries were notable for a period of catastrophic floods during which the whole coast line from Calais to Jutland underwent considerable transformation.' Just as it did, in fact, on the other side of the North Sea and Channel at the same time.

Off the Dutch part of the Frisian Islands chain some underwater work has been done in recent years. The Nederlandse Bond Voor Onderwatersport failed to find the Roman Castle off Brittenburg, but they located the Roman Temple of Nehellenia 1 kilometre to seaward of the coast in 4 metres of water at high tide and also a castle, lost around 1600, only 100 metres off the present shore in 2 metres of water at low tide. The first was off Domburg on Walcheren, and had obviously been salvaged soon after inundation, only a few broken stones being visible. The latter was off Zierikzee, Schouwen Duiveland, where the pattern of a building could be discerned, as well as broken stones and much pottery buried deeply in mud. There were few volunteers to excavate it. The location methods used were neat. Old maps and a good deal of documentation was available and where old buildings, mainly churches, still existed on land, this gave a roughly accurate indication of direction. These two sites are roughly opposite the Thames Estuary, but the President of the Club, H. A. v Vlimmeren, told me in 1963 that they had had a look at a site out in the North Sea itself but that 'the sea is very wild at that particular place and very turbid, which does not induce us to start searching there!'

305

Some known submerged sites in the North Sea and English Channel. As the normal wind direction is from the south-west, it can be seen how the water will build up during gales in the eastern end of the Channel and, after passing round Scotland, also on both sides of the North Sea, causing unusually high 'Storm Tides' dangerous to sea coast defences.

Edinburgh

Belfast

YORKSHIRE

Hull

Dublin

LINCOLNSH

Caernarvon Bay

Liverpool

Cardigan Bay

WALES

London

HAMPSHIRE   SUS

Southampton   Portsmouth   S

Plymouth

Hayling   Sels

CORNWALL   Isle of Wight   Brack

Scilly Isles

Cherbourg

NORMAND

Brest   BRITTANY

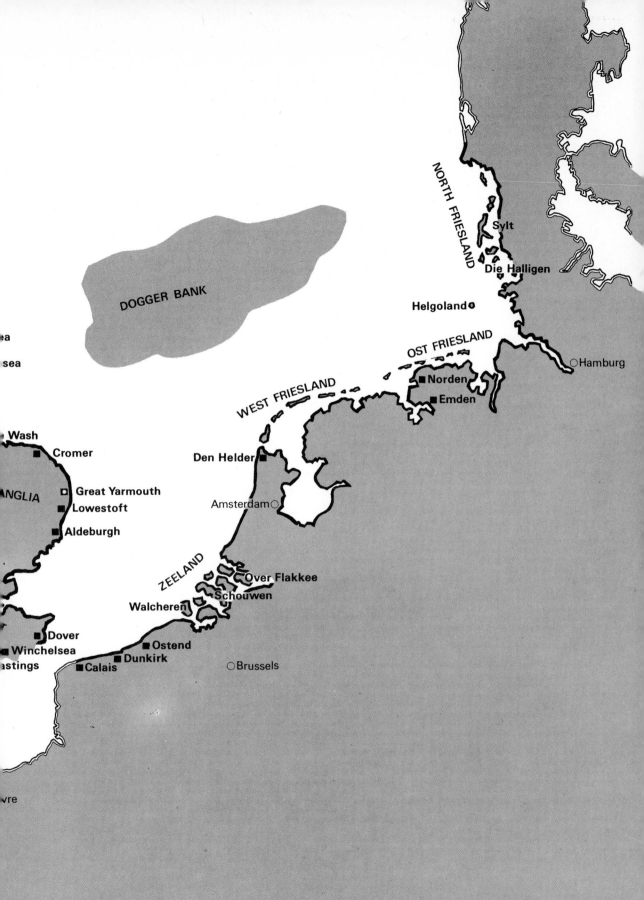

DOGGER BANK

NORTH FRIESLAND

Sylt

Die Halligen

Helgoland o

OST FRIESLAND

WEST FRIESLAND

Norden

Emden

o Hamburg

e Wash

Cromer

Great Yarmouth

Den Helder

ANGLIA

Lowestoft

Amsterdam o

Aldeburgh

ZEELAND

Over Flakkee

Schouwen

Walcheren

Dover

Winchelsea

Ostend

astings

Dunkirk

Calais

o Brussels

vre

o Paris

It will be recalled that the modern local historians were worried by the size of the disaster which must have taken place at Old Hayling, if the old historians were correct in placing the church originally in the centre of the island and now two miles out to sea. They never really looked at the evidence, because they were convinced that this could not be. This understandable doubt had already been completely removed by work carried out in the Netherlands by Professor G. D. van der Heide of the Directie van de Wieringermeer, the organisation responsible for studying the bed of the Zuyder Zee as, area by area, it was reclaimed from the sea. In effect, underwater excavation on land. In 1962 the Professor kindly sent me a copy of his *Zuyder Zee Archaeology*, reprinted in English from *Antiquity and Survival*. A great part of the Zuyder Zee was actually created by the basic factors which inundated Hayling and at the same period, and when such an area became dry land and could be excavated in the normal manner fairly easily, the proofs were plain to see. Villages, forests, and ships side by side—and the ships never earlier than about 1400 (except the remains of a prehistoric canoe from an earlier inundation). I was hardly overwhelmed by surprise to learn this, but as it was causes above all in which I was interested and as I already suspected the reasons, I wrote to the Professor to ask for his findings. He replied:

'In answer to your letter of the 8th of February I want to tell you that the sites in the Zuyder Zee were lost in the end of the Middle Ages by fresh-water flooding direct from the glaciers of Switzerland. But this was surely not a particular situation in this territory, but a part of a long-term sea-level rise as you wrote in your letter. In the Zuyder Zee we found the influence of climatical changes. Undoubtedly was that not only a question of melting of the ice of the glaciers of Switzerland, but also of the land ice of the polar area. In Holland there is mostly thought of climatical changes perhaps together with changes of the axis of the earth. Of course there are several theories about this question. We have to do in the South-Western part of Holland with two different problems: the sinking of the subsoil (perhaps at first a question of shrinking of the sediments when drying, too) and a rising of the sea level. In the Northern provinces of the Netherlands there is somewhat rising of the subsoil.'

In the circumstances of the excavations very precise work was possible, and fairly exact datings by artifacts and so on could be obtained, going back a very long time indeed. The pattern was of submergence and emergence phases, as shown opposite.

The fluctuations in historic time are very noticeable and, although the inundations were of fresh water from melted glaciers, they correspond well with the documented inundations; coming in a little later than the established period 1250–1425, but providing a most excellent reason for the migration of some of the Saxons to England after A D 400, although many of these came from further north and their legendary starting point is in the North Frisians, on Süderstand, and quite definitely, by name-association with the East Frisians in the Emden area. In his letter, the Professor mentioned that he thought the twelfth century A D marked the end of the regression period and that the transgression period probably

Emergence	*Submergence*
200,000 B C	
(Riss)	
	120,000 B C
	(Riss-Würm) SALT
20,000–9000 B C	
(Post Würm and Palaeolithic)	
	4000 B C
	(Mesolithic) FRESH
2000–1500 B C	
(Neolithic and Early Bronze)	
	1400 B C
	SALT
500–0 B C	
(Late Bronze and Iron Ages)	
	A D 400–900
	FRESH
A D 900–1400	
(Middle Ages)	
	A D 1400–1600
	FRESH
	A D 1600–1932
	SALT

started at the end of the thirteenth century. It would be surprising, however, if the records matched precisely over a large geographical area, partly because of the many subsidiary factors also at work, of which *isostatic* change is merely the most obvious. One which has not been considered is that of changes in oceanic circulation resulting from there being, for a start, more water to play with, so to speak, but with incalculable effects on the current systems. The geologists rather tend to think, write and speak of *eustatic* change as if what they were dealing with was water going up and down in a bucket, or at best a pond. Of course, it is nothing of the sort. The oceans are an enormous circulatory system of immense power and complication, hardly at all understood at present, but most definitely affecting the climate; indeed, it has been suggested by some theorists that they work like a thermostat, controlling the temperature, and switching themselves on and off as required. That also is a little too simple, because sometimes the boiler goes wrong; recently, for instance, Mediterranean water welled up in the North Sea, and also recently, there have been marked changes in the water content of the western end of the English Channel. If these fluctuations are taking place in a phase of relative stability, what is likely to happen if sea level rises or falls considerably, thus altering, for a start, the shape of the coastlines and also of the submerged contours? With this thought in mind, Holinshed's descriptions might well be re-read, with profit. The smallest part of the earth's surface is earth; by far the largest part is water, and sea water at that, in continuous motion controlled, or at least acted upon, by the earth's rotation upon its axis and its flight through outer space in relation to the pull of various heavenly bodies, principally the sun and the moon. When the sun and the moon come into line with the earth, then the earth experiences strong, or 'spring' tides. The ultimate causes of alternations in sea level must lie in outer space, perhaps in some gigantic heavenly rhythm.

This idea was postulated as long ago as 1912 by O. Pettersson in his paper *Climatic Variations in Historic and Prehistoric Time*, and modern enquiries have merely added additional possible factors to the scheme of things which he put forward. In doing this, he had to undertake historical research into emergence and submergence phases, which did clearly show climatic changes, as one would expect; perhaps the most interesting throwing light on the early voyages of the Vikings across the North Atlantic, by re-reading their sailing directions in conjunction with references to the danger, or otherwise, of meeting drifting ice. Again, the dates coincide very closely with the results of work which had not even been done when he wrote his thesis. From the ninth to the twelfth centuries inclusive, the Vikings took a northern route and do not mention being hindered by ice, so presumably it was not melting and breaking up into drifting bergs. From the thirteenth century onwards, however, navigators are warned to expect much ice drifting in the sea off Greenland, but nothing drastic is suggested, which would indicate the start of a melting period which would cause sea level to rise. By the end of the fourteenth century, however, fundamental avoiding action has had to be taken; the northern route is closed and they must steer south-west to avoid the dangerous, drifting ice; which would imply that the north polar ice cap at least was in full melt. Once more, therefore, from yet another unexpected angle we have evidence pointing to roughly 1200 or so to 1300 and after, with the first really strong indication around 1300. Just the period when Prior Reynard told the commissioners that the first great inundation had taken place at Hayling.

But why did the ice melt? Fluctuations in solar radiation is one modern theory, which could well be a major factor. Fluctuations in oceanic circulation and temperatures is another, also quite possibly a major factor. Possibly merely coincidence is that recent discovery concerning the earth's magnetism. In Saxo-Norman times magnetic north was between 25 and 30 degrees east of true north, but by 1300—again that date! —it had altered sharply by that amount, so that true north and magnetic north virtually coincided. At the moment, geophysicists tend to rule out a great change in the axis of the earth as an explanation of this, and prefer to think in terms of some alteration in the earth's core. But a change there certainly was, and at a coincidental time.

Pettersson was in fact an oceanographer, studying tidal motions, fluctuations and rhythms in the seas surrounding Sweden from 1891 onwards; so he thought in terms of oceanography, when he found those patterns significant. But the introduction he wrote to his thesis was history:

'In the last centuries of the middle ages a series of political and economic catastrophes occurred all over the then-known world. They synchronise with occurrences of a startling and unusual kind in the kingdom of Nature. The coasts of Iceland and Greenland became blocked by Polar ice. Frequent volcanic eruptions occurred in Iceland and the surrounding seas. Violent storm-floods devastated the coast of the North Sea and Baltic. In certain cold winters Öresund and the Baltic were frozen over and the lucrative Hanseatic herring fishery of the early middle ages which had been carried on in the Baltic and Öresund ceased altogether. All these events are recorded in ancient chronicles which also depict the social and economic state of the communities, which were greatly influenced by these violent climatic variations and their consequences: famine and disease. . . . The Icelandic chronicles from the fourteenth and fifteenth centuries abound in descriptions of catastrophes. . . . Simultaneously there occurred violent floods and inundations of the European continent and winters of unexampled severity. Such was that of the year 1332–1333 described in the history of Olaus Magnus. . . .' I must confess I read all this (in 1960) with great interest because Pettersson, looking out on the world from the viewpoint of Sweden was quoting catastrophes and inundations I had never heard of, while he had never heard of the almost identical catastrophes and inundations I already knew a good deal about in my part of the world; and the dates and the details were the same. It was the sort of independent check I rather like.

Pettersson's theories were suggested to him by his discovery of a phenomenon he called 'submarine waves' entering the Baltic in periodic rhythms which fluctuated in most complicated patterns which proved to coincide with the relative positions, distances, and angles of the sun and moon to fixed points on earth. Eventually, he postulated a pattern taking just under 2000 years to go from peak through low to peak again; like an enormous spring tide of immense duration, succeeded by a weak neap tide of long duration, with, of course, inner fluctuating patterns. As he explained, 'The tide-generating force of the sun and moon, which governs the range of the tide, increases in our latitudes with their declination and proximity to the earth and is greatest when each of the heavenly bodies attains its maximum of declination and proximity to the earth simultaneously. This happened as to the sun about 1328 (Bohlins calculation) when the perihelion of the earth and the wintersolstice occurred on the same day. At the time of the wintersolstice 600 years ago the tide-generating force of the sun must have had an absolute maximum.'

Another calculation showed him that the moon would have exerted its strongest influence on the North Sea area of earth at the end of the fourteenth century. Considering the maximum effect to be obtained by a combination of the effects of sun and moon, Pettersson arrived at A D 1369 very roughly. He passed his figures for revision to an astronomer, Mr. Strömberg of Stockholm Observatory, and these showed that: 'the absolute maximum of the tide-generating force must occur about 3500 BC, 1900 BC, 250 BC, A D 1433, A D 3300'. This enormous force would of course quite definitely break up a large part of the polar icecap, and cause it to drift to warmer waters, where the ice would melt, besides the incalculable effects of altering oceanic circulation. Alterations of climate would certainly occur, the effect of the very high winter spring tides be increased, and bad weather might well coincide with these on many occasions, as it does today. The theory therefore passed the first test, that of historic evidence. The inundations of North-West Europe were associated with climatic changes and most unusual tides and weather. Theories as to *isostatic* movement, *tectonic* change, compaction of sediments, and so on, fall at this first fence. They complicate the picture, but they do not serve to explain it basically. The next stage is to test Pettersson's theories by putting his chronology alongside all the other chronologies, obtained in different ways by other people for slightly different geographical areas. That is: Pettersson from tidal and astronomical observations in the Baltic, Van der Heide for sediment and artifact evidence from the Zuyder Zee; Green from sediment and artifact evidence for East Anglia, myself for the Hampshire/Sussex coast from historical evidence. (Pettersson's historical enquiries gave approximately the same results for dating as did my own; these are shown in brackets).

Pettersson (peaks)	Van der Heide	Green	McKee
3500 BC	4000 BC	—	—
1900 BC	1400 BC	—	—
AD 250	AD 400–900	500–100 BC	AD 400–500
AD 1433	AD 1400–1600	AD 1250–1600	AD 1250–1425
(AD 1300–1500)			

It is quite clear that, the further back we go in time, the shakier does the evidence become, which is only to be expected. This may partly explain the discrepancies. But partly also it must be that some of the data is missing, or has been incorrectly read, or that there are other factors at work. The latter will be partly geographical, very broadly speaking, in that the inundation dates which I gave for Hampshire and Sussex—1250–1425—would have to be extended after 1425 if the coasts of either East Anglia or Ost-Friesland were to be considered from purely historical evidence; indeed they might well be extended to 1500 or even 1600. A reason for that can be suggested in their geographical location, which makes them more susceptible to effects of storm-tides than the Channel coast, or to the horizontal erosion resulting from an increase in sea level being more severe there, or to the effects of *isostatic* change. All these factors together, and possibly others, may well be at work to modify the main causation, by making its effect either more or less severe. Some can be purely local. For instance, Hayling Bay is a protected site, as it lies in the lee of the Isle of Wight during the prevailing south-westerly gales, whereas the adjacent Bracklesham Bay is wide open to the effects of a south-westerly and the difference in the seabeds (their basic geology being the same) is astounding. Neither, of course, are affected by northerly gales, as they then lie close under the lee of the mainland. If a

312

change in climate meant also a change in the direction of the prevailing winds, this could have a most drastic effect. But for the period I was interested in, A D 1250–1425, the correlation of the dates was remarkable; Hayling was merely one small example of a process which had affected at least all North-West Europe.

One item from Pettersson which struck a chord was the herring. I lived four years in Hamburg, where they have the pirate admiral Klaus Störtebecker ('Nick Tosstankard') as a folk-hero, instead of Robin Hood; and his story and that of the entry of the herring in vast numbers in to the Baltic were one and the same, for his pirate fleet preyed on the herring fleets and the Hanse trade routes. That the herring should enter the Baltic during an inundation period, and leave it afterwards, had suggested to Pettersson that they came in with the giant submarine waves which, during the critical cosmic periods, flowed under the fresh water with sufficient force to break over the sill of the Cattegat and into that brackish sea. Orthodox historians are still puzzled as to why the herring left the Baltic, 'turning up their dainty noses from the Baltic to the British coast', as Fisher puts it; and failing to realise that this unexplained retreat from former haunts coincided with the end of an inundation period. As we know now, the Isle of Wight 'cut-off' being a first-rate example, the chemical content, temperature, salinity and turbidity of the water, among other factors, determine the biological range of a particular area. An inundation, with an inrush of largely salt water, would so alter that range, and drastically. There would be wholesale massacre, followed by colonisation of the area by new species. Exit, the old fauna and flora. Enter, the new. The process would be reversed, when the inundations came to an end. Exit the herring, in search of something to eat and congenial conditions in which to seek it. Exit also the great Hanseatic herring fleets, and with them, the decline of their trade routes which, from Bruges to Novgorod, had been the second most important such network in the world. We might well call the herring, in such circumstances, an 'indicator fish', and the clue so provided, not so much by the inrush as by the retreat, is most indicative. For *isostatic* change is tending to raise land level in the Gulf of Finland but should, theoretically, be depressing it on the low-lying sea coasts of Denmark.

And here a word of warning to underwater archaeologists. Your time is short. The Baltic will become a saltwater sea again. The sunken ships still almost completely preserved since, say, 1450, will disintegrate, literally eaten away by the invading range of natural life which enters with the seawater of the oceans.

The Scilly Isles: changes of
sea level.

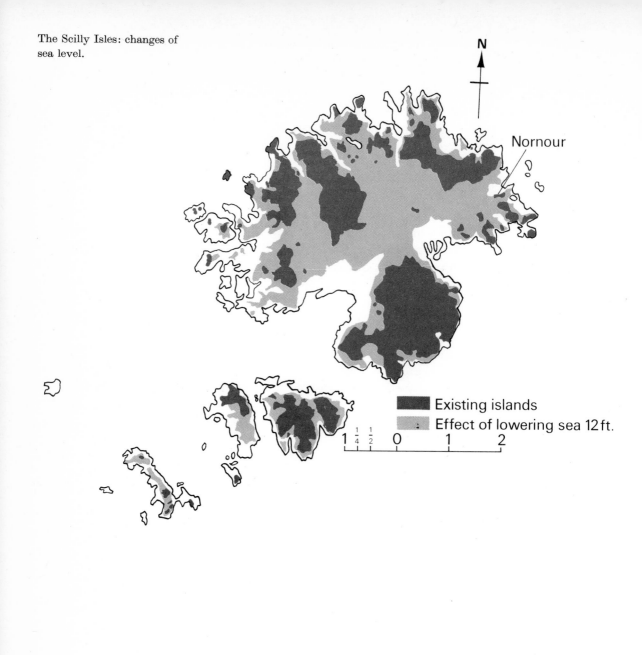

N

Nornour

Existing islands
Effect of lowering sea 12 ft.

1 ¼ ½ 0   1   2

17
The drowning of the pirate city

Legends of bells: Hayling, Wales, Port Royal
Ys and the Scilly Isles

We had begun our investigation by enquiring, 'Is there any truth in this "Church Bells under the Sea" story?' This was shorthand. We did not really believe in the bells. Who could, at 14 feet low water? After a careful scrutiny of all the smallest and lowest and most modest Saxon or Norman churches in the vicinity, I was convinced that there was not one of them, and that included Warblington, which would not show the bell at high tide, let alone low tide, if placed temporarily on Church Rocks. Even on a more deeply submerged site, there was the question: Could one hear, in air, a bell which was tolling under the sea? Probably not, because there would be no medium which could conduct the sound from the one world to the other. We were unable to establish this scientifically because no one would lend us a church to submerge. The only remaining avenue of research was documentary: to locate a 'Church Bells Ringing Under the Sea' legend and analyse it. This proved extraordinarily difficult because, not to put too fine a point on it, there were no such legends. With one single, solitary exception—Port Royal in the West Indies.

Apart from this, the legends pointed in the opposite direction; as did whatever evidence was available. The Hayling legends were all quite definite: this or that artifact, recovered from the beach or the bay a long time ago, is said to have come from the old church under the sea. An excellent legend, in fact, for it fitted both the facts and commonsense. And, of course, it was repeated across the North Sea on Sylt, with the salvaged altar screen in Westerland Church. And, moreover, fitted the clearly 'robbed' or salvaged nature of those few sites which had actually been examined underwater. Two of the Hayling artifacts were already in churches. In St. Peter's Church the largest bell 'is supposed to have been washed up from the old church under the sea', according to the Guide Book. In St. Mary's Church there are two fonts, one Norman and the other Saxon, the latter in a poor state of repair and being in fact the base of a Saxon cross re-used to make a font, with the old Saxon carving still faintly visible. In J. P. Williams Freeman's pioneer work *Field Archaeology of Hampshire*, written before the First World War, he states: 'Many years ago, whilst some dredging operations were being carried on at Jacob's Well near Church Rocks the Font was dredged up and cast upon the beach, when after a considerable time it was removed to Westbourne Church and eventually to the present Parish Church of South Hayling.' The truth of both the attributions has been disputed by later historians, on one technical ground or another, and it is no part of my purpose to seek to prove that they came from the sea; but rather to prove the nature of the local legend. About the third artifact there is no doubt, for the present Vicar discovered it and I helped him check the story attached to it, in 1963. According to expert opinion, it is probably 'part of a "Cross Shaft" of the period about A D 900 or a little later, of primitive or local Saxon or Viking art'. It was then mounted upside down as the base for a sundial in the grounds of the former Mosquito Research Institute on Hayling's Sea Front Road, founded by the late Mr. J. F. Marshall, and it was the resemblance of the carvings to those on the Saxon font in St. Mary's, which caused the Vicar to make enquiries. The best evidence we could get from

The second (Saxon) font in St. Mary's Church, South Hayling, supposed to have been 'dredged up' at Church Rocks in the nineteenth century.

the relatives of Mr. Marshall was that, in his widow's lifetime, but not within their memory, the stone had been purchased from a man who had found it on the beach opposite the Crescent, that beach being further seaward than the present beach. And with that we had to be content. Nevertheless, here once again was the same sort of artifact and the same sort of story as in the legend; but in this case no legend. This inclined me to assume that the disputes on technical grounds concerning the bell and the font were probably worthless quibbles and that these also had come from the sea. 'Washed up on the beach,' however, might well be really 'trawled up in the bay and dumped on the beach'; because this was how, using an oil drum for a lift, Harknett and myself had raised the first big block from Church Rocks, *towing* it ashore behind his motorboat, dumping it on the beach, and hauling it with ropes up to the car park. It is now,

317

with other Church Rocks masonry, in my garden and will doubtless cause future historians to dispute its origin. To the obviously salvaged artifacts, including the piscina and much of the stonework at the Dovecote still standing in the grounds of the former Grange associated with the old Priory, no legends are attached; local archaeologists, however, are of the opinion that they came from the submerged Priory Church soon after inundation and that the extension to the Dovecote (made of the salvaged material) implies an increase in population at the Grange, easily explained by the presence there of the displaced monks.

This research was short-circuited early on by the discovery that someone had already done the work for me, the historian Ernest Morris in his out-of-print book, *Legends o' the Bells: being a Collection of Legends, Traditions, Folk-Tales, Myths, etc., centred around the Bells of All Lands.* In spite of the title, it is a thorough and serious work. The legends connected with water came under four broad headings:

1. Bells Tolling under the Sea, as a result of Land Submergence.
One example only, Port Royal, submerged by earthquake, 1692. Sailors anchored over the submerged town claimed that their anchors caught in buildings and that they sometimes heard bells tolling.

2. Bells Tolling from Villages Submerged in Lakes.
A number of stories, all from Wales, the bells being said to belong to churches, cathedrals, or castles.

3. Lost Bells, Tolling under the Sea or under Rivers.
The majority of the myths come into this category, with the variations forming a pattern, and occurring in all countries. 'Lost by ship or boat wreck while in transit' is one variation, 'Hidden underwater to save them from robbers' another, 'Stolen by pirates subsequently wrecked' yet another. In rivers, there is often a deep, scoured hole on a bend called usually the 'bell-hole' or 'bell-pool' (there is one of these at Bosham, near Hayling, the raiders being Vikings, according to local legend). The detail that the bells could be heard ringing underwater by no means always occurs.

4. Bells Tolling to give Warning.
Fairly frequent, and not to be doubted; instances include the Armada. But the only flood warning quoted was that for the great flood of 1571, from the 200 ft. high tower of Boston Church, Lincolnshire, which reared up out of the floods (as described in the poem by Jean Ingelow). One could add, 'False invasion alarm, Portsmouth area, 1940' to the list, when the ringing of the church bells was to be the official warning and somebody got excited.

This was interesting, but soon afterwards I discovered that I had been wrong to dismiss the 'tolling of the bells' so easily, for the *Royal Naval Diving Magazine,* spring, 1964, carried a genuine story of tolling bells and divers, led by Lt.-Cdr. W. Y. McLanachan, whom I had met during the disposal of the Church Rocks 'mine'. His divers had been called to the villages of Derwent and Ashapton to destroy by explosive the tower of a
318

submerged church because the tolling of the bell on windy nights was intolerable to the villagers. The mythical story to the life! With but one significant correction. The church stood in a man-made lake recently created as a reservoir and the bell tower stood well out of the water, the bells being tolled by the wind and ringing in air. This could well happen where a natural inundation was concerned.

One has to be careful with legends, of course, but is rather too easy to be sceptical and so to dismiss without investigation what are in fact faint but genuine clues. An excellent example of the difficulties is provided by F. J. North's book *Sunken Cities*, in which he deals with all the Welsh tales of submerged coastlines and buildings submerged in lakes, and disposes of them all by argument. It is bitterly cruel to throw cold water on sites already submerged in it. Looking at his evidence, I am of the opinion that it in fact refers to two genuine coastal inundations, that of the late Middle Ages and that of the late Roman period; plus lake inundations at least worth looking at. Mr. North's main targets, late-Welsh fairy tales, were hardly worth shooting at. However, the handling of the evidence generally does raise a few pertinent points for future enquirers. Mr. North points out, with truth, that most of the flood stories are basically similar, even down to the type of incidents described; and then infers that this must be because one fairy-tale writer copied another. This happens, of course. But, equally, all inundation stories are, and must be, basically similar, down to points of detail. A great deal of innocent fun is had with the stories of how survivors are said to have floated past on a bed or a cradle or some other unusal life-raft; this may not be copying, however, but merely storyteller's automatic selection of the unusual incident rather than that which everyone would take for granted, people escaping to the roof of a house, for instance. Why should one disbelieve the bed or the cradle method of flotation in medieval times, when the *Sunday Express* of 5 February 1967, could headline a story of the Canvey Island floods of 1953: 'LINDA, THE FLOOD BABY WHO FLOATED TO SAFETY IN HER PRAM, IS 14 NOW'. To prove that Linda existed, they printed her picture. Are we to infer that the journalist got his information, not from Linda, but from some obscure document concerning medieval Wales? Similarly, Mr. North points out as a suspicious circumstance, that the flood stories always contain the tale of a man on a horse who makes for high ground and, arriving before anyone else, is first with the news. But if such an inundation occurred nowadays, would anyone make for low ground? And if no one did, then who would be most likely to arrive first on the high ground—the man driving the Mark X Jaguar, or the crippled old lady hobbling along on foot?

Mr. North is forced to rely on such arguments, because his sole open water investigation was made from a rowing boat at low tide on one site which, being a geologist by profession, he declared a natural feature. No doubt it was, but as any archaeologist or builder will testify, man often makes much use of natural features in his constructions and therefore we have to be very careful before we write them off. Indeed, one has to be more careful before reporting 'negative' than in reporting 'positive', because a positive result will be followed up and a mistake soon discovered; not so with a negative. So a little optimism is in order, particularly as without hope, you will not find. The lake stories, especially, require an underwater investigation, because remains of buildings of sorts are beginning to turn up in lakes elsewhere, over a very wide area indeed. Published results include the work of Zbigniew Bukowski in Lake Pilakno, Poland, for the Institute of Material Culture of the Polish Academy of Sciences in Warsaw, which showed traces of an early La Tène settlement, not on the shores of the lake but out in the water. The most up-to-date report is *Wyniki Podwodnych Badan Archaeologicznych W. Jeg. Pilakno, Pow, Mragowo, W., 1962 Roku*. Very recent, unpublished work includes the excavation of a pre-Etruscan village of about 800 BC in Lake Bolsena, Italy, for details of which I am indebted to Miss Helena Wylde; and a survey of Loch Lomond, in Scotland, which showed the existence of four completely artificial islands or cranogs and one natural island which had been extended artificially, in association with Samian ware of the first or second century A D, for details of which I am indebted to Major Hume Wallace.

Just as Mr. North was provoked into deriding all submergence stories in Wales, because a number of fairly-recent fairy tales could be easily exposed, so it seems that Mr. Dugan in his *Man Explores the Sea*, already quoted, was tempted to strike out at the concocted tales traditionally associated with what is called in England the 'Silly Season', and thus to deny the existence altogether of a submerged Port Royal, let alone its bells tolling under the water. He wrote, in 1956: 'The American version is the sunken pirate city of Port Royal, supposed to have slid into the Caribbean when an earthquake and fire struck the wicked down. Diving expeditions to walk the streets of Port Royal are a traditional hot-weather newspaper item in the United States.' There was a sub-stratum of truth here, in that, as was subsequently shown, a great deal of silting had taken place on the site and any diver who went down to investigate the legend in the twentieth century was not going to see very far, and what he would see, would be mud. But to assume from this that there was no sunken Port Royal was going much too far. The author of *Legends o' the Bells* had entered the tolling bells as a legend, but the submergence of Port Royal as a fact, by no means a quibbling distinction, as the postage stamps showed when the present author wrote to Robert Marx in 1967 for news of Port Royal and the real low-down on the bells story. Mr. Marx's reply was adorned with a beautiful Jamaican blue 5/- postage stamp, showing diving-ship and artifacts and labelled: 'Port Royal Exploration of Sunken City'. He was able to enclose a 73-page report which he had made for his employers, the Institute of Jamaica, entitled: *Excavation of the Sunken City of Port Royal: December 1965–December 1966: a Preliminary Report*. The report was dated March, 1967, and showed that 60 per cent at least of the original sunken city was now under the land, not the sea, and that the remaining underwater portion, amounting to about 1½ million square feet, had been covered with seabed sediment, except for a few walls near the 'Church Beacon', which were

320

The sunken town of Port Royal: members of the excavation team lifting ashore a brass cannon so coral-encrusted that it is hardly recognisable even above the water.

probably a part of Fort James, not a church. The proposed area of excavation totalled 480,000 square feet of sunken town, situated on a gentle slope which went down to 60 feet.

I had previously left Port Royal severely alone in my enquiries regarding submerged sites because, although I did not know very much about it, what I did know was sufficient to show that it was a special case, of no direct relevance as far as causation went with any site I knew of in north-west Europe. Mr. Marx's preliminary report for the Jamaican Government, who are financing the massive excavation, makes this very clear. 'Port Royal lies in an earthquake belt that extends from eastern Mexico through Cuba, Jamaica, Hispaniola and Puerto Rico (geologically unrelated to the volcanic region that runs through the Lesser Antilles to the South American continent),' he wrote. Further, the town had been built on unconsolidated material of dead coral, loose sand and so on, forming a sandspit alongside Kingston Harbour, with the nearest solid

321

bedrock being of limestone 60 feet down below apparent ground level. 'Such a shaky foundation,' writes Marx, 'might have been simply a nuisance in itself, but the inhabitants of Port Royal insisted upon making things worse by building their houses, stores and taverns several stories high. And in a severe earthquake like that of 7 June 1692, the results were both disastrous and, to a geologist, a foregone conclusion: tall buildings, resting on nothing more solid than loose, water-logged sand, and a few feet above sea level, at the edge of a steeply sloping sea bed, were bound to slide or topple down the slope and sink beneath the sea.' In some geological reconstructions, Port Royal is shown as being built on a kind of coral-supported shelf projecting out over nothing in particular.

Why anyone should ever have thought there was no truth in the story of submergence is a puzzle. The affair did not occur around 120,000 BC, but began at 11.40 a.m. on 7 June 1692, continuing for some hours of repeated earthquake tremors, followed by 'tidal' waves, and although more than 2,000 lives were lost, there were also a great many survivors who could speak and write, and did. Some of them were required to produce reports. Additionally, accurate plans of the town had been made and still existed. The latter very much simplified the work of the archaeologists, who are at present conducting a large-scale 'emergency dig', because the site of Port Royal may be threatened by future schemes to improve the modern Kingston Harbour. Mr. Marx is in charge of this and his historical studies show that Port Royal has had a longer history of underwater salvage and excavation than any other site known. Two factors contributed to this. The first was that the submergence was graded from easy to not-too-difficult. After the inhabitants had recovered from the sum total of the disaster, 2,000 deaths by drowning, 3,000 deaths by disease consequent upon it, they found Port Royal partly out of the water, partly in the water but with some of the buildings sticking out of it, and partly completely submerged to a depth then of less than 50 feet. The second factor was that Port Royal had been a pirate town, its inhabitants engaged in the 'wracking' or 'wrecking' business, which was divers' parlance then for stripping wrecked vessels of easily-get-at-able valuables. This is not so easy as it sounds, but with the right equipment and sufficient experience, a great deal can be done; and the locals had that equipment, or could improvise it, and possessed plenty of experience. Mr. Marx writes: 'The deepest part of the city lay under less than fifty feet of water, and most of it under twenty feet. Some used diving bells, which allowed them to remain submerged for an hour or so; the rest were free divers, and according to reports were capable of reaching depths of 100 feet and remaining submerged as long as five minutes. Besides diving, the other methods of salvage used on the site were dredging and fishing. To dredge they lowered heavily weighted fishing nets and dragged them over the sea floor, snagging loose items. To fish they first spread oil on the surface of the water to make it smooth so that they could see clearly to the bottom, and then used long poles or ropes with hooks attached.' As it happens, the latter method was in current use in the Portsmouth area up to 50 years ago, for the salvaging of dummy 800 lb. shells fired from coastal batteries

322

Three of Bob Marx's divers with a coral-encrusted brass pot recovered from the ruins of Port Royal, with bricks from a submerged building concreted to it.

at practice, and photographs exist of the men and their equipment, which consisted of 'pricker' pole and tongs; they were called 'Shotters', who had to be both anglers and engineers. The poles were 40 feet long.

As Marx points out, the early salvagers at Port Royal had the best chance of finding the valuables which certainly existed, because they knew more or less exactly where to look. 'We also know that salvage continued on a large scale for several decades after the earthquake. However, our own excavations have revealed that the walls of many buildings collapsed during the earthquake itself, and the salvagers apparently did not bother with attempts to raise and recover what lay beneath. They also by-passed items of minor importance to them, such as pottery, glassware, and clay smoking pipes, that lay in the open on the sea floor. The area located between Forts James and Carlisle, where the wealthy merchants had their wharves, warehouses and homes, all sank within a matter of minutes in thirty to forty feet of water. But the area to the south, between Forts James and Charles sank gradually, and the upper parts of these buildings remained above water for years, submerging only gradually as their weight caused them to sink into the soft sand of the seabed and the seabed itself to subside. In 1859 a Royal Navy helmet diver, who was at Port Royal making repairs to an English warship, made several prolonged dives on the site and reported that the walls of many buildings, including Fort James, were visible above the sea floor (Jeremiah D. Murphy, *What a Diver Found in 1859*). And as late as 1880, an English scientist visiting Jamaica stated that on clear days many of the buildings could still be seen from the surface through a glass-bottomed bucket (Harry E. Vendryes, *Port Royal's Sunken Treasure*). No salvage attempts or observations of the sunken city have been recorded for the first half of the present century, and during that period the site disappeared almost completely below the bottom sediment.' Apart from modern silting from modern causes, Marx was able to pin-point the earthquake of 1907 as also responsible, in that it brought down many of the still standing walls which when he excavated them, proved to have trapped underneath them artifacts which clearly dated to the nineteenth century, not the seventeenth.

'The first recorded exploration of Port Royal in this century,' he continues, 'was in the summer of 1954. Mr. Cornel Lumiere, a producer of underwater films, and Mr. and Mrs. Alexis Dupont, of Wilmington, Delaware, spent a week exploring the site, although with little success until the last day, when they discovered an arched doorway near Fort James with ten steps leading up to the entrance. The following year I made a brief visit to the site and was directed to the spot where the archway had been located. Sediment had already covered all the steps and most of the archway, and I understand that by the time Mr. Edwin Link arrived on the site in 1956 no traces of the archway remained above the sea floor. A full account of his successful expedition in 1959 was published in the February 1960 issue of *National Geographic Magazine* and need not be repeated here. The results indicated not only that Port Royal was one of the most important marine archaeological sites in the western hemisphere but also that a long-term program of excavation would be required to do it justice. In the fall of 1965, I was contracted by the Jamaican government to direct such a program, after a series of recent developments had convinced the government that the excavation should begin without delay.' Thus the present excavations are large-scale, long-term, local-based and cannot be compared to anything done previously, as these were in the nature of 'soundings', or preliminary reconnaissance. Even so, the area is so large that it can be dealt with only by small sections at a time; and it is extremely difficult. Excavation to a depth of 12 feet below seabed level, with nearly nil visibility, and trenches tending to slide or cave in, present problems of orderly recording which have not yet been fully solved. Even if they could be, the cost might be prohibitive.

Among the ruined buildings have been found two large ships, not yet fully excavated. Provisionally, they have been identified. One appears to be the vessel indicated in an anonymous account written shortly after the earthquake and the tidal wave which followed: 'In this dreadful
324

typical day's haul from
ort Royal, including a
ooden musket butt,
wter plate, two pewter
d one silver spoon, an
on cooking cauldron,
veral wine glasses, a
own-glazed mug, a small
lftware vase, a band rim
a pewter charger and a
ece of brass.

concussion several ships in the harbour were drove into the town and lost, one whereof was a French Prize, which was drove into the market place, and there lost.' Another vessel appears to be a British warship, the frigate *Swan*, fifth rate, 32 guns, which was being careened at the time when the tidal wave struck on the heels of the earthquake and seems to have stranded on the ruins, partly above water. She is probably the vessel referred to by a survivor, who stated: 'At length I got a canoa, and row'd upon the great sea side towards my house where I saw several men and women floating upon the wreck.' The wreck found by Marx was among the buildings and had had her keel fractured in several places, which is consistent with a ship bodily carried over the buildings of a town and deposited among them. The brass and copper artifacts found on and around this shattered hull are marked with the broad arrow denoting British Government property to marine archaeologists. Ex-convicts would probably not agree.

The object of the excavations as a whole, planned to last twenty years, if modern development does not before then destroy the site, is to chart accurately the sunken city for comparisons with the existing town plans; to gain information on the design and construction of the buildings of the pirate capital; to recover the surviving building materials and artifacts with a view to the reconstruction of the most important buildings and the display of the artifacts, which necessarily cover a much wider range than would those in use at sea in a sunken ship. The word 'reconstruction' is used in the literal sense: it should be possible to dismantle some of the submerged buildings and reassemble them again on land as a unique portrayal of the old Port Royal of the pirates.

325

In my second letter to Mr. Marx, of 3 March 1967, I asked specifically what sidelight his investigations threw on the legend of the bells of sunken Port Royal, in view of the fact that it was, to my knowledge, the only site submerged in the sea to which such a legend was attached. I asked: 'What is the date of the legend? Is it possible that the tops of some buildings still showed after the earthquake? Or, alternatively, did sailors hear (through the hull of their ship) wreckage being washed about on the seabed below them? Or is there no truth in it all?' As Mr. Marx had the full answer, it is worth quoting in full.

'The legend of the church and church bell ringing at Port Royal is still believed here. The church did sink into the sea during the 1692 earthquake, but at a location about a quarter mile from where the people today believe it is and now the part where the old church sunk into the sea is actually covered over by land and a modern hotel is built on top of it. The legend about the church and bell began about 1840–1845, when a large bronze church bell was fished up in some fishing nets at Port Royal. It is now on display in the Institute of Jamaica. In the area where the bell was found several high walls were seen sticking up through the bottom sediment and the local people just assumed that it was a church. Shortly after, a navigational beacon was erected over the site: named "Church Beacon". In 1859 a British helmet diver named Murphy, who was stationed at Port Royal, explored around the "Church Beacon" and wrote a long article for a local paper, explaining that it could not be a church as he found it to be the walls of a fort with cannon still in their emplacements. It is actually the site of Fort James. Many others have written telling how it could not be the church, but the locals still aren't convinced. The church bell, we believe, came off a shipwreck, of which there are many around the "Church Beacon".'

Less than a dozen years of undersea exploration have translated the mythical Port Royal, the 'hot weather' story of 1956, into the Government excavation of 1966, with its elaborate plans to bring up the remains of important buildings, brick by brick, and rebuild them on the land, brick by brick. Very muddy, very expensive, quite unromantic. The real thing. Twelve-thousand artifacts already, and tons of bricks.

What now of all the others? The shining legends of a summer sea? Are they now also likely to have a depressingly material reality? I fear they are. I can now look back over all the legendary references I used to collect and put my finger, almost infallibly, on the clues that matter, which pin the problems to a board of known principles. We had asked the right questions and had accumulated the critical answers. Perhaps after all it had been right to dismiss the bells with contempt and think only of the church. Had it been submerged? If so, why? But of all the 'submerged city' stories, the delicate texture of the romantic tale of sunken Ys, off Britanny, is the one whose loss will be most regretted.

The French writers are always inspired by the dream of Ys or Is. Philippe Taillez, one of Cousteau's pioneers, wrote in his book *To Hidden*

Depths: 'At Douarnenez, in that splendid Breton bay which on fine summer days is reminiscent of Provence, I searched endlessly up and down for the town of Is. It was not there, and people told me—to console me—that the same story of a princess, bells and a submerged town is to be found along the whole coast of Europe from the North Sea to the Baltic.' Two other French divers, Pierre de Latil and Jean Rivoire, wrote in their book *Man and the Underwater World:* 'Melodious voices are once again heard, mingling this time with the sound of bells, to remind the sailor of the swallowing up by the vengeful waves of the town of Is, for the Atlantic, the dark and terrible Atlantic, has engulfed a whole city. If you go back to the sources of these poetic visions, which still remain alive in our folklore, you will find no written text from which they emanate. For instance, in the *Roman d'Is* the sea plays only a subordinate, background role, and we meet it only in the final episode. It was only subsequently that poetic imaginations invented the story of the drowned city. What still remains in the folklore preserved in men's minds is well described in a passage from Renan. Today it is forgotten, but in the days of our grandfathers it was famous:

"You are shown the site of that legendary city at various places along the coast and the local fishermen will tell you strange stories. In times of storm, they will assure you, you can see the spires of submerged churches in the hollows of the waves, and when the weather is calm you can hear the sound of bells rising from the depths, still calling the faithful to service. Sometimes I pause to lend my ear to those vibrations which seem to rise tremblingly from infinite depths like voices from another world. Above all, as old age approaches, I have found pleasure during a restful summer listening to those far-off sounds from a vanished Atlantis."'

Yet another French diver who went to look for Ys, only half-believing, was Philippe Diolé, who wrote a wonderfully atmospheric piece about the delusion in his book *4000 Years Under the Sea*, half-mocked it, but concluded: 'What would be really comic would be to find that the city of Ys had actually been, all the time, in the precise spot where the diver had failed to see it! A fine finish, that, to a legend born in the fifth century! Maybe, some neophyte of our craft may find himself in luck's way, and come upon the Palace of King Gralon or the bedchamber of Dahut of Armorica.'

Re-opening the book, I can see that I underlined *fifth century*, and noted it in the margin. And then entered it on a map of the North Sea and Channel where, in the Western Approaches, such a site would be an extension into the Atlantic of the Breton peninsula almost due south of where the legendary 'lost land of Lyonesse' forms an extension of the Cornish peninsula to the Scilly Isles. O. G. S. Crawford, the famous land archaeologist who pioneered the technique of site-location by aerial photography, which shows sites as crop shadow lines which cannot be seen in close up when actually standing on the soil, had tried for Lyonesse and failed. But my map and the date sequences painstakingly collected pointed to a legend with a basis. The tales of Ys dated to the fifth century A D. The late-Roman period for Britain, towards the beginning of a submergence-by-fresh-water-flooding phase for the Zuyder Zee. The chronologies did not match exactly, for two different geographical areas, but they did overlap; and moreover, the overlap included the fifth century A D. Submergence was widespread at the particular point in time when the legendary Ys had suffered its mythical submergence. The improbable legend probably did have a basis of reality. What was required was more evidence, which meant more investigation and less cynicism.

Off Britanny there is a kelp jungle discouraging to divers, but many people have had a nibble at the Scillies, the obvious counterpart in Cornwall to Ys. They are a maze of islands which, if sea level dropped somewhat, would become a coherent land mass admirably placed for sea trading purposes at a hub of routes. This became a virtual certainty in the early 1960s, after the discovery by land archaeologists of a Roman trading post on one of the islands. It was this which suggested to a group of divers from Guildford Branch of the B.S.-A.C. that an integrated, land and underwater expedition be organised for 1964. They decided to camp on the island of Arthur, associated in legend with 'Arthur's Harbour', the personage referred to being King Arthur, rather a legendary figure himself, but associated with the 'drowned land of Lyonesse'. Modern historical enquiry makes him a Count of the Saxon Shore carrying out a rearguard action against the barbarians at about the time the Romans left Britain officially, or around the fifth century A D. Jerome O'Hea was the first to dive and in a couple of minutes had found 'Arthur's Harbour'. It was a 30-yards long natural breakwater, which had been artificially levelled at top and sides to convert a natural feature into a quay wall. It was isolated and did not connect with the land, there being a gap between its shoreward end and the mainland. This certainly suggested Mediterranean influence in its design, the gap being planned in to provide a scouring rush of water which would prevent silting. The first structure on land, a probably Iron Age hut, was soon found when Nigel Cope fell into it. The expedition plotted on land nine Megalithic tombs dated to about 2000–1000 B C, plotted a system of field walls which were laughable for isolated waterless islands, but made sense if sea level had at one time been lower and there was one large island instead, and dated one of these walls to the period 550 B C—A D 43, before the Romans came. Evidence for Roman occupation there already was, and the expedition's report, written by R. Kingsford-Curram, came to one conclusion dating one inundation: 'The fact that, after A D 500 at the latest, Arthur was a small, waterless island and, although perhaps used for grazing, would not have justified the effort involved in the erection of a system of field walls.'

The inundation was therefore dated to the fifth century A D and the legendary King Arthur, whoever he was, is also dated to the fifth century A D. And the legendary King Gralon, supposed to have lived on the exactly adjacent peninsula on the opposite side of the Western Approaches, is supposed to have had his palace of Ys inundated by the sea in the fifth century A D.

Oddly, one of the three submerged sites derided by Mr. North is called Lys Helig, is said to lie near Anglesey off the coast of Wales, and is associated with a minor 'king' (or large landowner) called Helig whose estates

328

are supposed to have been submerged in about the sixth century A D. Take the 'L' out of Lys and you have Ys. This may mean a migration of people rather than of legends, for there is increasing archaeological evidence to show that something strange was happening to sea levels throughout the period of Roman occupation in Britain as well as in immediate post-Roman times. Signs point to at least three periods of inundation, but in the absence of documentary details it is difficult to differentiate between a really solid submergence and a merely temporary disaster. At any rate, the thesis that all submergence legends must date far back into prehistory, because there is no evidence more recent than that, is no longer tenable. However, one does not show picture postcards to a blind horse, and no cynics will be convinced; and this is a good thing, because the reason for the existence of cynics at all is to spur other people on to secure firm evidence through investigation and other kinds of tiring labour, usually manual. The main land mass of the British Isles is a triangle roughly, and if a number of inundated sites were examined all along all three sides of the triangle, the evidence would be most interesting. We should have the facts we require to separate *eustatic* change from *isostatic*, because the tilting or bending must be from the highlands, generally in the west and north of the triangle. This would affect the depths of dated submerged sites, and this would provide fairly good evidence, although something less than precise unless the height above sea level of the former land surfaces could be established. The point being that, in the south-west, *isostatic* change would tend towards submersion, while in the north-west it would theoretically have the opposite effect.

Perhaps one of the most important contributions which diving can make to archaeology is a study of the divers themselves, considered as a prototype prehistoric community, which in fact they are. We have seen already that scholars were convinced that no prehistoric hunters could successfully tackle a mammoth, and that an actual discovery proved them wrong. What the scholars really meant, subconsciously, was that they themselves could not successfully tackle a mammoth on its own ground with prehistoric equipment; and in this assumption they may have been right. In praiseworthy endeavours to put themselves literally in their ancestors shoes they employ hiking clubs to put on Saxon war kit and do a timed route march, which may be considered as a number of steps in the right direction, but is essentially amateur, as the hikers are civilians; real infantry are driven, and only after a lot of barrack-square barking to induce conditioned reflexes. They also practise primitive agriculture themselves, which again, although certainly an advance in technique, still cannot avoid the accusation of amateurism. One elderly man and five college girls do not make a prehistoric family agricultural team, any more than the Little Wopping Hikers Club can really represent a Saxon war band or a Roman Legion out on business. Scholars have studied primitive bushmen in their native haunts, and even filmed them during the first part of the chase; and that, inevitably, is as far as they get. To keep up from that point on, would require roller-skates. Physically, they cannot stay with the bushman during the actual chase; nor, even if they could, would their observations be of the slightest interest to anyone, especially not to the hungry. Hunting is a highly technical matter.

At the moment, this seems to be the point at which archaeological analysis of primitive hunting communities breaks down most seriously. First of all, the danger is impossible to simulate. In army exercises troops used often to be fired on with live ammunition, the bullets missing by a foot or so; and sometimes not; nevertheless, the gulf between being fired at by someone who is aiming to miss you, and being fired at by someone who is trying to kill you, is psychologically immense. To re-create a mammoth-hunt, requires a real mammoth not a scholarly one, and it requires also that the scholar leave his bazooka behind. Now, it is only underwater that such a situation may in modern times be genuinely created. Because most underwater hunters, barring a few advanced Australians and Americans experimenting with powerheads, encounter dangerous beasts without the protection of law and armed with what are essentially prehistoric weapons—variations of the knife, the spear, the catapult, and the bow-and-arrow. After a time, they get very expert and then go out after the big game, often only for 'kicks', not because the monster is edible. This vicious streak in the human male, plus the highly competitive 'ace' mentality, are most often forgotten by scholars, but are nevertheless quite basic to the subject, as is, of course, pure brute force and size. The bones of the slain mammoths were all of young beasts; they wouldn't take on the big ones. Additionally, where many enemies are concerned, there is the value of split-second highly technical teamwork, as shown by Polynesian natives who hunt edible fish in competition with sharks and employ relays of divers in a planned pattern, much as fighter formations fly stacked up in inter-locking layers for mutual protection in their aggressive role. This principle, which is one of pure aggression in all its aspects, is almost always neglected; the most scholars can postulate is that primitive man, in order to kill something larger than himself, dug a pit and put stakes in it; which may be partly the case, but generally would come under the heading of: How to starve the tribe to death in one scholarly lesson. A much better lesson is to watch a collection of spear-fishermen in action: the novices are no good, often they fail even to see any fish, but the 'aces' are mighty men indeed. It will be observed that also there is an 'ace' mentality: success is partly psychological. And also, that they 'think' fish beforehand. Self-indoctrination. This is no laughing matter, for it works. For fish, lost outboard motors and archaeological artifacts. It is the one critical key to success.

A prehistoric hunting party was most unlikely to resemble a meeting of the Royal Society; they would be equally intelligent, at least as brave, and a good deal quieter and more serious; excluding inferior strains such as the Neanderthalers, of course. Considered as a viciously aggressively, highly-intelligent, long-experienced fighting force, led by mighty, some-times boastful big men, or 'aces', but containing also a number of novices and semi-trained hunters, they would most certainly bear comparison with, say, a normal club outing of the B.S.–A.C. and, indeed, with many other underwater organisations all over the world. If this conception is basically accurate, then it is the nearest we are likely to get to the real thing, except perhaps a fighter squadron, where the risks would, however, be too high to bear strict comparison. At any rate, it is a more useful concept than the standard archaeological explanations for, say, pre-historic cave-paintings. These depict basically the hunted animals, some-times with arrows stuck in them, and occasionally a complete hunt; and are always interpreted as basically religious, the worship of the beasts whose existence is essential to the welfare of the community. This is, of course, pure assumption without evidence or inference of any kind. But the previous analogies, if correct, would enable us to draw quite other assumptions, not necessarily fully accurate, but at least worth thinking about. They could be scholarly paintings: that is, commissioned carvings to enable the hunting instructor to make his points and ram home his lessons. These are all basic, to begin with: you don't just point your bow in the general direction of the target and loose the string, that's pure waste of arrowheads. You must learn to remember and to recognise the various vital points of all possible targets, and especially the angle at which they become exposed. And in the case of a fast animal running across your front—sit up at the back there, you dozy man!—you must aim off for full deflection; and, remember, practise your snapshooting, you may only have a second or so as he moves from one bit of cover to the next. After this, the instructor will go on to describe the habits of the various animals, and, finally, the tactics of team attack on a big one. For all of this, the cave carvings would be very useful. Equally, of course, they could be the equivalent of the battle picture on the regimental wall, or even the photograph of 'that monster bass I got off Bolt Head'.

From a careful study of primitive diving communities around the British Isles, one might guess that the scholars' interpretations are generally too complicated, too sophisticated. For instance, if Brian Evill could have been fossilised a few years ago, when he had purchased a new suit and had decorated it in yellow tape with the sign of a lobster, what would future scholars make of this find? Clearly, that the man had been a member of a tribe of lobster-worshippers, because, you see, if he puts on the sign of the lobster, this must surely mean that he wishes to partake of the strength, skill, and cunning of his mighty opponent. This must also mean that the scholar who postulates the theory is a man of sensi-tivity and great intelligence. Simply to say that divers need to mark their suits individually, so that they can be sorted out of the chaos in the boat after the trip, and that the personality who chose the lobster was a famed lobster catcher, would gain a scholar no kudos; it would merely be true. And if somebody fossilised me, what would a scholar make of it? The valuable equipment, cameras and so on, marked with the mystic sign 'McK'; the lesser items inscribed with a rough circle (made out of old gardening-glove material); with the surely significant exception of the rear end of the neoprene trousers, taped in a vaguely Viking, or runic, pattern. What reputation could possibly be made by speculating that this might represent the repair to the slice I ripped out of my trousers at a vulnerable point, by catching it on a cleat as I slipped overboard? Surely none. It would be a far, far better thing to deduce by the significant runes my religious beliefs and the way I voted at the last election.

The scholars are also very interested in the habits of hunting parties, and can be heard speculating on whether they took food with them, and if so, how much and what was it, did they camp or not? and so on. The briefest acquaintance with a genuine underwater hunting community will convince that this is the directly wrong approach to the subject. The correct question to ask is: What was the prey and what were its habits, where was it likely to be found, and so on? Because the habits of the hunters are based on the habits of the hunted, as anyone who cares to may see for himself. Then, too, the apparently brutal initiation ceremonies of young warriors are explained in the wrong sequence, the sociological theory being that it is to give the youth adult status in the tribe, whereas it is much more likely that this was a practical test, laid on merely because if a battle, a hunt, or indeed any risky, skilled enterprise was in prospect, it was more than the team dare afford, to have a coward along. Or, for that matter, an unfit man.

A close study by scholars of a practical hunting community in modern times, formed of articulate men, may perhaps avoid the publication, in about A D 3067 of a much-admired monograph concerning a strange tribe, established tentatively as British, and worshipping the jerboa, or desert rat, which after many years in the wilderness of North Africa, in about A D 1944 crossed over to the continent of Europe in search of the dwindling jerboa herds upon which its economy was so dependent. And of their strange association there with the Lion Men (15th Scottish Division) and the Wild Boar People (30 Corps). But what on earth will they make of SHAEF?

The underwater world owes so much to archaeologists already, that this is surely the least we can do for them in return.

And what have they done for us? They have shown us that the archaeological site of the future—pioneered in 1967 at Yassi Ada—will resemble a big engineering project in full flow. As tightly planned and timed as the most careful of 'set piece' battles, employing a mass of mechanical equipment, with an array of scientific gadgets ranging all the way from the electronic instruments which will have made the first 'soundings' to the complicated conservation laboratories which will stabilise the more fragile material. At airlift level the operation will seem all very remote from history, but precisely because it is more efficient, the results will bring us very much closer to history. It will mean also that because of the expense only the most important sites will be dealt with in this manner, the others left untouched. And this means that the reconnaissance stage will be extremely important, so that two men in a boat will still play the first and most vital part, provided that they possess both the interest and the knowledge.

SELECT BIBLIOGRAPHY

Marine Archaeology, ed. Joan du Plat Taylor (Hutchinson, 1965)

Under the Mediterranean by Honor Frost (Routledge & Kegan Paul, 1963)

Deep-Water Archaeology by Frédéric Dumas (Routledge & Kegan Paul, 1962)

The Lost Ships by Peter Throckmorton (Cape, 1965)

Archaeology Under Water by George F. Bass (Thames & Hudson, 1966)

Diving for Treasure by Clay Blair (Barker, 1961)

Proceedings: Fifth Annual Convention of the Underwater Society of America (CEDAM, 1965)

The Undersea Challenge: Second World Congress of Underwater Activities (B.S.–A.C., 1962)

'Zuyder Zee Archaeology' by G. D. van der Heide (reprint from *Antiquity and Survival*, The Hague)

'Climatic Variations in Historic and Prehistoric Time' by O. Pettersson (*Ur Svenka Hydrograpisk-biologiska Kommissionens Skriftet*, vol. V, pp. 1–25)

Helgoland (Herman Haag Verlag, Hamburg)

Excavation of the Sunken City of Port Royal: A Preliminary Report by Robert F. Marx (Institute of Jamaica, 1967)

Investigations at Kenchreai 1963 by Robert Scranton and Edwin Ramage (Athens)

'Discoveries at Kenchreai' by Robert L. Scranton (*Chicago Today*, 1966)

'Shallow-Water Excavation at Kenchreai' by Joseph W. Shaw (*American Journal of Archaeology*, 1967)

'Motya: A Phoenician Trading Settlement in Sicily', by Joan du Plat Taylor (*Archaeology*, 1964)

Cambridge Expedition to Sabratha 1966: Report (University of Cambridge, 1967)

Anglo/Israeli Underwater Archaeological Expedition 1966: Preliminary Report by Alexander Flinder (B.S.–A.C.)

The Warship Vasa by Anders Franzén (Norstedts, Stockholm, 1966)

Vasa: The King's Ship by Begt Ohrelius (Cassell, 1962)

On Resurrecting a Wreck by Lars Barkman (Stockholm, 1967)

'Corrosion Problems in Marine Archaeology' by Ora Pataharju (Scandinavian Corrosion Congress, Helsinki, 1964)

'Preservation of Metals from a Sea Environment' by Gale Wever (*Underwater Technology*, 1967)

To Hidden Depths by Captain Philippe Taillez (William Kimber, 1954)

Man and the Underwater World by Pierre de Latil and Jean Rivoire (Jarrolds, 1956)

4000 Years Under the Sea by Philippe Diolé (Sidgwick & Jackson and Editions Albin Michel)

Whitstable, Seasalter and Swalecliffe by R. H. Goodsall (Cross & Jackman, 1938)

INDEX

(For ship names, wreck names, wreck sites, and all associated technical information, see under Ships)

Fliedner, Dr. Siegfried, 143
Flinder, Alexander, 270, 333
Florida, 164, 166–7, 171, 174–6, 187–90
Focke-Museum, Bremen, 143
Fort Cumberland Preservation Society, 240
Forth of Firth, 260
fossils, 255
Franzén, Anders, 39, 93–4, 143–5, 155, 160, 183, 195, 197, 333
Fraser, John Williams, 8, 10, 13–14, 63
Freeman, J. P. Williams, 316
Frisia, Frisians, Friesland, 128–9, 281, 302, 304–8, 312
Frost, Honor, 88, 263, 333
Fullager, John, 65

Galbraith, Professor, 165
Gargallo, Piero, 96, 99
Garnett, R. H. T., 257
Geological Survey, London, 284–5
Gerkan, A. von, 261–2
Giannutri, 102–3, 117–20
Gibraltar, 257–8, 272
Giglio, 83–4, 102–20, 265
Glasgow, Tom, 216
Goodrich Papers, 4–5
Goodsall, Robert H., 5, 333
Gosport, 25; fishermen, 36, 45–6; Lit. and Phil. Soc., 18
Gozo, 258
Gralon, King, 328
Green, Charles, 304, 312
Greenhough, M., 128
Greenland, 310–11
Greenland, A. J., 128
Gregory, A., 285–6, 290
Grenville, Roger (*Mary Rose*), 41
Greynville, Sir Richard, 152
gunnery, 181–2
Gustav III, King of Sweden, 156

Hafemann, Dr. Dietrich, 260
Haifa, 270–1
Hale, Roger, 103, 107–10, 116, 119, 204
Hall, Capt. Basil, 6, 16, 57–61, 178
Hall, Dr. E. T., 270–2
Hall, George, 55–6, 63, 65–6
Hamble River, 133–8, 242
Hamburg, 313
Hampshire Telegraph, 6, 26, 29–30, 57
Hanseatic League, 143, 156, 311, 313

Harknett, Maurice, 207, 209, 211, 213, 220, 224–8, 234, 238–9, 241, 287–92, 317
Harris, Corporal David, 65
Hass, Hans, 81
Hastings, 302–3
Havana, 173–6
Hayling Island, 186–7, 237, 239, 274–318
Heide, Professor G. D. van der, 140–3, 308–9, 312, 333
Henderson, Robert, 238–9, 242
Henry I, 132–3; IV, 301; V, 135–6; VIII, 35–6, 38–44, 75, 153, 216–17, 248
Heligoland, 281, 304, 333
Helsinki, Finland, 155–6, 158
Herne Bay, 127
Hicks, James, 4–5
Hispaniola, 173–5
Hogarth, David, 261, 278
Holinshed, 43, 303, 309
Homer, 89–90
Honduras, 173–5
Hooker, John, 41
Horse Sand, 28, 194, 201
Horsey, S., 37, 58
Hudson, W. H., 278
Humphry, John, 128
Hurst, Robert, 224–5
Hutchins, Roger, 283–7
Hydrographer of the Navy, 222–3

Ice Ages, 254, 259–61
Iceland, 311
Imperial College, London, 257
Indians, North American, 256–7
Inman, James, 182
Isis, 266–70
Isle of Wight, 25, 128, 197, 211, 216–8, 259–60, 301, 312–13
Israel, 270–2

Latil, Pierre de, 327, 333
Lee, Alan, 203–4, 206–7
Leeward Isles, 166, 171–5
legends, 81–2, 130, 133, 138, 252, 262, 277, 316–21, 326–9
Ligurian Studies, Inst. of, 119–20
Linder, Elisha, 94, 270
Link, Edwin, 167, 324
Lisle, Lord (John Dudley), 217–19
List, Sylt, 304
Little, Midshipman Thomas, 27
Lomond, Loch, 320
London, Hiram, 56

Longcroft, C. J., 297–8
Looe, Cornwall, 167
Looe Channel, Selsey, 167, 255, 280
Looe Key, Florida, 167
Lulworth, Roman finds, 124–5, 128
Lumière, Cornel, 324
Lyonesse, 327–9
Lys Helig, 328–9

magnetometer, proton, 226–8, 236,
    240, 270–2
Magnus, Olaf, 311
Maida, Battle of, 50
Majer, W.O.B., 248
McKee, Alexander, 21, 64, 83
McKee, Arthur, 166–7
McLanachan, Lt.-Cdr. W.Y., 318–19
Malta, 258
Maltini, Raniero, 272
Marienhafe, 304
Marke, Dr. Paul, 237, 239
Marseilles, 114
Marsden, Peter, 125–6, 134
Marsh, Sgt. Samuel, 14, 57, 178
Marshall, J. F., 316–17
Martin, Frank, 276, 286
Matanceros, Punta, Yucatan, 167
Matanzas, Cuba, 167
Marx, R. F., 164–76, 320–6, 333
Meijers, Johannes, 304
Methone, 96–8, 141, 146, 221
Mexico, 166, 173–5, 256
Milgate, Jack, 277, 284, 292
Millar, Maj.-Gen. Sir William, 37
Millerchip, John, 221
Mills, John D., 235–47
Mitchell, Corporal Henry, 53–4
Mixon, Selsey, 280
Möhne-See, 275
Monson, Admiral Sir William, 44,
    152–3, 211, 214, 220
Moody, Herbert, 134
Moore, Sir John, 50–1
Morris, Ernest, 318
Morrison, Ian, 216, 260
Motya, Sicily, 109, 264–5, 271, 333
Munich (München) Underwater
    Club, 106, 119
Murphy, Jeremiah D., 324, 326
Mussolini, Benito, 103, 124

Naish, F. C. P., 134
Naish, George P. B., 126–7, 134
Naples, 262, 272
National Maritime Museum,
    Greenwich, 128, 167, 221

Nautical Archaeology, Committee
    for, 134, 221–3, 232, 248, 270
Nautical Research, Society for, 248
Nederlandse Bond Voor
    Onderwatersport, 305
Nehellenia, 305
Nelson, Horatio, 50, 150, 152, 168,
    198, 217, 219
Nemi, Lake, 103, 124
Nesmith, Robert I., 188
Newman, William, 261–2
Newport, I. o. W., 45
nitrogen narcosis, 108–11
Nombre de Dios, 173
Norden, 305
Norderney, 128, 281
Northney, 128
North, F. J., 319–20, 328–9
North Sea, 281, 304–5, 311

Oakley, Dr. Kenneth, 259
Oglander, Sir John, 301
O'Hea, Jeremy, 328
Ohrelius, Cdr. Bengt, 145, 333
Oppenheim, M., 211
Ordnance, Board of, 18, 26,
    35–48, 52, 55
Oseberg, 129
Owers Bank, Selsey, 198, 255, 280
    302

Padwick, William, 299
Pagham, Selsey, 302
Panama, 173
Paris, Matthew, 303
Pasley, Major-General C. W.,
    48–70, 178, 200, 204, 211–12,
    234; career, 50–2; reports on
    diving helmets, 6, 8, 12, 14,
    62–5; experiments with
    underwater demolition, 50–6,
    194, 207; plans to demolish
    Royal George, 55
Pataharju, Ora, 155, 158, 333
Patent Office, London, 7, 9–14
Paul, Peter, 235
Peru, 171–5
Peterson, Cdr. Mendel, 167, 178–82
Petterssohn, O., 310–3, 333
Philip II, King of Spain, 173
Phipps, William, 18, 176
Phoenicians, 264–5
photogrammetry, stereo, 132, 216
Pilaknno, Lake, Poland, 320
pinger probe, 94, 235–48
Pitt-Rivers, General (Lane Fox,
    A. E.), 22, 140

340

Revenge, galleon, Azores (1591), 149–50, 152

Riilahti (Rilax), Finland, battle wrecks (1714), 158

Riksnyckeln, warship, Stockholm (1628), 143

Roskilde Fiord, Denmark, Viking wrecks, 130–2

Royal George, 108 guns, Spithead (1782), 4–5, 8–9, 14, 18–20, 26–38, 42, 55–70, 74–5, 151, 194–7, 201, 203–14, 220, 222–3, 257. Court Martial findings, 30–2

Ruotsinsalmi (Svensksund), battle wrecks (1789–90), 156–8

Saale, German freighter (1967), 185

San Antonio, Bermuda (1621), 180–1, 183

San Francisco Xavier, Florida (1715), 190

Sankt Nicolai, Russian frigate, Svensksund (1789–90), 157–8

St. Mary, wineship, I. o. W. (1314), 196

St. Tropez, France, stone-cargo wreck (2nd cent. AD), 81–2, 96

Scire, Italian submarine, Haifa (1942), 272

Scole, Le, Giglio (*c.* AD 400), 103, 106–10

Silver Shoals, West Indies, Span. treasure ship (1641), 18, 176

Spargi, Sardinia (2nd cent. AD), 78, 120

Swan, frigate, Port Royal (1692), 325

Taranto, Gulf of, sarcophagi wreck (3rd cent. AD), 96–7, 233

Thetis, frigate, Cape Frio, Brazil (1830), 53

'Titan', France (1st cent. BC), 78

'Tobermory Galleon', Mull (1588), 58, 235–6, 238

Turku (Abo), Finland (1629), 158

Vasa, galleon, Stockholm (1628), 16, 39, 41, 61–2, 141–55, 158, 160, 198, 248, 333

Venerable, 74 guns, Torbay (1804), 18

Vigo, Plate Fleet (1702), 53, 176

Viking ships, 128–38

'White Ship', Barfleur (1120), 132–3

William, coal brig, Thames (1837), 52–5

Withern, bucket-dredger, Langstone (1909), 228–9

Yassi Ada, Turkey, Byzantine wrecks (5th–6th cents. AD), 78, 90–4, 97, 102, 178, 198, 332

Zuyder Zee, 140–3, 146, 197, 308

Shipwrecks (itemized information):
causes, 79–81, 102, 104, 114, 116, 164, 166, 183–7
'closed communities', 26–7, 61–2, 153–5
'closed finds' ('time capsules') (*sic*), 26–8, 118

concretions, 16, 91, 108, 116, 135, 206–8, 258

conservation, 132, 146, 153–4, 157, 178, 200–1, 206–7

deterioration, 32–3, 37–8, 57–61, 66–70, 87, 89, 91, 96–102, 126, 130–2, 136–7, 140, 143–60, 164, 178–9, 182, 196–7, 224–5, 228–32, 272, 313. *See also* Deterioration of materials

disputes: archaeologists—divers —nautical historians, 76–8, 82, 87–9, 120, 138, 157, 164–5, 179, 252, 277, 294

identification, 26–8, 39, 42–5, 135, 140, 143, 158, 167–9, 180, 182, 188, 204–7, 209–14. *See also* Legends

legal protection, Finland, 157; Mexico, 168–9; general, 178; Florida, 189; Great Britain, 248

pillage and destruction, 103, 107–10, 133, 156–7, 165, 167–9, 178, 182–3, 189–90, 248

seabed signs, 68–70, 88–9, 91, 112–16, 140–3, 158–60, 188–9, 197, 205–10, 212–14, 221, 224, 226, 230–5, 240

seabed signs, scholarly interpretation of ('Oh, it must have fallen overboard'), 4, 26–8, 38, 81–2, 90, 112–16, 133–5, 144, 155, 213–14, 217, 231, 257, 262, 277–8, 286, 317–20, 326–9

search techniques, 80–1, 92–4, 140, 143–5, 164–5, 169, 183, 187–90, 194–5, 203–4, 219–20, 222–3, 225–7, 235–48

shallow water, 97–102, 130–2, 124–38, 140–3, 158, 183–90, 224–5, 229–34, 281

shipworms, 126, 130, 145, 228–9

Survey, 126, 135, 141–3, 158, 165, 189, 197–8

Shoreham, 302

Sicily, 96, 98, 102, 233, 264–5

sidescan sonar, 93–4, 241–8

Sidon, 263

Siebe, Augustus, 8, 14–16, 21, 62–5

Sieveking, Dr. G. de G., 254

Silver, John, 255

Simpson, Rev. F. S. W., 302

Skelton, John, 65

Smith, John, 55–6, 62

Smith, Sir Sidney, 270

Smithsonian Inst., 167–8, 178–80

Soc. for Nautical Research, 248

Solaini, Piero, 272

Solent and 'Solent River', 25, 201, 257

Southampton, 61, 135, 137–8

South Downs, 257

South Saxons, 128, 255, 302

Southsea Castle, 8, 26, 28, 47, 65, 75, 195, 206, 217

Spatola, Francesco, 98

342